COMPETITION AND INNOVATION IN POSTAL SERVICES

**Topics in Regulatory Economics
and Policy Series**

Michael A. Crew, Editor
Graduate School of Management
Rutgers University
Newark, New Jersey, U.S.A.

Previously published books in the series:

Rowley, C., R. Tollison, and G. Tullock:
  Political Economy of Rent Seeking

Frantz, R.:
  X-Efficiency: Theory, Evidence and Applications

Crew, M.:
  Deregulation and Diversification of Utilities

Shogren, J.:
  The Political Economy of Government Regulation

Hillman, J., and R. Braeutigam:
  Price Level Regulation for Diversified Public Utilities

Crew, M.:
  Competition and the Regulation of Utilities

Einhorn, M.:
  Price Caps and Incentive Regulation in Telecommunications

COMPETITION AND INNOVATION IN POSTAL SERVICES

edited by
Michael A. Crew
Graduate School of Management
Rutgers University
Newark, New Jersey, U.S.A.

and

Paul R. Kleindorfer
The Wharton School
University of Pennsylvania
Philadelphia, Pennsylvania, U.S.A.

Kluwer Academic Publishers
Boston/Dordrecht/London

Distributors for North America:
Kluwer Academic Publishers
101 Philip Drive
Assinippi Park
Norwell, Massachusetts 02061 USA

Distributors for all other countries:
Kluwer Academic Publishers Group
Distribution Centre
Post Office Box 322
3300 AH Dordrecht, THE NETHERLANDS

Library of Congress Cataloging-in-Publication Data

Competition and innovation in postal services / edited by Michael A. Crew and Paul R. Kleindorfer.
    p. cm. — (Topics in regulatory economics and policy series ; 8)
    Proceedings of a conference in honor of Rowland Hill, held at Coton House, the Post Office Management College, on July 22–25, 1990, and sponsored by the British Post Office.i.
    Includes bibliographical references.
    ISBN 0-7923-9147-0 (alk. paper)
    1. Postal service—Congresses. 2. Postal service—Great Britain--Congresses. I. Crew, Michael A. II. Kleindorfer, Paul R. III. Hill, Rowland, Sir, 1795–1879. IV. Great Britain. Post Office. V. Series: Topics in regulatory economics and policy ; 8.
HE6011.C62   1991
383 '.4—dc20   90-28437
                                                                         CIP

Copyright © 1991 by Kluwer Academic Publishers

All rights reserved. No part of this publication may be reproduced, stored in a retrieval system or transmitted in any form or by any means, mechanical, photo-copying, recording, or otherwise, without the prior written permission of the publisher, Kluwer Academic Publishers, 101 Philip Drive, Assinippi Park, Norwell, Massachusetts 02061.

Printed on acid-free paper.

Printed in the United States of America

CONTENTS

Authors and Discussants — vii

Preface and Acknowledgements — ix

Foreword — xi
    Sir Ron Dearing

1 Rowland Hill's Contribution as an Economist — 1
    Michael A. Crew and Paul R. Kleindorfer
    Comments — 13
    Martin J. Daunton

2 International Postal Reform: An Application of the Principles of Rowland Hill to the International Postal System — 17
    James I. Campbell, Jr.
    Comments: International Postal Reform — 33
    Roger Tabor

3 Peak-Load Pricing of Postal Service and Competition — 37
    Michael A. Crew and Paul R. Kleindorfer
    Comments: Sorting-Out Prices — 57
    David de Meza

4 Assessing the Welfare Effects of Entry into Letter Delivery — 61
    Ian Dobbs and Paul Richards
    Comments — 89
    Norman Ireland

5 Delivering Letters: Should it be Decriminalized? — 93
    Saul Estrin and David de Meza
    Comments: Bagging the Mail — 109
    Charles K. Rowley

6 A Comparative Analysis of Wage Premiums and Industrial Relations in the British Post Office and the United States Postal Service — 115
    Michael L. Wachter and Jeffrey M. Perloff
    Comments — 139
    Frank Rodriguez

7 Productivity and Cost Measurement for the United States Postal Service: Variations Among Regions J.R. Norsworthy, Show-Ling Jang, and Wei-Ming Shi	141
Comments Thomas A. Abbott	169
Comments Donald J. O'Hara	173
8 Postal Newspaper Delivery and Diversity of Opinions Ulrich Stumpf	177
Comments Frank A. Scott, Jr.	189
9 Competition in Postal Service Roger Sherman	191
Comments: Marginal Experiments, Unintended Results Michael R. Frierman	215
10 Is Postal Service a Natural Monopoly? John C. Panzar	219
Comments Michael Waterson	229
11 Postal Rate-Making Procedures and Outcomes in Various Countries Robert Albon	233
Comments John Haldi	251
12 Postal Service and Less Developed Countries David E. Treworgy and James A. Waddell	253
Comments Robert M. Pike	271
13 Competitive Strategy for New Zealand Post Elmar Toime	275
Comments Ian Steele	283

AUTHORS AND DISCUSSANTS

Thomas A. Abbott, Assistant Professor of Economics, Graduate School of Management, Rutgers University

Robert Albon, Senior Lecturer in Economics, Australian National University

James I. Campbell, Jr., Special Counsel, International Express Carriers Conference

Michael A. Crew, Professor of Economics and Director of the Center for Research in Regulated Industries, Graduate School of Managment, Rutgers University

Martin J. Daunton, Professor of History, University College London

David de Meza, Professor of Economics, University of Exeter

Sir Ron Dearing, Former Chairman, British Post Office

Ian Dobbs, Senior Lecturer in Economics, University of Newcastle Upon Tyne

Saul Estrin, Senior Lecturer in Economics, London School of Economics

Michael R. Frierman, Assistant Professor of Economics, Graduate School of Management, Rutgers University

John Haldi, President, Haldi Associates, Inc.

Norman Ireland, Professor of Economics, University of Warwick

Show-Ling Jang, George Mason University

Paul R. Kleindorfer, Universal Furniture Professor of Decision Sciences, Wharton School, University of Pennsylvania

J.R. Norsworthy, Professor of Economics, Rensselaer Polytechnic Institute

Donald J. O'Hara, Principal Economist, United States Postal Service

John C. Panzar, Professor of Economics, Northwestern University

Jeffrey M. Perloff, Professor of Economics, University of California, Berkeley

Robert M. Pike, Professor of Sociology, Queen's University

Paul Richards, Economic Advisor, British Post Office

Frank Rodriguez, Senior Economist, British Post Office

Charles K. Rowley, Professor of Economics, Center for Study of Public Choice, George Mason University

Frank A. Scott, Jr., Associate Professor of Economics, University of Kentucky

Roger Sherman, Brown Forman Professor of Economics, University of Virginia

Wei-Ming Shi, Rensselaer Polytechnic Institute

Ian Steele, Marketing Information Manager, British Post Office

Ulrich Stumpf, Economist, WIK Institute, Bonn
Roger Tabor, Director—Corporate Planning Department, British Post Office
Elmar Toime, Group Manager—Marketing, New Zealand Post
David E. Treworgy, Consultant, Price Waterhouse
Michael L. Wachter, Professor of Economics, University of Pennsylvania
James A. Waddell, Partner, Price Waterhouse
Michael Waterson, Professor of Economics, University of Reading

PREFACE AND ACKNOWLEDGEMENTS

This book resulted from a conference held at Coton House, the Post Office Management College, July 22-25, 1990. Coming at the one hundred and fiftieth anniversary of the Penny Post, the conference, as well as discussing some important current topics, honored the contribution of Sir Rowland Hill. Honoring Hill is by no means without controversy. As the papers here illustrate, Hill will remain a controversial figure as long as there is mail! Other issues addressed by the Conference included entry of competition, the nature of natural monopoly in postal service, regulation of postal service, privatization versus public monopoly, and the effect of the monopoly on labor unions, to mention just some of the major issues. As a result of this conference, it seems clear to us that mail service has been taken for granted for too long by economists and that a considerable potential exists for further study. We would expect more research, as well as other conferences on postal economics and postal issues, to follow.

The Conference and this book were made possible by support from the British Post Office, who provided the use of the fine facilities at Coton House. The Center for Research in Regulated Industries, The Huntsman Center for Global Competition, and the International Express Carriers Conference provided additional support. We would like to thank our sponsors not only for the financial support but also for their insights, advice, and encouragement. In addition to providing the use of Coton House, Paul Richards and Roger Tabor of the Post Office were very helpful in making suggestions for papers and discussants and providing contacts with persons in postal services throughout the world. Jim Campbell of the International Express Carriers Conference, in addition to support and the paper included in the book, provided useful advice and comments.

Special thanks are due to Sir Ron Dearing who provided a highly stimulating keynote address and wrote the Forward to the book. We would also like to thank our speakers and discussants whose papers comprise the book. In addition, the other participants at the conference contributed to the often lively discussion. Finally, we would like to thank Linda Brennan, Administrative Assistant in the Center for Research in Regulated Industries. She copy-edited the papers and managed the Ventura desktop publishing system used to generate camera-ready copy. In addition, she took care of most of the many details involved in conference administration.

FOREWORD

Any Chairman of the British Post Office dwells in the shadow of Rowland Hill, and, if he were an honest man, he probably from time to time, while singing the praises of Rowland Hill, as is his due, thinks a silent thought of sympathy for his predecessor Colonel Maberly, the head of the Post Office, the Champion of established orthodoxy, the leader of the Professionals, who had to endure the irresistible force of Hill's arguments combined with his skills as a pamphleteer, agitator, and political propagandist.

My favorite passage of the book *Royal Mail* by Martin Daunton (1985) shows how much the Post Office of the day needed a Rowland Hill to challenge Colonel Maberly and all that he stood for. I quote from a passage describing how the Colonel, when he arrived at about 11:00 a.m. and while enjoying his breakfast, listened to his private secretary reading the morning's correspondence.

Daunton records:

> The Colonel, still half engaged with his private correspondence, would hear enough to make him keep up a running commentary of disparaging grunts,
>
> "Pooh! stuff! upon my soul!" etc.
>
> Then the clerk, having come to the end of the manuscript, would stop, waiting for orders; and there would ensue a dead silence, broken by the Colonel who, having finished his private letters, would look up and say:
>
> "Well, my good fellow, well!" "That's all sir." "And quite enough too. Go on to the next." "But what shall I say to this applicant, sir?" "Say to him? Tell him to go and be damned, my good fellow!" (p. 21)

When, after seven years in the Chair at the Post Office, I moved onto other things, I thought that I had left the shadow of Rowland Hill behind me. My chosen new career was in education. But it was not long before I discovered that here, too, Hill had been a major reformer, rather than an obscure schoolmaster in a small private school in Birmingham, as I had thought. He is in the front rank of names in the history of British education, having made innovations that were decades and, indeed, a century before their time. For example:

> At Bruce Castle we are told that originally eleven hours per week were devoted to science. This makes an astonishing contrast with what other schools were doing at the same period of time and even during the next

---

This Foreword is based on the Dinner Speech given by Sir Ron Dearing at the conference "Competition and Innovation in Postal Services" on July 24, 1990, at Coton House, Rugby, England.

> hundred years or more, in spite of the efforts of various Government Commissions and Committees to bring science into its rightful place within the education system.
>
> As late as 1936 the Science Masters' Association, the official professional body, could only suggest a minimum of three hours per week for pupils up to sixteen years of age. (from *Rowland Hill* by Colin Hey, 1989, p. 19)

And so, it seems my lot to live perpetually in the shadow of this great man, and I owe it to him not just to express a profound debt on behalf of all who have followed him, but also to recognize that his thinking remains valid and to discuss whether we should be taking his ideas a step further forward. By this I mean a system of prices that is consistently related to cost—if you like—at the margin.

I raise this issue not out of any deep reverence for the principles of economics, but because, as a practical manager, I am conscious (1) that if people do not know what things cost, they make bad decisions; and (2) that for technological, economic, and political reasons—not to mention self-inflicted wounds by the worlds' Post Offices—the monopoly is being progressively eroded and, if the Post Office is to continue to be successful—whether as a so called monopolist or not—it needs fair pricing systems that help it to compete fairly, rather than foster the development of strong competitors.

International Pricing

When I left the British Post Office in the Autumn of 1987, I was asked to lead a small international task force to enable the Post Offices of the advanced world, in particular, to provide better international services. Our goal was to offer stronger competition to the powerful, fast-growing private sector courier firms, remailers, and, increasingly, facsimile.

As the Chairman in Britain, I confess that there had been so much to do at home that it was not until the last year or so of my tenure of office that I began to think seriously about international services. These, under the aegis of the Universal Postal Union (UPU) with around 170 member States, seemed inextricably locked into an almost immutable, highly complex worldwide system of such complexity that practically every country, except at the quinquennial gatherings of the UPU, left it to a small number of experts versed in the regulations of the UPU.

But during this last year, a number of chairman and chief executives of the Post Offices' of Western Europe—the CEPT—were becoming increasingly frustrated and concerned, as they lost markets on a huge scale to the international private sector operators. They decided they must do something about it, not least to establish the facts.

We knew that our basic services were often inadequate in quality. What few of us appreciated was how we were virtually handing our business over to the private sector by a system of international charging (land rates in the case of parcels; imbalance charges in the case of letters), which often, if not usually, bore a doubtful relationship to costs.

Parcels

To be specific, for international parcels, the charge made by the receiving country to the despatching country for handling an incoming parcel bore no consistent relationship to the charge for handling a comparable parcel for carriage within the country. In all nine countries surveyed, the parcel received from abroad bore a higher charge, ranging across the nine countries from 10% more to 100% more. Such pricing must tend to encourage bulk posting from abroad directly into the inland stream and raise the question of whether land rates were too high to enable the Post Offices in the despatching country to compete on an equal basis with the private sector. That was three years ago, and, doubtless, the world has since moved on, but that example illustrates my point about the need for soundly-based pricing policies by Postal Administrations.

Variable service quality for ordinary parcels, as opposed to express parcels where service was highly competitive, coupled with such pricing added to the difficulties facing government-regulated public service institutions in innovating new services in response to developing market needs. This situation fostered the creation of major multinational concerns concentrating on high-value, high-price courier services and remailing. This was the rational market response to the stupidities in postal charging that enabled the private sector to act as intermediary between postal services, usually with the assistance of a third postal administration, at profit for modest effort.

Add to that, the developing threat from facsimile, which must be greatest for international mail, where the certainty and speed of facsimile, coupled with its increasingly low cost, give it such competitive advantage.

The task force reported to a very concerned group of chairmen and chief executives of the Post Offices that, unless there were reforms, their international business would progressively decline. It also told them that, the more the international private sector operators gained in strength, the more inroads they would make into the post offices' basic inland services, since they would have developed the collection and distribution network to make such a further development a feasible.

This is one of the amplest demonstrations of the danger of not pursuing rational pricing policies and not realizing market opportunities. Rowland Hill, had he been with us today, would have been just the man—by his tireless energy, his powerful advocacy, his determination to overcome obstruction, and his courage—to have secured reform.

I am glad to say that the task force has had some effect and that there have been changes to world international pricing practice. Had we had a Rowland Hill, I think they would have been more profound than those yet realized.

Inland Prices

The papers in this volume, as I have read them, have been concerned with rational pricing, whether between various classes of mail or between mail destined to go from town to town as opposed to mail beginning or ending in a rural area.

In the papers, there is criticism of uniform inland pricing. I think it is a fair summary to say that, while in principle, the arguments for differential pricing have been well made, there are counter arguments of the kind made by Roger Tabor of the United Kingdom and others, that the administrative costs of operating differential pricing for rural and town mail may outweigh the economic gain. I am sure, in the absence of definitive evidence one way or the other, that debate will continue.

But, I suspect that it is a debate which will not be determined by economic argument, but by what I would describe, for want of a better word, as politics.

As the papers make clear, Rowland Hill did not advocate uniform delivered pricing. His economic analysis led him only to conclude that there should be uniform pricing for primary delivery form town to town, leaving scope for differential pricing for delivery from postal towns to delivery points, especially those in rural areas.

Rowland Hill did not get his way. The political attraction of uniform pricing, with the benefits that gave to rural areas, was too great.

I note from Roger Sherman's paper on the United States Post Office that political thought was much the same in the United States. I quote from his paper:

> No one doubts that a mail monopoly was created in the United States to foster cross subsidization, mainly to have eastern cities support mail services to the nation's frontiers.

So far as I know, what is wrongly called the Rowland Hill principle of uniform inland pricing is applied pretty well across the whole of the world. I guess a combination of politics and administrative feasibility—convenience if you like—was the reason, rather than a multinational deliberate misreading of Rowland Hill's texts.

The Practical Chairman's View

Let me offer you, as best as I can remember it, the practical attitude of a Post Office Chairman when these kinds of issues came across his desk.

In my own case, I was conscious of virtually no pressure from outside to have differential pricing between town and rural areas, and life has a lot to do with pressures. I was conscious of the administrative problems. It is all very well to say that it is only necessary to add a suffix to the postcode to secure the necessary differentiation. However, having struggled throughout the whole of my Chairmanship to get postcode usage up to 70% in Britain, I was all too aware that any addition to the postcode, which was widely unpopular, would get short shrift.

But there was another reason. Here I would quote from another of my favorite texts, namely Nicolo Machiavelli:

> ... it ought to be remembered that there is nothing more perilous to conduct, or more uncertain in its success, than to take the lead in the introduction of a new order of things. Because the innovator has for enemies all those who have done well under the old conditions, and lukewarm defenders in those

who may do well under the new. This coolness arises partly from fear of the new. Thus, it happens that whenever those who are hostile have the opportunity to attack they do it like partisans, whilst the others defend lukewarmly, in such wise that the Prince is endangered along with them.

I have found again and again in life that Machiavelli's advice to his Prince is true, as Mrs. Thatcher has found in recent months over the Poll Tax. The Chairman of the Post Office taking an initiative in making such a recommendation would have been excoriated and, no doubt, eviscerated.

I now turn briefly to our decisions in Britain during my seven years Chairmanship on widening the differential between first class and second class post.

The 1st Class/2nd Class Differential

The Post Office's judgement that a continuing rise in first class mail prices, in relation to second class mail, is justified under the Ramsey principle, is now being questioned. But there is another telling factor in our mind. We were having particularly severe difficulties in securing an adequate standard of service for first class mail, and the tendency of the volume of first class mail to expand faster than that of lower categories of mail was a source of continuing anxiety to us in terms of service standards. It therefore seemed rational, given the magnitude of our problem and in the face of labor supply difficulties, to use pricing to limit switching from second to first class mail.

The Monopoly

I am sure that the Machiavelli principle would weigh heavily with any government in a decision on the postal monopoly. I suspect that the one of the main reasons why governments have not pressed ahead with the opening up of postal services to competition, through the ending of the monopoly, has been their concern with maintaining services to rural and suburban areas at a low price. There are other ways, as outlined in the papers in this volume, such as providing a subsidy to the Post Office to enable it to continue to provide such services, possibly financed by a tax on the private sector competitor entrants. However, I can imagine Ministers balking at such a measure because of future pressures from the private sector operators to reduce the subsidy and the danger of it becoming a charge to the Exchequer.

One day, perhaps, governments will be ready to address their minds to such a possibility, but I suspect that a condition precedent would be evidence that the private sector is really interested in providing a large scale postal service. When the present Conservative Government came into office, Sir Keith Joseph, who some view as the designer of Thatherism, instigated an investigation of the case for, and the feasibility of, ending the postal monopoly in Great Britain. His inquiry showed that there was little interest in the subject, in spite of the very strong complaints about the Post Office at that time, and, most significantly, that there was no significant private sector operator, actual or potential, who was interested in coming into the mass mail business. And I must say, as someone who now spends part of his time in the board rooms of the private sector, that I can understand why private sector concerns are much more interested in operating at the high-price, high-margin end of the market. I understand that the main mail users in Britain are more interested in a better monopoly postal service than in one provided by competing concerns.

Therefore, in Britain, given that the Royal Mail is an institution dating back three and half centuries; that, with all its faults, there is much affection for it; that is has kept its price increases below the Retail Price Index for a decade; that there is no great stirring by the private sector to come into the mass mail business; and that there is much potential trouble for government in taking action that would disturb existing interests, I suspect that the privatization of the mail will not become a top political priority, unless the postal service causes a degree of dissatisfaction that creates real pressure for change.

Change

But that is far from my wishing to say that there is no need for change or that competition would be damaging. Indeed, I often said, as the Chairman of the Post Office, that my greatest handicap was that of being a monopolist. It was a handicap because it meant that I had to be subject to continual—meaning daily—control by the Department of Industry, which had a staff of capable people entirely devoted to the oversight and control of my affairs. It also meant that there was no direct threat to the job security of postal workers, which Sherman in his paper relates to the high wages of postal workers in United States. I would not say at all that postal workers in Britain have high wages relative to those in the private sector. I would say that monopoly, with an associated, powerful trade union, has led to pressures for work practices that increase job numbers and income levels, through their influence on the scale of overtime working.

I was also conscious, as a manager, of the extra zest and commitment that comes to management from competition. I remember when one of the courier firms decided to make a major attack on part of our business through a well-conceived franchise operation. The response from within the business was electric, and the jolt that gave to us was of long lasting benefit.

Measures

As Chairman of the Post Office, I always refused to get drawn into the issue of privatization, but, in case the Post Office is to remain a publicly-owned monopoly, you and I would share an interest in ways in which it could become more effective.

I have mentioned pricing in connection with international mail services.

Within the United Kingdom system, during my period of office, we decided to split the Post Office into four separate businesses, each with its own accounts with proper charging between businesses. My successor has continued to take this forward, and, as a result, cross subsidization, whether deliberate or accidental, has been progressively ended, as the accounting systems have been developed to produce valid methods of charging. I can recall few issues that raise more tensions than this change—as I find it is also the case when the same happens in large concerns in the private sector.

I strongly favor knowing costs for sub-services within the mails, so that rational pricing policies can be pursued within the framework of practical administration and practical politics. A very important part of practical politics is that there should be no dramatic changes—that is one of the best ways of making no progress at all.

I would also strongly favor continual development of products in relation to market needs, and I have been interested to read what the New Zealanders are doing. I am sure that it is wrong for any postal service to think that there is any particular virtue about the systems that it has in place. All of my experience points to the constantly changing nature of the market and to the advantages of continually identifying market needs and providing the right services at an economic price.

If I might be allowed a purely personal comment, I would want to change the relationship between Post Offices and their governments. This would be so even though they remained in public ownership. As the British Government has said many times, it is not the best owner of a business—party and political pressures force Ministers, however good their intentions, to be interventionalist. I do not think that any of the papers in this volume recognized the scale of government involvement in Post Office affairs, including their pricing decisions.

I have long been attracted by the concept of the Government in Britain setting aside its own de facto powers to control prices and services by setting up an office of Postal Prices, as has already happened for the Telecommunications and Water Industries, with the Post Office being set a five year objective of RPI-X (plus or minus a Quality factor, which would exist to reward or punish the Post Office for superior or inferior service, compared with its target).

But it would be wrong to see the Post Office as concerned only with costs. Cost minimisation is not economically efficient. It can lead to perverse decisions. The RPI-X formula, which is now becoming widely recognized as an instrument for controlling monopoly prices, needs to be supported by profit targets, preferably in the form of return on capital, with incentives to managers and the workforce to achieve and exceed such targets, through a meaningful and, indeed, generous system of profit sharing.

There also need to be real penalties for failure. In Britain, when a public enterprise has failed to deliver the goods, the Government has picked up the tab. Afterward, all has continued as in the past, no doubt after some months of critical investigation and the production of new strategies and financial forecasts.

Lest you think that I say the following with all the advantages of no longer being involved in a nationalized institution, may I say that I have been advocating this for at least ten years. If by mismanagement a public board gets into the kind of situation which in the private sector would lead to bankruptcy or a rebellion by shareholders, then the board should lose its job. An incoming board would have a clear mandate form government to take whatever action necessary, however painful, to put things right.

One of the great inhibitors to any such brave course of action has been the near impossibility of recruiting sufficient able people to the boards of public corporations. To be able to recruit in the face of such sanctions would be doubly difficult. The solution is the private sector one, to pay the rate of the job. To the credit of the present Government, on occasion they have done this and often with tremendously successful results.

Conclusions

The Post Offices of the world are proving remarkably resilient to challenge. Under its present chairman, I know that the British Post Office is more than willing—and able—to meet the challenge of new competing technologies. But if we—and I still identify with the Post Office—aim to prosper, we must recognize the implication of this growing competition, not least in rationally structured and fair, yet highly competitive, pricing policies. Of course, I welcome the progress being made internationally on that front since I left the scene, but there is more to be done.

Therefore, I greatly welcome this volume and the associated conference, with its emphasis on competition and pricing, and I hope you will meet, from time to time to continue to extend these challenging ideas. We can only gain from vigorous, informed debates between the practical thinkers and the thinking practitioners.

There is one more element in my package, and it is that conferences, like the one this volume resulted from, of international experts should be encouraged. We should welcome and encourage research into the nature of costs in postal services. Too little has been done. We should also welcome experiment. Indeed, it is by experiment and by the experience that comes from experiments and research throughout the postal world, where we are all engaged in very much the same business, that we can best advance.

A number of countries, of which Britain is of course is one, have been engaged in new initiatives over the last year. We have all been interested in what is happening in New Zealand.

I therefore congratulate the contributors to this volume and the attendees at the conference for coming together. I am so pleased that Britain was chosen for the conference. I do encourage all to continue work in the spirit and tradition of Rowland Hill, however uncomfortable that may be for the Colonel Maberlys of the day.

SIR RON DEARING
Former Chairman,
British Post Office

1
ROWLAND HILL'S CONTRIBUTION AS AN ECONOMIST

Michael A. Crew
Paul R. Kleindorfer

In 1840, with the introduction of the Penny Post in England, modern postal service was born. The era of cheap, ubiquitous, and rapid communication had begun. Rowland Hill is credited with the major role in introducing the Penny Post and is regarded as the father of modern postal service. Hill was an educator, business man, reformer, and economist. His contribution as an economist stems not from his fundamental thinking and sculpting the discipline of economics, but from his brilliantly successful application of microeconomic analysis to the important practical problem of pricing and organizing postal service. Indeed, we are hard-pressed to think of any other application of microeconomic theory that has had such a widespread and long-lasting impact. Of course, Hill's contributions are those of a practical economist and are not of the same character in shaping the discipline as the fundamental works of early economist such as Adam Smith, David Ricardo, and Thomas Malthus.[1]

Hill's contribution rests mainly on his pamphlet with the unpromising title *Post Office Reform*, which first appeared in 1837 marked *private and confidential*. It is because of the impact of this pamphlet and his success in applying its ideas that Hill should be ranked with the major leaguers in economics.

Although Hill's ideas were a resounding success and have stood the test of time, there has been surprisingly little attention given to evaluating his contribution to economics.[2] Thus, the purpose of this paper is twofold, to evaluate the contribution of Rowland Hill as an economist and to note that some of his important ideas that had not formerly been applied now may be very relevant in an age of high-technology communications.

The paper has four sections. Section 1 contains a brief summary of Hill's proposals. Section 2 is the main critique, commentary, and evaluation of his economic ideas. Section 3 discusses how some of his ideas may be applied to current problems of mail service. Finally, section 4 is by way of concluding discussion.

1. Some Highlights of Rowland Hill's Proposals for Postal Reform

The mails in England in the 1830s were in a mess. Mail service was very unreliable and expensive.³ Clearly Rowland Hill's (1837) *Post Office Reform* pamphlet owed a considerable amount of its success to its timeliness. It not only set out his proposed reforms but also employed economic analysis to justify his proposals and accounting data to provide detailed cost analysis and forecasts of the effects of his proposals. *Post Office Reform* is remarkably advanced for its time, foreshadowing a lot of modern economics in that it employed well-crafted theory to a practical problem and forecasted the effects of its proposals by employing real data.

As the letter monopoly was used as an important source of tax revenue, the pamphlet begins with, by the standards of the day, a very sophisticated discussion of the notions of price elasticity and optimal taxation.

> The best test to apply to the several existing taxes for the discovery of the one which may reduced most extensively, with the least proportionate loss to the revenue, is probably this: excluding from the examination of those taxes, the produce of which is greatly affected by changes in the habits of people, as the taxes in spirits, tobacco, and hair powder, let each be examined as to whether its productiveness has kept pace with the increasing numbers and prosperity of the nation. (1837, 1-2)

He then demonstrated that between 1815 and 1835 the tax revenue from letters had remained unchanged, while population had increased by approximately one third. He made a similar comparison with stage coach duties, which were set at a much lower rate, and showed that they increased by 128 percent over the same period. Finally, he argued that "...reduction in postage to a considerable extent, would produce an increase of revenue" (p. 9).

Hill's proposal, as Coase (1939) clearly demonstrated, was in many major respects different from, and much more radical than, what emerged with implementation of the Penny Post in 1840.[4] A very radical departure was his strong denunciation of the postal monopoly.

> There can be no doubt that if the law not interpose its prohibition, the transmission of letters would be gladly undertaken by capitalists, with all that economy, attention to the wants of their customers, and skillful adaption of means to the desired end, which is usually practiced by those whose interests are involved in their success. But the law constitutes the Post Office a monopoly. Its conductors are, therefore, uninfluenced by the ordinary motives to enterprize and good management; and however injudiciously the institution may be conducted, however inadequate it may be to the growing wants of the nation, the people must submit to the inconvenience; they cannot set up a Post Office for themselves." (Hill 1937, 7)

Hill's proposal and the cost analysis underlying it were fundamentally different from the Penny Post. He argued that the uniform postage of one penny should be charged not for mail service as we know it, but for what he called "primary distribution." Primary distribution did not necessarily include delivery to individual addresses. As Hill defined it, *primary distribution* consisted of "...the transmission of letters, etc, from post-town to post-town throughout the United Kingdom, and the delivery within the post-towns." This should be contrasted with "... *secondary distribution*, or that distribution which proceeds from each post-town, as a centre, to towns of inferior importance, and to country places" (p. 11).

To be exact, Hill's proposal for primary distribution was:

> If, therefore, the charge for postage be made proportionate to the whole expense incurred in the receipt, transit, and delivery of the letter, and in the collection of its postage, *it must be made uniformly the same from every post town to every other post town in the United Kingdom.* (p. 16, emphasis in the original).

Hill envisaged that secondary distribution would be priced and provided separately, with "..the central authority of the Post Office...relieved of nearly all care with respect to the secondary distribution of letters...which would in each instance be regulated in exact accordance with the wants of the district" (p. 48-49).

Hill performed a detailed cost analysis which showed that costs, at least for primary distribution, did not vary much with distance, contrary to intuition and the prevailing view at the time. He therefore argued that uniform postage was the logical pricing policy to apply to primary distribution. Hill did not make a specific proposal concerning secondary distribution, which he viewed as being open to a wide variety of delivery arrangements, including competition.

Before 1840, postage could be prepaid or paid by the recipient. Hill analyzed the high transactions costs of this procedure and argued that postage should always be prepaid. Similarly, his cost analysis showed that "...the expenses of receipt and delivery are not affected by the weight of each letter within moderate limits..." (p. 17). This led him to argue for an abolition of the practice of charging by the sheet for a letter, which he noted caused high transactions costs.

2. Critique of the Economic Analysis of Postal Reform

Although his contributions were ahead of their time and were not properly understood, Hill was sufficiently pragmatic to accept major compromises to his original proposals because he saw that the 1840 Penny Post was a considerable improvement over the status quo. While clearly he would not have used the term, he proved to be an able practitioner in second-best optimality. The striking example of this is his adoption of uniform pricing for both primary and secondary distribution, which was clearly not what he proposed. Recall he proposed uniform pricing only for primary distribution. More generally, "What he advocated was not uniformity, but uniformity in so far as it was justified by costs" (Coase 1939, 430). He was apparently correct to compromise, given the success of uniform pricing of mail all over the world for a century and a half. Indeed, uniform pricing was so successful that it quickly became overused. The dangers arising from excessive application were recognized by one of the great economist of the time, Jevons.[5]

The success of uniform pricing and its improper imitation illustrate a major problem faced by economists. Like modern economists, Hill was rather careful to state the conditions under which his system of uniform pricing was to apply. He compromised and allowed it to be extended in its application. When it became a success, there were attempts to extend its use still further. Uniform pricing offered another tool for redistribution for politicians who have used uniform pricing as a tool for cross subsidy.[6] Indeed, only in the last twenty years have public utilities begun to make significant departures from uniform pricing and have economists really become serious in developing tools to analyze the inefficiencies of cross subsidies.

Hill was one of the first to toil in the vineyard of applied economic analysis. At the time, the tools available were very limited. Assumptions are critical simplifying tools in theory and applied economic analysis. Hill used them well in *Post Office Reform*. Unfortunately, as with many instances of where economic theory is applied, the non-economist pays insufficient respect to the limiting assumption. Clearly this was the case with Hill's proposal. He was in favor of competition, and his scheme was for primary distribution and the competition. In the end, postal service blossomed on the basis of uniform pricing and monopoly.

Hill was an unusually clear thinker and a fine intuitive economist. He was very clear on the nature of optimal taxation. "...[I]t is exceedingly important that great care and judgment should be exercised in the selection of the tax to be reduced, in order that the maximum relief may be afforded to the public with minimum injury to the Revenue" (p. 1). Modern day tax reformers in the United States Congress could take a lesson from Hill. He at least saw the relevant tradeoffs when taxes were changed. In addition, he saw the effect of different elasticities. While it is going too far to say that he intuited Ramsey's (1927) famous inverse elasticity rule, he did get the basic idea that taxes on mail were too high for the elasticities involved.

He addressed, at least implicitly, the cross-subsidy issue. This is why he was clear to make the distinction between primary and secondary distribution. He saw secondary distribution as "a source of loss" (p. 46). Envisaging, as he did, some competition in mail service, he saw the desirability of not attempting to tax secondary distribution. "...Let the whole weight of taxation be thrown on the primary distribution and let each department of secondary distribution just defray its own expenses" (p. 47).

Hill's proposal is an early contribution in transactions costs economics. His analysis showed that the transactions costs of collecting postage when the letter was delivered far exceeded the alternative approach of prepayment by the sender. He found that payment by the recipient not only caused high costs, arising from the postman's having to collect money when he delivered the mail, but also because of the complex operations that had to be performed on the mail stream in the office. He found that a considerable number of operations had to be performed on a letter in the mail processing facility prior to its transportation to its destination. By requiring prepayment and considerable simplification in the rate structure, namely the Penny Post, transactions costs were cut dramatically. He found a situation where, because of lack of innovation, there had been a complete failure at institutional innovation, with the consequent dramatic increase in transactions costs. Hill's study also makes clear the importance of such operations, known as mail processing in the United States and as sorting in the United Kingdom. His approach is, in addition, a contribution from a methodological point of view. He makes it clear that, to study institutional economics, it is critically important to study the operations of the institutions concerned. Hill's analysis might be considered a very early antecedent to the work of Commons (1934), Coase (1937), and the modern contributions of Williamson (1975; 1985). Of these, only Coase was apparently influenced by the thinking and work of Rowland Hill.

While Rowland Hill's contributions to economic analysis were clearly major, his record as an administrator at the Post Office received low ratings from his contemporaries in the Post Office and from Martin Daunton's (1985) history of the Post Office since 1840. Daunton's bottom line was that "Propagandists do not necessarily make good administrators and Hill created twenty years of acrimony and tension within the Post Office which probably hindered rather than helped the successful development of the Penny Post" (1985, 35).

Criticisms of Hill were at two levels, personal and technical, which we will discuss in turn. At the personal level, Daunton provides a comprehensive and humorous summary of the comments of the Hill detractors. Certainly the most articulate was the great victorian novelist, Anthony Trollope. Daunton concludes his chapter on Hill with a quote from Trollope: "I never came across anyone who so little understood the ways of men—unless it was his brother Frederic" (1985, 35). As quoted in Daunton (1985, 5), Trollope made no attempt to hide his personal antipathy for Hill:

> "feuds—such delicious feuds! I was always an anti-Hillite ... believing him to be entirely unfit to manage men or arrange labour. It was a pleasure to me to differ from him on all occasions; —and looking back now, I think that in all such differences I was right."

The picture that appears from Daunton is that Hill was an arrogant and extremely difficult man with whom to do business.

Most of the detractors were contemporaries who had good reason to speak ill of Hill. He was placed in a position of few pamphleteers and economists. Most of us just criticize, safe in the knowledge that there is little chance that our proposals will be adopted and an even smaller probability that we will be required to implement them. The position would be too challenging for most people and clearly Hill had his problems. He was placed in the position of having to work with and, in the case of Lt-Colonel W.L. Maberly, for the very people he had criticized in his pamphlet. His whole pamphlet was critical of the status quo, and the changes he proposed were not perceived to be to the benefit of entrenched management. For example, the following remarks would not endear him to postal management. "...the Post Office...as a means of distributing the correspondence of the country, is, at present, lamentably inefficient" (p. 40). Recall that he also attacked the notion of the postal monopoly. Any management that has tasted the fruit of monopoly prefers that arrangement to the chill of competition. Hill, with his pamphlet and with his tenure at the Post Office, clearly created a lot of friction and shook things up. This was clearly not before time. [7]

Some criticism was also made at a technical level of Hill's predictions as to the benefits of his scheme. Again, Daunton provides a review of these criticisms. The main criticism concerned his revenue projections. Recall that he argued that, because of elastic demand, total revenue would be increased by lowering price and that net revenue would also increase as a result of the institutional innovations and the resultant reduction in transactions costs.

> [T]hese increased facilities, together with the greatly reduced charges, would have the effect of increasing the number of chargeable letters, in all probability, at least five and a quarter fold; which increase ... would produce the four-fold increase of business, for which, as it has been shown, the present establishment of the Post Office, with a slight addition, would suffice. (p. 50)

Daunton (1985, 23-24) reports that the five-and-a-quarter-fold increase in volume was achieved by 1853. Through this period, the average cost of a letter fell dramatically by a half in 1840 and by over two thirds by 1853. Over the period, net revenue did fall from about £1.5 million to about £.5 million in 1840 and eventually rose to almost £1.2 million in 1853.

Even though Hill's claims made in *Post Office Reform* were somewhat more optimistic than the actual results, the results indicate the smashing success of the Penny Post. They show Hill to be a great practical economist. Admittedly, it took thirteen years. But this was quite a short time to achieve a greater than five-fold increase in volume. Moreover, *Post Office Reform* was silent on how long it would take to get the projected increase in volume. Obviously, it was not expected to occur overnight.

The problem with just examining net revenue or profit, along the lines of Hill's critics, is that such a test is inappropriate. Elementary economic theory castigates profit maximizing monopoly as inefficient because it restricts output. Hill recognized this point clearly, and indeed one of his major criticism was that the Post Office restricted output by charging (taxing) too much. Thus, Hill's achievements in economic terms need a more acceptable measure of economic efficiency than profit maximization. The success of his work becomes much more obvious if some measure of welfare is employed. Moreover, this approach seems consistent with Hill's thinking. In *Post Office Reform*, he seems to be reaching for a welfare measure beyond the simple revenue and costs concepts available to him. This is apparent in his notion of "the best test"[8] for optimal taxation. He clearly saw the need to weigh consumers' gains and losses against the revenue of the taxes. In addition, it is clear that he had some wider notion of the public good in mind, for example "...the Post Office assumes the new and important character of a powerful engine of civilization; capable of performing a distinguished part in the great work of National education, but rendered feeble and inefficient by erroneous financial arrangements" (p. 7).

Let us, for illustrative purposes, perform a naive welfare analysis. The analysis is based upon a simple notion of efficiency. For example, policy A is judged to be more efficient than policy B if the net benefits of policy A are greater than the net benefits of policy B. Net benefits are defined as the sum of benefits and costs, weighing consumers and producers' benefits equally. Consumer benefits are measured by the simple Marshallian consumer's surplus, and producer benefits are revenues minus cost or profit. (In the Penny Post case, tax revenue and consumer benefits are weighted equally.) We use the data provided by Daunton (1985, 23, Table 1.1) and repeat it below in table 1, for 1839 and 1840, the year before and the year of the Penny Post, respectively. The data show a dramatic increase in demand over this short period. For simplicity, we assume linear demand. We calculate that the net gain from the Penny Post in its first year was a little over £1.7 million. The gain to consumers (Marshallian consumer's surplus) was about £2.8 million, far outweighing the loss in revenue of over £1.1 million.[9] While we do not provide estimates of the monetary value of net benefits over longer periods of time, because stability of parameters would make such estimates less meaningful, volume grew dramatically and cost declined dramatically in the first decade of the Penny Post. In any case, the estimates provided here just for first year net benefits provide strong vindication of Hill's arguments.

Table 1. Simple Calculation of the Net Benefit from the Introduction of the Penny Post—1839-1840

		1839	1840
Letters	(millions)	75.9	168.8
Revenue	(million £)	2.39	1.36
Cost	(million £)	0.76	0.86
Net Revenue	(million £)	1.63	0.50
Average Cost	(£)	0.010	0.005
Average Revenue	(£)	0.031	0.008
Average Revenue[a]	(pence)	7.56	1.93
Consumer's Gain[b] from Price Reduction	(million £)	2.87	
First Year Net Benefit[c] from the Penny Post	(million £)	1.74	

[a] Recall in the days of pounds, shillings, and pence (£sd) there were 240 pence in a pound.
[b] Consumer's Gain is measured by the additional consumer's surplus $CS = Q_{39} (P_{39} - P_{40}) + \frac{1}{2} (P_{39} - P_{40}) (Q_{40} - Q_{39})$.
[c] Net benefit (NB) is obtained by deducting the difference in the net revenue between 1839 and 1840 from the additional consumer's surplus (CS), resulting from the price cut in 1840.

Our conclusion is that Hill's economic analysis and proposals in *Post Office Reform* were notable for their high quality and practical impact. His advocacy of postal reform and his practical work of implementing drown the jeers of his contemporaries in the Post Office. Fortunately, Anthony Trollope is remembered for his Barsetshire and other novels and not for his carping about Rowland Hill's eccentricities and deficiencies.

3. Applying Rowland Hill's Ideas to Present-Day Postal Problems

Rowland Hill's success as a reformer and father of modern mail service arose not only from the innovative nature of his work but also from the timeliness. The time was ripe for an innovator. In some ways, now the time is as ripe for innovation in postal service, as it was in 1837. While, in some respects, the current situation is just as challenging as that confronting Hill in 1837, we must be careful in drawing too close a comparison between today and Hill's situation. What is clear is that innovative thinking is called for. While some innovations are being generated both from inside and outside postal administrations, as some of the later papers will reveal, it is our opinion that there is scope for much more innovation and that the experience and contribution of Rowland Hill has application to today's problems.

The first lesson from Rowland Hill's experience is that existing postal management should be open to new ideas from outsiders. As Daunton's account reveals, Hill faced considerable opposition from postal management of the day. In the current situation, postal managements can afford to take this same attitude only at their peril. This is because postal service, despite its statutory monopoly, is faced with considerable competition and the likelihood of more competition. Express services, certainly in the United States, have made dramatic inroads in the United States Postal Service's (USPS) Express Mail service, and also have had some impact on their First Class mail. Similarly, United Parcel Service, unlike the case in Britain, has taken most of the parcel business away from USPS. Competition from telecommunications is only just beginning to have an impact on traditional mail service, since FAX machines are not ubiquitous and have not yet made great inroads into traditional sources of mail demand. Indeed, the FAX machine is only just starting to make an impact on traditional mail service. However, in many cases, FAX has a considerably lower marginal cost than traditional mail service. For example, FAX transmissions using local calls are likely to be of significantly lower cost than the mails.

The question of how to react to competition is perhaps the vital one for mail service today. One approach would be to attempt to employ regulation or other powers of government to strengthen postal monopoly. This would clearly be against the thinking of Rowland Hill, who stated the inefficiencies of the postal monopoly and preached the benefits of competition. Even the most entrenched postal management sees little chance that this would happen. The other alternative is to go the competitive route. Postal administrations could agree to the abolition of the monopoly and simultaneously seek the abolition of regulation. Currently, postal service faces varying degrees of competition, from very little direct competition in services, where there is a statutory monopoly, to considerable, for example in the case of express or parcel service. The regulatory process provides an opportunity for competitors to reduce USPS's ability to compete in these areas by intervening in rate hearings.

In other respects, Hill's ideas might be applied to today's problems. Recall that his actual proposal was not adopted. His scheme was radical in that it was for *primary distribution*. Perhaps the time has come for the consideration of a radical scheme like this. If the postal monopoly were ended, in the United States this would mean that the mail box could be used for other materials other than postage-paid mail; there would be an incentive for other delivery services to compete with deliveries. In some instances, the existing local networks of national postal services would be strong competitors and would continue very much as presently. In other instances, postal service faces problems. Some local delivery is very expensive and loses money. Currently, with its common carrier obligations, a national postal administration has no choice but to deliver to places where the costs far exceed the uniform price charged. Under competition, with the end of common carrier obligations, such cross subsidies would be eliminated, and a scheme very much like Hill' system of primary distribution might suffice.

Absent a move by legislators to open up mail service to competition, major changes in philosophy are required. Postal administrations have to respond to competition where it is obvious. For example, in the United States "mailing shoppes" are being set up. They provide services such as mail boxes and FAX machines, and they sell stamps, usually at a slight premium over face value. They are open convenient hours and provide friendly service in attractive facilities. Stamps in the United States are not available in machines as often as one might expect, and foreign visitors are surprised to find that they are normally charged a big premium from those machines over face value. These cases indicate that there may be new market opportunities for postal services.

FAX may be an instance where postal administrations are slow to respond. For example, the USPS is renting space to FAX machine owners in their lobbies. In view of the considerable potential impact of FAX on traditional mail services, a more aggressive approach may be warranted. The opportunities for post offices are considerable. Post offices might offer competition to messenger service with FAX. I have a FAX machine, but the recipient does not. I can FAX to his local post office and have it delivered by messenger, or by the next regular delivery, or have him pick it up at the post office. This is a means of expanding postal business and making it relatively less attractive for the recipient to get his own FAX machine, because he has service from his local post office. Post offices have existing ubiquitous networks that are currently available. They have a strong first mover advantage.

4. Concluding Discussion

The FAX example is just one idea for postal administrations. The basic notion is that they need to become more market-oriented. This means becoming more responsive to the needs of their customers—which Hill noted the postal monopoly was not, more innovative in the services they offer, and much more cost conscious. Hill's other contribution was his recognition of the importance of communications. The world is communications hungry. Despite the great advances in telecommunications, postal service has continued to grow. By innovating and moving into new postal markets, postal services can continue to share in the growth in the demand for communications. The papers in this volume will address inter alia innovations in postal service, including such issues, as competition, privatization, productivity, internal efficiency, technological change, compensation of unionized labor, efficient pricing, innovative marketing of postal services, and so on. The papers therefore strive to continue the innovative spirit of Rowland Hill, the father of modern mail service.

Notes

1. Hill certainly was an avid reader of Adam Smith and an able practitioner of a subset of Smith's theories. See Hill (1880, 23).
2. With the exception of Ronald Coase (1939; 1947).
3. "...a Londoner might receive his mail from three letter-carriers. The charge for local letters within the central area of London was twopence, and there was also an outer area in which there was a charge of an extra penny. (Daunton 1985, 5-6)
4. We would like to emphasize our debt to Coase. His early articles were an important contribution to the wave of debate on optimal pricing that took place in the 1940s. His contributions of the inefficiencies of uniform pricing systems (Coase 1939; 1947) are especially noteworthy. It is a shame that it took so long for this kind of thinking to have an impact on public pricing.
5. As early as 1883, much to the chagrin of the great economist, Jevons, there were proposals for uniform rates for many industries. "I can imagine no grounds for the notion except for the great success of Rowland Hill's penny postage." Jevons (1883, 369). See Coase (1939, 434) for details.
6. Crew and Rowley (1988; 1989) examine the use in regulation of cross subsidy as device for obfuscation. Their arguments derive in part from Peltzman (1976) and Tullock (1967).
7. Hill also effectively had "the last laugh" on his detractors. He received the honors of Freedom of the City of London and burial in Westminster Abbey in 1879. He was given the life pension of full salary and a special Parliamentary grant of £20,000 in 1864. For a strongly opposing view of Hill to that of Daunton, see Hey (1989).
8. Hill (1837, 1-2) cited above in full on page 2 of this paper.
9. Crew and Kleindorfer (1985) provide details and technical derivations of these types of welfare assessments.

References

Coase, Ronald H. 1937. "The Nature of the Firm." *Economica* 4 (November): 386-405.
Coase, Ronald H. 1939. "Rowland Hill and the Penny Post." *Economica* 6 (November): 423-35.
Coase, Ronald H. 1947. "The Economics of Uniform Pricing Systems." *The Manchester School* 15 (May): 139-56.
Commons, John. 1934. *Institutional Economics*. Madison, Wisconsin: University of Wisconsin Press.
Crew, Michael A., and Paul R. Kleindorfer. 1985. "Governance Costs and Rate of Return Regulation." *Journal of Institutional and Theoretical Economics* (March).
Crew, Michael A., and Charles K. Rowley. 1988. "Toward a Public Choice Theory of

Monopoly Regulation." *Public Choice* (March).
Crew, Michael A., and Charles K. Rowley. 1989. "Feasibility of Deregulation: A Public Choice Analysis." In *Deregulation and Diversification of Utilities*, edited by M.A. Crew. Boston: Kluwer Academic Publishers.
Daunton, Martin J. 1985. *Royal Mail: The Post Office Since 1840*. London: Athlone Press.
Hey, Colin G. 1989. *Rowland Hill: Genius and Benefactor, 1795-1879*. Londno: Quiller Press.
Hill, Sir Rowland, and George Birkbeck Hill. 1880. *The Life of Sir Rowland Hill and the History of the Penny Post*.
Hill, Sir Rowland. 1837. *Post Office Reform*.
Jevons, William Stanley. 1883. *Methods of Social Reform and Other Papers*. London: Macmillan.
Peltzman, Samuel. 1976. "Toward a More General Theory of Regulation." *Journal of Law and Economics* 19 (August): 211-240.
Ramsey, Frank P. 1927. "A Contribution to the Theory of Taxation." *Economic Journal* 37 (March): 47-61.
Tullock, Gordon. 1967. "The Welfare Costs of Tariffs, Monopolies and Theft." *Western Economic Journal* 5 (June): 224-232.
Williamson, Oliver E. 1975. *Markets and Hierarchies: Analysis and Antitrust Implications*. New York: Free Press.
Williamson, Oliver E. 1985. *The Economic Institutions of Capitalism: Firms, Markets and Rational Contracting*. New York: Free Press.

COMMENTS
Martin J. Daunton

Rowland Hill has been the subject of hagiography rather than biography, and it is all too easy to point out that the idol is made of clay (Hey 1989; Daunton 1985). Such cynicism can easily go too far, and Michael Crew and Paul Kleindorfer show that the penny post did produce a net consumers' gain to set against the reduction in net revenue. But it their calculation correct? A large number of "contraband" letters were carried in 1839, and much of the increase in the mail in 1840 was a transfer from private carriers (Gregory 1987, 142-8). As a result, the net benefit from the penny post in the first year was less than Crew and Kleindorfer suggest. Further, the fall of the Post Office's revenue had serious implications for government finance, which meant that other taxes, which potentially offered a greater net consumers' gain, could not be reduced. The fiscal circumstances in which Hill wrote his pamphlet in 1837, and into which the penny post was introduced in 1840, were complex. Income tax had been abolished, and the government relied upon a regressive tax system based upon import duties, assessed taxes on items of conspicuous consumption, stamp duties, and indirect excise duties on beer, salt, and so on. The government was anxious to make concessions at a time of social unrest. It could cut its expenditure in order to shed various taxes and duties, or it could shift the tax regime in a progressive direction by reintroducing the income tax, which was a politically dangerous maneuver. In 1837, the year of Hill's pamphlet, the budget moved into deficit. The Chancellor of the Exchequer, Thomas Spring-Rice, was skeptical about the financial viability of Hill's scheme and wrote to the Prime Minister that "I can never be a party to the reduction of the postage by law without the contemporaneous imposition of an equivalent tax;" it would be "a measure of reckless daring—for which I confess I have not courage. I dot not think it would be honest" (Brown 1958, 61). Nevertheless, the government brought in the bill in 1839 because they could not afford to lose radical votes in parliament. A reduction in the net revenue of the Post Office by 1.13 million between 1839 and 1840 was a major element in the deficit of 1.8 million in 1840/1, and the lack of sympathy towards Hill in not altogether surprising.

In 1840, F.T. Baring (who had succeeded Spring-Rice as Chancellor) failed to balance the budget by increasing assessed taxes and customs and excise duties; in 1841, he adopted an alternative strategy. By cutting import duties, he hoped that revenue would rise as a result of increased consumption, which was Hill's contention on the penny post. It was to be linked with a revision in the corn law, which produced an agricultural reaction. What Baring did *not* wish to do was to introduce an income tax. The budget of 1841 was rejected, the Whigs lost power, and the new Tory government seized the financial nettle. Peel's budget of 1842 reintroduced the income tax, both to deal with the deficit, and to place the tax regime on a more socially acceptable basis at a time when the Anti-Corn Law League, Chartism, and the "condition of England" question were causing alarm. In 1839, Peel had supported the penny post but had argued that it should not be introduced without creating a new tax to cover the loss of revenue; he hinted that an income tax would be the most sensible financial strategy.

Clearly, the penny post was at the heart of a debate over the deficit and taxation. The penny post exacerbated the Whigs' budgetary difficulties and contributed to their defeat. It was to be the yield on Peel's income tax which allowed the budget to return to surplus and permitted the reduction of other duties and taxes, marking a shift towards direct taxation and a social contract which tied classes together rather than produced conflict. Hill's single-issue pressure group politics forced the Whigs to take action which they felt to be undesirable, and Hill himself showed no grasp of the wider political and fiscal implications of his proposal. The animosity of politicians such as Baring towards Hill is perfectly understandable (O'Brien 1988; Mathias and O'Brien 1976; Hilton 1977; Gash 1986; and Matthew 1979).

Hill argued that important consideration in determining rates was cost: since transport was a small item in total costs within the "primary distribution," it followed that the charge for a letter should be the same regardless of distance. His opponents started from a different assumption: rates should not be determined by the cost, so much as by what the customer would pay. Here distance *was* a relevant consideration. Hill's opponents were not simply obscurantist, for they had an understanding of the nature of the demand for mail services. In 1784, 1797, 1801, 1805, and 1812 postage rates were changed so that they increased more for longer distances. "Distance is the chief ingredient," argued J.W. Croker in 1839, "of any and every system of post-office charge... The intrinsic value of the conveyance of a letter... is exactly equal to the time, trouble and expense which is saved by the correspondent—of which the best, if not the only measure is distance." This was the view of Lt. Col. Maberly and the Post Office. The relevant consideration was not cost by rather the benefit to the consumer which varied by distance. Although the extent of the contraband mail suggests that rates had become too high, largely under the pressure of war finance, it should not be assumed that Hill's opponents could not make a reasoned case for postal rates determined by distance (Gregory 1987, 132-5).

There was certainly nothing original about Hill's view that a reduction in taxation might increase the yield. This had been argued by Henry Parnell in *On Financial Reform* of 1830, in which he claimed that "when a tax has been carried to an excessively high point, the reducing of it is not necessarily followed by a reduction of revenue." Parnell's tract had influence upon a group of Whigs and Radicals, especially at the Board of Trade. One outcome was the Select Committee on Import Duties of 1840 which built upon the work of George Porter, the head of the Statistical Department of the Board of Trade who was, like Hill, associated with Charles Knight, the publisher of *Postal Reform.* Porter broke new ground in analyzing the price elasticity of consumption of tea, sugar, and coffee which underlay the Select Committee of 1840, Baring's budget of 1841, and Hill's campaign for the penny post. Hill and the postal reformers were, therefore, in no sense original in the discussion of price elasticity and optimal taxation, but were part of a strand of thought present among the Whigs in the 1830s (Brown 1958).

There is no doubt that the Post Office needed reform in the 1840s, and this was part of the shift in policy which was affecting many government departments. Hill was a small part of this trend. It is possible to have sympathy with Hill in facing such bastions of the old regime as Maberly, but the more interesting question is his divergence with the new generation within the Post Office, such as John Tilley and Frank Scudamore, over such issues as the determination of wages, rates for the carriage of mail by railway and ships, and the justification for moving into new directions such as the Post Office Savings Bank. The new men saw Rowland and Frederic Hill as unnecessarily restrictive in their attitudes, threatening the continuity of service by a rigid attitude to wage rates and mail contracts, and frustrating the movement of the Post Office into socially desirable ventures. It is in these debates of the 1850s and 1860s that Hill was in a more real sense moving into new territory than in the 1830s. The opponent of the Post Office letter monopoly could argue for the nationalization of the railways, because they destroyed the competition of stage coaches and placed large monopolies in private hands. In this case, public ownership or regulation of their rates was essential—the market could not be allowed to fix the rate for the carriage of letters, whether by monopolistic railways or oligopolistic steamship companies. This was part of a debate over how to deal with the emerging public utilities of gas, water, and public transport in the cities of Britain which led to complex regulations over prices, and to municipal ownership. The Post Office was to remain deeply involved in this question, leading to the acquisition of the telegraphs and the telephones. Hill is a point of entry into a debate over the nature of a mixed economy, which is a central feature in the history of Britain.

My contention is that, despite a modest welfare gain from the penny post, the loss of postal revenue *did* matter at a time of tension and controversy over the fiscal regime, when taxation was at the heart of social and political conflict. Hill's grasp of the wider issues was weak, and he is an object lesson of the dangers of pursuing a single issue without a sense of balance and proportion. Neither were his ideas original; far from being one of "the major leaguers in economics," he was derivative and lacking in originality.

References

Brown, Lucy. 1958. *The Board of Trade and the Free Trade Movement, 1830-42*. Oxford: Clarendon Press.
Daunton, Martin J. 1985. *Royal Mail: The Post Office Since 1840*. London: Athlone Press.
Gash, Norman. 1986. *Sir Robert Peel: The Life of Sir Robert Peel after 1830* (2nd edition). London: Longman.
Gregory, Derek. 1987. "The friction of distance? Information circulations and the mails in early nineteenth-century England." *Journal of Historical Geography* 13: 130-54.

Hey, Colin G. 1989. *Rowland Hill: Genius and Benefactor, 1795-1879*. London: Quiller Press.
Hilton, Boyd. 1977. *Corn, Cash and Commerce: The Economic Policies of the Tory Governments, 1815-30*. Oxford: Oxford University Press.
Mathias, Peter and Patrick K. O'Brien. 1976. "Taxation in Britain and France, 1715-1810: a comparison of the social and economic incidence of taxes collected for the central government." *Journal of European Economic History* 5:601-50.
Matthew, H.G. Colin. 1979. "Disraeli, Gladstone and the politics of mid-Victorian budgets." *Historical Journal* 22: 615-43.
O'Brien, Patrick K. 1988. "The political economy of British taxation, 1660-1815." *Economic History Review* 2nd series 41:1-32.

2

INTERNATIONAL POSTAL REFORM:
An Application of the Principles of Rowland Hill to the International Postal System
James I. Campbell, Jr.

> Cheap postage! What is this men are talking about? Can it be that all my life I have been in error?
> —Sir Francis Freeling, Secretary, British Post Office (Harlow 1928, 190)

Although many nineteenth century figures are better known than Rowland Hill, few had a more beneficial effect upon civilization. His thoughtful analysis of the British Post Office resulted in the establishment of the first inexpensive, universal system for communications available to all members of society. Modern post offices allude romantically to Persian messengers and Roman couriers, to seventeenth century proclamations and ringers of bells in cockaded hats. But these allusions are fundamentally misleading to the modern mind. What we think of as postal service began in 1840, a magnificent English innovation soon copied by all countries in the world.

Modern postal service has become so commonplace that we forget its significance. We take for granted—indeed we can hardly cope with—the possibilities of cheap universal communications. To appreciate the work of Rowland Hill we must imagine a world without telecommunications, when one's only connection to the outside world was by the physical delivery of messages and newspapers. In overall social importance, the development of cheap, universal postal service was as significant in its way as more technologically spectacular inventions such as the telephone and television.

The essence of Hill's approach was, I believe, that he refused to accept the correctness of traditional assumptions about the postal business or yield to political "realities." Rather, he thought through his ideas logically and carefully and forced his opponents to do the same. Today, discussions about postal policy on both sides of the Atlantic are replete with statements such as "You may be right, but of course we must recognize political facts of life." The first lesson that I take from Rowland Hill is that governmental and industry officials—whether in Brussels or Washington or anywhere else—must concentrate their attention upon the truth, not political realities, if they are to earn what Hill nicely refers to as "the gratitude and affection of the people."

For me, it is interesting to speculate what would have happened if Hill's proposals had been rejected and the British Post Office left unreformed in 1840. Perhaps Rowland Hill would have started a private delivery company to put his ideas in practice. Of course, Hill Express would have started on a small scale. From the beginning, however, Hill would have introduced prices based upon actual costs, so that delivery rates between major cities would have been uniform. And he would have simplified procedures such as prepayment of charges, elimination of unnecessary supervisory work, expedited delivery procedures, and so forth.[1]

No doubt the British Post Office would have tried to close Hill Express for violating the postal monopoly. Having proven his ideas on a small scale, Hill would likely have argued his case to Parliament. The Post Office would have surely replied that Hill Express was "cream skimming" the most profitable routes, taking advantage of anomalies in postal tariffs, and failing to provide the traditional security measures. Scholars and experts would have been invited to comment about whether Hill's ideas would be viable for the entire postal system. And the Post Office would have noted that in any social situation, there are so many variables that it is impossible to prove that disasters will not occur if conditions change.

Perhaps. But, of course, all of this is mere speculation. I raise it only by way of prologue.

Despite the general acceptance of most of Rowland Hill's ideas, several participants in the conference question whether national postal policies have applied fully Hill's teachings or, indeed, whether they comply with still more esoteric economic criticisms. Rather than push into this crowded field, I would like to place before you the suggestion that there remains a most interesting and important realm of postal policy which is almost completely unenlightened by, and is quite ripe for, Rowland Hill's reforms. I am referring to the international postal system.

To give you a sense of scale, the United Kingdom postal system in Hill's day transmitted an estimated 126 million items. The international postal system of today handles about 6.4 billion items (excluding the Soviet Union), about 50 times as many. In 1837, the fastest coaches from London to Edinburgh took about 60 hours. Today, air transportation from London to Sydney takes about 24 hours. In operational terms, then, the international postal system is substantially denser and more compact than the British postal system of 1837. Compared to today's national postal systems, the international postal system is about the same size as the Italian post office, and a bit smaller than the Canadian.

I would like to suggest to the conference a few simple propositions about the international postal system: (1) it has never embraced the basic reforms of Rowland Hill; (2) it is extremely important in overall commercial and social development;

and (3) it presents a postal system in which fundamental reform is feasible and especially timely.

To support my suggestions, I shall examine seven aspects of current international postal policy using Hill's famous 1837 paper (Hill 1937) as my basic text, with annotations drawn from the experience of the private international express industry. I do not intend my comments to be definitive in a scholarly sense; on the contrary, my purpose is to experiment with these ideas, to offer hypotheses, and to encourage further analysis by others more qualified than I.

1. Relatively Poor Performance of International Postal Sector

Hill began his study of the British Post Office by asking "whether its productiveness has kept pace with the increasing numbers and prosperity of the nation." He noted that, in the preceding two decades (1815-1835), population had increased by 31 percent whereas postal revenues had actually declined by 1 percent. He found this particularly remarkable considering that revenues from the stagecoach tax, a seemingly closely related industry, had increased by 129 percent (Hill 1837, 2-4).[2]

The circumstances of the international post today are remarkably similar, at least to the untutored eye. According to estimates by the Universal Postal Union[3] (UPU), during the last decade (1977-1986), the volume (pieces) of international letters (LC) handled by the 28 major non-communist post offices decreased by 6 percent and the volume of printed matter (AO) increased by only 4 percent. This poor performance contrasts with increases, during the same period, in domestic postal traffic of 32 percent for letters (LC) and 68 percent for printed matter (AO). Like Hill, we can look to seemingly related industries for confirmation that something is amiss. During the same decade in which international postal traffic stood still, international aviation (world passenger kilometers) and international telecommunications (telephone calls between the European Economic Community (EEC) and the United States, both directions) grew by almost 100 and 500 percent, respectively. These figures are summarized in table 1.

It should be noted that the relatively poor performance of the international post is in no way explained by the recent phenomenon of remail. Since remail is by definition eventually posted somewhere, a loss in one post office's account will show up as a gain in another post office's account, not affecting the total.[4] Moreover, remail of letters did not develop to any substantial degree until after 1986, the year the United States Postal Service withdrew objections to international remail based upon the United States postal monopoly.

According to Hill's approach, then, it would appear possible that the international postal system has failed to keep pace with modern commerce and may be in need of fundamental reform.

Table 1. Relatively Poor Performance of the International Post			
	1977	1986	Change
Intl Post (OECD)			
Letters (LC) bil.	3.9	3.7	-6%
Printed (AO) bil.	1.3	1.4	+4%
Domestic Post (OECD)			
Letters (LC) bil.	107.8	142.5	+32%
Printed (AO) bil.	64.6	108.3	+68%
Intl Aviation (World)			
Sched. mil. tonne-km	46.7	89.6	+92%
Intl Telecomm (US-EEC)	36.6	219.3	+499%
Sources: UPU, *Five-yearly Report on the Development of the Postal Services, 1977-1981*, Tables XIV, XV, XVIII, XIX (1984); UPU, *Five-yearly Report on the Development of the Postal Services, 1982-1986*, Graphs T1, T4, T13, T16 (1989); International Civil Aviation Organization, *Civil Aviation Statistics of the World*, Table 1-13 (1986 ed, 1988 ed.); U.S. Federal Communications Commission, *Statistics of Common Carriers* Table 15 (1977 ed.), Table 13 (1986 ed.).			

2. Division of Distribution into Primary and Secondary Areas

The second step in Hill's analysis was an intuitive simplification. He divided the business of the Post into "primary" and "secondary" distribution systems. "Primary distribution" was defined as distribution within and between major towns. "Secondary distribution" included distribution "to towns of inferior importance, and to country places." According to Hill's (1937, 10-13) calculations, primary distribution accounted for about 61 percent of the whole (by revenue). The reforms advocated by Hill pertained mainly to the primary distribution area.

At the governmental inquiry into Hill's proposals, Hill himself was followed by two witnesses from the Post Office. The first said he did not understand the distinction between primary and secondary distribution, and the second testified that he understood it and saw no advantages. Finding the concept too technical to explain in the face of postal opposition, Hill withdrew this portion of his proposal (Coase 1939, 423, 432). Writing a century later (1939), Professor Coase (1939, 435) commented:

> There is indeed good reason to deplore the abandonment of the distinction between primary and secondary distribution. It ... might have led to a rational discussion of price policy and its relation to costs. As it is, the magic word "uniformity" has been substituted for thought.

Most, I think, would agree that Hill's distinction between primary and secondary distribution remains an economically sound idea.[5] The analogous approach in the international area is clear. Of total international mail, about 80 percent circulates between the developed countries.[6] Hence, as in England in 1840, it is possible to improve the entire system by concentrating on primary distribution. In the international postal system, we may tentatively define the primary distribution system as including all traffic among the 24 OECD countries or the UPU's similar list of 28 "free market industrialized countries."

Of course, dividing the world into "big guys" and "little guys" is not automatically popular. Indeed, as recently as 1979, the UPU explicitly rejected a carefully reasoned proposal to divide the "terminal dues" charge into a two tier system which distinguished between developed or less developed countries.[7]

Recent events in the international postal world, however, suggest the growing acceptability of such an approach in two key areas. First, the 1989 UPU congress made a U-turn and agreed to a two tier terminal dues system. Second, about 20 major post offices have decided to coordinate postal policy more closely under the umbrella of a Dutch company called Unipost.

It should be noted that in both cases, the international postal system's embrace of this Rowland Hill concept has come entirely by way of reaction to the competition posed by the private express system.[8] As we shall see, this is not the only instance in which competition has forced the international postal system to rediscover Hill's principles.

3. Adaptation of Price to Cost

After his grand division of the postal system into primary and secondary distribution, Hill analyzed postal costs guided by the principle that prices should reflect actual costs (plus a uniform tax in Hill's day).

The most famous application of this approach was Hill's advocacy of a uniform postage rate within the primary distribution area. Prior to 1840, British postal rates varied according to distance and a host of other transportation factors. Postal historian Alvin Harlow (1928, 180-181) writes:

> [I]n 1813 and thereafter, the city [of London] rates were twopence and threepence, and the weight limit four ounces. There were numerous surcharges throughout the kingdom. For example, a single letter of one quarter-ounce weight going from London to Dublin, about three hundred and twenty-five miles, paid one shilling fourpence [24 pence] of which twopence was steamer postage across the Irish Sea from Holyhead, one penny for crossing the Conway Bridge and another for crossing Telford's bridge across the Menai Straits... The general result was that the post had become a convenience only for the well-to-do, and that even they avoided the payment of postage whenever and by whatever means possible.

Undaunted by this seeming complexity, Hill carefully examined postal costs in the primary distribution area and concluded that, contrary to conventional wisdom, the cost of transportation between major towns was an insignificant fraction of the total cost of delivery. For this reason, Hill argued, the postage rate "must be uniformly the same from every post town to every other post town in the United Kingdom" (Hill 1837, 16).

Because of frequent misstatement of Hill's principles today, it is worth emphasizing that uniformity of price was simply a consequence of conforming prices to costs, not a goal in itself. Hill did not advocate uniform postage rates to secondary towns, for he saw clearly the economic error of such an approach and believed that "every branch of the Post Office ought to defray its own expenses" (Hill 1837, 46). We might summarize Hill's views of secondary distribution by saying that the institutional costs of the post office should be borne by the primary distribution system while secondary distribution costs should be tailored to the needs of individual communities and priced at marginal cost (Hill 1837, 46-48).[9]

Given the subject of my paper, Hill's views on international postage rates are especially interesting. He wrote (Hill 1837, 48):

> For the sake of simplicity in accounting for postage, it is very desirable that the rates of charge should be the same for Foreign and Colonial as for Inland letters; that is to say, that a Foreign or Colonial letter not exceeding one ounce in the British Isles should be conveyed from any post town in the British Isles to the Foreign or Colonial *port* [emphasis by Hill] for one penny. *The conveyance in the foreign country or colony being of course subject to the arrangements there established* [emphasis added].

Hill's insistence on conforming price to cost also led him to advocate abolishing postage rates for "packets" which depended upon the number of sheets of paper in the envelope. Hill (1837, 17) reasoned:

> Again, the expenses of receipt and delivery are not much affected by the weight of each letter, within moderate limits; and, as it would take a nine-fold weight to make the expense of transit amount to one farthing [one quarter penny], it follows *that, taxation apart, the charge ought to be precisely the same for every packet of moderate weight, without reference to the number of enclosures* [emphasis by Hill].

Thus, Hill's basic principle that postal prices should reflect costs may be seen in three pricing policies. We can restate them as follows: (1) the cost of transportation between large cities does not vary proportionally with distance and is small relative to collection and delivery costs; (2) postal charges for delivery in a foreign country should be based upon the cost of delivery by the foreign post; and (3) postal charges for shipments of multiple letters handled as a single shipment should be based upon cost factors and not simply the number of letters.

Let us consider the international postal system in regard to each policy.

3.1. Charges for International Transportation

While many post offices contract individually with international carriers, the matter of correctly costing international transportation comes up when post offices forward each other's mail, either to another post office or to a city removed from the port of import. For example, what should the French post office charge the British Post Office for transporting English mail from Calais to Germany? Or from Calais to Lyons? In UPU terminology these charges are called "transit charges" and, for air transportation, "air conveyance dues."

At the very first congress of the Universal Postal Union in Berne in 1874, the matter of "transit fees" occasioned the "longest and most acrimonious discussion" (Codding 1964, 29). Some post offices argued there should be no charge for forwarding mail, citing Rowland Hill, who of course would never have supported such a thing.[10] Other post offices, who were so situated that they had large amounts of transit mail, insisted upon being repaid (or better, overpaid) for costs incurred.

In the end, the twenty one predominately European countries agreed upon a common transit fee schedule under which transit charges varied depending upon weight, distance, type of conveyance, and the nature of the mail. Table 2 presents the figures.

Table 2. First UPU Transit Fees (1874)		
Distance and Means	Letters (LC)	Printed Paper (AO)
0-750 km by land	2 gf/kg	0.25 gf/kg
750+ km by land	4 gf/kg	0.50 gf/kg
0-300 n.mi. by sea	0 gf/kg	0 gf/kg
300+ n.mi. by sea	6.50 gf/kg	0.50 gf/kg
Europe to U.S./India	Negotiated	Negotiated
Source: Codding (1964, 29-30). Note: "gf" refers to gold francs; "n.mi." refers to nautical miles.		

It requires no special knowledge of nineteenth century economics to recognize this as a political solution rather than the economic one that Rowland Hill would have advocated. It seems highly likely that a 20 kilogram bag of letters costs a little more to transport by ship than a 10 kilogram bag; in any case, the sea voyage for a bag of letters was certainly not 13 times as costly as for a similar bag of newspapers.

Today, UPU transit charges, and air conveyance dues, still vary according to weight and distance, even though the costs of transport tend to vary more by volume and number of pieces.[11] Moreover, unlike the UPU of 1874, the modern UPU convention makes no allowance for variations in cost around the world. The same schedule applies to America and India as to France and Germany.

Within the last two or three years, however, the outbreak of international remail competition between post offices, aided by the private express industry, has caused some post offices to reconsider this inflexible and cost insensitive approach. A 1987 UPU "Study on Remailing" notes:

> *The remail firms' flexibility in obtaining favorable air transportation rates is another major competitive advantage* they have over postal administrations. For longer distances they pay air freight rates which are much lower than UPU conveyance rates. For shorter distances, where the UPU air conveyance rates are comparable to, or even lower than, air freight rates, they submit their mailings to a postal administration which is willing to cooperate by dispatching the items as its own mail, at the usual UPU air conveyance rate.[12]

At the UPU congress last December, the Secretary General acknowledged the assistance of the private express industry in bringing this matter to his attention when he described the situation to the man from IATA (International Air Transport Association) as "the onslaught of the competition."[13]

Despite recognition that air transportation charges (the most important transport element today) do not reflect actual costs, the UPU Executive Committee has so far rejected proposals either to move to individually negotiated arrangements or to accept a slightly more cost related ("digressive") air conveyance schedule.[14]

3.2 Charges for Foreign Postal Delivery

Delivery of mail in a foreign country, Hill thought, should be "subject to the arrangements there established." However, the UPU has never accepted this Hill precept either. Indeed, the UPU's approach has been exactly the opposite. The basic principle of the UPU has been that British mail should be delivered in foreign countries, from Afghanistan to Zimbabwe, for the delivery cost incurred by the British Post Office in England! Put another way, the UPU's basic premise has been that the mail flow between two post offices is the same in both directions, in quantity and content, and that delivery costs are the same in both countries; as a result, neither post office would charge the other for local delivery.

In the UPU's 1897 Washington Congress, some post offices noted that they received more mail than they sent out. At the 1906 Rome Congress, the Italian post office demonstrated that it delivered 320,000 printed papers from abroad and sent out none. It was not until 1969, however, that the UPU introduced a correction for traffic imbalances. The correction charge, called "terminal dues," was a fixed amount per kilogram.[15]

This uniform, weight based delivery terminal dues charge, however, is fundamentally flawed. Most basically, it applies equally to all post offices, despite the fact that, according to a 1988 UPU survey, actual local delivery costs around the world vary by a factor of 16 or more (depending upon LC or AO).[16] One can just imagine Rowland Hill shaking his head in amazement!

A second problem with the terminal dues rate is that it ignores the number of pieces of mail, even though local delivery costs obviously vary more by number of pieces than by weight. The 1989 UPU Congress finally addressed this second issue, but only halfway. It set different per kilogram charges for letter mail (LC) and printed matter mail (AO) based upon the assumption that there are 46 letters and 5.6 printed papers in each kilogram of mail.[17]

This limited reform was the direct result of the "problem" posed by remail competition. The problem with remail is that large mailers can use the private express system to shop among post offices, tendering their mail to those post offices that reduce international postage rates to marginal costs. Since terminal dues are the major component of marginal costs for international mail, the post offices agreed to raise terminal dues among themselves as much as possible.

Spurred by the competitive threat, some post offices have gone even further, embracing an approach very much like Rowland Hill advocated in 1837. These post offices are prepared to levy a charge for the delivery of foreign mail based upon the domestic postage rate. The domestic rate is discounted by a percentage, about 40 percent, reflecting the absence of collection costs for foreign mail. This system has been operating among the four Nordic post offices since the first of January, 1990, and I understand other European post offices may be negotiating similar arrangements. Indeed, as a result of a complaint filed by the International Express Carriers Conference, the European Commission may soon rule that some such approach is required in the European Community. If the Commission so rules, I have no doubt the international postal system will be the better for it.

3.3. Discounts for Packets of Letters

Unlike the British Post Office of the 1830s, the modern international postal system has never charged for the transmission of letters based upon the number of sheets per envelope. But it has done something similar. For letters collected at a single point—a post office or sender's office—the collection cost is more or less the same for one letter or for many letters. Yet the international post has traditionally been very reluctant, more so than the national post, to allow discounts for large mailers who save the post office collection costs.

Again, we may note that, in the last two years and in response to private competition, the international postal system has lowered prices for large mailers. A 1988 UPU survey found that 88 percent of responding post offices had accepted the need to lower prices.[18] Indeed, there is a danger that the international postal system will reduce prices to predatory levels. New Article 12bis of the 1989 UPU Convention authorizes post offices to

> give preferential rates to major users [not less than] those applied in the internal service of items presenting the same characteristics.

A quick reference to Rowland Hill suggests to me that this provision would allow a relatively low (unit) cost postal administration, such as the Royal Mail or United States Postal Service, to reduce international postage rates to well below actual cost.[19]

4. Simplification of Postal Operations

A fourth major theme of Hill's review of British postal operations emphasized the gains to be won from simplifying operations and procedures. He analyzed the inefficiency of letter carriers collecting postage. Hill also described in detail the complicated clerical work demanded by the old tariff, requiring "a vigilance rarely to be met with." And he lamented the large number of supervisors necessary to guard against fraud. These observations led Hill to recommend, among other things, that all postage be prepaid and that the number of "receiving-houses" be expanded.

Today, hardly any international mailer is aware that postage used to be collected from the addressee, but there are still somewhat similar anachronisms to be found. For large international mailers, for example, the traditional method of paying postage is very cumbersome. Postage must be calculated on an individual piece basis and affixed to each letter. And the prepayment of foreign postage for business reply cards was impossible. Private express companies, however, introduced the possibility of paying for large mailings of similar items on the basis of total weight. Shippers could accumulate charges and pay against monthly invoices, as with most other businesses. Prepaid international business reply cards were also introduced. Such simplified payment procedures are in fact quite important for large customers. Here again, the international postal system has been forced by the competitive threat to introduce similar features, to the benefit of the mailers.[20]

5. Postal Management and Postal Monopoly

Overall, Rowland Hill was not favorably impressed with the quality of management at the British Post Office. He wrote (Hill 1837, 40):

> The Post Office has too generally lagged behind other institutions in the progress of improvement, instead of being, as it might be, an example to the country of skilful and energetic management.

Hill's 1937 paper carefully explains his view that the fault lay more in the system than in the individuals. The first flaw in the system was, he felt, the postal monopoly, which exercised an enervating influence upon postal management. He said (Hill 1837, 7):

> There cannot be a doubt that if the law did not interpose its prohibition, the transmission of letters would be gladly undertaken by capitalists, and conducted on the ordinary commercial principles, with all that economy, attention to the wants of their customers, and skilful adaptation of means to the desired end, which is usually practiced by those whose interests are involved in their success. But the law constitutes the Post Office a monopoly. Its conductors are, therefore, uninfluenced by the ordinary motives to enterprize and good management; and however injudiciously the institution many be conducted, however inadequate it may be to the growing wants of the nation, the people must submit to the inconvenience; they cannot set up a Post Office for themselves.

Hill also blamed the political and legal circumstances which created a divided system of management. The worst evils were caused by the Legislature, which had no management responsibility. The Postmaster General was the chief executive, but he was a political appointee who at best could only "acquire a general knowledge of the vast and complicated mechanism." And the most knowledgeable executive, the Secretary, "[had] not the requisite authority for effecting such improvements as he may think necessary" (Hill 1837, 40-41).

If one looks at today's international postal system with the same skepticism that Hill brought to the British Post Office of 1840, it is possible that one would likewise conclude that the political and legal system has produced a management structure that is less than optimum. The management of the international postal system consists of about a thousand senior executives (there were some 900 delegates to the last UPU congress) physically located in the international affairs departments of about 170 post offices as well as UPU headquarters in Berne, Switzerland.

Management decisions are taken in meetings of the UPU's various committees as well as meetings of the nine regional postal unions. The central staff, the UPU's International Bureau, has only very limited power to manage the system, or even gather the data needed for management. Even allowing for the large geographic distances and the differences in language and culture—a problem equally faced by the international express companies—this appears to be a rather complicated management structure for a postal system smaller than the Canadian post office.

Like the British Post Office of 1840, the international postal system is also insulated from competition by legal protection: national monopoly laws, favorable customs procedures, antitrust immunity, and so on. In 1987, Mr. Mostafa Gharbi, Assistant Deputy-General of the UPU, wrote an article in the UPU's official magazine which should have earned him renown for courage and wisdom. Mr. Gharbi's theme was "deregulation, a postal modernization factor." He wrote:

> A wind of change is currently blowing through postal administrations which, having long been ensconced in the comfort provided by monopoly, have suddenly noticed that they are being seriously threatened by private firms that have started to compete with them...
>
> It is a fact that top postal executives have long tended to give preference to the means provided by regulations in order to solve the management or operational problems facing their administrations. For this purpose, the Post has at its disposal an arsenal of legal texts .... However, it is being realized ever more clearly that too many regulations can retard progress and restrict initiative and the ability to adapt to new situations.[21]

Rowland Hill would have applauded these insights. And I sense that more and more postal officials, especially younger ones, are beginning to suspect the appropriateness of competition at the international level (leaving the national level to one side). But I may be wrong.

The "winds of change" stirred by the private express industry are beginning to be seen not only in regulatory philosophy, but also in management structure. Twenty of the largest post offices have established a separate international management organization, Unipost. And the UPU itself has, for the first time, authorized its Executive Council to modernize regulations without waiting for the next plenary congress. While I believe there are fundamental legal problems in both cases, in both cases I would also concede that the post offices are rightly searching for a more unified and flexible management structure for the international postal system.

6. Elasticity of the Demand for Postal Services

With an eye towards his governmental audience, a major selling point in Hill's 1837 paper was his proposition that the demand for postal services is elastic. A decrease in postage would result in an increase in revenue. Whether or not Hill was correct in this proposition is unclear to me.[22] However, this seems a bit beside the point. Hill was right in that, in some sense, a drastic postage reduction was far less costly in net terms than previously thought and yielded much greater public benefits. Hill's instinct to price postal services as low as possible appears to have been vindicated.

It is my impression that the international postal system has been unsympathetic to Hill's low price instinct, although a quantitative study would be most interesting. Codding (1964, 238) recounts numerous debates between high postage and low postage advocates at UPU meetings, with the high postage side almost always victorious (except just before World War I). Most post offices appear to take the view that international postal rates should be set to reap extraordinary profits, since international rates are less politically sensitive than national rates and the mailers are generally well heeled. Like Adam Smith, I have the feeling that it is too much to expect groups of post offices in a collective meeting to reduce rates.

Within the last two or three years, however, the private express companies, acting in concert with individual post offices have become rate cutters for international postage rates. A substantial fraction of all international mail is now being transmitted for 50 percent or less of previous rates. Has this led to a beneficial increase in total international mail volume? Again, I quote excerpts from a 1988 UPU study:

> In the period from 1979 to 1986, when the world's population, level of economic activity, tourism, and international trade rose, international mail volumes declined... Postage-rate increases...were widespread.... Most administrations indicated [in answer to a questionnaire] that they face competition. Moreover, the competition is growing.... Most respondents believe the overall market (postal volumes plus privately carried volumes) for LC-type products is increasing.... also...for AO-type products....[23]

The obvious implication of these observations is, of course, that competition has led to postage reductions, which in turn have led to the first upturn in international mail traffic for a decade. However, more analytical work is certainly needed in this area.

7. Importance and Practicality of Reform

Finally, Hill was very concerned to persuade his readers that postal reform was both important and politically practical. On the matter of importance, indeed, Hill (1837, 7) was eloquent:

> When it is considered how much the religious, moral, and intellectual progress of the people would be accelerated by the unobstructed circulation of letters and of the many cheap and excellent non-political publications of the present day, the Post Office assumes the new and important character of a powerful engine of civilization.

I imagine that the present conference hardly needs to be persuaded of the importance of the exchange of documents. But it may be useful to note that, in the much more complex world of 1990, the corresponding "engine of civilization" is the communications and delivery infrastructure as a whole. When Hill's reforms had reshaped the British Post Office, it was the basic means of exchanging messages and small parcels between citizens. Today, the citizens of the world require a multiplicity of similar tasks, at various service levels, from a complimentary network of post offices, telecommunications administrations, and private delivery companies (express and non express).

It must be true that, from the public policy standpoint advocated by Hill, what is important today is to ask whether we are making the best use of the international communications and delivery system as whole, in order to ensure that we are not depriving ourselves of the efficiencies and benefits Hill discovered absent from the British Post Office of 1840.

Hill (1837, 54) ends his paper by arguing the political practicality of his ideas, naming names of supporters, and concluding that "the proposed reform, if undertaken by the Government, would not meet with opposition."

I cannot end my paper quite so sanguinely. We have already seen tremendous opposition to reforms in the international delivery system (leaving communications to others), not least from post offices who seem to have forgotten some of Hill's lessons. Nonetheless, fundamental reform does seem practical, for three reasons. First, international traffic comprises only 1 to 8 percent of the postal business, so the most drastic international reforms will not endanger the financial viability of any post office. Second, the European Community's 1992 program has created an opportunity, which otherwise would never arise, to rethink in detail the appropriate public policy towards relations between different postal systems. Third, the United States is in the remarkable position of being the largest supplier of both postal and private delivery systems and Chairman of the Universal Postal Union for the next five years. Logically, at least, the Bush Administration is positioned to play a very positive role. Of course, as in England in 1840, reform, however practical, will in fact occur only if demanded by the users and other leaders of society.

In closing, I would like to repeat that my purpose, in view of the occasion, has been to get an old coat out of Rowland Hill's intellectual closet and try it on today's international postal system. I would encourage others with more specialized skills to straighten it up and apply patches where necessary. Then we can all stand back and judge how well it fits. Perhaps, indeed, it will be seen to fit only to the extent that the international private express industry has, like Rowland Hill 150 years earlier, been successful in persuading the postal system to rethink the nature of its business.

Notes

1. Of course, to be fair, we must assume that Hill Express would have paid the same overall level of tax as the Post Office.

2. In the early nineteenth century, postal rates were viewed more as taxes than as charges for services rendered. According to Hill, postal revenues overall were about three times total costs.

3. The Universal Postal Union is an intergovernmental organization that was formed in 1874 to develop common rules for the exchange of international mail. The major UPU agreement is an international treaty called the "Universal Postal Convention." The UPU, which now includes virtually all governments in the world, convenes a "congress" every five years to revise and readopt the Convention and other agreements.

4. Although remail could transfer volume for one post office's international account to another post office's domestic account (so called "ABB remail").

5. By this, I mean only that, as with many types of economic activity, most postal transactions are concentrated in a relatively few number of markets. The pricing policies suitable for a few reasonably homogenous high density markets do not necessarily apply to many diverse low density markets.

6. More precisely, 76 percent for LC mail and 82 percent for AO mail according to 1979 Congress of the Universal Postal Union, Document 7, Annex 1, Attachment 14, Table 4.7. "Developed countries" in this study referred to 24 free-market industrialized countries. Although out of date, this well done study of the terminal dues problem by the Canadian Post Office remains very informative. No more recent study is known for this particular datum, but there is no reason to believe the proportions have changed significantly.

7. For those fortunately innocent of UPU terms, "terminal dues" are the charges that post offices levy each other for the local delivery of foreign mail (local delivery meaning exclusive of long haul transportation, such as air transportation).

8. It should also be noted that although both examples show a new spirit of economic realism on the part of the post offices, in both cases, the actual agreements pose serious issues under the competition laws.

9. This summary involves a little interpolation, as Hill was not very detailed in explaining his ideas for secondary distribution.

10. Hill did not support differences in postal charges to customers for letters circulating between major towns because the average transportation was only one thirty sixth of a penny. This is not at all the same thing as saying that post offices should not charge other post offices for substantial, clearly identifiable transport costs for bulk mail. Hill's support for proper costing of postal services would presumably have led him to support cost related transit charges between post offices. The question of whether these transit charges were significant enough compared to total costs to justify differences in the ultimate postage rates to mailers is a quite different question.

11. UPU Convention (1984), arts. 63, 83.

12. UPU Terminal Dues Roundtable, 6-7 April 1989, Annex 3: CE 1988/C4 - Doc 9/Annex 1 (emphasis added) (hereafter this roundtable is referred to as UPU TD Roundtable). The several annexes to this work paper provide a detailed analysis of the phenomenon of remail competition among post offices and the postal responses to it.

13. UPU 1989 Washington Congress, C6 - Rep 3, p. 2 (1 December 1989).

14. UPU 1989 Washington Congress, Doc 63.

15. It makes no difference whether one considers this a charge levied against all international mail or only against the "imbalance" arising out of bilateral exchanges.

16. UPU TD Roundtable, Annex 4: CE 1988/C 5 - Doc 8, p. 7. Even within the European Community, postal delivery costs appear to vary by a factor of three or more, judging from variations in both postal cost data and first class LC postal rates.

17. This simplifies the matter somewhat. The 1989 UPU terminal dues provision is very complicated. It contains a correction mechanism for kilograms that contain more than 55 LC items per kilogram or more than 7 AO items per kilogram, although it is unclear to me how this will be administered. It also retains the flat rate per kilogram for bilateral postal markets in which the traffic is less than 150 tonnes per year in either direction. Furthermore, the 1989 convention allows post offices to agree upon alternative terminal dues agreements on a bilateral basis.

18. UPU TD Roundtable, Annex 2: CE 1988 /C 5 - Doc 9, p. 12.

19. The domestic postal rates of a low cost post office are, plainly, far below the actual costs of delivery incurred by a high cost foreign post office. In addition, of course, domestic rates do not include international transportation costs, as international postage rates should.

20. If, in accordance with new arrangements, terminal dues vary both by number of pieces and total weight, then both private express companies and post offices will have to introduce tariffs based upon the number of pieces as well as weight. However, the procedures will still be simpler for the mailer than traditionally required by the international post.

21. Union Postale (1987) p. 11A.

22. According to Hill, the overall tax on the postal system was about 200 percent of costs. Some fifteen years after Hill's reforms were introduced, postal revenues had more or less returned to previous levels, but one has to allow for changes in the tax rate and inflation in order to assess whether, even over

this period, Hill's postage reduction paid for itself.
  23. UPU Terminal Dues CE 1988/C 5 - Doc 9, p. 3.

References

Coase, R.H. 1939. "Rowland Hill and the Penny Post." *Economica* (November): 423-435.
Codding, G.A., Jr. 1964. *The Universal Postal Union*. New York: New York University Press.
Harlow, Alvin F. 1928. *Old Post Bags*. New York: D. Appleton and Company.
Hill, Sir Rowland. 1837. *Post Office Reform*.

COMMENTS:
International Postal Reform
Roger Tabor

This paper is a stimulating contribution to an area of postal activity which is not often discussed. It is certainly the case that postal administrations throughout the world could work more effectively together. It is equally true that many of the competitive anomalies that have arisen in the postal world, which for so long has been the object of exclusive privilege within the boundaries of each country, take place in the international arena, where they have been stimulated by unsatisfactory arrangements for a country of posting to compensate the country of delivery of an item of mail.

As a postal operator myself, I would gladly acknowledge the part competition has played in inviting reconsideration of previously immutable positions. Even "remailing"—the activity of private operators in helping mailers to enter the world's postal system at the most effective point—albeit anathema to postal people, has done us a service in highlighting the economic nonsense of the terminal dues system.

The United Kingdom has indeed been a prime mover in seeking to reform the settlement arrangements between administrations known as terminal dues. The most recent change at the Universal Postal Union (UPU) in 1989, which the United Kingdom advocated, was able to overcome the apparent stigma associated with dividing countries into developed and less developed, by including a differential arrangement based on the volume of the mail flow.

It may be instructive at this point to consider some illustrative figures. Table 1 compares, in very round terms, what the British Post Office might have expected to receive on various different bases of terminal dues currently available. The likely delivery costs for incoming foreign mail with which the figures should be

Table 1. Terminal Dues (TDs)		
Example: 20g letter for United Kingdom delivery		
		Pence
Posted in U.K.	(Price)	15/20
Receivable under TDs:		
Old UPU	(weight only)	4
CEPT	(weight + per item)	12
Nordic	(60% domestic tariff)	9/12[a]
New UPU[b]	(weight by stream)	13
[a] rises with inland tariff		
[b] large flows		

compared will be broadly in the 10p to 13p range, depending on the approach to costing used. The table uses values for a 20 gram letter, as a significant proportion of incoming mail posted abroad into the United Kingdom is at the lightweight end of the market.

It is evident from this that the old UPU formula produced a very low price for delivery in Britain of bulk letters which have been posted in another country. Since the costs to a despatching administration of collecting an item, sorting it to the country concerned, and despatching it abroad are only a small part of the cost of sending a letter, one could surmise that the total cost to an administration, say, elsewhere in Europe, of an item of bulk mail to the United Kingdom could be as little as 8p. This would permit the foreign country to undercut the British Post Office's price for delivery within the United Kingdom even with discounts for bulk.

Competition is, of course, not only about price, and the whole service offering has to be correct. International private operators are also able to take advantage of any differential quality of service as between domestically posted bulk mail, often in a deliberately "deferred" service, and incoming foreign items. But it is inescapable that private operators have been able to assist postal customers to exploit anomalies in international charging, and that the price differential will have been influential in that. The new UPU terminal dues arrangements are due to be brought in in 1991, and we must now wait and see whether they have the significant impact on this situation which, prima facie, they appear to do from these figures.

But the main theme of Jim Campbell's paper is to suggest that Rowland Hill's economic principles could be, but have not been, applied to international mail.

His paper does, at one point, seek to distinguish between "truth" and "political reality." Those of us who work in public sector organisations may recognise two distinct forms of reality by these words, but reality they both are. While economic theory can guide the policy maker, it must frequently be tempered by political judgement, and the relative attractiveness of an economic proposition is conditioned by the probability of securing its acceptance and implementation by those in power.

In a way, the problem here may arise from a "big country" perspective. It may seem strange, to one accustomed to the scale of domestic letter operations in the United States, that mail from Athens to London has to be treated with an entirely different frame of reference to that applying between Dallas, Texas, and New York.

Fernando Toledano of the European Commission described the situation in Europe. Here we have a collection of comparatively small—some tiny—nation states. All have their own post offices with autonomy within the country, and there are at least two schools of thought among them about whether the guiding principles for the mail should be primarily economic/competitive or primarily a matter of public service.

Even in the relatively liberal United Kingdom, state ownership of the Royal Mail is not currently an issue. Corporatisation is widespread (often wrongly described as privatisation, which implies a change of ownership), but there is little immediate prospect of organisational change so radical as to permit a European Post Office, never mind one for the whole world! This existence of national boundaries must accordingly influence our response. We must therefore consider how the act of its crossing a border can influence our judgement about the economies of a letter.

Let us consider what actually happens to a piece of mail. Typically it is collected from the firm or street collection box, and it is taken to a sorting office (sorting center) where it is sorted for despatch to a distant destination. It is then conveyed possibly to an intermediate office where it will be sorted again or perhaps directly to the sorting office which serves the delivery region of its destination. At that distant sorting office, it will be sorted to the local delivery center, where it will then go through the final process of being prepared for the postman to take it out and deliver it. Mail circulation follows these general principles in most countries, although, of course, my model is based on personal knowledge of the United Kingdom. We can simplify this in terms of figure 1.

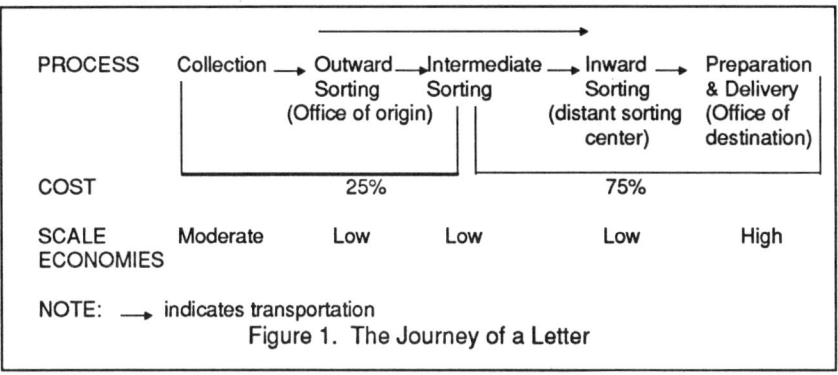

Figure 1. The Journey of a Letter

An international letter goes through substantially the same processes, although it typically passes through two intermediate offices which are specially designated for the exchange of international mail, one (outward) in the country of posting and the other (inward) in the country of delivery.

This enables us to look at an international letter as if it were two truncated inland ones. Figure 2 keeps each within the bounds of national sovereignty, while remaining true to Rowland Hill's view that handling of a letter in a foreign country should be "subject to the arrangements there established."

These figures include very rough proportions of the operational staff costs of handling a letter and a note about the relative contribution that each of the processing activities makes intuitively to economies of scale. (The intuition is supported by unpublished studies within the British Post Office. This analysis suggests that the "inward" part of a letter's journey, within the country of destination, is both more costly and more likely to benefit from economies of scale than the "outward" part in the country of posting.)

This would be important from a regulatory policy viewpoint, since if there is a case at all for a monopoly or other protected market position, it seems to rest in the avoidance of wasteful competition, through the exploitation of economies of scale and scope which might exist if there were only one network provider. This case is

PROCESS	Collection	Outward Sorting (office of origin)	Office of Exchange (country sorting)	Office of Exchange (inland sorting)	Inward Sorting (distant sorting center)	Preparation & Delivery (office of destination)
	LETTER IN COUNTRY A			LETTER IN COUNTRY B		
COST	25%			75%		

NOTE: ⟶ indicates transportation

Figure 2. An International Letter as Two Inland Letters

strongest at the delivery end. Any delivery manager realises that the economics of his operation rely on the routes being filled to capacity so that the number of drops per call is maximised and idle route mileage is reduced.

In satisfying the condition of deliveries being as "full" as possible, incoming international mail is of equal importance to inland. Take it away, and the unit cost of delivering the remaining (inland) mail would rise. If therefore one accepts the principle that the economics of delivery, the maintenance of a universal service, and the provision of service at an economic price, do require a degree of market protection for the postal service, then it would apply no less to an incoming foreign item. Such a letter has very similar cost characteristics to an inland letter posted in the immediate locality of the inward international office in the destination country.

On the outward side, an international letter has the characteristics of an inland letter addressed to someone residing at the outward international office of exchange. But we see from the exhibits that it avoids the activities which both generate most returns to scale and cost the most in absolute terms. The case for competition here would therefore seem more compelling. Competition is already effectively established at the level of the outward international letter in the remail context. I agree with Jim Campbell that this competition is stimulating a response from some Post Offices. In the United Kingdom, it has already prompted critical reviews of our service quality, our operating costs, and our product portfolio. And on the outward side, our efficiency gains would seem, on the basis of this analysis, to be less threatened by structural loss of economies of scale. The competitive playing field will, however, be more level when the terminal dues payments we receive for delivering mail from other countries more closely compensates us for our costs.

But if a case for regulated non-market services exists at all for letters—and a lot of evidence, and a lot of history says that it does—it *also* applies to *delivery* of international mail. Indeed, it is hard to conceive that a domestic monopoly could be enforceable if delivery of international mail in the same country were allowed: it would be hard to stop a private firm delivering letters in the street and judge from the outside of the envelope where the letter had originated, particularly if they chose to make it so.

3
PEAK-LOAD PRICING OF POSTAL SERVICE AND COMPETITION

Michael A. Crew
Paul R. Kleindorfer

Introduction

As we argued in our earlier paper, the United Kingdom Post Office has a long and distinguished tradition of innovation going back to the reforms of Rowland Hill. On September 16, 1968, the Post Office introduced another major innovation, the two-tier pricing system. Peak-load pricing thus became universal in the Post Office. Without fanfare, in one stroke, peak-load pricing was applied completely to one industry. Despite the many exhortations for peak-load pricing in electricity, telephone, and other industries, in no other industry has peak-load pricing been so extensively applied as in the Post Office.[1] While the practical experience of peak-load pricing gained by the Post Office has been considerable, the significance of the two-tier pricing systems has generally been missed in the literature of academic economics. The analysis provided by economists of the peak-load pricing problem in postal service has been limited to testimony by John Panzar (1984) and our recent paper with Marc Smith, (Crew, Kleindorfer, and Smith 1990, C-K-S).

The purpose of this paper is to expand the scope and application of C-K-S to include some important problems now facing postal services. C-K-S provides a net benefit maximizing (allocative efficiency driven) model of postal service. While such a welfare-optimizing framework is consistent with the traditional notion of marginal cost pricing, it does not reflect some of the major problems faced by postal services. For example, it ignores the issues of breakeven and competition. Therefore, in this paper, we will examine Ramsey optimal peak-load pricing for postal service and some effects of competitive entry.

We begin with a simplified overview of the peak-load, breakeven and competitive problems in postal service. While our analysis is partially motivated by the two-tier policy of the United Kingdom, our results are intended to be applied more generally to postal service. Section 2 develops the Ramsey results for a general model with limited deferrability. Section 3 provides an analysis of minimum cost operations for postal service, emphasizing the structure of marginal costs when limited deferrability of service for one class is possible. Section 4 examines some issues of competition. Section 5 provides a concluding discussion.

1. Motivation and Overview of Analysis

The peak-load problem exists in postal service for the same reasons that it exists in other industries—because mail has to be processed within a short time of its arrival and because it does not arrive uniformly over time. Thus, the essence of peak-loads, namely non-storability and periodic fluctuations in demand, mean that a peak-load problem exists in postal service. The solution to the peak-load problem in postal service, along the lines of the two-tier system of the United Kingdom Post Office, is not the classic application of peak-load pricing, namely, time-of-day pricing, but rather service-differentiated pricing. The United Kingdom Post Office offers either First Class (next business day delivery) or Second Class (delivery after two business days). The peak-load problem is therefore resolved by offering service-differentiated pricing that takes advantage of the limited deferrability that is possible in mail service. As in C-K-S, we examine in detail the peak-load problem in postal service, including a comprehensive statement of the peak-load problem for the diverse technology case. However, in the interest of continuity, we do not prove these results in the text, but leave it to the interested reader to consult Appendix A.

Peak-load pricing for the postal service allows for more cases than traditional peak-load pricing. The latter has just a firm peak and a shifting peak. Service differentiated pricing allows, in addition, a firm peak in the off-peak period. This occurs when it becomes efficient to defer processing of the deferrable class of mail (Second Class) to such an extent that the off-peak period optimally becomes the period when most mail is processed. The results for a simple technology are stated in section 3.

The welfare-optimal results provided in Crew, Kleindorfer, and Smith (1990) do not take into account problems of breakeven and competition. Section 2 provides Ramsey pricing results, while section 3 links these to minimum cost operations. In Section 4, we provide a very simple model of competition. Competition derives from capture of a part of postal business by a competitor, e.g., external presorting of mail, in which one or more steps in mail processing is performed before mail is delivered to the postal system. We analyze the appropriate discounts to be allowed for such external operations, since excessive discounts will encourage inefficient entry into the presort business. We characterize optimality conditions for these discounts and for regular full-service mail and derive results for several special cases.

2. The Ramsey Peak-Load Model with Limited Deferrability

Our model is derived from the traditional Boiteux-Steiner peak-load model following the treatment in C-K-S. We extend this analysis to allow deferred processing of some demand. The resulting analysis leads to service-differentiated marginal cost pricing under welfare maximization and to a variant of the inverse elasticity rule under a Ramsey breakeven constraint.

We assume two classes of mail: "First-Class" mail is denoted $C1$ and "Second-Class" mail by $C2$. A typical day is considered, which is divided into two equal-length periods. Demand from both classes arrives in both periods. We assume that the first period (the "night shift") is the peak period for $C1$ demand. $C1$ must be processed in the period it arrives, while $C2$ processing may be delayed one period. For each class, uniform prices (P_1 and P_2) must be charged, i.e., prices not varying with time of day.

We assume a heterogeneous population of consumers denoted by $\theta \in [0,1]$, where the number of consumers of type $\leq \theta$ is given by the distribution function $F(\theta)$, which is assumed to have a continuous density $f(\theta)$. Consumers of type θ have preferences for postal services x and a Hicksian aggregate m, as represented by a separable utility function

$$U(x, m; \theta) = V(x; \theta) + m, \qquad (1)$$

where m is the numeraire and $x = \{x_{it} \mid i = 1,2; t = 1,2\}$; x_{it} represents demand for service i in period t. Consumers know that $C1$ receives better service than $C2$ and therefore the willingness-to-pay function V in (1) satisfies

$$\frac{\partial}{\partial \gamma} V(x_{11} + \gamma, x_{12}, x_{21} - \gamma, x_{22}; \theta) > 0, \quad \text{for all } \theta; \qquad (2)$$

$$\frac{\partial}{\partial \gamma} V(x_{11}, x_{12} + \gamma, x_{21}, x_{22} - \gamma; \theta) > 0, \quad \text{for all } \theta. \qquad (3)$$

The implication of (2)-(3) is that every consumer θ prefers $C1$ service in either period to $C2$ service.

Denote $P = (P_1, P_2)$. Since over time uniform prices prevail and since the budget constraint is obviously binding given (1), demand $x(P; \theta)$ for consumer θ is determined as the solution to

$$\underset{x \geq 0}{\text{Maximize}} \; [V(x; \theta) - \sum_{i=1}^{2} P_i \sum_{t=1}^{2} x_{it}(P; \theta)] . \qquad (4)$$

Assuming that V is concave and monotonic increasing implies the usual characterizing conditions for demand $x(P; \theta)$. In particular, $\partial V/\partial x_{it} = P_i$ whenever $x_{it} > 0$. Since (2)-(3) imply that $\partial V/\partial x_{1t} > \partial V/\partial x_{2t}$ for $t = 1,2$, demand for $C2$ will vanish unless $P_1 > P_2$. Market demand is given by

$$X_{it}(P) = \int_0^1 x_{it}(P; \theta) \, dF(\theta) \tag{5}$$

and satisfies $\partial x_{it}/\partial P_i < 0$, for all i,t. We denote the vector of market demands by $X(P) = (X_{11}(P), X_{12}(P), X_{21}(P), X_{22}(P))$.

We assume the service provider is a welfare-maximizing monopolist, subject to a breakeven constraint on producer profits, with the traditional social welfare function W = total revenue plus consumers surplus minus total cost, which can be represented as the difference between aggregate willingness-to-pay and total cost, i.e.,

$$W(P) = \int_0^1 V(x(P; \theta); \theta) \, dF(\theta) - C(X(P)), \tag{6}$$

where $C(X)$ is the minimum cost of producing the vector X, subject to applicable service constraints for $C1$ and $C2$. We assume C is convex.

Profits are constrained as follows:

$$\Pi(P) = \left(\sum_{i=1}^{2} \sum_{t=1}^{2} P_i X_{it}(P) \right) - C(X(P)) \geq \Pi_0. \tag{7}$$

Using $\partial V/\partial x_{it} = P_i$, the first-order conditions $(\partial W/\partial P_j = 0; j = 1,2)$ for maximizing W subject to the breakeven constraint (7) are

$$\sum_{i=1}^{2} \sum_{t=1}^{2} (1+\mu) \left(P_i - \frac{\partial C}{\partial X_{it}} \right) \frac{\partial X_{it}}{\partial P_j} + \mu \left(\sum_{t=1}^{2} X_{jt} \right) = 0, \quad j = 1,2, \tag{8}$$

where $\mu \geq 0$ is the dual variable associated with (7).

We first note that if the constraint (7) is nonbinding ($\mu = 0$) and if $MC_{it} = C_i$ for $i,t = 1,2$, then $P_i = C_i$ is the unique solution to (8). Thus, with non-time varying marginal costs, first-best prices equal marginal costs. However, marginal costs of mail processing operations typically vary as a result of night-time labor premiums. Because of this, even the unconstrained welfare-maximizing solution to maximizing (6) is complex (see C-K-S).

To solve the first-order conditions (8), we need some additional assumptions. What we assume is that the only cost difference between period 1 and period 2 processing is that variable costs are higher in period 1, the night shift, by a constant proportion, than corresponding variable costs during the day shift. This corresponds essentially to a labor premium for the night shift. Under this assumption, we provide a model in the next section for which

$$MC_1 = \frac{\partial C}{\partial X_{11}} > MC_2 = \frac{\partial C}{\partial X_{it}}, \quad (i,t) \neq (1,1), \tag{9}$$

i.e., premium period ($t = 1$) $C1$ marginal costs MC_1 are greater than non-premium marginal costs MC_2, and marginal costs are equal to MC_2 for every class and time period other than for peak period ($t = 1$) First-Class ($i = 1$) demand. The intuitive rationale for (9) is that the deferrability of $C2$ mail allows it all to be processed with X_{12} (period 2 $C1$ mail) in the non-premium period where lower unit costs arise. Assuming (9) holds and denoting $\delta = MC_1 - MC_2 > 0$, we can rewrite (8) as

$$[P_1 - MC_2 - \delta]\left[\frac{\partial X_{11}}{\partial P_j}\right] + \sum_{(i,t) \neq (1,1)}[P_i - MC_2]\left[\frac{\partial X_{it}}{\partial P_j}\right] = -k\sum_t X_{jt}, \quad j = 1,2, \tag{10}$$

where $k = \mu/(1 + \mu) \geq 0$ is the Ramsey number. Using Cramer's Rule, (10) can be solved to obtain

$$P_1 = MC_2 + \left(\frac{\delta}{\Delta}\right)\left[\left(\frac{\partial X_2}{\partial P_2} \cdot \frac{\partial X_{11}}{\partial P_1}\right) - \left(\frac{\partial X_2}{\partial P_1} \cdot \frac{\partial X_{11}}{\partial P_2}\right)\right] - \left(\frac{k}{\Delta}\right)\left[\left(X_1 \cdot \frac{\partial X_2}{\partial P_2}\right) - \left(X_2 \cdot \frac{\partial X_2}{\partial P_1}\right)\right] \tag{11}$$

$$P_2 = MC_2 + \left(\frac{\delta}{\Delta}\right)\left[\left(\frac{\partial X_1}{\partial P_1} \cdot \frac{\partial X_{11}}{\partial P_2}\right) - \left(\frac{\partial X_1}{\partial P_2} \cdot \frac{\partial X_{11}}{\partial P_1}\right)\right] - \left(\frac{k}{\Delta}\right)\left[\left(X_2 \cdot \frac{\partial X_1}{\partial P_1}\right) - \left(X_1 \cdot \frac{\partial X_1}{\partial P_2}\right)\right] \tag{12}$$

where

$$\Delta = \left(\frac{\partial X_1}{\partial P_1} \cdot \frac{\partial X_2}{\partial P_2}\right) - \left(\frac{\partial X_1}{\partial P_2} \cdot \frac{\partial X_2}{\partial P_1}\right) \tag{13}$$

and where X_i denotes total class i demand, i.e.,

$$X_i(P) = X_{i1}(P) + X_{i2}(P), \quad i = 1,2. \tag{14}$$

Analyzing further the solution (10)-(11), we show in the Appendix that if (9) holds, if $C1$ and $C2$ are substitutes ($\partial X_{it}/\partial P_j \geq 0$, for $j \neq i$) and if own-price effects dominate, i.e.,

$$\frac{\partial X_1}{\partial P_j} + \frac{\partial X_2}{\partial P_j} < 0, \quad j = 1,2, \tag{15}$$

then the Ramsey-optimal prices in (11)-(12) must satisfy

$$P_1 > Max\,[P_2, MC_2]. \tag{16}$$

Thus, (16) implies that the price for first class mail, P_1, is greater than the price of second class mail and P_1 is also strictly greater than MC_2, the marginal cost of processing $C2$. It is also straightforward to show that $P_1 \leq MC_1$ when $k = 0$, i.e. at the first-best solution.

Perhaps surprisingly, (12) does not imply that $P_2 \geq MC_2$ in general. Two special cases are interesting, however.

First, if $X_{12} = 0$, then $X_1 = X_{11}$, so that (11)-(12) imply for this case that

$$P_i - MC_i = -\left(\frac{k}{\Delta}\right)\left[\left(X_i \cdot \frac{\partial X_j}{\partial P_j}\right) - \left(X_j \cdot \frac{\partial X_j}{\partial P_i}\right)\right], \quad i,j = 1,2, i \neq j. \tag{17}$$

Since the right hand side of (17) is clearly positive unless $k = 0$, we see for this case that $P_i \geq MC_i$, $i = 1,2$, with $P_i = MC_i$ if and only if $k = 0$.

Second, when demands for $C1$ and $C2$ are independent ($\partial X_{it}/\partial P_j = 0$ for $i \neq j$), then the term in the first [ ] in (12) vanishes and $P_2 \geq MC_2$. In the independent demand case, we can solve (11)-(12) directly to obtain

$$P_1 = \alpha MC_1 + (1-\alpha)MC_2 - \left(\frac{kP_1}{\eta_1}\right); \quad P_2 = MC_2 - \left(\frac{kP_2}{\eta_2}\right), \tag{18}$$

where $\eta_i = (\partial X_i/\partial P_i)/(X_i/P_i)$ is own-price elasticity for class i and where $\alpha \in [0,1]$ is given by $\alpha = (\partial X_{11}/\partial P_1)/(\partial X_1/\partial P_1)$. If we interpret $\alpha MC_1 + (1-\alpha)MC_2$ as the average marginal cost of $C1$, then (18) is in the classic inverse elacticity form. The form of the pricing rule for P_1 is a simple Ramsey extension of the welfare-optimal uniform pricing rule for time varying demand (Crew and Kleindorfer (1986, p. 52)).

3. A Peak-Load Cost Model with Diverse Technology

We now turn to an examination of the structure of marginal costs and present sufficient conditions under which (9) is valid. We use a two-period, diverse technology peak-load model. First, some notation.

i = denotation for class i ($C1$ or $C2$);
t = time period, 1 or 2;
h = technology type designator, 1 or 2;
X_{it} = Ci demand arriving in period t, as given by (5), with $X_i = X_{i1} + X_{i2}$, the total Ci demand over the cycle;
b_h^t = variable cost of technology h in period t, where we assume that

$b_h^1 = (1 + \rho) b_h > b_h = b_h^2$; ρ may be thought of as a night-time premium;

Y_{it} = Quantity of Ci processed in period t;
Q_h = Capacity of type h (i.e., maximum processing capacity of type h available in either period);
q_{ht} = Quantity produced on capacity h in period t;
β_h = Cost per unit of capacity of type h.

We assume that technology 1 is capital-intensive, while technology 2 is a flexible, labor-intensive technology with $b_2 > b_1$ and $\beta_1 > \beta_2$. When technology 2 is purely labor intensive, $\beta_2 = 0$ and only variable costs obtain for technology 2. Adapting Crew and Kleindorfer (1986, 45), we require that the technologies satisfy the following efficiency conditions:

$$\frac{\beta_1 - \beta_2}{2+\rho} < b_2 - b_1 < \beta_1 - \beta_2. \tag{19}$$

If the left-hand (respectively, right-hand) inequality in (19) is violated, then it can be shown that only technology 2 (respectively, 1) need be used in an optimal solution.

Marginal costs for the specified diverse technology are derived from the following cost minimization problem:

$$Minimize \sum_t \sum_h b_h^t q_{ht} + \sum_h \beta_h Q_h \tag{20}$$

Subject to:

$$Y_{1t} = X_{1t}, \quad t = 1,2 \tag{21}$$

$$Y_{21} + Y_{22} = X_2, \tag{22}$$

$$\sum_h q_{ht} = Y_{1t} + Y_{2t}, \quad t = 1,2, \tag{23}$$

$$q_{ht} \leq Q_h, \quad \forall h,t. \tag{24}$$

$$\text{All Variables} \geq 0. \tag{25}$$

We show in the Technical Appendix that the solution to (20)-(25) satisfies $Y_{21} = 0$ at optimum. This means that $C2$ mail will never be processed in the first (premium) period. From (21)-(22), therefore, exactly X_{11} is processed in the first period and exactly $X_2 + X_{12}$ is processed in the second period.

Three cases are possible: either there is a firm peak in period 1 ($X_{11} > X_2 + X_{12}$), a firm peak in period 2 ($X_{11} < X_2 + X_{12}$), or a shifting peak ($X_{11} = X_2 + X_{12}$—equal output in both periods).[2] If ρ were zero, the solution to (20)-(25) would be analogous to the cost minimization problem in traditional peak-load pricing (with X_{11} replacing peak-period demand and $X_2 + X_{12}$ replacing off-peak demand), for which the solution is known (e.g., Crew and Kleindorfer (1986)). The presence of $\rho > 0$ complicates matters somewhat. The important point to note is that we need only deal with two marginal costs, as assumed in (9): MC_1 reflecting marginal cost of processing (of $C1$) in the first (premium) period and MC_2 reflecting marginal cost of processing (of all other mail) in the second period.

To provide some intuitive background, let us first consider the case where only one technology, say 1, is available. Then the solution to (20)-(25) is straightforward. The optimal capacity Q_1^* is

$$Q_1^* = Max [X_{11}, X_2 + X_{12}], \tag{26}$$

the maximum of the processing requirements in periods 1 and 2. Marginal costs are given in table 1 below.

Table 1. The Simple Technology Case

Peak Period	Relative Demands	MC_1	MC_2
Period 1	$X_{11} > X_2 + X_{12}$	$(1 + \rho)\, b_1 + \beta_1$	b_1
Shifting	$X_{11} = X_2 + X_{12}$	$(1 + \rho)b_1 < MC_1 < (1 + \rho)b_1 + \beta_1$	$b_1 < MC_2 < b_1 + \beta_1$
Period 2*	$X_{11} < X_2 + X_{12}$	$(1 + \rho)\, b_1$	$b_1 + \beta_1$

*A peak in period 2 can only occur if $(1 + \rho)\, b_1 > b_1 + \beta_1$.
Note: $MC_1 > MC_2$ and $MC_1 + MC_2 = (2 + \rho)\, b_1 + \beta_1$ must hold for all cases.

Table 1 has several features deserving comment. First, note that (9) is satisfied for this case so that welfare optimal prices are given by (11)-(12). Next note that the sum of marginal costs for periods 1 and 2 is always equal to $(2 + \rho)\, b_1 + \beta_1$, the cost of a unit of capacity utilized fully in both periods. The firm peak cases (1 and 2) are clear from the marginal costs given in table 1. For the shifting peak case, the result can be shown as follows. With only technology 1 available and knowing that $Y_{21} = 0$, (20)-(25) reduces to the following minimization problem for the optimal capacity Q_1:

$$\underset{Q_1}{\text{Min}} \left\{ [(1 + \rho)\, b_1 X_{11} + b_1(X_2 + X_{12})] + \beta_1 Q_1 \right\} \qquad (27)$$

Subject to:

$$Q_1 \geq X_{11}; \qquad (28)$$

$$Q_1 \geq X_2 + X_{12}. \qquad (29)$$

Of course, the solution to (27)-(29) is just (26). Moreover, a simple Kuhn-Tucker analysis of (27)-(29) shows that the sum of the dual variables for (28) and (29), which are the marginal costs MC_1 and MC_2, equals $(2 + \rho)\, b_1 + \beta_1$.

We note in table 1 that a period 2 firm peak can only occur if $(1 + \rho)\, b_1 > b_1 + \beta_1$, i.e. $\rho b_1 > \beta_1$. For suppose that $(1 + \rho)b_1 \leq b_1 + \beta_1$ and that $X_{11} < X_2 + X_{12}$. Since $(1 + \rho)\, b_1 \leq b_1 + \beta_1$, it is less costly to shift some processing of X_2 from period 2 to period 1 (yielding $Y_{21} > 0$). Cost savings from these shifts will continue until processing is equalized in both periods. At this point, marginal costs would be $MC = [1 + (\rho/2)]\, b_1 + (\beta_1/2)$, identical in both periods. Thus, any incremental demand in either period would be split between the two periods equally, if need be by shifting the C2 processing schedule. But with equal marginal costs in both periods, as noted after (7) above, equal prices would result and (2)-(3) would then imply that C2 demand would vanish. Given our standing assumption that $X_{11} > X_{12}$, this means that a firm peak in period 2 (implying $X_{11} < X_2 + X_{12}$) is not compatible with the cost condition $(1 + \rho)\, b_1 \leq b_1 + \beta_1$ at the optimal prices defined by (11)-(12).

Many of the properties of the single-technology case continue to hold for the case of diverse technology, which we now consider. We distinguish two cases employing the following cost relationships:

$$(1 + \rho) b_2 + \beta_2 \leq (1 + \rho) b_1 + \beta_1; \tag{30}$$

$$(1 + \rho) b_1 + \beta_1 < (1 + \rho) b_2 + \beta_2. \tag{31}$$

Equation (30) implies that it is cheaper to use technology 2 to meet an additional unit of demand in period 1 (the premium period) than to use technology 1, while the converse obtains under (31). Note that when $\rho = 0$, (19) implies that only (30) is possible.

Case 1: (19) and (30) obtain
From (19), technology 1 is optimal for meeting any smooth demand over both periods (since the cost of producing a unit of output in both periods using technology h is $(2 + \rho) b_h + \beta_h$). Moreover, from (19) and (30), technology 2 is cheaper than technology 1 in supplying a unit of output in either period 1 or 2 alone. Thus, technology 1 will be used for that part of demand that continues over both periods, and technology 2 will be used for the remaining demand in the peak period.

Case 2: (19) and (31) obtain
It is optimal here to use only technology 1 when a firm peak obtains in period 1 (i.e., when $X_{11} > X_2 + X_{12}$). This is seen as follows. From (19), $(2 + \rho) b_2 + \beta_2 > (2 + \rho) b_1 + \beta_1$, so that technology 1 should always be favored in place of technology 2 in meeting a steady demand for both periods. For processing a unit of demand in a single period, technology 2 is also dominated when there is a firm peak in period 1. This follows from (31) for period 1 processing. For period 2 processing, $b_2 > b_1$ implies that technology 1 is also favored over 2 if only period 2 processing is considered (as long as period 1 drives capacity).

Based on the above principles, and the noted fact $Y_{21} = 0$, we establish in the Technical Appendix the solution given in tables 2 and 3 for optimal capacities and marginal costs for the various cases noted above. The optimal operating policy is to utilize capacity in merit order (i.e., in increasing order of variable cost b'_h) in each period, with demands specified by the solutions to (11)-(12) at the indicated marginal costs MC_1, MC_2.

The parameter Γ in table 3 is given by

$$\Gamma = (2 + \rho) b_1 + \beta_1 - (b_2 + \beta_2), \tag{32}$$

so that, from (19), $(1 + \rho) b_1 < \Gamma < (1 + \rho) b_2$. We show in the Technical Appendix that a firm peak cannot occur in period 2 unless $\Gamma > b_2 + \beta_2$. When $\Gamma \leq b_2 + \beta_2$ (or equivalently $(2 + \rho) b_1 + \beta_1 \leq 2(b_2 + \beta_2)$), technology 2 does not provide sufficient advantages to be used as a peaking technology in period 2 and either a period 1 peak or a shifting peak results.

Table 2: Summary of Optimal Capacity Policies			
Peak Period	Relative Demands	Q_1^*	Q_2^*
Period 1:Case 1	$X_{11} > X_2 + X_{12}$	$X_2 + X_{12}$	$X_{11} - (X_2 + X_{12})$
Period 1:Case 2	$X_{11} > X_2 + X_{12}$	X_{11}	0
Shifting Peak:Case 1	$X_{11} = X_2 + X_{12}$	X_{11}	0
Shifting Peak:Case 2	$X_{11} = X_2 + X_{12}$	X_{11}	0
Period 2*	$X_{11} < X_2 + X_{12}$	X_{11}	$(X_2 + X_{12}) - X_{11}$
*A peak in period 2 can only occur if $\Gamma > b_2 + \beta_2$.			

Table 3: Summary of Marginal Cost Results		
Peak Period	MC_1	MC_2
Period 1:Case 1	$(1 + \rho) b_2 + \beta_2$	$\Gamma - \rho b_2$
Period 1:Case 2	$(1 + \rho) b_1 + \beta_1$	b_1
Shifting:Case 1	$\Gamma < MC_1 < (1 + \rho) b_2 + \beta_2$	$b_1 \leq \Gamma - \rho b_2 < MC_2 < b_2 + \beta_2$
Shifting:Case 2	$\Gamma < MC_1 < (1 + \rho) b_1 + \beta_1$	$\Gamma - \rho b_2 < b_1 < MC_2 < b_2 + \beta_2$
Period 2*	Γ	$b_2 + \beta_2$
*A peak in period 2 can only occur if $\Gamma > b_2 + \beta_2$.		
Note: $MC_1 > MC_2$ and $MC_1 + MC_2 = (2 + \rho)b_1 + \beta_1$ must hold in all cases.		

The reader should note from (32) and table 3 that, wherever the peak falls in either Case 1 or 2, $b_1 \leq MC_2 < MC_1$ and $MC_1 + MC_2 = (2 + \rho) b_1 + \beta_1$, just as in the single-technology case of table 1. In particular, (9) is satisfied for all cases here. Thus, (11)-(12) provide the appropriate characterizing conditions for optimal service-differentiated prices, with marginal costs as determined above. We now consider the relationship between (11)-(12) and these marginal cost results in more detail.

First, as noted, the sum of the marginal costs $MC_1 + MC_2$ is the same in all cases (namely, $(2 + \rho) b_1 + \beta_1$). Defining the differential $\delta = MC_1 - MC_2$, as in (11)-(12), we can therefore express the marginal costs for all cases as

$$MC_1 = \frac{m + \delta}{2}, \quad MC_2 = \frac{m - \delta}{2}, \text{ with } \delta > 0 \text{ and } m = (2 + \rho) b_1 + \beta_1. \tag{33}$$

Now note from table 3 that MC_2 (respectively, MC_1) increases (respectively, decreases) as we proceed through the three sub-cases: firm peak in period 1, shifting peak, firm peak in period 2. Thus, $\delta = MC_1 - MC_2$ decreases as we proceed from period 1 peak to shifting peak to period 2 peak. Intuitively, one also expects that the corresponding price differential $P_1 - P_2$ must be decreasing as δ decreases. While we have not been able to verify this conjecture, we can show (see the Technical Appendix) that as δ decreases, prices $P = (P_1, P_2)$ change in such a manner that the quantity

$$G(\delta) = X_{11}(P(\delta)) - (X_2(P(\delta)) + X_{12}(P(\delta))) \tag{34}$$

is nonincreasing, where $P(\delta)$ is the price vector (11)-(12) corresponding to marginal costs MC_1, MC_2 satisfying (33) for a given $\delta > 0$.

Thus, there are exactly three cases:

1. If $G(\delta) = X_{11} - (X_2 + X_{12}) > 0$ at the prices $P(\delta)$ corresponding to the marginal costs in table 3 for the period 1 peak, then there is a firm peak in period 1 (and note that decreasing δ further would only increase the peak).

2. If $G(\delta) = X_{11} - (X_2 + X_{12}) < 0$ at the prices $P(\delta)$ corresponding to the marginal costs in table 3 for the period 2 peak, then there is a firm peak in period 2.

3. If $G(\delta) \leq 0$ at the period 1 peak prices and $G(\delta) \geq 0$ at the period 2 peak prices, then the optimal solution is a shifting peak, which occurs at the marginal cost differential δ (and prices $P(\delta)$) at which $X_{11} - (X_2 + X_{12}) = 0$.

Because $G(\delta)$ is nonincreasing and continuous, exactly one of the above three cases will occur. Thus, the indicated sub-cases, together with $G(\delta)$ and $P(\delta)$ from (11)-(12), are the necessary conditions for an optimal solution. Since the premium (night) shift (period 1 here) is typically the peak period for mail processing operations, the primary results of interest above for current postal operations are those corresponding to a firm peak in period 1.

To summarize, we have verified appropriate conditions under which (9) is valid, so that Ramsey-optimal prices for the diverse technology considered here are given by (11)-(12) and satisfy (16). The key to (9) is that limited deferrability of $C2$ allows it to be processed during non-premium hours (period 2 here) and allows moreover for the processing schedule to be smoothed out, thereby achieving cost economies through peak shaving and less reliance on high variable cost technologies.

4. Competition and Ramsey Pricing

In this section, we consider a variation on the Ramsey problem in which the postal authority faces competition in some aspect of its service. Postal service consists of many steps (facing, presorting, barcoding, sorting, delivery to postal walks, etc.), and competition comes typically in the form of external suppliers doing some of the mail processing steps external to the postal authority. Since this saves the postal authority resources, a prima facie case for a discount exists for those who elect to use an external supplier to perform one or more of the steps required for postal service. We address here is the nature and magnitude of this discount, e.g., for external presorting.

The thrust of our model is the following. Preferences for postal service are as described earlier (equations (1)-(3)). But a customer can either subscribe to full service, in which presorting is done by the postal authority, or the customer can hire his own presorting equipment and only use the postal authority for basic mail service. We assume that basic service is sold at a discount below full service. We assume that it costs the customer something to set up for external presorting, e.g., buying equipment and training operators, and that these costs are sunk. Just as in competitive bypass in telecommunications, these sunk costs imply that larger customers will find it more economical to switch to external presorting. The number of such customers who decide to switch will, of course, depend on the difference in the price between full and basic service, i.e., on the presort discount. We are interested in the determination of Ramsey-optimal prices and presort discount.

Let $P = (P_1, P_2)$ denote the price of full service (full service includes the cost of all operations) for $C1$ and $C2$ and let $p = (p_1, p_2)$ denote the price of basic service for $C1$ and $C2$. The price the customer actually pays if external presorting is used is then $p + s = (p_1 + s_1, p_2 + s_2)$, where $s = (s_1, s_2)$ is the vector of unit costs of external presorting. We assume that the customer also incurs a sunk cost of S in setting up for external presorting operations.[3]

If a customer θ uses full service, his demands are given by $x(P; \theta)$ as determined by (4). If a customer elects external presorting, then his demands are given by the solution to

$$\text{Maximize } (V(x; \theta) - (p + s) x), \quad x \geq 0 \qquad (35)$$

where we have used the vector notation

$$(p + s) x = \sum_i (p_i + s_i) \sum_t x_{it}. \qquad (36)$$

Clearly, a customer will elect external presorting precisely when the benefits of so doing exceed the setup cost S, i.e., when

$$(V(x(p + s; \theta); \theta) - (p + s) x(p + s; \theta) - S) \geq (V(x(P; \theta); \theta) - Px(P; \theta)). \qquad (37)$$

To proceed further, we make the assumption that the function

$$\gamma(P, p; \theta) = V(x(p + s; \theta); \theta) - V(x(P; \theta); \theta) \qquad (38)$$

is increasing in θ for each fixed P, p with $(p + s) \leq P$.[4] Clearly, unless $(p + s) \leq P$, no basic service will be demanded. The import of this assumption is that the larger the customer (i.e., the larger θ), the larger the willingness to pay for presort discounts. Assuming $\partial \gamma / \partial \theta > 0$, and noting from preference maximization (4) that $\partial V(x(P; \theta); \theta) / \partial x_{it} = P_i$, we see that

$$\frac{\partial}{\partial \theta} (V(x(p + s; \theta); \theta) - (p + s) x(p + s; \theta) - V(x(P; \theta); \theta) + Px(P; \theta))$$

$$= \frac{\partial}{\partial \theta} (V(x(p + s; \theta); \theta) - V(x(P; \theta); \theta)) = \frac{\partial}{\partial \theta} \gamma(P, p; \theta) > 0, \qquad (39)$$

so that, from (37), if customer θ prefers external presorting at prices (P, p), then so does every customer $\theta' > \theta$.

Define $M(P, p)$ as the market share of the postal authority in presort service. Clearly, $M \in [0,1]$ is just the largest customer type which still finds it preferable to have the postal authority presort its mail. For every $\theta > M$, (37) is satisfied. From (37) and monotonicity of indirect utility in prices, we see directly that $\partial M/\partial P_j < 0$, $\partial M/\partial p_j = \partial M/\partial s_j > 0$.

Let the total cost function $TC(X, Y_2)$ for the postal authority depend on the demand for full service ($X = (X_{11}, X_{12}, X_{21}, X_{22})$) and on demand for basic service ($Y_2 = (Y_{11}, Y_{12}, Y_{21}, Y_{22})$), where

$$X_{it}(P, p) = \int_0^M x_{it}(P; \theta)\, dF(\theta) \tag{40}$$

and

$$Y_{it}(P, p) = \int_M^1 x_{it}(p + s; \theta)\, dF(\theta). \tag{41}$$

We assume the following form for $TC(X, Y)$:

$$TC(X, Y) = C(X + Y) - c(Y), \tag{42}$$

where $C(X)$ and $c(Y)$ will be assumed to arise from cost minimization problems similar in structure to that of Section 3, where $c(Y)$ as the total cost to the postal service of presorting Y, a cost which is avoided for Y by external presorting. We note that $c(Y)$ may be greater or less than the competitive market presort cost sY.

We can now state the constrained welfare maximization problem of interest. Define W and Π corresponding to (6)-(7) as follows:

$$W(P, p) = \int_0^M (V(x(P; \theta); \theta) - Px(P; \theta))\, dF(\theta); \tag{43}$$

$$+ \int_M^1 (V(x(p + s; \theta); \theta) - (p + s)x(p + s; \theta) - S)\, dF(\theta) + \Pi(P, p);$$

$$\Pi(P, p) = \int_0^M Px(P; \theta)\, dF(\theta) + \int_M^1 px(p + s; \theta)\, dF(\theta) - C(X + Y) + c(Y). \tag{44}$$

The first (respectively, second) term in (43) is consumer surplus for those consumers who demand normal (respectively, only basic) service. The third term is postal authority profits $\Pi(P, p)$, as shown in (44). We assume that external presorting is competitive, so zero profits obtain from that activity.

Taking first-order conditions for maximizing (43) subject to (44), and using $\partial V/\partial x_{it} = P_i$ as in (8), yields the following for optimal prices P and p:

$$\frac{\partial W}{\partial P_j} + \mu \frac{\partial \Pi}{\partial P_j} = -X_j(P,p) + [V(x(P;M);M) - Px(P;M)]f(M)\frac{\partial M}{\partial P_j}$$

$$- [V(x(p+s;M);M) - (p+s)x(p+s;M) - S]f(M)\frac{\partial M}{\partial P_j}$$

$$+ (1+\mu) \cdot \left(\sum_{i=1}^{2}\sum_{t=1}^{2}\left(P_i - \frac{\partial C}{\partial X_{it}}\right)\frac{\partial X_{it}}{\partial P_j} + X_j(P,p) \right.$$

$$\left. + \sum_{i=1}^{2}\sum_{t=1}^{2}\left(P_i - \frac{\partial C}{\partial Y_{it}} + \frac{\partial c}{\partial Y_{it}}\right)\frac{\partial Y_{it}}{\partial P_j} \right); \tag{45}$$

$$\frac{\partial W}{\partial p_j} + \mu \frac{\partial \Pi}{\partial p_j} = -Y_j(P,p) + [V(x(P;M);M) - Px(P;M)]f(M)\frac{\partial M}{\partial p_j}$$

$$- [V(x(p+s;M);M) - (p+s)x(p+s;M) - S]f(M)\frac{\partial M}{\partial p_j}$$

$$+ (1+\mu) \cdot \left(\sum_{i=1}^{2}\sum_{t=1}^{2}\left(P_i - \frac{\partial C}{\partial X_{it}}\right)\frac{\partial X_{it}}{\partial p_j} + Y_j(P,p) \right.$$

$$\left. + \sum_{i=1}^{2}\sum_{t=1}^{2}\left(P_i - \frac{\partial C}{\partial Y_{it}} + \frac{\partial c}{\partial Y_{it}}\right)\frac{\partial Y_{it}}{\partial p_j} \right), \tag{46}$$

where $X_j = X_{j1} + X_{j2}$ and $Y_j = Y_{j1} + Y_{j2}$. Now note from the definition of the marginal consumer M (see (37)) that the second and third terms in both (45)-(46) cancel, leading to the first-order conditions for optimal P_j and p_j, $j = 1,2$:

$$(1+\mu) \cdot \left(\sum_{i=1}^{2}\sum_{t=1}^{2}\left(P_i - \frac{\partial C}{\partial X_{it}}\right)\frac{\partial X_{it}}{\partial P_j} + \sum_{i=1}^{2}\sum_{t=1}^{2}\left(P_i - \frac{\partial C}{\partial Y_{it}} + \frac{\partial c}{\partial Y_{it}}\right)\frac{\partial Y_{it}}{\partial P_j} \right) + \mu X_j(P,p) = 0 \tag{47}$$

$$(1+\mu) \cdot \left(\sum_{i=1}^{2}\sum_{t=1}^{2}\left(P_i - \frac{\partial C}{\partial X_{it}}\right)\frac{\partial X_{it}}{\partial p_j} + \sum_{i=1}^{2}\sum_{t=1}^{2}\left(P_i - \frac{\partial C}{\partial Y_{it}} + \frac{\partial c}{\partial Y_{it}}\right)\frac{\partial Y_{it}}{\partial p_j} \right) + \mu Y_j(P,p) = 0 \tag{48}$$

While (47)-(48) have a strong resemblence to (8), little is known about the solution to (47)-(48), even for the welfare-optimal case. Since total costs $C(X+Y)$ for full service depend symmetrically on X and Y, it is clear that $\partial C/\partial X_{it} = \partial C/\partial Y_{it}$. From this, we can derive the solution for the welfare-optimal case (where $\mu = 0$) for which the marginal costs for each class are constant. Denoting $\partial C/\partial X_{it} = C_i$ and $\partial c/\partial Y_{it} = c_i$, we see that the solution to (47)-(48) is given by

$$P_i = C_i \text{ and } p_i = C_i - c_i.$$ (49)

Thus, in this case, the postal authority sets the presort discount for class i at exactly the unit cost c_i of presorting. If $c_i \leq s_i$, the prevailing unit cost in the market, then the postal authority will capture the entire market. If $c_i > s_i$, then some market share will be lost to competitors, with the magnitude of market share loss depending on $c_i - s_i$ and S. We see from (49) that in this case $P_i = p_i + c_i$.

Interestingly, even when marginal costs are constant for each class, the Ramsey solution need not satisfy $P_i = p_i + c_i$. The presort discount under Ramsey pricing will depend on market share dynamics and on the relative unit cost advantage $(c_i - s_i)$ enjoyed by the postal authority over the competition.

When marginal costs are not constant, then one would expect that presort discounts would depend on the magnitude of the peak problem, with larger discounts given to ameliorate peak loads. Such discounts would be further emphasized to the extent a capital intensive technology were used for presorting. Clearly there would be no point in providing significant presort discounts for demands that were processed in the off-peak period, if spare capacity were present off peak. The detailed analysis of these issues awaits further research.

5. Conclusions

In this paper, we have extended the results of our earlier paper (C-K-S) on peak-load pricing in postal service (or service-differentiated pricing) to include the effects of Ramsey pricing and competitive entry. Aside from being a familiar generalization of the welfare-maximizing framework, the Ramsey results are of potentially practical significance to postal services.[5] This is particularly so now that postal services are facing increased competition.

We have attempted to address the issue of competitive entry by means of a model where entrants perform some of the processes that make up mail processing. For example, they may presort the mail. The problem has some similarities to that of bypass faced by telephone companies. One difference compared to telephone companies is that pricing flexibility is assumed here. The postal authority is assumed to have freedom to lower prices, and the entry of competitors is not a function of prices of certain products being set artificially high to support cross subsidies. Presorting may also be a source of some benefits. For example, in the traditional firm peak case, the effect of competitive processing may be to reduce the amount of peak capacity and to improve utilization. Where there is a shifting peak, the discounts may be more complicated. This and other aspects of discounts provide potentially fertile opportunities for future research.

Technical Appendix

Proof of (16)

We first show that $P_1 > P_2$. From (11)-(12), we compute

$$P_1 - P_2 = \left(\frac{\delta}{\Delta}\right)\left[\left(\frac{\partial X_1}{\partial P_2} + \frac{\partial X_2}{\partial P_2}\right)\cdot\frac{\partial X_{11}}{\partial X_1} - \left(\frac{\partial X_1}{\partial P_1} + \frac{\partial X_2}{\partial P_1}\right)\cdot\frac{\partial X_{11}}{\partial P_2}\right]$$

$$-\left(\frac{k}{\Delta}\right)\left[X_1\left(\frac{\partial X_1}{\partial P_2} + \frac{\partial X_2}{\partial P_2}\right) - X_2\left(\frac{\partial X_1}{\partial P_1} + \frac{\partial X_2}{\partial P_1}\right)\right] \quad (A1)$$

Since C1 and C2 are substitutes, $\partial X_{11}/\partial P_2 \geq 0$; and, since own-price effects dominate cross-price effects ($[\partial X_1/\partial P_j + \partial X_2/\partial P_j] < 0$, $j = 1, 2$), $\Delta > 0$ in (13) and (A1). Since $\partial X_{11}/\partial P_1 < 0$ and $\delta > 0$, the first term in (A1) is therefore positive. Suppose now that $P_1 \leq P_2$. Then, by (2)-(3), $X_2 = 0$ and the second term in (A1) is also positive, contradicting our assumption that $P_1 \leq P_2$. Thus, it must be that $P_1 > P_2$, as asserted. Similar reasoning applied to (11) implies $P_1 > MC_2$, so that (16) follows.

Finally, it is straightforward to show that $\Delta \geq B$, where B is the term in the first [ ] in (11). Thus, given the definition of $\delta = MC_1 - MC_2$, it follows that $P_1 \leq MC_1$ when $k = 0$. Without further assumptions, the first term in [ ] in (12) may be either positive or negative, so that P_2 need not be greater than MC_2 in general.

Q.E.D.

Proof That $G(\delta)$ is Continuous and Nonincreasing in δ

The argument in the text, together with the proof that follows, establishes that the optimal prices $P = (P_1, P_2)$ must satisfy the necessary conditions (8) and (10), and the marginal costs in (10) must satisfy (9) and (33). We wish to show that any solution P compatible with these conditions allows precisely one of the three cases indicated in tables 1 and 3. To this end, we define $G(\delta)$ as

$$G(\delta) = G(X(P(\delta))) = X_{11}(P(\delta)) - (X_{12}(P(\delta)) + X_2(P(\delta))), \quad (A2)$$

where $P(\delta)$ are the prices determined by the solution to the necessary conditions (8) or (10) with δ defined by (33). We must show that as the differential $\delta = MC_1 - MC_2$ increases, with the sum $MC_1 + MC_2$ held constant, the function $G(\delta)$ is continuous and nonincreasing. Continuity follows directly from the continuous differentiability of the demand function $X(P)$ and the implicit function theorem applied to (11)-(12) and (7), if (7) is binding. To show monotonicity, we first use (33) to rewrite the first-order conditions (10). Define the functions $F_j(P, \delta)$ as follows:

$$F_j(P, \delta) = \frac{\partial W}{\partial P_j} + \mu\frac{\partial \Pi}{\partial P_j}, \quad j = 1, 2, \quad (A3)$$

where, from (10) and (33),

$$\frac{\partial W}{\partial P_j} = \left[P_1 - \frac{m+\delta}{2}\right]\left[\frac{\partial X_{11}}{\partial P_j}\right] + \sum_{(i,t) \neq (1,1)} \left[P_i - \frac{m-\delta}{2}\right]\left[\frac{\partial X_{it}}{\partial P_j}\right]$$

and

$$\frac{\partial \Pi}{\partial P_j} = \left[P_1 - \frac{m+\delta}{2}\right]\left[\frac{\partial X_{11}}{\partial P_j}\right] + \sum_{(i,t) \neq (1,1)} \left[P_i - \frac{m-\delta}{2}\right]\left[\frac{\partial X_{it}}{\partial P_j}\right] + \sum_t X_{jt},$$

with $W(P)$ the welfare function given in (6) and Π the profit function given in (7). Furthermore, define $F_3(P,\delta)$ as the constraint (7), i.e.,

$$F_3(P, \delta) = \Pi(P, \delta) - \Pi_0. \tag{A4}$$

The claim we wish to establish is that $G(\delta)$ is nonincreasing along the path of prices $P(\delta)$ determined as the solution to $\{F_k(P, \delta) = 0 \mid k = 1,2,3\}$. This then establishes that for if marginal costs satisfy (33), then precisely one of the three cases, $G(\delta) < 0$, $G(\delta) = 0$, or $G(\delta) > 0$, obtains for the prices $P(\delta)$ solving (10).

Consider the comparative statics with respect to δ of the system of equations $\{F_k(P, \delta) = 0 \mid k = 1,2,3\}$. This yields, via the implicit function theorem, the following system of equations:

$$\begin{bmatrix} W_{11} + \mu\Pi_{11} & W_{21} + \mu\Pi_{21} & \Pi_1 \\ W_{12} + \mu\Pi_{12} & W_{22} + \mu\Pi_{22} & \Pi_2 \\ \Pi_1 & \Pi_2 & 0 \end{bmatrix} \begin{bmatrix} \frac{\partial P_1}{\partial \delta} \\ \frac{dP_2}{d\delta} \\ \frac{d\mu}{d\delta} \end{bmatrix} = -\begin{bmatrix} \frac{\partial F_1}{\partial \delta} \\ \frac{dF_2}{d\delta} \\ 0 \end{bmatrix} \tag{A5}$$

where subscripts in (A5) denote partial derivatives with respect to prices P_1, P_2. Denote by H the 2×2 submatrix in the upper left-hand corner of (A5). H is the Hessian of $W + \mu\Pi$, which is negative semi-definite by the second-order necessary conditions for maximizing (6) subject to (7). Thus, pre-multiplying (A5) by the row vector $[\partial P_1/\partial \delta, \partial P_2/\partial \delta, d\mu/d\delta]$ and noting from (A5) that

$$\Pi_1\left(\frac{\partial P_1}{\partial \delta}\right) + \Pi_2\left(\frac{\partial P_2}{\partial \delta}\right) = 0, \tag{A6}$$

we obtain

$$-\left(\frac{\partial F_1}{\partial \delta}\right)\cdot\left(\frac{\partial P_1}{\partial \delta}\right) - \left(\frac{\partial F_2}{\partial \delta}\right)\cdot\left(\frac{\partial P_2}{\partial \delta}\right) = (\nabla P_\delta) H (\nabla P_\delta)^T \leq 0, \tag{A7}$$

where ∇P_δ is the row vector $[\partial P_1/\partial \delta, \partial P_2/\partial \delta]$ and where the inequality follows from the negative semi-definiteness of H. Now note from (A2)-(A3) that $-\partial F_j/\partial \delta = [\partial G/\partial P_j]/2$, so that the left hand side of the inequality in (A7) is just

$[\partial G/\partial \delta]/2$. Thus, G is nonincreasing in δ.

Q.E.D.

Proof of Entries in Tables 2 and 3

We proceed with each case separately. We will use in these proofs the basic principles for Case 1 (where (19) and (30) hold) and Case 2 (where (19) and (31) hold) discussed in the text. Optimal solutions are as follows:

Firm Peak in Period 1—Case 1: $X_{11} > X_2 + X_{12}$

$$Q_1^* = X_2 + X_{12}; \quad Q_2^* = X_{11} - (X_2 + X_{12}). \tag{A8}$$

$$MC_1 = MC_{11} = (1 + \rho) b_2 + \beta_2,$$

$$MC_2 = MC_{it} = \Gamma - \rho b_2, \quad (i,t) \neq (1,1); \tag{A9}$$

where the parameter Γ is defined by (32). To see (A9), note that increasing X_{11} will occasion adding a unit of technology 2 (the peaking technology) and using it to process the additional unit of X_{11}. Thus, $MC_1 = (1 + \rho) b_2 + \beta_2$. Similarly, if $X_2 + X_{12}$ increases by a unit, the increase will be met by a corresponding unit increase in the capacity of technology 1. But this increase in technology 1 capacity will then also be used in period 1, leading to a total increase in technology 1 costs of $(2 + \rho) b_1 + \beta_1$, while saving $(1 + \rho) b_2 + \beta_2$ in technology 2 costs, i.e., $MC_2 = \Gamma - \rho b_2$. From (19), (30), (32), and (A9), $b_1 \leq MC_2 < \Gamma < MC_1$.

Firm Peak in Period 1—Case 2: $X_{11} > X_2 + X_{12}$

$$Q_1^* = X_{11} > X_2 + X_{12}, \quad Q_2^* = 0, \tag{A10}$$

$$MC_1 = MC_{11} = (1 + \rho) b_1 + \beta_1,$$

$$MC_2 = MC_{it} = b_1, \quad (i,t) \neq (1,1). \tag{A11}$$

As argued in the text, Case 2 implies that only technology 1 will be used when there is a firm peak in period 1. The marginal costs are clearly given by (A11) and table 3 for this case.

Firm Peak in Period 2: $X_{11} < X_2 + X_{12}$

$$Q_1^* = X_{11}; \quad Q_2^* = (X_2 + X_{12}) - X_{11}; \tag{A12}$$

$$MC_1 = MC_{11} = \Gamma,$$

$$MC_2 = MC_{it} = b_2 + \beta_2, \quad (i,t) \neq (1,1). \tag{A13}$$

Assume that $X_{11} < X_2 + X_{12}$. We wish to distinguish two competing cases: where all $C2$ demand is deferred to period 2 (leading to a firm peak in period 2) and the case where some $C2$ demand is processed in period 1. In the case where all demand is deferred, the marginal cost of any processing in period 2 is simply $b_2 + \beta_2$. The cost of shifting one unit of $C2$ demand from period 2 to period 1 (which then would be processed using technology 1 in period 1) is given by

$$\Gamma = [(1 + \rho) b_1] - [b_2 - b_1] + [\beta_1 - \beta_2]. \quad (A14)$$

The first [ ] in (A14) is the cost of processing the transferred unit in period 1, the second [ ] is the cost saving associated with using technology 1 rather than technology 2 to process an additional unit in period 2 with the added technology 1 capacity, and the final [ ] represents incremental capacity costs. If $\Gamma > b_2 + \beta_2$, then it makes no sense to shift any processing to period 1. Thus, when $\Gamma > b_2 + \beta_2$ and $X_{11} < X_2 + X_{12}$ at the prices determined by (A13) and (11)-(12), a firm peak in period 2 occurs.

Now consider the case $\Gamma \leq b_2 + \beta_2$. In this case, (A14) implies that processing of some $C2$ demand should be shifted to period 1 until processing in both periods is equalized by these shifts. Beyond the point where processing is equalized, further shifts would give rise to a firm peak in period 1, with incremental costs of such additional shifts equal to $(1 + \rho) b_1 + \beta_1$ or $(1 + \rho) b_2 + \beta_2$, depending on which technology is used to process the quantities shifted. But both $(1 + \rho) b_1 + \beta_1$ and $(1 + \rho) b_2 + \beta_2$ are greater than $b_2 + \beta_2$, the unit cost of processing with technology 2 in period 2. So, when $\Gamma \leq b_2 + \beta_2$, it is optimal to shift processing to period 1 until equal processing occurs in both periods. But equal processing loads in both periods implies from (19) that only technology 1 will then be used and *equal* marginal costs in both periods obtain, namely $MC = MC_{it} = (1 + (\rho/2)) b_1 + (\beta_1/2)$, since a small increase in any demand will be processed by first smoothing the increased demand across both periods and then using technology 1 to meet the half-unit increase in each period. As noted following (7) in the text, however, equal marginal costs ($\delta = 0$) yield equal prices ($P_i = MC$ for $i = 1,2$). And equal prices imply from (2)-(3) that $C2$ demand will vanish. Given our standing assumption that $X_{11} > X_{12}$, we see that $X_{11} < X_2 + X_{12}$ cannot obtain at optimum when $\Gamma \leq b_2 + \beta_2$.

Shifting Peak: $X_{11} = X_2 + X_{12}$

$$Q_1^* = X_{11} = X_2 + X_{12}, \quad Q_2^* = 0, \quad (A15)$$

$$MC_2 < MC_1 \text{ and } MC_1 + MC_2 = (2 + \rho) b_1 + \beta_1 \quad (A16)$$

First note that equal processing in both periods implies (A15)—only technology 1 will be used. Therefore, the marginal costs are derived from the problem (27)-(29) and satisfy (A16) as argued in the text. We see from (A9), (A11), (A13) and (A16) that (33) holds for all possible cases. Note that $MC_1 \leq MC_2$ is not feasible for a shifting peak since at $\delta = 0$ (i.e., $MC_1 = MC_2$) prices are equal and, as noted above, this leads to a firm peak in period 1. Further decreasing δ would only increase the peak in period 1 further since $G(\delta)$ is nonincreasing, as shown above.

Now, if $G(\delta)$ in (34) is negative at the period 1 peak prices corresponding to (A9) or (A11) and is positive for period 2 prices corresponding to (A13), then the monotonicity of $G(\delta)$ and (33) establish that the marginal costs for the shifting peak case must be between those for the period 1 peak and period 2 peak, as shown in table 3. Note that when $\Gamma \leq b_2 + \beta_2$, $G(\delta) > 0$ at the prices determined by (A13) since $\delta \leq 0$ in (33) when $\Gamma \leq b_2 + \beta_2$ and, as we saw above, at $\delta = 0$ (a fortiori, at $\delta < 0$), a firm peak in period 1 obtains.

Q.E.D.

Notes

The authors acknowledge helpful comments from David de Meza at the Conference.

1. Before our own exhortations for peak load pricing, e.g., Crew and Kleindorfer (1971; 1979), there were many proponents of peak load pricing for other industries including electricity, for example, Boiteux (1949), Little (1953), and Steiner (1956). Only Electricite de France comes close to the Post Office in its early and universal application of peak-load pricing.

2. The reader will note that $X_{11} > X_2 + X_{12}$ is equivalent to $X_{11} > (X_1 + X_2)/2$, the average class demand.

3. Since this is a single-period model, it is appropriate to think of S as the annuitized, single-period value associated with the sunk investment required to use external presorting.

4. This is satisfied, e.g., when $V(x; \theta) = a(\theta) V(x)$, with $a(\theta)$ monotonic increasing in θ.

5. Frank Scott (1986) examines the role of Ramsey pricing in the United States Postal Service.

References

Boiteux, Marcel. 1960. "La tarification des demandes en point: application de la theorie de la vente au cout marginal." *Revue Generale de l'electricite* 58 (August 1949): 321-40; translated as "Peak Load Pricing." *Journal of Business* 33 (1960): 157-79.

Crew, Michael A., and Paul R. Kleindorfer. 1979. *Public Utility Economics*. New York: St. Martin's Press.

Crew, Michael A., and Paul R. Kleindorfer. 1986. *The Economics of Public Regulation*. Cambridge, MA: MIT Press.

Crew, Michael A., Paul R. Kleindorfer, and Marc A. Smith. 1990. "Peak-Load Pricing in Postal Services." *Economic Journal* (September): 793-807.

Gravelle, H. 1976. "The Peak-Load Problem with Feasible Storage." *Economic Journal* 86 (June): 256-77.

Little, I.M.D. 1953. *The Price of Fuel*. Oxford: Oxford University Press.

Panzar, John C. 1984. "Rebuttal Testimony on Behalf of American Newspaper Publishers Association." Postal Rate Commission, Docket R84-1, Washington, DC, May 25.

Scott, Frank A. 1986. "Assessing USA Postal Ratemaking: An Application of Ramsey Pricing." *Journal of Industrial Economics* (March): 279-290.

Steiner, Peter O. 1957. "Peak Loads and Efficient Pricing." *Quarterly Journal of Economics* 71 (November): 585-610.

COMMENTS:
Sorting-Out Prices
David de Meza

Crew and Kleindorfer have performed a first-class service in extending the theory of public utility pricing in ways that are particularly relevant for postal administrations.

There are two innovations. The first is an analysis of optimal policy when it is not worth establishing separate prices for different services. For example, the cost of handling first-class mail varies with the time of posting, but the transactions costs of charging on this basis are probably high relative to the benefits. The problem is, therefore, to determine efficient tariffs subject to the constraint that two products with different costs must be sold at the same price. The other issue addressed is the appropriate discount if customers themselves undertake a costly processing stage, such as sorting.

In interpreting the pricing results, the easiest case to consider is that of independent demands. Prices must then be closen to satisfy (18). Suppose that the profit constraint does not bind, so $k = 0$. The optimal price of first-class letters is then a weighted average of the constant marginal cost of processing peak and off-peak mail. This looks like a simple extension of the first-best pricing rule. But there is a twist. At first sight, the weights on the two marginal costs should equal the proportion of peak to off-peak traffic, implying that the revenue raised equals variable cost. In fact, it is easily shown that this is true only if demand is equally elastic in the two periods. If peak demand is relatively inelastic, less weight should be given to peak-period marginal cost in setting price. The reason is straightforward. If peak demand is inelastic, the efficiency loss from setting price below marginal cost is low. It is more important to set the common price close to marginal cost in the stream for which usage is more sensative to price. So, assuming peak demand is inelastic, even with constant marginal cost, optimal pricing does not recover operating costs. The case for allowing a loss-making post office is strengthened if it is not feasible to adopt time-of-day pricing.

A striking feature of the general pricing equations (11) and (12) is their complexity. It would be unreasonable to expect reliable estimates of all the parameters required to set fully optimal prices. What would therefore be interesting to know is whether getting prices right much matters. Many optimal pricing simulations suggest that the welfare gain from moving from some form of average-cost pricing to Ramsey prices is modest (e.g., the table in Estrin and de Meza in this volume). Indeed, this view is implicit in the notion that it is inefficient to charge a supplement for peak-time collections, a policy which does not appear to involve enormous administrative problems. Nevertheless, there is at least one reason for thinking that postal prices have an important efficiency role. Certainly in the short run and probably in the medium run, the Post Office faces inelastic factor supplies. So, if there is a sustained surge in demand for, say, first-class mail, the choice is either to let the quality of service deteriorate or to raise prices. Errors in pricing leading to the wrong quality of service do potentially have significant welfare effects.

In addition to responding to permanent demand change, there is also the problem of coping with day-to-day fluctuations in the volume of mail and in processing capacity. These typically occur at too short notice to make appropriate input or price adjustments. In fact, there is a formal similarity between the analysis of Crew and Kliendorfer and the random demand problem. They consider two products with different costs but of necessity having equal prices. Interpret demand in different states as the distinct products and the probability of the states occuring as a scale parameter. Marginal cost will be highest in the high demand states for it is in these states that capacity costs are relevant. Since cross-price effects between states are absent, equation (18) will be the relevant one. Crew and Kleindorfer have therefore solved two problems for the price of one. Which thought leads on to the question of quantity discounting itself.

So far the concern has been to set the best possible prices subject to meeting a revenue target and requiring that per unit charges do not vary with the amount a customer buys. Both in principle and in practice, utilities may wish to issue tariffs with the property that price per unit depends on the quantity purchased. The efficiency gain from moving from simple Ramsey prices to such non-linear tariffs often exceeds the gains from switching to Ramsey prices from average cost pricing. There is some presumption that efficient non uniform pricing will involve quantity discounting, even if there are no economies in handling bulk orders. To see why, consider a simple case of two firms differing only in that the demand for a utility's services by one of them is double that of the other. The small firm buys nothing if price exceeds £3, 1 unit at any price between £3 and £1, and 3 units at a price of £1 or less. The large firm's demand is exactly twice as high buying 2 units at £3 and 6 units at £1 or less. The utility's marginal cost is constant at £0.5. A first-best solution has firms using the product to the point that another unit is worth less than its production cost. So, a fixed per unit price of £1 is efficient with 9 units being sold. The utility's suplus over variable cost is £4.5 and the firms enjoy a total surplus of £6, making an aggregate benefit of £10.5. But suppose that to cover fixed costs the utility must earn more than £4.5. Profits are maximised at a price per unit of £3 at which the utility's surplus over variable cost rises to £7.5, and the firms get no net benefit.

Consider next non-linear pricing. A fully efficient solution has the small firm buying 3 units and the large firm 6 units. Let the utility offer 3 units for £4.99 and 6 units for £7.98 but make available no other deals. The small firm gains a 1p profit from accepting the 3 unit offer but a £2.98 loss from the 6 unit offer. In contrast, the large firm has a profit of £2.01 from the 3 unit offer but on the six unit offer pays £2.02 less than its total benefit of £10. So the efficient allocation is achieved, the net revenue to the utility is £8.47 and the users' surplus is £2.03. Relative to linear pricing, the utility obtains considerably more revenue without causing any loss in efficiency. Indeed, in this example efficient non-linear pricing yields the utility more revenue than even the profit maximising (and inefficient) linear prices. Notice that, despite the demand of the large firm being a multiple of that of the small firm (and so even if direct price discrimination were feasible, under linear pricing it would not be desirable), the utility offers to supply twice the volume for only 60% more.

Should the utility require to earn more than £8.47, even with non uniform pricing, some inefficiency must be introduced. Suppose it offers 1 unit for £2.99 or 6 units for £9.98. The small firm buys the single unit, the large firm 6 units, the utility earns £9.47, and the users have a surplus of £0.03. Increasing the utility's revenue by £1 causes aggregate gain to fall by £1 but it is still £2 higher than in the linear pricing solution, in which the utility earns only £7.5. This price schedule has even more drastic quantity discounting than the previous one. It costs only 3 1/3 times as much to buy 6 times the volume.

Crew and Kleindorfer do not directly analyse non-linear pricing. However, the problem of determining discounts for pre-sorted mail has elements in common. The reason is that in their setup all firms face the same fixed cost in installing sorting equipment. Hence, only larger firms find it worthwhile to do so.[1] Setting the discount for sorted mail is thus akin to being allowed a single step in an otherwise linear price schedule. Crew and Kleindorfer find that, if the revenue constraint is not binding, the discount for sorting should equal the Post Office's cost saving. But if this special case does not apply and there is a net revenue target, the equations are difficult to interpret. However, the non-linear pricing perspective does suggest some presumptions. If the number of small firms is low relative to the number of large firms, it is attractive for the Post Office to charge a lot for small quantities of mail so as to be better able to exploit the large firms. In this case, the discount for sorting should be high. With only a few large firms, it is desirable to approach the efficient level of sales to the small firms, for stopping short in order to make the offer less attractive to large firms and thereby increase what they will pay for the high volume deal does not raise much extra revenue. Quantity discounts should consequently be low, which in this context implies modest discounts for sorting.

As an illustration, return to the numerical example, assuming that the Post Office must earn a net revenue of £5. With linear pricing and no discount for sorting, this requires a per unit price of £2.16. Summing across firms and the Post Office, aggregate surplus is £7.5. Now suppose a sorting machine comes on the market at a cost of £1.6 and with no running costs. For the sake of a dramatic example, suppose pre-sorting does not save any Post Office costs. The tariff schedule is changed to £2.5 for unsorted mail and £1 for sorted. The large firm has a gross gain of £3 if it pre-sorts and so it buys the machine, whereas the small firm gains only £1.5 so it does not. The Post Office sells one unit at £2.5 and 6 units at £1 and so meets its revenue target. With the small firm enjoying a surplus of £0.5 and the large firm of £4-£1.6=£2.4, aggregate welfare rises by £0.4 as a result of the discount for sorting. The massive discount is beneficial despite there being no gain whatsoever to the Post Office in having presorted mail. The reason is simply that a discount for sorting is a second-best alternative to a quantity discount. Which suggests that it needs careful thought why a quantity discount is itself not feasible.

Note

1. Computer-addressed bulk mail shots are in effect sorted in house at very low cost, whatever the volume involved. The model probably does not fit this case very well.

4

ASSESSING THE WELFARE EFFECTS OF ENTRY INTO LETTER DELIVERY

Ian Dobbs
Paul Richards

1. Background: The Structure of the UK Post Office and Operating Environment

The United Kingdom Post Office is a statutory corporation organized into three main businesses—letters, parcels, and counters. The counters business was established as a wholly owned subsidiary, Post Office Counters Ltd., in October 1987. The letters and parcels businesses are not separate legal entities, but they have their own internal accounts and are organizationally distinct. The Post Office derives its powers mainly from Section 7 of the Post Office Act 1969; it has the power to provide the various services specified there which include postal services, banking services, and services for Government. Section 59 of the British Telecommunication Act 1981 (BT Act 1981) requires the Post Office in exercising its powers to have regard to (1) efficiency and economy; (2) the social, industrial and commercial needs of the United Kingdom with respect to the matters subserved by its powers; (3) the desirability of improving and developing its operating systems; and (4) developments in the field of communications and banking. Additionally, The Secretary of State at the Department of Trade and Industry (DTI) has the power (HMSO 1969) to direct the Post Office to do work of any kind for government departments and local authorities.

Monopoly rights in the Post Office reside solely in the carriage of letters, undertaken by the letters business (now known as Royal Mail) under Section 66 of the BT Act. An important development of the 1981 BT Act was that a letter was defined in law (prior to this there was no definition or legal precedent) as

> Any communication in written form which -
>
> a) is directed to a specific person or address;
>
> b) relates to the personal, private or business affairs of, or the business affairs

of the employer of, either correspondent; and

c) neither is to be nor has been transmitted by means of a telecommunication system,

- and includes a packet containing any such communication.

Under the BT Act (1981), the Post Office has the exclusive privilege of conveying letters from one place to another and of performing all the incidental services of receiving, collecting, and delivering letters throughout the United Kingdom. Exceptions to this are given in Sections 67 to 69 of the Act. Section 67 details eleven general classes of acts not infringing the postal privilege, e.g., the conveyance and delivery of a letter personally by the sender; Section 68 details the operation of licenses granted by Government to other individuals to perform postal activity; Section 69 deals with suspension of the postal privilege. Licenses have been granted to all charities for the conveyance of Christmas cards, and, under earlier legislation, a license was granted to facilitate document exchanges to operate. A general license was also made suspending the postal privilege until the year 2006 for conveyance of a letter for which a charge of at least £1 is made. In the United Kingdom during the 1970s (and particularly following a strike in 1970), the courier industry grew very rapidly and the license to convey at £1 or over granted under the BT Act established legality on a development which had been taking place for some time. The Post Office has never had any exclusive rights regarding parcels.

Under Section 59 of the BT Act (1981), monopoly rights are paralleled with a general duty of the Post Office concerning the provision of letter services

> ... so to exercise its powers, as to provide, throughout the United Kingdom (save in so far as they are provided by other persons or the provision thereof is, in its opinion, impracticable or not reasonably practicable) such services for the conveyance of letters as satisfy all reasonable demands for them.

and the general duty thus extends to all classes of mail including those at over £1.

The BT Act (1981) does not confer power on the Secretary of State to significantly alter the nature of the Post Office's exclusive privilege, e.g., by reducing the £1 limit to zero, and current legislation does not give the basis for the permanent suspension of the letter monopoly itself, which would require primary legislation. Against this background, this paper deals with the potential impact of deregulation in the areas covered by the exclusive privilege in the letters business. It does not address the problems that domestic deregulation could imply for the handling of incoming and outgoing foreign mails, although this is a serious issue which would also need to be examined.

2. Defining the Issues on Deregulation

The issue of whether the provision of letter services should be subject to greater competition and, in turn, whether this would be of net benefit in some welfare sense is now considered. Some of the principal factors to be taken into account include

1. The nature of entry: why entry should occur when the market is opened up, which parts of the letters market would be most vulnerable to entry.

2. The competitive environment: How would the costs, prices, and services of the incumbent and entrants change under competition. How might the market structure change over time.

3. Assessment of costs and benefits: How should the changes be assessed to determine benefits. How the gains and losses of different customers should be evaluated.

4. Alternative approaches to deregulation: whether different methods of deregulation would yield better solutions and whether they have different measures of risk associated with them; the role if any of governmental or other regulatory agency on the incumbent and new entrants; whether any other industries offer a reliable guide as to the likely experience of deregulation in postal services; whether separate account should be taken of whether customers express a preference in favor of deregulation.

3. Proposals Concerning Deregulation

Table 1 sets out some of the arguments put forward in recent publications on this topic. Of these, the publications by Senior (1983), Albon (1987), Clarke (1988), and Mason (1988; 1989), are polemical in style; Estrin and de Meza (E&M, 1988) is exceptional in subjecting the issue to an economic analysis of the welfare effects of entry. The Mail Users Association/Association of Mail Order Publishers (MUA/AMOP 1989) publication is also noteworthy in that it comes from important customers of the Post Office. The Union of Communication Workers (1990) also addresses the issues of ownership and regulation but invokes economic arguments for monopoly retention. The economic content of the publications in favor of deregulation is usually rather spartan, but they still merit consideration, as do the solutions they propose. Whilst all are dismissive of any justifications for retention of the status quo, the solutions proposed range from total freedom to quite complex arrangements involving regulatory bodies and regional franchises. Some authors put forward a multitude of solutions, seemingly advocating some sort of combination of them as the likely "best" solution. The E&M Report (1988) is radically different from all of the others in that it explicitly attempted to estimate the gains and losses of deregulation. However, it should be noted that its exact recommendations do not appear to have been explicitly assessed in the analysis of the Report itself and, as such, appear to have been based on ad hoc intuition rather than a specific evaluation of the potential benefits.

Since the major review of the monopoly in 1979 by the United Kingdom Government, which led to the reforms in the 1981 Act, successive Secretaries of State in the DTI have reviewed the value of the monopoly but not deregulated, despite intense press speculation. More recently, the Government re-affirmed its commitment to the monopoly, stressing the need for universal service and uniform pricing. Overall, it is clear that the free marketeers have not yet convinced either

Table 1. Recent Publications on the United Kingdom Postal Monopoly

Author	Title	Institute	Monopoly Justifications Considered	Proposed Solution(s)
Senior	Liberating the Letter. 1983	Institute of Economic Affairs	Natural monopoly. Protect rural services. A social service.	Relieved of obligations of service and monopoly
Albon	Privatize the Post. 1987	Center for Policy Studies	Natural monopoly. Cross-subsidize rural operations.	Complete monopoly removal regional franchises. Tax on urban traffics to subsidize rural services.
Clarke	Ending the Post Office Monopoly. 1988	Aims of Industry	—	Suspend monopoly but perhaps experiment in rural areas first.
Mason	Enlightenment. 1988	Adam Smith Institute	—	Set up a single competing service.
Mason	Privatizing the Posts. 1989	Adam Smith Institute	Cream-skimming of urban traffics.	New regulatory authority; Regional franchises Duopoly solution Common carriage delivery.
Estrin & de Meza	Should the Post Office's Statutory Monopoly be lifted? 1988	LSE/DHL	Unsustainable natural monopoly	Reduce £1 limit Post Club Tax entrants
—	Deliver Us from the Post Office. 1989	Mail Users Association	—	Radical change in management structure.
—	The Last Post? 1990	Union of Communication Workers	Natural monopoly	

the Government or many important Post Office customers that introducing a free-for-all would be desirable.

4. The Nature of Entry Under Deregulation

The way in which deregulation might unfold will be strongly influenced by the costing structure of postal delivery; Appendix 1 describes some fundamental economic characteristics of the letters business in the United Kingdom including its cost structure, markets, pricing policy, and the way in which regulation has impacted on its performance and behavior during the 1980s. Appendix 2 comments on some claims made that the letter service does not display any natural monopoly characteristics. These are drawn upon in the discussion below.

There are at least five reasons why entry might occur under deregulation -

Cost Reduction. (1) The entrant has access to cheaper factors of production such as labor or capital which the incumbent cannot or is unwilling to employ. (2) There is structural inefficiency by the incumbent and the entrant produces the same product but cheaper. (3) An operator in another area can achieve some economy of scope and the incremental costs of postal services are less than the stand-alone costs. This might particularly be relevant if "cross-selling" was possible to an existing customer base.

New Services. (4) The existing product range is inadequate and some new service can be provided.

Pricing Structure. (5) The incumbent has a pricing structure in which the structure of costs is not well reflected in the structure of prices and selective entry ("cream-skimming") is feasible.

In practice, it is unlikely that an entrant would come in solely for one of these reasons—it would be more plausible that a combination of factors would apply. The likelihood of entry for any or a combination of these reasons will depend upon the practices and performance of the postal administration in question, the extent of restriction that applied prior to deregulation, and the willingness of entrepreneurs to enter. Concerning the willingness to take risks, it is a feature of postal services that the financial consequences of failure following entry at the simplest level-for local traffics-are likely to be very low. Local markets are therefore likely to be highly contestable. To run a truly national network, significant set-up costs would have to be incurred on buildings and marketing expenses, and, although many of the fixed assets could be re-sold at exit, some significant costs would inevitably be associated with failure, primarily those which would be incurred in an on-going operation.

Table 2 gives some hypothetical possibilities of entry in which the market is crudely segregated by service standard. In broad terms, it is suggested that the following might be feasible:

Overnight Services. For overnight services, it is highly likely that local traffics would be vulnerable not only from customers who already sort their traffic by postcode (and the segregation costs would therefore be minimal) but possibly also

Table 2. Possible Types of Entry into Postal Markets

Reason for Entry	Service Standard		
	Overnight	2-4 Days	Slow Service
Lower Costs		Where cost synergies of supply; linked franchises	Advertising material
New Service	Semi-premium service; City links; Business traffics	Consignment services	
Different prices	Local services	Niche markets; Packets	

from members of the public. A small private operator could offer this service and possibly offer a facilities management service to companies to sort the traffic. In addition, it has often been postulated that there might exist a gap below £1, but above First Class at 20 pence, for a semi-premium service offering a higher standard of assurance than the First Class traffic but less than courier price (typically at £10 an item). E&M (1988) appeared to be skeptical about this but advocated lowering the £1 limit to encourage any innovation that might be possible. The sort of individual who might try to innovate here could include express parcel carriers, courier firms, or perhaps local franchises linked together in some way or some other type of distributor. The local operator would probably also make use of cheaper labor such as casuals or part-timers, although, if a high-quality service is being offered with early delivery, then such opportunities might be limited. The operator offering a new value-added high-assurance service would probably employ similar labor to that of the postal administration, and any cost advantage would ensue from better use of labor rather than the factor price as such.

Standard Service. For a standard service, there are several possibilities. If a number of cheap local networks were established, then conceivably they might be linked to form a rival national service. The logistical problems involved here should not be underestimated due to the difficulties of devising a system of transfer payments, counting traffic, and capacity planning under conditions of stochastic demand. It is possible that other distributors of goods (particularly to businesses in conurbations) might be tempted to offer some delivery service, providing quality assurance was not too high and incremental costs low. It is also likely that in many countries "niche" markets exist for particular traffics which are regular and which may pay comparatively high margins under published tariffs, e.g., office-to-branch traffics which could be lost to a dedicated operation.

Slow or Intermittent Services. For very slow or intermittent services, such as unaddressed mail and some direct mail, it is clear that the primary source of competitive advantage would be through accessing cheaper labor such as casual workers, retired individuals, newspaper deliverers, etc. It may also be possible that this source of labor could deliver other types of mail requiring higher assurance which is scheduled but not time-critical.

Complete deregulation could impact on an incumbent postal administration from a number of ways. Different segments of traffic would be vulnerable from different entrants and, depending upon how well they succeed, would potentially weaken the administration to further competitive entry. Assigning degrees of vulnerability and magnitudes to the various traffics is difficult and, to an extent, speculative; certainly in the United Kingdom local traffics would be regarded as highly vulnerable, in that a service could be offered to large customers broadly similar to the current service by undercutting the uniform price.

5. The Competitive Environment: Expectations and Reactions

Many of the proponents of deregulation also promote privatization and believe that the spur to maximize profits will make major cost reduction possible for postal administrations. Bishop and Kay (1988) argued that privatization per se is neither a necessary nor sufficient condition for productivity improvement, and many of the poorly performing nationalized industries raised their performance whilst in the public sector during the 1980s. Whilst it is easy to ignore the privatization issue as being purely political, the potential for productivity improvement is important in the context of competition. However, assessments of the likely magnitude of slack to be removed are difficult to make in network industries, such as postal services, where there are acute problems in measuring workload.

Rather than simply assume that free markets will be the most efficient structure, it is possible to describe a formal model of the competitive environment, as for example that by E&M (1988), who looked at the consequences of postulating Cournot and Bertrand models of letter supply. The Cournot and Bertrand models prescribe competition according to specified reaction functions or rules. Cournot— each firm takes the output of other firms as given and decides on a level of output, with price adjusting to clear the market. Bertrand—each firm takes the price of the others as given and adjusts its own price with output clearing the market.

E&M (1988) examined Cournot and Bertrand duopoly (2-firm) models. These models can be thought of as either representing the initial, short-run behavior following deregulation or a long-term solution in which only two suppliers are licensed to offer postal services. Competition on Cournot lines is hard to envisage for postal services; the idea of firms choosing quantities and those quantities determining price does not align well with the reality that the posting decision is not determined by the provider of the service but by the individuals paying for the service. In this sense, the Bertrand model-which is a more aggressive form of competition-seems more meaningful than Cournot. However, given the assumption that the Post Office continues to be regulated and subject to the same financial target as at present, then a Stackelberg leader-follower model may be even more appropriate than the Bertrand model. The point is that in a single-product duopoly model, the Post Office as incumbent, subject to regulatory control on profitability, has no degree of freedom over its marketing strategy. If another firm enters the market at a certain price (or quantity), and holds this, then the Post Office must (eventually) respond by adjusting its price in order to attain the regulatory target. The potential entrant can reasonably be expected to know enough about Post Office cost and demand structures and the nature of the regulatory control to effectively predict the (eventual) Post Office reaction to the act of entry. A sophisticated potential entrant would clearly take into account the Post Office reaction in determining the optimal price/output at which to enter, and, indeed, in deciding whether to enter at all. Thus, it seems reasonable to cast the *entrant* as leader and the *incumbent* as follower in a Stackelberg model.

In deciding whether entry occurs, and if so whether it is welfare beneficial, critically depends on whether it is assumed that the entrant is assumed to be sophisticated (i.e., a Stackelberg leader) or not. Thus, E&M (1988) undertook an extensive sensitivity analysis of the single product duopoly case and concluded (p. 84):

> In summary, of the 28 cases we have considered, the only instances of disadvantageous entry involved very close substitutes and unrealistically high cost advantages for the entrant. There is no real efficiency case for a statutory monopoly here.

In fact, of the 28 cases they examined, entry occurred in 14 cases, and entry was welfare improving in 11 of these, so their conclusion looks reasonably robust. However, as we have argued above, it may be more reasonable to assume that the entrant is sophisticated, and if so, this radically changes the above conclusion. Part of our recent program of work has involved reproducing the Estrin and de Meza results and extending their model to consider the von Stackelberg case. Our calculations for the Stackelberg model suggest that in all their 28 cases entry is profitable, yet in 26 of these, there are adverse welfare consequences. Thus, a change in the expectations assumption leads to a diametrically opposite conclusion (namely, that the Post Office needs to be protected against harmful competition).

In more general terms, competition might expect to result in changes to the following:

The Pricing Structure. As noted in Appendix 1, the United Kingdom Post Office has made a price distinction in terms of perceived market willingness to pay for different service standards and there is a very high degree of transparency in pricing. It is possible to envisage alternative pricing structures which would be more discriminatory between customer types, traffic types, and the extent of competition. Pricing might become less transparent with discounting purely for volume reflecting bargaining power rather than costs.

Costs. The extent to which competitive pressures would induce downward pressure on costs is an empirical issue. In terms of pure factor prices, it is not clear that, in the United Kingdom at least, there is great scope for factor price reduction given trends in staff wastage and significant problems of recruitment and retention in over half the country. Whether other types of labor could be substituted for traditional labor (male full-timers) in sufficient quantities to make a material difference to costs is also unclear. It is possible that competitive pressure would improve productivity performance, but the extent of potential productivity improvement possible is hard to assess and this needs to be weighed against any disbenefits of deregulation.

Service Standards. There are acute difficulties which postal administrations face in establishing pricing structures which accurately reflect both costs and customers' willingness to pay, taking quality of service (QofS) into account. The cost structures are complex because of economies of scale, network relationships, and joint output variabilities. Where competitive entry is not likely to be high and if it is difficult to enforce complex price schedules reflecting different customers' willingness to pay, then making adjustments to service standards to better align costs with prices is one alternative strategy.

Given the many uncertainties as to how the market might develop, one way of considering their impact is to postulate scenarios to cover the range of plausible outcomes:

1. A dominant firm remains. The postal administration as "first mover" realizes significant economies of scale, manages to price discriminate by cost and markets, adjusts quality of service, and is reasonably profitable and pays competitive wages. The general price level is probably significantly above that under the current regulatory environment.

2. A dominant firm with significant competitive "fringe". Competition is widespread at the local level and in a number of other strategic markets. The dominant firm is able to survive offering a national service but with much reduced market volume, and profitability is much less than in case (1).

3. A fragmented industry with sufficient competition to reduce the financial viability of the dominant firm so as to threaten its survival. No player can realize significant economies of scale and coverage of service is patchy with no national service at near current price levels. Under this scenario, there would be a significant failure rate, high mergers, and low industry profitability.

Certainly in the United Kingdom there is no evidence that any entrant would attempt to replicate the incumbent by offering a national service at a uniform price, and this does not feature in the three scenarios above.

The key issue arises as to how the market might develop over time. Scenarios (1) and (3) probably represent plausible steady-state solutions; certainly it is difficult to see how a fragmented industry in (3) with low profitability could induce any company to take the risk to attain dominance with a national service, whilst always having a very active competitive fringe. Scenario (2) would probably be regarded as the best outcome by many, in which the dominant firm is able to realize sufficient economies of scale to ensure viability and offer a national service but still have the pressure to reduce costs and lower prices. There are two key questions here: (1) How likely is it that scenario (2) would move either to scenario (1) or scenario (3)? (2) What incentive would there be for a dominant firm to retain a national service?

To the extent that there are uncertainties surrounding these questions, in the short term at least, there would need to be some regulatory controls.

6. Measuring Welfare: The Costs and Benefits of Deregulation

Welfare benefits are usually assessed by reference to consumer surplus, i.e., the savings to the customer from having had to pay less than he was willing to pay for the service, and also to industry profitability. In the case of postal services, there are two particular features which may complicate and limit the applicability of this approach: (1) The consumption of the service is a joint demand of recipient and sender, but only the sender pays. (2) The vast bulk of traffic is sent by firms and not households, and firms do not gain consumer surplus in the conventional understanding.

Traffic from firms engenders consumers surplus, at least in part, via "flow-through". That is, the postal price influences firms' final product prices and hence consumers surplus. Whether firms operate in competitive or non-competitive markets, it is a tricky task to assess the associated welfare consequences from these sources. (See e.g., Brown and Sibley (1986).)

Two studies, Albon (1989) and E&M (1988), have considered the welfare gains from alternative pricing structures. Albon (1989) considers the gains from the Post Office altering its pricing structure in its current state, whilst E&M (1988) also consider the impact on consumer surplus of competitive entry from different pricing structures and potential profits for an entrant. Some question surround the Albon (1989) study; first, his Ramsey-pricing solution is not based on marginal costs but on a form of allocated costs. (Although marginal costs for the United Kingdom Post Office have been estimated (Post Office 1986), Tabor (1987), reports the results of a separate exercise involving cost allocation and Albon (1989) appears to have used these values.) Second, the high real price elasticities employed (at -0.9 for First and Second Class relative to retail prices) do not align with any previous studies and are seriously adrift from the values estimated by Neary (1975) or Cuthbertson and Richards (1991). In fact, Albon (1986) originally estimated the welfare gains of adopting a more cost-related tariff to be £65m (in 1985-86 prices), assuming annual benefits were capitalised in perpetuity. In 1989, this estimate was raised more than threefold to roughly £200m (still at 1985-86 prices) based on a very much higher and somewhat implausible price elasticity.

While aligning prices more accurately to costs usually brings welfare gains, E&M (1988) reject the assertion that breaking the current uniform tariff would necessarily be welfare improving, partly on the grounds that benefits from a Ramsey pricing solution should be based on the measure of marginal costs of the current network rather than allocated costs or stand-alone costs. Further, taking into account the likely problems of administering a complex set of tariffs, they considered that the gains were unlikely to outweigh the losses.

The argument usually attributed to the Post Office and to governments for maintenance of uniform pricing (e.g., Albon (1986)) is that the rural lobby has significant political influence. Irrespective of whether this is true or not, the arguments for not having a "rural" tariff are strong on purely economic grounds:

1. On equity considerations, it is not especially material, as the vast majority of

posters send mail to a variety of locations including what might be classified as rural. Whilst undoubtedly there are some posters whose mail is perhaps more weighted toward rural communities, e.g., farming suppliers, it is difficult to believe that they constitute a material segment of posters, who need to be singled out for special treatment. Similarly, private individuals frequently holiday in rural areas and post or receive mail there. Whilst traffic posted in rural areas costs more to collect, this is usually undertaken jointly with delivery and is not a particularly significant cost.

2. The costs of administering a rural tariff are likely to greatly outweigh any conceivable benefits, as E&M (1988) point out. Indeed it was the very reforms that introduced the Penny Post which swept aside cumbersome and unwieldy procedures involving surcharges and the like. In this respect, Albon (1989) is simply incorrect in asserting that

> it would be virtually costless for letters to be divided into four categories. It is difficult to see that the additional handling administrative and customer compliance costs of a Ramsey pricing structure for inland letters would be prohibitive. In fact they are likely to be trivial compared with the expected efficiency gains.

There are a number of acute problems in offering complex tariffs of the type Albon (1989) envisages:

1. Not all mail is handled through mechanized letter offices (and particularly from rural areas), and currently First and Second Class traffics are largely separated manually not automatically (except where large customers pre-sort traffic). At the outward despatching stage, it is unimaginable that a properly enforced four way tariff involving rural items could be implemented without significantly reducing service standards.

2. The confusion and problems of a rural tariff for the vast majority of posters would be such that many posters would either deliberately or inadvertently ignore it. (Experience of overseas mails tariffs bears this out.) The administrative problems of surcharging the rural recipient rather than the sender are equally formidable where one could easily envisage large numbers of individuals refusing to pay, diverting mail to neighbors, etc.

3. There would be significant anomalies in the pricing of international mails, with the possibility that posting some letters to rural areas in Europe would cost less to post than letters to some areas within the United Kingdom. This would be hard to rationalize to customers.

4. The definition of what constitutes a rural address is to a large extent arbitrary and would be likely to alter over time; this would require constant revision to the pricing structure and informing customers.

While the problems of a rural tariff are more or less insurmountable and not cost effective, it is less clear that a tariff for locally posted and delivered items would be so difficult to implement for some customers. The marginal cost difference at the local level between First and Second Class items is comparatively small, and it could be argued that a uniform service at a single price should be offered.

However, there would still be significant costs of implementation and boundary anomalies, particularly as operational boundaries do not typically align with other administrative areas. Certainly, in the United Kingdom there is no obvious groundswell of customer demand for breaking the uniform tariff, and the statutory body representing consumer interests-the Post Office Users National Council-recently argued (1989) that its retention reflected the clear balance of user views.

Regulation bringing more overtly cost-related pricing structures is unlikely to be important purely on equity grounds. But, deregulation might bring about significantly less transparency in pricing, if there was much greater attention given to customers' willingness to pay. It is not hard to envisage the development of overt and covert pricing, with a published tariff which the general public and small posters would face, whilst large customers would use their bargaining power to obtain better deals. In effect, this would result in non-uniform pricing, i.e., price discounts for volume. It is theoretically possible that this would yield net benefits compared with a uniform Ramsey pricing solution, although, in practice, covert pricing of this type would probably cause considerable public disquiet and might even be regarded as anti-competitive.

A proper assessment of the benefits of deregulation should include not only the impact of relative and overall prices changing but also service standards. Measurement of the service-price trade-off is extremely difficult to establish. Although, in the United Kingdom there are two basic services which differ in speed of delivery, they each include a range of traffics which have very different levels of quality assurance related to the exact route taken by the traffic itself.

In conclusion, there is little convincing evidence that different price structures would yield material gains to welfare either compared to an "ideal" Ramsey solution or the current pricing structure. For the majority of posters, letter traffics by their nature are not amenable to complex tariffs which distinguish origin of posting and destination of delivery, and it is not obvious that any major class of customer suffers materially under current pricing arrangements or would stand to gain significantly under a different pricing structure under competition.

7. Alternative Approaches to Deregulation

The foregoing discussion suggests the following problem for the would-be deregulator:

1. Currently the incumbent is strictly controlled and regulated. To permit open competition would of necessity imply at least some relaxation of these controls in the long-term, if the market is to function freely.

2. Entry into the market is most likely in the short-term where either prices are not well aligned with costs or economies of scope are achievable or specific types of customers or traffics are targeted.

3. For some parts of the country or types of traffic, it is unlikely that significant competition would develop either at the early stages or in the longer-term, including "rural" traffics and traffics to areas of low population density or social deprivation.

4. The incumbent has economies of scale/scope which it may not be able to use to prevent entry. Where a price niche is discovered ("cream-skimming") and the incumbent's traffic is lost for the "wrong" reason (i.e., it is simply impossible to implement a complex price schedule effectively), then customers may experience a general rise in prices. Every customer would have an incentive to be served by a niche entrant if it had a significant proportion of traffics in that stream making segregation cost-effective, but collectively this could be self-defeating if the incumbent lost economies of scale and was obliged to raise other prices disproportionately.

5. On the other hand, the incumbent might be able to use its economic power very effectively by introducing selective pricing, such as discounts for volume, local tariffs to prevent entry, reductions in service where competition did not develop, and raising the general level of prices and profits.

6. The potential losses from deregulation need to be weighed against the potential improvements in operating efficiency, which are themselves difficult to assess.

The deregulator therefore needs to devise a set of rules which will permit transition from the current state to another state, in which presumably there is greater competition while maintaining continuity of a national service. The uncertainties involved are enormous, but it is highly likely that, irrespective of the method of deregulation, the incumbent would be expected-or obliged-to offer a national service or be a postal service of last resort, at least in the transition period.

There are a great number of ways to deregulate including: (1) a free-for-all and total deregulation; (2) lowering of the entry price and/or further exemptions of traffics; (3) restricted competition by area or type of traffic; (4) explicitly regulated competition, such as the duopoly in United Kingdom telecommunications of British Telecom (BT) and Mercury, or regional franchises, as currently in television; (5) an output tax on all entrants; and (6) setting a minimum price. It may even be possible to combine these as some commentators have suggested.

Of these, it is highly unlikely that options 1, 5, and 6 would be front-runners. The first would have the advantage of being simple to implement and having a lasting impact, but it would be high-risk and probably only invoked at the end of a deregulation process. Options 5 and 6 could be difficult to legislate and simply unenforceable in practice (in effect the position would be turned back 150 years when high and complex tariffs resulted in massive illegal evasion). The next least plausible option is probably introducing restricted competition under option 3 perhaps at the local level or for certain types of traffic. This would give customers a limited increase in choice but be subject to boundary problems, and, if the cream-skimming hypothesis has any merit, it is unclear that customers would benefit overall. Opening competition to certain types of letters, e.g., based on content, is appealing at first sight but, in practice, would be subject to practical difficulties, particularly as many letters contain a variety of contents, e.g., financial mail, advertising, etc.

The most likely routes for deregulation would appear to be: (1) a development along BT/Mercury lines in which another distributor of mail is licensed to offer a service, possibly with access to parts of the incumbent's network; (2) adjusting the entry price; or (3) the regional franchise solution.

The franchise model for postal services faces the problems of establishing trading relationships with each franchise (or another transmission company responsible for trunking) and the setting and achievement of quality standards for outward and inward mail. Whilst existing arrangements for mail movements between different parts of the country would serve as an initial benchmark, to formalize them in a contract would be less straightforward, particularly if changes to the network structure were necessary. A further difficulty in the short-term would be to find sufficient organizations, apart from the incumbent postal operators, capable of bidding for the franchise with a track record of financial and operational competence. In short, the regional franchise solution has significant practical difficulties if greater competition is the aim, largely because franchisees would need to trade with each other with formal contracts to cover costs and ensure service standards were maintained. In terms of customer choice, this solution is not particularly appealing if the franchisee has a local monopoly for then all that will have been achieved is to replace a single, unified monopoly with a series of smaller, local monopolies. This solution would also pose problems for many customers, who prefer to be able to interface with a single part of an organization to discuss matters such as service standards than have to deal with a multitude of suppliers who trade with each other.

A much simpler solution would be to license a single rival to offer a national service, perhaps by deliberately trying to divide up the existing traffics between the incumbent and a rival or by simply allowing the competitive process to work in some way to enable entry. To the extent that the rival is obliged to use some part of the incumbent's network, customers' choice is perhaps not extended significantly, and, in particular, there would be no possibility of an uninterrupted service or real alternative in the event of industrial action. Further, there would be the usual problem of establishing fair terms for use of the network. Assuming that a rival could be selected and did not need to use the incumbent's network, what is the economics of this solution? E&M (1988) examined some simple Bertrand/Cournot models of this type of entry, and we are currently developing a further range of models of this type (including Bertrand, Cournot, competitive fringe, and Stackelberg, along with various forms of regulatory regimes for the Post Office). Our work to date on these models suggests that a fairly general conclusion for this type of simulation is that it is not at all difficult to construct "plausible" cases in which a licensed duopoly can be shown to be harmful to consumers in a welfare sense. It quickly becomes clear that the choice of regulatory regime is likely to be critical in determining whether entry is beneficial or harmful. Furthermore, in a licensed duopoly, there is the interesting question of whether it is desirable to also regulate the entrant-something which is not the case in telecommunications in the United Kingdom at present. Analysis of the duopoly option in this way illustrates the basic issues to be addressed, but it does not give unequivocal guidance on the benefits of this form of market structure or whether more than one alternative licensed operator would be desirable. The practical difficulties of such a solution would be in establishing fair terms for competition, who should bear obligations of service, and who the rival should be. (If the rival was an international express company, it would thereby gain an enormous strategic advantage on its rivals.)

To legislate and ensure choice in service, such as through the duopoly solution, may be more difficult for letters than for telecommunications, particularly if complex transfer charging is involved. It is also apparent that Oftel, the regulatory agency for telecommunications in the United Kingdom, is now (Oftel 1990) raising a very fundamental issue as to whether competition per se will be beneficial for telecommunications, it having had the clear remit to promote competition to date. In the Financial Times of June 28 1990, the Director General of Oftel reports that

> while competition had improved the lot of consumers in the UK, it could also "decrease the value for money"... The Government would have to weigh the advantages of improved efficiency stemming from competition against the disadvantages of lost economies of scale. Improved efficiency might not outweigh the loss of economies of scale... "I do suggest that the viability of differing levels of competition is an open question that needs to be assessed as part of the duopoly review."

The alternative approach to deregulation involves the setting of the price limit as a barrier to entry. There are a number of ways of interpreting this form of regulation:

1. As a means of stimulating greater direct competition to replicate or better the existing incumbent's service.
2. To encourage or permit market entry in new types of provision in which a different type of service is permitted.
3. A means of promoting better cost or price control of the incumbent with only the threat of potential entry.

If the intention of the barrier to entry is to be effective, then at a given level of service it is not obvious what margin above current tariffs will suffice. The United Kingdom £1 limit in 1981 was clearly set at a relatively high level presumably to deter entry, not only at the basic weight step, but at much higher weight steps also. However, it has not been raised in value since then. The consequence of entry at below the prevailing limiting entry price will depend upon the nature of the service being offered. To the extent that a "new"' service of some type is provided, then the extent of traffic loss from the existing incumbent's services may be limited. If the service is only slightly differentiated and traffic migrates up from a standard or First Class service, the higher cost and price of the First Class service from a lower volume may be compensated by the benefit of the new service, if a significantly higher quality of service is offered. This raises the issue of establishing the customer valuation of different service standards.

An advantage of this form of deregulation is that it can be partially controlled by relaxing the entry price slowly to see the impact. The other key advantage of this approach would be to prevent either of the two undesirable market structures of a dominant firm abusing its power or the other extreme of total fragmentation. The disadvantage is that it would be difficult if not impossible to reverse retrospectively if the outcome was deemed unsatisfactory. It is also unclear to what extent the existing financial controls and general regulation of the incumbent could be retained, and the loosening of regulation of the incumbent may not easily integrate with this form of deregulation.

Of all the deregulatory approaches, adjusting the entry price is potentially the least risky, if it is used cautiously. To the extent that a modest reduction in the minimum entry price induces little response, then no harm may be done but likewise little good. A more drastic reduction in the limit would offer greater chance of entry (although not of the cream-skimming kind if retained above the incumbent's price) and perhaps segment the market; the extent to which this would be beneficial or not is difficult to discern. The closer the limit comes to current tariffs, the greater the potential impact and the problems of regulating not only the incumbent but also the rivals. In short, this method is potentially attractive for the deregulator providing it is not too drastic in its effects, i.e., it is used as a controlled and limited deregulation. To a considerable extent, this appears to be the main thrust of the E&M Report (1988). If significant competition is desired, then ground rules for competition need to be addressed and whether the incumbent should still be given obligations of service.

It is interesting to compare letter services with other industries which have been deregulated. In the United Kingdom, the closest parallel is probably buses, the background to which is contained in a Government White Paper (1984). This paper perceived competition as the cure for a declining moribund industry which received significant subsidies and was unresponsive to customer needs. In essence, the Government abolished the restrictions on entry (outside London) and the provision of commercially unviable routes (largely rural) were to be franchised. A further perceived beneficial consequence of competition was the elimination of cross-subsidy, and it was apparent that internal cross-subsidy was much more important than external subsidy (although subvention was very important for rural services and Sunday services). While it is too early to be certain of the impact of subsequent deregulation in 1987, the following appear (Association of Metropolitan Authorities 1990) to have happened:

1. Where some services were already relatively good, such as on key radial urban routes, they have been augmented further.

2. Conversely, rural routes have only been continued where subsidy from local authorities has been available, and many of these are under threat.

3. Overall passenger mileage has continued to decline.

4. There have been some moves to greater industry concentration with some takeovers being referred to the Monopolies and Mergers Commission. Competition is now as much or more in the "Boardroom" than on the streets.

5. In the initial stages at least, there were acute problems (Brown 1987) particularly as rival companies would not co-operate to issue joint timetables (and individual timetables were altered frequently) or transferable tickets.

There are some striking similarities with letter services, but differences also. The greatest similarities are probably the internal geographical cross-subsidization and the sensitivity to real price (quoted at -0.3), but there are many differences:
1. The bus companies did not attempt to offer a national service.
2. The deregulation process was intended to retain a fragmented industry.
3. The industry was inherently weak with (it is claimed) poor cost control.
4. The equity argument in favor of competition to eliminate cross-subsidization was probably more cogent given that different individuals benefitted from the distortion of prices.
5. Pricing can be tailor-made to individual bus routes.

In broad terms, whereas a regulated letter service is obliged to be universal, deregulation in buses was deliberately focused on breaking up joint operations. But in some ways the consequences of deregulation would probably be similar, namely entry has occurred where demand is relatively high but little interest would be given to sparsely populated areas.

The outcome of bus deregulation certainly gives some pointers as to the likely impact of deregulation in letter services: some customers gained and others lost; operating efficiencies have probably improved; entrants have configured their services to particular traffic types; and there has been some conflict in information provision which has resulted in disruption to customers. Probably the greatest difference between buses and letters is the service being offered. Bus journeys tend to be localized and most travellers have little interest or need to know about the provision of services outside their area, whereas posters of letters need to be sure that all of their letters can be delivered.

The likely benefits and disbenefits of complete deregulation are speculative and it is not difficult to hypothesize that, taking into account the nature of letter service cost structures and the limited opportunities for accurate pricing, a fragmented industry could result from a free-for-all. In short, in the absence of regulation, a unified service could disappear. With a high degree of deregulation, market entry might occur for good reasons (e.g., higher efficiency, new services) or bad ones (e.g., cream-skimming). To devise rules that only ensure the former and not the latter would not be straightforward, and many of the ideas suggested by free-market commentators are clearly impractical in part or in whole.

In this context, it is interesting to note that the Mail Users Association Paper (1989) rejected complete deregulation:

> Lengthy discussions also took place around a second option - the repeated calls for an end to the letter monopoly....Although these proposals have much to commend them, a survey of AMOP and MUA members rejected the implicit consequence of a multi-carrier service.
>
> Members felt that such fragmentation would:-
> * Reduce the quality of service to rural users.
> * Put pressure on rural prices.
> * Increase complexity.
> * Dilute economies of scale.
> * Still leave the general public without a real choice.

* Raise serious problems about security - eg., registered mail
* Cause problems after 1992 and the growth of continental traffic.

In addition, our research found no instance of any other major industrial country having more than one national letter carrier and several private UK carriers doubted their own ability to offer a genuinely national next day letter delivery service at an economic price.

Economic theory is equivocal on whether it is desirable to protect a natural monopoly industry, such as the letter service; there are arguments both for and against (as discussed in this paper). The problem, thus, becomes one of trying to put numbers to these arguments in order to assess whether the pros outweigh, in welfare terms, the cons. Unfortunately, even highly stylized models (such as the duopoly models discussed above) at best give only some insight into the magnitude of possible benefits and costs and their determinants; organizational, incentive, information, and dynamic effects are central to the evaluation but are notoriously difficult to pin down empirically.

In conclusion, there are no easy solutions to the deregulation issue which are not high risk to customers and service standards. If a free-for-all is ruled out as too risky, then the basic problem is to establish fair rules of competition which need to co-exist with an obligation for universal service. The absence of such an obligation opens up the serious possibility of fragmentation, whilst the presence of a universal service obligation imposes a cost on the incumbent which, in practical terms, can only easily be met with simple tariff structures and protection from entry.

Appendix 1. Some Economic Characteristics of Postal Supply and Markets in the United Kingdom

Aspects of the Cost of Supply

The collection, conveyance, and distribution of letters is a complex network business. In many ways, it is something of a paradox in that it can be operated with virtually no capital equipment and the individual processes involved-of collecting, sorting, bundling, etc.-are extremely simple tasks. At this level, it might be thought that the issues of establishing whether there are economies of scale and the business is a natural monopoly should not be a problem. But this superficial perspective misses the subtlety of network optimization possible under different levels and mixes of traffic.

The United Kingdom last formally reviewed the structure of costs in 1986 (Post Office 1986) following a series of recommendations by the Monopolies and Mergers Commission (MMC, 1984). The MMC made essentially three points about long run marginal costs (LRMC) in this context:

1. Business strategy. They did not believe that the Post Office knew enough about its cost structure to be certain that a policy of growth would lead to lower average costs (Recommendation 3). 2. Detailed cost structure. A "national model" should be developed of the LRMC of providing the various streams of traffic to form a basis for tariff setting and discounts (Recommendation 4).

3. Cost information systems. The accounting systems needed strengthening to provide information on both average and marginal costs. (Recommendation 21).

The Post Office's response (Post Office 1986) gave results of analysis of historic cost performance, operational research modelling of cost behavior, analysis of accounting costs, and a survey of local managers' views of cost variability. Some of the key conclusions were as follows:

1. Over a plausible range of traffic variation, there were significant economies of scale and a rule of thumb would indicate that costs would rise by .6% for every 1% of traffic growth.

2. Areas demonstrating significant economies of scale include collection, delivery, conveyance, and some management overheads. Sorting also shows some economies of scale when traffic growth permits direct despatching between offices cutting out the need for intermediate handling.

3. Viewed at the national level, there was no evidence of cross-subsidy between the major streams and particularly between First Class and Second Class mails, both of which more than covered their LRMCs.

4. Short run marginal cost (SRMC) (defined as cost reaction possible within 1 year of traffic change rather than 5 years for LRMC) could be greater or less than LRMC depending upon the state of the network and the magnitude of the traffic change. If an implied cost for quality of service failure was allowed for-which would be likely if traffic rose and resources could not ensure service standards were met-then it would be quite feasible to imagine SRMC significantly above LRMC. (The Mail Users Association paper (1989) quoted that "members have estimated postal delays could cost British commerce as much as £17.5 million per day or over £4 billion per annum". This cost amounts to roughly double total revenue of the entire United Kingdom inland letter service.)

These conclusions-which corroborated the findings of a number of previous investigations undertaken by independent management consultants-were based on very specific assumptions:

1. The nature of the traffic change; its composition and presentation to the Post Office would not alter.

2. The number of delivery points was fixed.

3. Factor prices were held constant, and labor and capital were in infinite supply at current prices.

4. The management on-costs of effecting change were ignored (or held constant in the sense that continuous change would imply a base cost).

All of those factors are critical to the results, and it is quite easy to see that altering any of them would yield a different result:

1. A greater volatility in demand would imply less efficient use of labor and equipment and raise incremental costs (assuming that it was the extra marginal traffic that was more volatile).

2. More household delivery points imply higher delivery costs, but this is not a function of traffic growth per se.

3. Under tight labor or capital markets, it might be necessary to pay premium

rates for additional resources and raise the general level of costs.

4. The costs of installing new equipment, re-optimizing delivery rounds, and finding new premises could be significant, although not enough to raise marginal costs close to average costs.

That there should, in principle, exist significant structural scale economies will not surprise any operator in the postal business. An ancillary, but more difficult issue concerns economies of scope, i.e., the degree of synergy from handling a range of products or services. This is not merely an interesting question in relation to the issue of natural monopoly, it is a practical problem which all postal administrations have to address in configuring their networks. In essence, the issue is an empirical one revolving around the inter-relationship of two factors (1) the handling characteristics of the traffics; and (2) the quality of service (QofS) constraints.

For many types of letters handled, it is possible to have common collections, sorting in the same buildings, common conveyance, and combined deliveries. To the extent that any of these functional areas enjoy economies of scale, they are likely to display economies of scope, and, for all practical purposes, the two economies are indistinguishable. (The same applies for given letter types but which are distinguished by origin-destination e.g., local letters and distant letters.) However, it is possible that some letters cannot be handled jointly, require dedicated facilities at one or more stages, and, thus, offer limited cost synergies. This can arise for two reasons:

1. It is impractical to combine them. Large or consignment letters may need specialized conveyance, sorting, and delivery facilities.

2. The customer QofS requirements prevent joint handling. The clearest example here is in the area of high-priced courier services guaranteeing early next day delivery. In these circumstances, the delivery function is severely time-constrained, and the opportunity to attain large scale economies from combining with other deliveries is very limited (at least within the delivery span itself). Similarly, the opportunity to combine conveyance with other traffics (or "piggyback") may be limited, since this may lead to the integrity of the system being threatened and make QofS failure more likely.

Even if economies of scope are sometimes limited in operating some services (and this will depend critically on the range of services offered), it is still likely that there are significant economies of scale in the specific services themselves. Setting up a national infrastructure inevitably implies a large set-up cost, and, where a high service standard is offered, this implies a comprehensive network of delivery offices and a high assurance trunking network. The logistical problems and costs of establishing a national network covering large distances probably constitutes a significant barrier to entry which would not be experienced at a localized level, e.g., on handling intra-town traffics.

One further aspect of cost functions, which is related to the discussion above, concerns distance. Rowland Hill is invariably credited with the insight that as conveyance costs constitute a small component of total costs, uniform pricing is

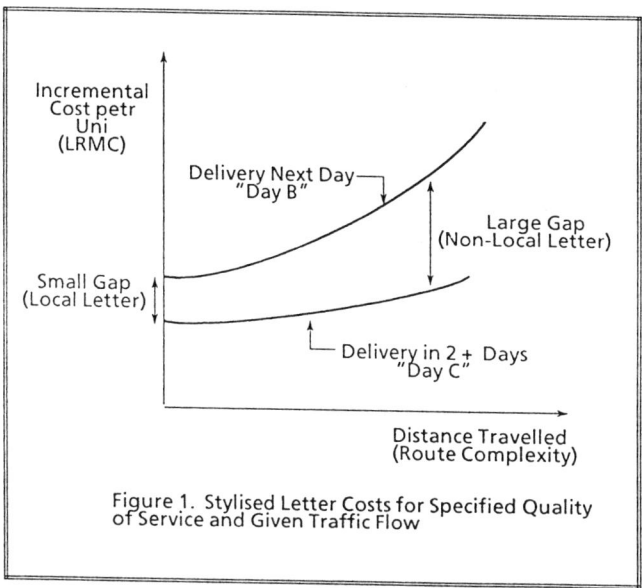

Figure 1. Stylised Letter Costs for Specified Quality of Service and Given Traffic Flow

justified. In some ways this is a misnomer. First, conveyance costs do not constitute the sole difference between local and non-local tariffs, as there are likely to be more handling costs. Second and more importantly, it is highly unlikely that local and distant traffics receive the same QofS. To attain the same QofS for non-local traffics as local traffics will depend upon the level of QofS being offered. Figure 1 illustrates this, in a loose way, where two services are offered-next day (Day B) and two or more days (Day C). At the local level, the difference between the LRMCs themselves of Day B and Day C service is minimal (in the United Kingdom probably around 1p under current arrangements). For longer distances-which is intended to proxy route complexity-the cost of the Day B service (at a high assurance level of 90% plus, say) is likely to be much greater. There are a number of reasons for this, including the costs of additional handling and the provision of facilities to cope with system failures. The cost of a Day C service will rise less steeply, as there is less difficulty in maintaining the integrity of a system which is not subject to such difficult time constraints.

For many postal administrations, it is typically difficult, if not impossible, to gauge the shape and level of these cost functions when substantial changes in QofS are envisaged, e.g., moving from 80% to 90% assurance. When long distances are involved, it is likely that there are insufficient transport infrastructures which could cope with the traffics being handled. Although it is possible to model transport movements, the models themselves tend to be large and complex and, when transport networks provide a joint service (e.g., for fast and slow streams), optimization becomes yet more difficult. The costing of hypothetical networks to specified assurance standards may be further hindered, as they tend to involve protracted negotiations with suppliers.

Whether customers view letters as, in some sense, different when classified by origin and destination is doubtful, given the complex way in which the postal network is organized. It is more likely that they perceive that they are buying a uniform service when purchasing a First (next day) or Second Class (within four days) stamp, even though local and non-local traffics have different costs and also very different QofS standards. (The United Kingdom Post Office now publishes QofS achievements broken down by district of posting and broad destination of letter.) In practice, most postal administrations have probably compromised with uniform pricing by giving a high QofS for local traffics (where cost is low) and poorer QofS for distant traffics (where costs are higher), and an implicit trade-off is therefore made for a given price between cost and QofS.

Aspects of Markets

It is feasible to think of letter traffic in a very narrow sense-hard copy communication, along the lines of the BT Act (1981), or, in a very broad way, as part of the market for communications. In the context of the impact of deregulation, it is probably helpful to have both perspectives in mind.

Specific classifications of the market which are helpful in assessing the potential impact of deregulation might include the following: (1) geographical origin and destination; (2) service standard (including overnight, two days, and longer service); (3) business/private origin and destination; and (4) contents and competing communications media. All of these factors may be expected to influence the ease of entry to new entrants.

Pricing and Financial Regulation

The United Kingdom Post Office has endured exceedingly tight control from Government since the late 1970s with stretching annual targets covering (1) the level of costs; (2) the level of profitability; (3) investment; and (4) Cash flow.

Table 3 sets out the performance of the Post Office against targets. It is readily apparent from (1) and (2) that these imply a general level of prices, and this is in

Table 3. Financial Performance of the United Kingdom Post Office

	Profit % On Turnover		Real Unit Cost Reduction %	
	Target	Achievement	Target	Achievement
1981-82	2.0	3.4	0	-.4
1982-83	2.8	4.9	<	<
1983-84	3.0	4.2	5.0	7.2
1984-85	4.3	4.3	<	<
1985-86	—	4.3	2.1	2.3
1986-87	3.25	3.1	<	<
1987-88	3.25	3.9	5.5	4.6
1988-89	3.25	2.5	<	<

Source: 1988-89 Report and Accounts

accordance with the 1978 White Paper (HMSO 1978a) on the control of Nationalized Industries. Targets are usually set over three years.

In practice, before changing prices, the Post Office is obliged to consult both with the body representing the consumers' interests-the statutory Post Office Users National Council-and also the Government. In effect, this gives Government the ability to maintain continuous pressure on financial performance as its agreement to a pricing proposal will facilitate or hinder achievement of the published financial targets, the attempted attainment of which is a legal obligation of the Post Office Board.

The letters business has been profitable since the early 1970s, when losses were imposed through anti-inflation policy. Profit targets in the 1980s have been calculated with respect to the capital base employed to ensure that Government, as shareholder, has earned a return roughly comparable to that which would pertain in the private sector. No explicit or implicit subsidies are given and no exemptions granted from general taxation.

On the structure of pricing, the Post Office is bound by general policy in the White Paper (HMSO 1978a) to ensure all services cover marginal costs (proxied by direct accounting costs in a subsequent White Paper (HMSO 1978b) and by the 1969 Act (HMSO 1969), which requires (Section 11) that, in respect of services for which it has exclusive privilege, no undue discrimination against any class of individuals is practiced.

In terms of the key services offered which have exclusive privilege, the following issues are pertinent to the structure of pricing policy:

1. Prices must cover at the minimum LRMC (even though the context of pricing in the three year target period is really more akin to an SRMC framework, in which the level of costs has to be controlled).

2. Public First and Second Class tariffs are set after consultation with the appropriate bodies. (In practice, there is generally little dispute about the structure of these prices.)

3. Discounts for pre-sorting mail (in or out of the monopoly) by most large customers are published and open to all such customers who meet the criteria. The discounts themselves are directly based on LRMC estimates of the cost savings realized by the Post Office for not doing this work; these savings are passed back in full to customers.

One issue which has attracted some comment concerns the price differential between First and Second Class; currently these are priced at 20 pence and 15 pence respectively. This price difference has grown somewhat since the early 1980s for the following reasons:

1. On the grounds of perceived customers' willingness to pay more for a premium service.

2. The margin has been deliberately widened to restrict the growth of the First Class proportion as the dramatic rise of First Class traffic in the 1980s was unanticipated, causing difficulties in meeting service standards.

Note that the overall level of postal prices is constrained under the target mechanism which relates to average costs and prices and not with reference to long-term sustainability and LRMC. In other words, prices must be set in an SRMC framework, and SRMC may be very different from LRMC, particularly when the implied cost of service failure is taken into account.

Compared with an estimated difference of about 2 pence in their respective LRMCs, a number of commentators have argued that there is cross-subsidization between First and Second Class, including Pryke (1981) and E&M (1988):

> That first class letters heavily subsidize second class seems evident. Whether this is a good or bad thing is much harder to evaluate ... The current cross subsidy is undesirable.

Neither Pryke (1981) nor E&M (1988) state exactly what they mean by cross-subsidy in this context, but on the conventional LRMC test they are clearly incorrect. Further, given the nature of postal networks it is most implausible that either service operated on a stand-alone basis would be cheaper, so there is no cross-subsidization from the Faulhaber (1975) definition either.

It is however, quite likely that an independent, stand-alone local service could undercut a uniform national price, as noted by the Post Office in 1979, particularly if a cheaper labor source could be employed. Thus, it could be argued that there is an element of geographical cross-subsidization. Whether it is worthwhile rectifying this is another matter. In a somewhat tendentious article, Molyneux and Thompson (1987) seem to assume that implementing an urban-rural price distinction would be both costless and beneficial; as discussed in the text, we would strongly dispute these assertions.

Appendix 2. The Natural Monopoly Argument

It is interesting to examine the economic arguments put forward by the proponents of deregulation. Senior (1983) puts forward three points.

> It is worth noting that, for the following reasons, the "letter" service does not constitute a natural or technical monopoly in economic terms: entry to the market by new suppliers is both cheap and simple, as the upsurge of courier companies in the past few years has demonstrated; postal services are labor-intensive and require few skills, so that new ones could quite easily be established from a large pool of unemployed workers; while there are economies of scale in handling postal traffic - a postman can deliver two letters to a house as cheaply as one - it is impossible to argue that a "letter" monopoly would develop naturally, any more than in the distribution of parcels or milk.

Unfortunately none of these arguments addresses the issues in a coherent way.

1. The first point concerning ease of entry has no bearing on whether the cost function of the incumbent has natural monopoly characteristics; what matters is whether the incumbent in these circumstances can repel entry.

2. It is not clear exactly what the second argument is propounding in terms of the supply function, but neither the skills level nor the state of the labor market

appear to be particularly relevant to whether the incumbent has natural monopoly characteristics.

3. Intriguingly, Senior believes that there are economies of scale in delivery but then appears to make an assertion (presumably based on intuition) that it would "be impossible to argue that a 'letter' monopoly would develop naturally." Again, this confuses the issues of whether a letter service has a sub-additive cost function and whether, in practice, market conditions would ensure that a single firm supplied the whole market.

Albon (1985) originally argued against the natural monopoly hypothesis by disputing whether it has economies of scale. More recently Albon (1987), he approaches the issue by casting doubt on the plausibility that letter services could display natural monopoly characteristics by reference to other industries which have been deregulated, (such as airlines and telecommunications), by the growth of mail courier services and because of multiple delivery of milk and newspapers. The difficulty in assessing the merit of Albon's more recent arguments is that the issues raised are very wide ranging, and, for the most part, tangential to the specific issue of postal services. Discussion of the relevance of bus deregulation in the United Kingdom is given in the text but some comments on the other examples cited, of couriers and milk delivery, is relevant here. Multiple supply, in couriers and milk delivery, does not demonstrate that a standard letter service cannot display natural monopoly characteristics because the issue revolves around economies of scope, as discussed in Appendix 1. It is likely to be the case that, as services provided to customers become more tailor-made to each individual customer's requirements, the opportunities to attain economies of scope are likely to decline as facilities and operations need to be configured toward dedicated requirements. The greater degree of heterogeneity in customer requirements implies the likelihood of more specialist operators, each attempting to maximize market share through realizing economies of scale. The degree of industry concentration in courier letter and parcel distribution probably varies widely according to the size of the market, ease of entry, and the extent of economies of scale and scope. But, without detailed assessment of each market, it is not obvious that the existence of multiple suppliers is particularly informative of the supply characteristics of the letter service (and as importantly, the sustainability of a single supplier under competition). Albon (1987) also quotes the milk example:

> Mail delivery, at present accounting for another thirty per cent or so of costs, is another area sometimes regarded as being "naturally" monopolistic, particularly delivery to households, and in country areas. While such country areas may have to be given special consideration, competition in delivery to suburban households and businesses does not appear to present any problems. Already houses have regular deliveries from one or more sources - postmen, milkmen, newsboys and a host of handbill deliverers. If there are economies of scope in deliveries, why aren't these functions integrated into a single operation in urban areas (as they sometimes are in rural areas)?

The obvious answer to this is that combining milk delivery with letter delivery in urban areas would be unlikely to ensure that service standards are attained for either product; it is also implausible that newspaper delivery could easily be assimilated with letter delivery (at least for the majority of ordinary letters). Re-configuring the delivery rounds to cope with traffic change would also be difficult and the same problems would apply to collections.

A further factor which is often overlooked here concerns consumer behavior; the drawback of the minimum cost natural monopoly solution is absence of consumer choice. But certainly some customers are clearly prepared to pay a premium price to retain choice (for example, some users of courier services in the United Kingdom make simultaneous use of multiple suppliers, perhaps partly to maintain a stronger bargaining position).

E&M (1988) correctly identify the theoretical requirements for monopoly protection as constituting the need to demonstrate that the supplier is an efficient but unsustainable natural monopoly; they acknowledge that this is difficult to establish unambiguously one way or the other. Unlike Albon and Senior, they take a neutral position on whether entry is desirable.

> This paper now examines the issues of whether deregulation is desirable. The point is that the case for allowing entry, even if not promoting it, is so widely accepted that it is more sensible to appraise the limited number of reasons why there might be gains from the state prohibiting competition than to focus on the many arguments why competition should be permitted. But it must be emphasized that even on narrow economic grounds there are logically impeccable arguments for legal restrictions on entry.

E&M (1988) structure their analysis by considering how competitive entry would impact on costs, outputs, and prices and by deduction, the impact on consumer welfare. In many ways, this is similar to the approach of the United Kingdom Post Office back in 1979, (Post Office 1979) in which the potential disbenefits of competition (from lost economies of scale) were compared with plausible improvements in operating efficiency.

Note

This Paper reflects the views of the authors but not necessarily those of the United Kingdom Post Office. The authors would like to thank Richard Adams, Barbara Duffner, Ian Reay, Ian Steele, and Tim Walsh for helpful comments on an earlier draft. The usual disclaimer applies.

References

Albon, R. 1985. "Competition or Monopoly in Australia's Postal Service?" Center for Independent Studies.
Albon, R. 1986. "A Cost-Related Pricing Structure for Inland Letters - the Cost and the Benefits."
Albon, R. 1987. "Privatize the Post." Center for Policy Studies.
Albon, R. 1989. "Some Observations on the Efficiency of British Postal Pricing, Applied Economics."
Association of Metropolitan Authorities. 1990. "Bus Deregulation : The Metropolitan

Experience."
Bishop, M., and J. Kay. 1988. "Does Privatization Work?" Center for Business Strategy, LBS.
Brown, K. 1987. "Private Buses Run into Timetable Problems." Financial Times (February 16).
Brown, S.J. and D.S. Sibley. 1986. "The Theory of Public Utility Pricing." Cambridge University Press, Cambridge, United Kingdom.
Clarke, P. 1988. "Opening Up the Post Office." Aims of Industry.
Cuthbertson, R., Richards, P. (1991 forthcoming) "An Econometric Study of the Demand for United Kingdom Inland Letters." Review of Economics and Statistics.
Estrin, S., and D. de Meza. 1988. "Should the Post Office's Statutory Monopoly be Lifted?" London School of Economics.
Faulhaber, R. 1975. "Cross-Subsidization: Pricing in Public Enterprises." American Economic Review.
HMSO. 1969. "The Post Office Act."
HMSO. 1978a. "The Nationalized Industries." Cmnd 7232.
HMSO. 1978b. "The Post Office." Cmnd 7292.
HMSO. 1981. "British Telecommunications Act."
HMSO. 1984. "Buses." Cmnd 9300.
Mail Users Association.1989. "Deliver us from the Post Office". London.
Mason, D. 1988. "Enlightenment." Adam Smith Institute.
Mason, D. 1989. "Privatizing the Posts." Adam Smith Institute.
Molyneux, R., and D. Thompson, 1987. "Nationalized Industry Performance : Still Third Rate?" Fiscal Studies.
Monopolies and Mergers Commission. 1984. "The Post Office Letter Post Service." HMSO Cmnd 9332.
Neary, P. 1975."An Econometric Study of Irish Postal Services." The Economic and Social Research Institute Paper No. 80, Dublin.
Oftel. June 1990. "Report of Director General of Telecommunications."
Post Office. 1979. "The Letter Monopoly, A Review."
Post Office. 1986. "Report of the Steering Group on the Long Run Marginal Costs of the Inland Letter Service."
Post Office Users National Council. 1989-90. "Annual Report."
Pryke, R. 1981. "The Nationalized Industries." Oxford.
Scott, F.A. 1986. "Assessing USA Postal Ratemaking: An Application of Ramsey Prices." Journal of Industrial Economics, 34. 279-290.
Senior, I. 1983. "Liberating the Letter." Institute of Economic Affairs.
Tabor, R. 1987. "Can Competitors Pass 'Go' with a Natural Monopoly?" Public Finance and Accountancy.(May)
Tabor, R. 1987. "Who Benefits from 'One Price for Everywhere'." Public Finance and Accountancy.(June)
Union of Communication Workers. 1990. "The Last Post?" London.

COMMENTS
Norman Ireland

I found reading the Dobbs and Richards paper (D & R) a rewarding experience: it was full of pertinent information and enabled me to at least claim to have grasped the essential background to a key issue. I cannot fault any of the factual statements, and my comments will be limited to what I consider to be the most important focus of the paper: how to approach an assessment of the welfare effects of entry deregulation.

When assessing entry deregulation, it is necessary to distinguish carefully between entry deregulation and the regulation of the industry conduct in other respects. Entry deregulation will provoke a level of entry which will depend on the post-entry regulatory regime. Further, the amount of entry will affect the extent of industry regulation (price regulation, etc.) that continues to be necessary. The questions that arise are (a) how far entry deregulation can replace conduct regulation and what is the nature of optimal conduct regulation? and (b) whether there are positive net benefits from entry deregulation? In their discussion, D & R do not put forward a clear scenario for the post-entry regulatory system, although they allude to a situation where the PO (Post Office Letters Business) acts as a follower in price setting, since it has to obtain some fixed profitability target. They also discuss possible changes in price discrimination and service quality levels. This highlights the problem with considering radical reforms: how much to keep constant in order to assess the crucial elements. The low overall elasticity of demand for letters (claimed by Cuthbertson and Richards (forthcoming)) seems to suggest that conduct regulation would need to continue, unless there was very significant entry. Conduct regulation leads however to low prices which limit potential competitive entry. This point is made by Bös and Nett in a current discussion paper (Bös and Nett 1989). It seems of particular importance, given the skimming activities of possible competitors. The PO is not a natural monopoly, since skimming of its most profitable lines is always likely to be attractive. On the other hand, conduct regulation may be more forcefully applied to the PO than to entrants (by requiring particular national quality and price standards for example).

As an illustration of the link between entry and conduct regulation, consider the D & R scenario whereby a competitive fringe eats into the dominant firm (PO) market. I find this the most convincing scenario proposed, although one should emphasise that the fringe will be concentrated at the most profitable market segments. However, the authors seem to suggest that the greater the fringe the lower will be equilibrium prices. In fact, there are some reasons for doubting this, based on the Salop (1979) model of price-setting competition. Alternatively in the D & R context, if the PO continues to be price capped subject to a zero profit constraint, the PO would have to raise prices elsewhere to replace lost revenue and maintain zero profits. If uniform prices were maintained, then all PO prices would have to be raised. Then the competitive fringe prices may also drift up. An Edgeworth cycle of unstable pricing may be observed. Basically, the customer has to pay for the lost economies of scale. Of course, in return the customers may enjoy more variety and the reduction of x-inefficiency. Nevertheless, it is a basic characteristic of entry that the entrant makes no allowance for the lost economies of scale of the incumbent, and that entry may occur when it is not socially desirable.

In contrast, suppose entry deregulation is combined with the removal of the requirement for the PO to charge uniform national prices and that entry deregulation produces price discriminatory practices, this may well lead to more market segmentation and to more monopoly power for the dominant firm. Restrictions on price differentials, transparent prices, and non-discrimination tend to promote true competition, and their loss may be regrettable. In particular, the social cost for consumers of acquiring information on complex postage rates for such a small expenditure item may be disproportionate: what is a worthwhile activity when spending a hundred dollars on an airline ticket may become simply irritating when spending less than a dollar on posting a letter.

The reverse connection between conduct regulation and entry is similarly important. D & R perceive advantages in a gradual reduction in the minimum price that competitors can charge. To scale down the entry deregulation has the advantage of easy reversal, but for just that reason it also maximises uncertainty of future structure. It is not possible for the regulatory authority to commit itself to a fully-credible timescale for future minimum price reductions, and the potential entrant may respond over-cautiously to such promises.

Any analysis of the entry question should incorporate three factors. These are (1) economies of scale in each market segment; (2) complementary costs (economies of scope): some fixed costs are common; and (3) variable profits across market segments. I have argued above that an additional factor that must be included very carefully is (4) a clear statement of the constraints on PO (and entrant) conduct after entry, particularly in regard to such matters as price differentials across segments and profit/sales/quality objectives. My final comment relates to a further essential characteristic of a model of entry into the PO. This is (5) a range of welfare criteria. Most analyses of PO deregulation appear to accept the welfare basis of linking price to cost. However, this makes no concessions to either the historical experience or the practicalities of policy. It may be thought undesirable to charge higher prices to those individuals living in remote areas of low population, or indeed there may be some services which have demand curves everywhere above average cost but where the social cost of non-operation is very high. To many policy makers, PO services are hardly distinct from education, health, or library services. Then policy objectives reflect the view that individuals should not be penalised for their geographic isolation. An analysis which is fundamentally utilitarian omits these considerations, and more general welfare analysis is needed to explain past policy and investigate current propositions for reform.

The D & R paper has been an important contribution to setting the menu for theoretical and empirical research. It is to be hoped that the methodology adopted for such research is able to incorporate all the above elements.

References

Bös, Dieter, and Lorenz Nett. 1989. "Privatization, Price Regulation and Market Entry. An Asymmetric Multistage Duopoly model." Discussion paper 303, Rheinische Friedrich-Wilhelms-Universität Bonn.

Cuthbertson, R., and P. Richards. (Forthcoming.) "An Econometric Study of the Demand for UK Inland Letters." *Review of Economics and Statistics.*

Salop, Steven C. 1979. "Monopolistic Competition with Outside Goods." *Bell Journal* 10: 141-156.

5
DELIVERING LETTERS: SHOULD IT BE DECRIMINALIZED?
Saul Estrin
David de Meza

1. Introduction

Throughout the world it is illegal to compete with the state Post Office in the collection and delivery of letters.[1] Is this an instance of the madness of crowds (of bureaucrats) or is there a good economic or other justification for outlawing competition? As background to discussing the substantive issues, we first provide a brief historical account of the evolution of the monopoly in Britain.

In the Middle Ages, private mail services co-existed with those of the Crown. Until the sixteenth century the state did not claim privileged rights over the conveyancing of post. The original motive seems to have been "national security" as Queen Elizabeth sought to suppress treasonable correspondence. In the seventeenth century, the raising of revenue became an influential justification for the postal monopoly but the emphasis had shifted towards the maxim of public service by the end of the nineteenth century. These new arguments for the monopoly were epitomised by an article in the Pall Mall Gazette in 1892:

> The sole reason why the Post Office has a remunerative monopoly is to enable it to include services which are unremunerative. Free competition in London or other large towns would make short work of the present Post Office rates. And if these rates are forcibly maintained, the country ought to get some compensation in the shape of a reasonably good service to every corner of the Kingdom, (quoted in Daunton 1985, p.49).

Of course, the case for the monopoly did not go unchallenged. One of the most eloquent and surprising critics was Rowland Hill himself. He advocated repeal of the legislation on the grounds that:

It implies the removal of an offence from our statute book and the probable rise of a wholesome competition wherever the service is performed with less than the greatest efficency and cheapness: a competition which more perhaps than any other external circumstance, would tend to compel the department to have due regard to simple merit in its offices and economic efficiency in all its arrangements", (quoted in Coase 1939, p.430).

Alfred Marshall, took a similar view. In two letters to The Times in 1891 (Coase 1961), he was concerned with the Post Office's "lethargy" and "slothful" behaviour and with the "vivifying" effect of competition causing its "stiff joints (to) become more supple."

The letter monopoly has been maintained to the present day, except that the Secretary for State for Trade and Industry now has power to suspend it, as indeed occurred temporarily during the 1971 strike when postal services were "licenced out" to private operators. Moreover, the 1981 British Telecommunications Act also enables the Minister to grant licences which render legal specific activities otherwise covered by the Post Office's exclusive privilege. This power has been invoked by the government to introduce some competition with Post Office letter services. In 1981, the statutory monopoly was weakened in two respects. First, licences were granted to charities to deliver Christmas cards. Second, the market for time sensitive valuable mail with a minimum charge of £1 was opened up to competition providing a legal basis for the de facto operations of many private courier services. In 1982, the monopoly was further relaxed when private document exchanges were given the legal power to operate (so that firms can rent a box into which correspondents can deliver letters by hand). Recently, (June 1989) the Prime Minister said "..greater competition would be good and we may have to consider ending the monopoly on the postal letter service...".

2. The Natural Monopoly Defence of Statutory Monopoly

The case for allowing competition in letter delivery is that to succeed, new entrants to the industry must offer at least some consumers a better deal. This may not be difficult since a Post Office protected against the rigors of competition has limited incentives to introduce new products or keep down the costs of existing services. The potential drawback of permitting new entry is that postal delivery is probably a natural monopoly. If the market is divided between several competing firms, economies of scale and scope may be lost and overall costs increased.

A standard criticism of this defence of the statutory monopoly is well expressed by Milton Friedman (1962, p.29):

> It may be argued that the carrying of mail is a technical monopoly and that a government monopoly is the least of all evils. Along these lines, one could perhaps justify a government post office but not the present law, which makes it illegal for anybody else to carry mail. If the delivery of mail is a technical monopoly, no one will be able to succeed in competition with the government. If it is not, there is no reason why the government should be engaged in it. The only way to find out is to leave other people free to enter.

This position is strongest if the postal market is contestable. A contestable market is one in which there are no sunk costs, so that a firm can realise the full value of its assets at any time—this effectively means that a firm considering entry into a contestable market does not face a risk of losing its assets if entry is unsuccessful or only short lived. Moreover, the incumbent is assumed to be unable to change price at short notice. In such a market, if the existing firm is inefficient, a new and more efficient firm will enter and take the whole market - so retaining the benefits of the economies of scale. In a contestable market there is only one firm in the market at any given time, but there is a constant threat of entry which ensures that the established firm does not exploit its market position by pricing high.

Even if the assumptions of contestability hold, Panzar and Willig's (1977) classic paper shows there are some circumstances under which a natural monopoly is vulnerable to entry (is unsustainable, in their terminology). The conclusion that natural monopoly does not justify a statutory monopoly is further weakened for if the assumptions of contestability fail even slightly the conclusions may be radically different (Schwartz, 1986). Moreover, the strict assumptions of the contestable market model are not particularly plausible in the case of postal services. Sunk costs are almost certainly important in practice. At first sight it may seem that all that is needed for a local letter delivery business is a van (that can be resold easily) and a few employees (who can be hired on weekly contracts). However, when the costs of planning (especially of collection and delivery routes) as well as advertising the service are considered, it is clear that these sunk costs are important and that any potential rival to the Post Office must be prepared to stay in the business on a long-term basis before committing itself to entry.

If economies of scale are important and the market is not contestable, the case for allowing competition is no longer clear cut. Suppose, as shown in the left-hand diagram of figure 1, that the monopoly Post Office faces the demand curve DD and the average cost curve AC which, being downward sloping, implies increasing returns to scale. As a nationalised industry, the Post Office does not set out to maximise profit, but can instead be assumed to seek to cover all costs including normal profits. The Post Office therefore sets price P^* delivering Q^* letters, determined by the intersection of the average cost and demand curves.

Now suppose that the statutory monopoly is abolished. Granted the Post Office remains in the market and continues to price at average cost; a commercial rival calculates that if it offers a superior service at price P, it can earn profits. When the new service is introduced some of the Post Office's customers switch to it and this means that the Post Office's demand curve shifts to the left, $D'D'$ in figure 1, so that its price increases to P'.

The bad news associated with the entry of the new firm is that the price of the existing service has risen because some of the economies of scale are lost. The good news is that a new product has appeared—in effect the price of the new firm's product has fallen from infinity to P. The overall change in consumer surplus can be measured in the usual way. In the right-hand graph, dd is the demand curve for

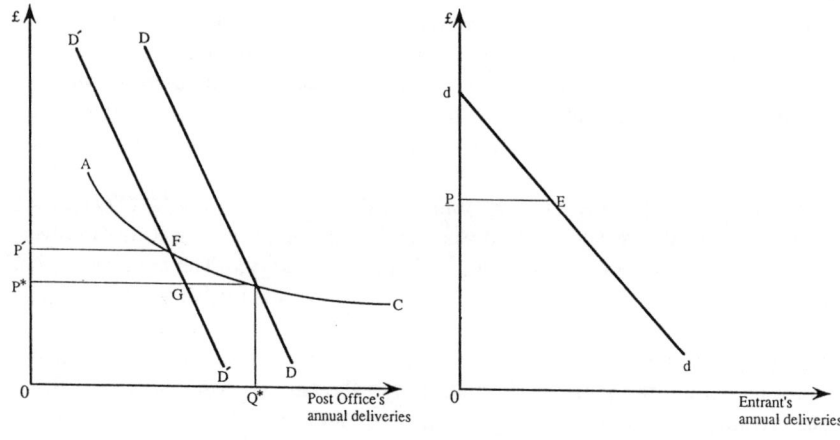

Figure 1.

the entrant's product given that the Post Office charges P^*. Were that the end of the story the consumer surplus generated by the new product would be the area dEB. But the left-hand graph shows the price rise from P^* to P' on the demand curve $D'D'$ which involves a loss of consumer surplus measured by the area $P'FGP^*$. So, consumers are harmed by entry if $P'FGP^* > dEP$. And this is more likely to be the case if economies of scale are strong, for then P' will exceed P^* by a lot; or if the new product is a good substitute for the existing service, for then $D'D'$ will be far to the left of DD and dd will be relatively elastic, making dEP small. If entry stimulates the Post Office to increase efficiency however, its average cost curve will shift down in the left-hand panel of figure 1, bringing P' closer to P^* and so making the case for competition stronger.

What this analysis demonstrates is that entry cannot be guaranteed to benefit consumers. To make further progress a more explicit treatment of the factors governing entry and the nature of post-entry competition is required.

3. A Theoretical Framework

There has been little discussion of sustainability outside the contestable market setting, despite its policy relevance. The question of whether in the presence of economies of scale there can be entry when all firms are profit maximisers, and of whether the equilibrium involves too much or too little entry, has been addressed. (Mankiw and Whinston (1986) provide a neat interpretation and extension of this literature). However, the analysis has not been adapted to the case when the incumbent is an average-cost pricer, or is set a target profit below the maximum attainable. As we show, this makes a considerable difference to the results. This is important in the present context for there can be little doubt that, despite the recent improvement in its returns, the British Post Office, like others around the world, does not seek to maximise profit. This follows indirectly from the form of regulation and directly from the fact that all estimates of demand elasticity put it well below unity. Hence, price is certainly below the profit maximising level.

Our basic model supposes an incumbent monopoly (call it the Post Office, (PO)) producing a single good. Average costs are declining at all outputs and the incumbent sells the highest output consistent with covering costs. There is one potential entrant (the rival, R) who can offer a product which may be a close or distant substitute to that offered by the PO. The production costs incurred by R may be either higher or lower than those of the PO. However, in contrast to PO, the rival seeks to maximise profits. In deciding whether to enter, R correctly anticipates the market share he will obtain and the equilibrium post-entry price. In order to make these predictions, the entrant must know the nature of post-entry competition. The two common models are Bertrand competition and Cournot competition, though both must be somewhat modified to take into account the fact that the PO is an average cost pricer. Under Bertrand competition, each firm maximises its objective function given the price of the other. This is rational if firms must decide on their strategy without knowing what their rival has chosen and if output can be adjusted at shorter notice than price. Bertrand competition is very aggressive. If the firms are selling close substitutes and there are economies of scale, it is typically the case that it is impossible for both firms to survive. Cournot competition is rather less cut throat, but is still far from being collusive pricing. Here, the firms make simultaneous output choices and prices are then set to clear the market. Implicitly, output must be chosen ahead of price. Neither model is fully satisfactory, but together they serve to indicate the range of outcomes. It is possible to analyse models in which one firm's choice is observed by the other firm prior to its own decision. However, it is generally difficult to explain what it is in the environment which gives one firm the advantage (or sometimes disadvantage) of being the first mover. More interesting than imposing an exogenous order of play would be to analyse markets in which the firms interact on a repeated basis and perhaps in which capacity can only be slowly adjusted. There is not yet a fully satisfactory theory to deal with such a case.

Returning to the static game, consider first the case of Cournot competition. Given that entry occurs, curve RR in figure 2 shows the profit maximising output of the rival, Q_R for various outputs of the Post Office Q_P. Similarly the curve PO shows how PO's profit maximising output varies with the production chosen by R. The case drawn is for the two firms having the same cost function. If both firms were profit maximisers, the equilibrium ouputs would be Q_P^* and Q_R^*, at least if

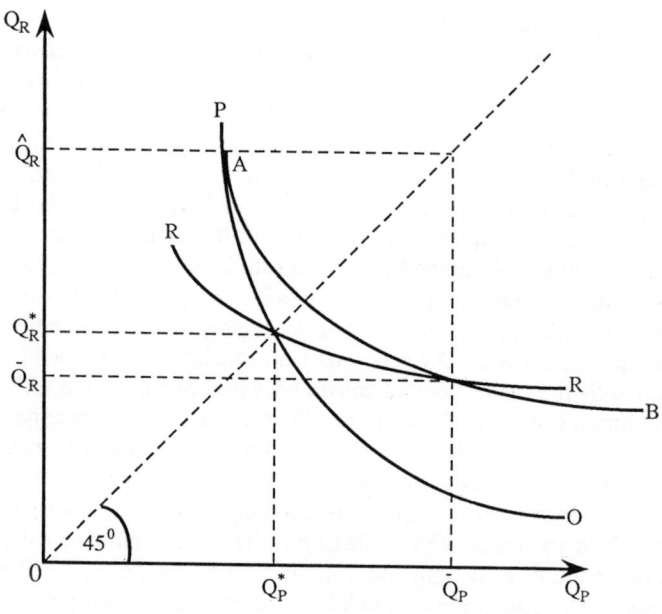

Figure 2.

both firms are covering costs at these production levels. The relative slopes of the lines *PO* and *RR* follow from standard and plausible assumptions concerning demand and costs.

Our purpose is to investigate entry possibilities if PO is an average-cost pricer. The implication of this is that at any Q_R at which the Post Office could make positive profits by restricting its own output, it will actually produce more than shown by PO, expanding until its profits are eliminated. In Figure 2, *AB* shows the reaction curve of the average-cost pricing Post Office. $\hat{Q}_R$ is the maximum output of R at which PO is actually able to cover its costs. Unless point *A* lies above the intersection of *RR* and *PO*, entry is not feasible. Equilibrium occurs at $\overline{Q}_R, \overline{Q}_p$ supposing that R is able to cover its costs when PO chooses $\overline{Q}_p$. That is, in the symmetric case the question is whether $\overline{Q}_p > \hat{Q}_R$. If this condition holds, the rival will not enter. If $\hat{Q}_R > \overline{Q}_p$, entry occurs and the question is then whether consumers gain. In Figure 2, $\hat{Q}_R = \overline{Q}_p$ so entry is just possible.

We have argued elsewhere (see Estrin and de Meza (1988)) that in the Cournot case, with a homogeneous product and economics of scale throughout, entry is impossible if the Post Office is at least as efficient as any potential entrant, and that if entry does occur, because the potential entrant is more efficient than the Post Office, the loss of economies of scale ensures that customer welfare will be reduced. This implies that repeal of the statutory monopoly would in all likelihood have no effect but, if it did, post users would suffer. Even if the Post Office is grossly inefficient, this conclusion applies.

The assumption that both firms sell an identical good is crucial to these results. If instead they offer imperfect substitutes, post-entry competition is less severe, making entry easier and, because a new product is created, the benefits to the consumer if entry does occur greater. Were the Post Office monopoly repealed it is indeed unlikely that entrants actually would offer the same service as the Post Office. A further route by which entry could lead to gains is if the Post Office is thereby stimulated to become more efficient causing its cost curves to shift down. This effect could more than offset the loss of economies of scale, even in the homogeneous product case.

To investigate further we simulate the effects of entry into the postal business. Before doing so we outline the model if the post-entry game is Bertrand.

Under Bertrand competition prices are the strategic variables. Hence, the reaction curve diagram now appears in price space and is shown in figure 3 where P_p is the Post Office's price and P_R that of the potential entrant. Thus, RR shows how the profit maximising rivals's price varies with P_p and line PO shows how the profit maximising Post Office price varies with P_R. It is not inevitable that these reaction curves be upward sloping. If they are, it implies that if the price charged by your competitor rises then it is profitable to take the opportunity to increase your own price. Two goods for which this is true are termed strategic complements. This is a fairly plausible assumption and is built into our subsequent simulations. However, the theory is a little changed if the goods are strategic substitutes.

Granted that both firms are profit maximisers, equilibrium prices in the symmetric case of figure 3 are $P_R^* P_P^*$, at least as long as each firm covers its costs at these prices. If the goods are close substitutes and there are economies of scale it is typically the case that there are losses where the reaction curves intersect. If so, it follows that no entry will occur. However, we now assume that profit maximising Bertrand duopolists can at least cover their costs.

We are interested in the case in which PO is an average cost pricer. The implications of this switch in behavioural assumption is that at any R at which the Post Office could make positive profits, it will actually choose a lower price than shown by PO. For average cost pricing, the PO's reaction curve is thus given by AB where $\bar{P}_R$ is the lowest rival price at which PO can cover costs. Curve AB is downward sloping reflecting the fact that the higher is P_R the further to the right is the demand curve faced by PO causing an average cost pricer with economies of scale to lower its price.

If entry does occur with average cost pricing, the equilibrium is $\hat{P}_p, \hat{P}_R$. The PO charges less than in the profit maximizing duopoly equilibrium and so profitable entry is even less likely. However, it could be the case that if the goods are sufficiently differentiated then at $\hat{P}_p, \hat{P}_R$ the rival does cover costs. If so, it will enter if allowed to do so. The Post Office will end up charging more as a result of

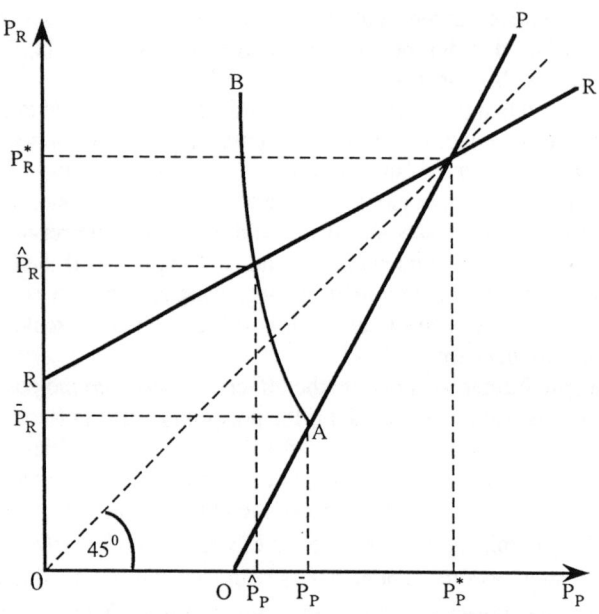

Figure 3.

entry, but since a new product is available in the market there is no a priori way of determining whether consumers are better off overall. In contrast to the Cournot model, if the two firms sell identical goods it is easy to see that in the presence of economies of scale there is never a pure-strategy equilibrium and so this case is not pursued.

4. A Summary of Simulations

The analysis so far suggests that statutory protection for the Post Office is never harmful and may actually benefit consumers because entry, while profitable for the new firm, could dissipate economies of scale, increase prices, and reduce consumer welfare. But these unambiguous results depend on the entrant offering an identical product to the Post Office. To investigate the tradeoffs when the Post Office and the entrant are offering heterogeneous goods, we undertake a simulation exercise.

$$C_i = F_i + a_i Q_i - b_i Q_i^2, \quad i = N, M \tag{1}$$

When Q_i is the firm output. Inverse demand functions are

$$P_i = a_i - B Q_i - \gamma Q_j, \quad i \neq j, \ i, j = N, M \tag{2}$$

The model was calibrated to own price elasticities of demand in the region of 0.2-0.5 and elasticities of returns to scale from 1.2 to 1.5. Under Cournot assumptions the only instances of disadvantageous entry involve very close substitutes and unrealistically high cost advantages for the entrant. With differentiated products cases of profitable and advantageous entry were possible under seemingly reasonable configurations. A representative case is of fairly modest scale economies with a 10% increase in volume raising costs by 7.5%. The entrant sells a fairly distinct product for in equilibrium it charges 60% more than the Post Office and yet still captures 20% of the market, earning in the process a 3.5% return on turnover. The loss of volume causes the Post Office price to rise by 4.5% but the opportunity to buy a new good means consumers are better off in aggregate by some 3.5% of their initial spending. Taken together, the simulations suggest no real case for a statutory monopoly, a conclusion which is reinforced if entry eliminates x-inefficiency.

We undertook a similar exercise for the case of Bertrand competition, using the same functional forms, with price rather than quantity as the strategic variable. Entry is quite rare. If a sufficient quality or cost advantage enables the entrant to make positive profits, there is a tendency for the Post Office to be able to survive. But when the Post Office and the entrant share the same structure of costs and economies of scale are not "too great," there is profitable entry which raises social welfare. However, it should be noted that there are some cases of welfare-reducing profitable entry with Bertrand competition. In particular, the entrant can survive with a low elasticity of demand (0.3 in the monopoly equilibrium), and modest economies of scale (1.25) but with its cost similar to the Post Office's at low levels of output but much higher as output increases. This might typify an entrant which is labour-intensive and employs a bespoke delivery system rather than a systematic delivery round. Entry strategies along these lines can be profitable but reduce consumer welfare.

Looking across all the cases, the general conclusion suggested by these single product simulations is that in the presence of an average cost pricing Post Office, permitting entry is rather unlikely to result in aggregate losses to the consumers and could well yield gains.

5. The "Cream Skimming" Defence of Statutory Monopoly

5.1. Should the Post Office Set Uniform Prices?

The most common defence of the statutory monopoly is that in its absence entry would be predominately attracted to the high profit relatively low cost routes and services. It would be left to the Post Office to reach those inaccessible locations with low volumes of mail that commercial operators spurn. Left with this costly rump, the Post Office would have to increase its charges substantially. If this is truly what happens, the question is, why would it be a bad thing?

The way the story is often told, it appears as though the commercial entrants would actually reap the high surplus that the Post Office currently earns on a subset of its services. It is implied that this involves a mere transfer from the presumably deserving public sector to an undeserving capitalist and so is undesirable on distributional grounds. In fact, there is no very good reason for thinking that the commercial operators would earn high profits. Even if the Post Office does not respond to entry by cutting its own prices on formerly high surplus services, the lure of such allegedly high profits would surely attract multiple entry and the profits would be competed away. So, the real issue is whether bringing prices more closely into line with costs is desirable.

Economists are prone to think that if prices reflect costs, efficiency will be served. Consumers will then only buy goods and services which are valued more highly than the alternative outputs which could have been produced with the resources used up in their production. However, it needs some thought as to the correct cost to relate prices. Suppose first that when deregulated, letter delivery were really a contestable market. The price of each service would then fall to the average cost of providing it. Deliveries to inaccessible rural location would cost more than to towns. But what is actually required for an efficient allocation of resources is that prices are proportional to marginal not average cost. A uniform tariff may get closer to achieving this than the average cost pricing emerging in a contestable market. The main difference between regions is in delivery costs (Tabor 1987) and these are also the primary source of economies of scale in the system. Suppose, in the extreme, that delivery costs are fixed with respect to the volume of mail delivered but higher in rural areas than in urban areas. Sorting and collection costs are the same everywhere. The marginal cost of mail posted to rural areas would thus be the same as mail posted to urban areas. A uniform tariff would thus be economically efficient (they would constitute Ramsey prices). But in a contestable market with freedom of entry, rural mail would be more expensive. Even ignoring any administrative costs, breaking the uniform tariff would be inefficient.

To investigate these matters more formally, let the average cost of each letter posted to the cheap region be

$$AC_L = a + bQ + \frac{F}{Q} \qquad (3)$$

and to the expensive region

$$AC_H = \hat{a} + \lambda bQ + \frac{\lambda F}{Q} \qquad (4)$$

where Q is letters per address. The proportion of addresses in the cheap region is α. The number of postings to each address is $Q = A - BP$ where P is the uniform price. It is straightforward to compute the change in consumer surplus from moving from a break-even uniform price to a multiple price scheme that breaks even for each region, as would arise in a deregulated contestable market.

Our model fails to take into account possible cost complementarities between the volume of deliveries in the two areas. However, these are not likely to be great and in view of the very small values for welfare changes generated by the model,

DELIVERING LETTERS: SHOULD IT BE DECRIMINALIZED?

Table 1

Uniform Pricing

	1	2	3	4	5	6	7	8	9	10	11
$\hat{\alpha}$	0.67000	0.60000	0.96000	0.60000	0.60000	0.60000	1.60000	0.60000	0.25000	1.60000	0.90000
α	0.67000	0.60000	0.48000	0.60000	0.60000	0.60000	0.80000	0.60000	0.25000	0.80000	0.50000
F	0.27000	0.32000	0.32000	0.37600	0.37600	0.37600	0.00000	0.32000	0.40000	0.00000	0.32000
b	0.00000	0.00000	0.00000	0.00000	0.00000	0.00000	0.20000	0.00000	0.10000	0.00000	0.00000
λ	2.66000	2.00000	2.00000	1.25000	1.25000	1.25000	2.00000	2.00000	2.00000	1.50000	2.00000
a	0.86000	0.75000	0.75000	0.75000	0.75000	0.75000	0.75000	0.75000	0.50000	0.75000	0.75000
β	0.30000	0.50000	0.30000	0.30000	0.50000	1.00000	0.50000	0.30000	0.30000	0.30000	0.20000
A	1.30000	1.50000	1.30000	1.30000	1.50000	2.00000	1.50000	1.30000	1.30000	1.30000	1.20000

Results

	1	2	3	4	5	6	7	8	9	10	11
Q_l	1.019553	1.04721	1.06594	1.00811	1.01473	1.03764	1.00000	1.02648	1.08161	1.06000	1.03836
Q_h	0.843592	0.80000	0.75905	0.97545	0.95355	0.84142	0.58333	0.90871	0.90566	0.82000	0.87346
P_l	0.934821	0.90557	0.78020	0.97298	0.97054	0.96236	1.00000	0.91175	0.72798	0.80000	0.80818
P_h	1.521359	1.40000	1.80316	1.08183	1.09289	1.15858	1.83333	1.30429	1.31447	1.60000	1.63272
Δ Surplus	-1.06809	-0.01751	-0.00632	0.00014	-0.00043	-0.00774	-0.16493	-0.00553	-0.00826	0.01800	-0.00155

even when costs are very different between regions, further sophistication will not alter the qualitative conclusions.

Table 1 reports the results. The first case uses Tabor's (1987) data that rural mail is 14% of the total mail (i.e., $\alpha = 0.86$), and costs some 48% more in total to process than does urban mail. Sorting costs are much the same in both areas ($a = \hat{a}$). The elasticity of returns to scale is 1.49, and demand elasticity is 0.3. Rural prices are 52% higher and urban prices fall by some 6.5% as a result of breaking the uniform tariff. Urban prices fall by so much because of scale economies. Although these price changes are large, the overall change in consumer surplus is small (1%) and negative for reasons discussed above. Various combinations of parameters are reported in table 1, but in all cases indicate that at best efficiency gains from setting prices at average cost for each region are small and may be negative.

These are maximal measures of gain from breaking the uniform tariff because it is plausible that if the Post Office were to maintain its comprehensive service, charging a differential between rural and urban mail would involve significant administrative costs. High cost areas or addresses would first have to be designated which would doubtless involve considerable controversy. An identifier could then be added to the post code. A system of monitoring whether the right identifier and correct postage paid for any particular address would have to be introduced. Finally, a procedure would have to be established to handle cases where the wrong postage had been paid. Confusion on the part of the public would probably result in a considerable volume of wrongly stamped mail, let alone intentional fraud. Moreover the extra costs incurred by users in determining correct rates and the time taken by counter staff in answering enquiries would be sufficient to outweigh what would anyway be small efficiency gains. The first class/second class tariff discrimination is much easier to police, understand and administer.

Rowland Hill himself favoured a two tier tariff structure, arguing that secondary distribution letters to places of inferior importance could be surcharged. He was only persuaded to drop this proposal to facilitate the passage of his other proposals. However the present analysis suggests that there is no justification for the Post Office to move from a uniform to a two tier tariff based on a differential delivery costs. This is true whether the Post Office retains its monopoly and were to unilaterally introduce the new scheme or whether it were forced on the Post Office as a result of deregulation in a contestable market.[2]

If the Post Office is committed to maintain its uniform tariff, the possibility of more serious losses from deregulation arise than those which occur in contestable markets. Assuming entry and exit are costly, as in our earlier modelling exercises, there is the possibility that entrants could profitably enter low cost services even though they are less efficient than the Post Office, because the uniform tariff means that on these services the Post Office maintains prices considerably above costs. Even if the rival is equally as efficient or more efficient than the Post Office, the encouragement to entry provided by uniform pricing may result in losses from the dissipation of economies of scale. We now extend our earlier models so as to address these issues (see Estrin and de Meza, 1988 for a fuller account).

In our simulations of this model, we find, as might be expected, that cream skimming increases the likelihood of profitable entry under both Cournot and Bertrand competition. Nonetheless, in most cases of successful entry, the Post Office and the entrant are offering products sufficiently heterogeneous that the total size of the market is expanded, the loss of economies of scale is more than matched by the gains for the new customers and overall welfare is increased. But disadvantageous entry is more likely in the case of cream skimming, particularly for Cournot competition. Typical patterns for disadvantageous entry are when economies of scale are assumed to be relatively low and the rival offers a similar product to the Post Office but has significant cost advantages. Cases of disadvantageous entry also arise with Bertrand competition.

To this point, we have argued that uniform tariffs have attractions, but if the Post Office does maintain them deregulation in a non-contestable market may well have significant welfare costs. But there is an important qualification to this argument in favour of the status quo. If the Post Office were allowed to break the uniform tariff should a competitor appear in a particular sub-market, then our earlier simulations suggest that it would be impossible to enter profitably by offering a similar product even if the entrant has large cost advantages. So it is possible that knowing the Post Office is allowed to break the uniform tariff would be an effective deterrent to disadvantageous cream-skimming entry. In practice the uniform tariff will never or seldom be broken and so the policy of permitting flexible pricing by the Post Office may be the best approach.

6. Policy Implications

The theoretical modelling and the simulations based upon it suggest that allowing one or more private firms to compete with the Post Office could be harmful even though it is perhaps more likely that benefits will accrue. That entry could lead to efficiency losses is, as always, the consequence of an externality; that is a cost imposed by the entrant's actions but bourne by other parties. The externality in question is that in diverting traffic from the Post Office economies of scale are lost and, the prices paid by the Post Office's remaining users must rise.[3] The loss involved is made more precise by the following equation:

$$E = \frac{A\eta^A}{1 + \varepsilon\eta^A} \tag{5}$$

where E is the external cost if the entrant attracts an extra letter from the Post Office as a result of a perceived quality or price advantage; A is the Post Office's average cost per letter; η^A is the elasticity of the Post Office's average cost and ε is the elasticity of demand.

At first sight diverting a letter from the Post Office entails an externality equal to the difference between average and marginal cost, for this represents the extra amount which must be raised from the remaining users if the Post Office is to continue to break even. However, the consequent price rise will cause a further loss of volume and therefore a second round of efficiency losses and so on. The more elastic is demand the larger will these repercussions be, as the equation shows. As an illustration, suppose elasticity of demand is 1.0, η^A is −0.2 and A equals 20, implying a marginal cost of 16. While the gap between average and marginal cost is only 4, equation (5) reveals that E is 5.

The three policies which will now be proposed are based on this externality perspective.

(a) Where externalities are present, the standard economic remedy is to tax them, at least if the tax itself is not too costly to administer and not subject to excessive manipulation by special interest groups. The application here is to allow letters to be conveyed by any operator for whatever price they choose, provided that the proceeds of a tax on each letter is paid to the Post Office to compensate for cream-skimming losses and reduced economies of scale. Thus, if the Post Office loses business it would be compensated financially and so able to maintain its current tariff structure. The competition would provide a spur to Post Office managers and workers to increase efficiency but would not harm them or the public. Giving the proceeds of the tax to the Post Office is not actually efficiency enhancing. Desirable entry is potentially precluded by the refund. But the distributional effects of entry will be tempered by the refund and the adverse consequences of miscalculating the tax will be minimised. Compensating the Post Office is a safety first approach.

At first sight, such a scheme may seem vulnerable to administrative problems. Private firms have an obvious incentive to under record volume and public resources would therefore have to be devoted to policing activities. Such difficulties may be overstated for, after all, it has not proved infeasible to collect VAT. However, there is an alternative means of implementing the tax proposal which may avoid some of these difficulties. Commercial carriers are prohibited from charging directly for a letter. Rather, the carrier sets the tariff he wishes and Post Office stamps to that value must be affixed to the letter. The carrier then feeds the letters through an electronic reader which registers their value and cancels the stamps to prevent them being re-recorded. At the end of each month the Post Office reads the machines and pays the firm the difference between the value of the stamps and the tax.

(b) A reduction in the minimum legal charge available to private delivery services from the present 1 to, say, 50p. Even at this price there is unlikely to be competition for the bulk mail services, so there would be little loss of Post Office economies of scale or problem with cream-skimming. Where externalities are low there is no case for supressing competition.

(c) Allowing post clubs to operate provided each member pays a significant annual levy to the Post Office. A post club involves setting up a network between members who contract to join for a minimum period. The point of the levy is twofold. Firstly, it would restrict membership to high volume users. Delivery and collection from such users is normally by means of a dedicated services, rather than as part of a general round. Economies of scale are thus unlikely to be very important. Secondly, the Post Office receives the levy to compensate for cream-skimming losses and so to keep prices down.

There is a sense in which schemes (a) and (c) involve compulsory franchising. Commercial firms do the Post Office's work for it but only when they can do so at less than the Post Office's marginal (not average) cost. Yet these schemes involve considerable decentralisation: were an explicit franchising scheme to be introduced with the Post Office choosing whether or not to contract out services, it would likely be biased against hiring outsiders. An independent agency would be unlikely to be sufficiently knowledgeable about what needs doing, nor to have much incentive to encourage innovative services which might prove to be failures.

That the revenues from schemes (a), and (c) is returned to the Post Office might seem to give management little incentive to improve performance. If the Post Office loses business, it is compensated financially. But it is difficult to see that there would be fewer incentives to efficiency than under a statutory monopoly. There could be no more effective indictment of management than that competitors are taking all the business. Moreover, if that does happen there will ultimately be fewer managers and those let go will hardly come on to the labour market with the best of recommendations. But, if stronger incentives for efficiency are required, part of the revenue could be directed to a separate body responsible for the provision of socially desirable, but unprofitable, postal services. The Post Office could compete with other companies in tendering to provide an even more direct spur to Post Office effort and, as many of the loss making burdens would no longer be the direct responsibility of the Post Office, it would enable them to keep their average charges down. But whether it is worth the cost of setting up and controlling a new bureaucracy is debateable. Channelling the money straight to the Post Office may be simpler.

Notes

The authors would like to thank Polly Vizard and Miguel Delgado for their research assistance and acknowledge helpful advice and comments from Robert Albon, Jane Black, Paul Richards, and Hugh Wills and participants at the Conference on Competition and Innovation in Postal Services in July 1990. Any errors remain the responsibility of the authors.

1. New Zealand is unique in having recently privatised its Post Office but at the time of writing has retained its statutory monopoly.

2. It is sometimes suggested that transaction costs will only be incurred in a deregulated competitive market if it is efficient that they should be. This is easily seen to be false. The market test of whether to stream customers is whether there is a group for whom supply costs are sufficiently below the average to cover the costs of identifying them. This test ignores the higher prices paid by the high cost users. Real resources are used up to what may be wholly or partly a redistributive role.

3. This may appear to be a pecuniary rather than a technological externality and therefore not a source of efficiency loss. However as the Post Office sets price above marginal cost the initial equilibrium is not first best and prices are not good measures of opportunity cost.

References

Coase, R.H. 1939. "Rowland Hill and the Penny Post." *Economica* 6 (November): 423-435.
Coase, R.H. 1961. "The British Post Office and the Messenger Companies." *Journal of Law and Economics* 4:12-65.
Daunton, M.J. 1985. *Royal Mail*. London: Athlone.
Estrin, S., and D. de Meza. 1988. "Should the Post Office's Statutory Monopoly be Lifted?" London School of Economics mimeo.
Friedman, M. 1962. *Capital and Freedom*. Chicago: University of Chicago Press.
Hunt, L.C., and E.L. Lynk. 1990. "An Empirical Examination of the Case for Post Office Divestiture in the UK." Mimeo.
Mankiw, N.G., and M. Whinston. 1986. "Free Entry and Social Efficiency." *Rand Journal* 17 (Spring): 48-58.
Panzar, J.C., and R.D. Willig. "Free Entry and the Sustainability of Natural Monopoly." *Bell Journal* 8 (Spring): 1-22.
Pryke, R. 1981. *The Nationalised Industries*. Oxford: Martin Robertson.
Schwartz, M. 1986. "The Nature and Scope of Contestability Theory." *Oxford Economic Papers* 38 (supplement): 37-57.
Tabor, R. 1987a. "Can Competition Pass 'Go' with a Natural Monopoly?" Public Finance and Accountancy (May 8).
Tabor, R. 1987b. "Who Benefits from 'One Price for Everyone'?" Public Finance and Accountancy (June 12).

COMMENTS:
Bagging The Mail
Charles K. Rowley

1. Introduction

Estrin and de Meza present a thoughtful and carefully reasoned case for allowing only a limited further deregulation of the bulk mail service in the United Kingdom. In their policy portfolio, the Post Office would remain under public ownership and would continue to pursue a policy of overall average cost pricing, based upon a uniform letter delivery price which discriminates between high and low cost spatial markets. Within this institutional perspective, three alternative reforms are postulated.

First, and least momentous, would be the lowering of the minimum legal charge to private delivery services from £1 to 50 pence. Since the lowered minimum price still significantly exceeds the typical bulk mail letter price, the statutory protection of the Post Office is little eroded by this reform. Secondly would be a policy of allowing "post clubs" to operate among high volume users, subject to the payment of a significant annual levy to the Post Office to recompense it for "cream-skimming losses. third would be a more general policy of allowing unlimited competition in the letter delivery service, but shackling competitors with taxes which would prop up the Post Office in direct proportion to its failure to meet competition.

In my judgement, Estrin and de Meza fail to establish a convincing efficiency case either for continued public ownership in the mail delivery service or for the retention of statutory limitations on free competition in the mail delivery market. In this comment, I shall address briefly some analytical and empirical limitations of their paper and outline some public choice reasons for skepticism concerning their proposed reforms. Finally, I shall direct attention to some public choice explanations of the statutory protection accorded to public service systems, not only in Britain, but worldwide.

2. The Argument from Market Failure

Estrin and de Meza characterize the British Post Office as a multi-output natural monopolist operating under cost conditions that would render it unsustainable in the absence of statutory protection, even if its pricing strategies were not constrained to the uniform letter delivery rate. They claim, moreover, that, although the delivery service is non-contestable in view of relatively high sunk costs that would impose capital losses on exit for failing new entrants, nevertheless new entry is likely in the absence of statutory protection and that such entry conceivably, though not certainly, would lower overall consumers' surplus by eroding the economies of monopolistic supply.

In order to eliminate the perceived external diseconomies of new entry, the authors propose the imposition of a Pigovian tax upon all effective new entrants to be paid directly to the Post Office to recompense it for forfeited economies of scale and scope. As the reader will perceive, the logic of this convoluted argument depends on a number of important propositions which are asserted rather than established in their paper.

A natural monopoly is said to exist in a particular market if and only if a single firm, in the absence of statutory assistance, can produce the desired output at lower cost than any combination of two or more firms. This condition is defined as strict sub-additivity of costs. In the case of the single-output firm, economies of scale are a sufficient (though not necessary) condition for strict sub-additivity of cost. In a multiple output market, such as that of letter delivery to rural as well as to urbanized customers, product-specific scale economies are neither necessary nor sufficient for strict sub-additivity to hold. Sub-additivity in the multiproduct context requires that there be economies of joint production, as well as the more usual economies of scale. These former economies are referred to as economies of scope. Yet even economies of scale together with economies of scope are not sufficient for general sub-additivity. A sufficient condition for sub-additivity to hold, in the multiproduct firm, is that its cost function is transray convex and characterized by universally declining ray average cost.

This leads to my first reservation. The authors present cursory arguments justifying the existence of product-specific scale economies; but no hard evidence. They merely assert the existence of economies of scope. Even if their assertions are correct, this does not imply that the letter delivery service is a natural monopoly. Much more complex reasoning and more difficult cost analysis is required to establish the basic propositions that a natural monopoly exists. Cost rays and cost transrays are difficult, if not impossible, to estimate in the absence of systematic fixed proportion output decline or expansion and of reductions or increases in the output dimensions catered for by a single firm. Not proven, is my judgement, on this proposition.

The authors secondly assert that the natural monopoly enjoyed by the British Post Office is unsustainable in the absence of statutory protection. They rest this judgement on perceived characteristics of the price vector and the actual cost conditions that characterize the organization under existing conditions of public ownership and statutory monopoly. Since these conditions are unlikely to hold in the private laissez-faire environment, their judgement must be treated with particular caution.

The announced prices of a natural monopolist are sustainable if the monopolist is financially viable at these prices and if no potential entrant can find a marketing plan whose expected economic profits cover the costs of entry. For sustainability to hold, in the absence of entry barriers, the natural monopolist must be X-efficient, that is it must produce its output vector at the lowest cost available to the industry.

Such a natural monopoly, under certain demand and cost conditions, will be sustainable if it selects prices that satisfy the conditions of Pareto optimality under a profit constraint i.e., Ramsey-optimal prices. In the absence of sustainability, the pressure of potential entry can lead to significant market instability.

The Post Office, if it is a natural monopolist, is unlikely to be sustainable in its present form, should statutory protection be removed. In the absence of competitive stimuli, it is unlikely to be X-efficient in production. Its pricing policy, which involves a uniform price irrespective of marginal cost, also leaves it highly vulnerable to cream-skimming new entry. For these reasons, Estrin and de Mesa have real cause for concern.

Such would not be the case, however, if mail delivery were to be privatized and released from its uniform price constraint. The profit motive, together with the re-emergence of property rights, would re-establish cost-reducing incentives. Cross-subsidization of prices would disappear and prices would be related to marginal cost in such a way as to minimize the risk of cream-skimming new entry. A two-tiered price structure, distinguishing urban from rural markets, would emerge. Certain delivery routes would be abandoned altogether as uneconomic. Others would rely upon central delivery stations with box numbers for individual clients, shifting the burden of collections from supplier to client sources. In the contestable market situation, unfettered laissez faire has a great deal to commend it, even in the natural monopoly situation.

Estrin and de Meza reject the notion, however, that markets catered for by the Post Office are contestable. They cite the importance of the costs of planning collection and delivery routes, as well as advertising as impediments to new entry; sunk costs that cannot be recouped upon market exit. In my view, such costs are not necessarily sunk, especially if the new entrants are diversifying into the letter delivery from unprotected express mail and bulk mail delivery markets with existing spatial market expertise and an established brand name. Moreover, if Estrin and de Meza are correct, what purpose does statutory prohibition on new entry serve, other than as a rent-protection device?

Estrin and de Meza, reluctant as they are to recommend a free market solution, rest their case on an unconvincing organizational and behavioral set of assumptions. They retain public-ownership for the hapless incumbent, which is viewed as retaining a uniform price structure, a commitment to total market coverage and a continuation of an X-inefficient cost function, even under the threat of cream-skimming, cost-efficient new entry. They envisage market adjustments that wipe out product-specific scale economies and scope economies with some ensuing loss of consumers' surplus. Even in the presence of non-contestability, new entry occurs in their analysis, as outside firms characterized by bounded rationality under-estimate the implications of high sunk costs for the exit decision. A Pigou tax, they argue, will compensate the Post Office and its customers and will lower incentives for market failure implicit in the new entry decision.

3. Arguments from Government Failure

The policy solutions addressed by Estrin and de Meza, designed to limit the damage to the Post Office from cream-skimming competition in the post-regulation, market environment, do not address the fundamental source of the problem, which is located in the public ownership of the Post Office. Public ownership seriously erodes individual property rights in mail delivery assets and thus weakens the incentive to monitor performance and, indeed, replaces wealth maximizing objectives with political objectives brokered by special interests in the political marketplace. It is small wonder that an organization whose policies are determined, in part at least, by the organized lobbying of the rural constituencies and the postal-workers unions adopts a discriminatory pricing policy and is inefficient. It is a yet smaller wonder that such an organization clings desperately to statutory protection from outside market forces.

The Post Office is vulnerable to market erosion, in the absence of statutory protection, because of government and not because of market failure. In a sense, it is an active cream-skimmer itself, garnering political rents for its principals, by dedicating its pricing policies to wealth redistribution goals. Its pricing policy is in a rent-seeking equilibrium, given existing institutions. The threat to this political equilibrium that laissez-faire poses is the impulse that has triggered rent-protecting lobbying by those interests that presently benefit from job protection and wealth redistribution. Such interests have expended real resources in rent-seeking, in support of public ownership and the uniform price. Even if they recognize the efficiency losses that the present equilibrium imposes, they themselves confront a transitional gains trap. By voting in favor of markets, they impose wealth losses upon themselves. Predictably, their lobbying is for the status quo. The rationally ignorant voter predictably may be no political match for the dedicated, wealth-protecting special interest lobbies.

Rent-seeking theory thus offers a powerful explanation of the pervasive existence of publicly-provided, statute-protected mail delivery systems. Such nurtured instruments now are under threat as a consequence of technological advances in communications which threaten market annihilation for the letter delivery system as a whole in the absence of vigorous reform. Ultimately, this wider threat will overwhelm the narrow, political constituency interests that favor the status quo. Better that the victory should be swift, allowing a private market in postal services to survive and to compete with the enemy from without on even terms rather than that the victory should be total, as current experience in Germany shows to be an almost universal consequence of socialist monopoly. Vacant sorting houses, unemployed former postal workers, and a slow-moving second-hand market in repainted vans and pick-up trucks is the predictable long-term alternative to privatization and laissez-faire in postal services.

The race between new information technology and political reform of the postal system predictably will be a close run thing. The Penny Post has proved to be a long-lived effective rent-seeking instrument, highly robust against its detractors' arguments. Predictably, justifications for its retention, such as those here advanced by Estrin and de Meza, drawn (however dubiously) from public interest rather than from public choice analyses will have little impact on the ultimate political outcome. If the Penny Post monopoly indeed is swept aside, the victory will lie with market forces, unleased by new technology, which destroy the very rents that the present political equilibrium seeks ineffectively to protect. Once there is no cream to skim, there will be no interest groups with any incentive to lobby the legislature to help them to bag the mail.

The real issue of significance for this debate is whether rent-seeking is dispersed in time, before the letter delivery service itself becomes non-viable, as potential customers adapt to alternative cost-effective methods of communication. I am willing to stake the out-house, but not the ranch, that such will prove to be the case and that some form of letter delivery service will survive the twentieth century.

Note

The Author gratefully acknowledges research support by the Lynde and Harry Bradley Foundation. Helpful comments on an earlier draft by Professors Estrin and de Mesa are also acknowledged.

6
A COMPARATIVE ANALYSIS OF WAGE PREMIUMS AND INDUSTRIAL RELATIONS IN THE BRITISH POST OFFICE AND THE UNITED STATES POSTAL SERVICE

Michael L. Wachter
Jeffrey M. Perloff

1. Introduction

This paper analyzes and compares the wage-setting mechanisms in the United States Postal Service (USPS) and the British Post Office. The United States comparability standard states that the USPS should pay wages comparable to those paid in the private sector:

> It shall be the policy of the Postal Service to maintain compensation and benefits for all officers and employees on a standard of comparability to the compensation and benefits paid for comparable levels of work in the private sector of the economy."[1]

The extent to which the Postal Service meets this standard has generated a considerable literature in the United States. We review the earlier studies and present an economic interpretation of the comparability standard, including an econometric methodology which addresses the comparability question. In extending our past research, we present new results, using the latest data available on the size of the Postal Service wage premium.[2] Our methodology relies on multivariate regression analysis of individual worker observations from the Current Population Survey of the Bureau of the Census. The data include industry and union status, as well as measures of education, occupation, region of the country, etc. Our approach tests for sample selection bias, and identifies the effects of union status and firm and establishment size on the wage premium.

The United Kingdom comparability standard covering the British Post Office is much less formal than the USPS standard.[3] The history of comparability rules dates back to the British Post Office arbitration award of 1927 which first declared that [postal] earnings should be set in terms of "fair relatives with outside industry."[4] Due to data limitations, however, we are unable to use the same econometric approach used for the United States. Instead, we must rely on data on the time trend of Post Office wages compared to private sector wages, the union premium in the United Kingdom, and information on regional pay differentials. In each case, we compare the United Kingdom data to the comparable United States data in order to draw inferences about British Post Office pay comparability.

2. Labor Law and Union Representation in Postal Labor Markets

Before discussing the econometric issues in estimating comparability, we describe the industrial relations systems in which the USPS and the British Post Office operate. Wage comparability does not take place in a vacuum, independent of union status or the relevant labor law.

2.1. Union Status of Postal Workers

The great majority of postal workers are unionized, both in the United States and in the United Kingdom. In the United States, four unions the (American Postal Workers Union AFL-CIO, the National Association of Letter Carriers AFL-CIO, the National Post Office Mail Handlers AFL-CIO, and the unaffiliated National Rural Letter Carriers Association) represent over 80 percent of postal workers, virtually all of the nonmanagerial and nonprofessional workers. The union representation follows occupational categories so that the postal clerks, city letter carriers, mail handlers, and rural letter carriers are represented by separate unions.

In the United Kingdom, five unions represent over 90 percent of postal workers. All five unions are constituent or associate members of the Post Office Unions' Council. The Union of Communication Workers represents most of the nonsupervisory-nonprofessional personnel. Smaller unions represent other postal crafts.

2.2. Labor Law

The union-management relationship is regulated very differently in the United States and the United Kingdom. In the United States, labor law is codified in the National Labor Relations Act (NLRA). This Act provides special protections to the bargaining process and to the resulting collective bargaining contracts. The NLRA is enforced by the National Labor Relations Board (Board) which has rule making powers and operates as an administrative law system. Although the Board decisions or rules can be overturned by a Court of Appeals or the Supreme Court, higher courts give deference to Board decisions.

There is no comparable unified labor law in the United Kingdom, although separate statutory rules have been adopted from time to time. Unions in the United Kingdom are not certified by the government and do not have the special protections enjoyed by United States unions. Whereas collective bargaining contracts in the United States enjoy special protections spelled out by the NLRA and the Board, collective bargaining contracts in the United Kingdom are often not legally enforceable obligations. The enforceability depends on whether they are incorporated into the individual employment contracts. However, some terms, including the collective bargaining machinery, are not considered capable of incorporation. In addition, no-strike pledges are not legally binding.[5]

Postal bargaining in the United States is regulated by the NLRA, but separate rules override certain NLRA rights. For example, postal unions in the United States do not have the right to strike. If collective bargaining reaches an impasse instead of a contract, the impasse is resolved through mandatory, binding arbitration. Since passage of the Postal Reorganization Act, postal unions did conduct local work stoppages in 1978 which resulted in the issuance of court injunctions and the discharge of a number of postal workers. More significantly, there have been no strike threats since the Professional Air Traffic Controllers strike of 1980-81 ended with President Reagan dismissing several thousand striking workers for conducting an illegal strike.

In contrast, in the United Kingdom, postal unions have the right to strike, a right enjoyed by workers in nationalized industries (as distinct from workers in the civil service). The result is that the British Post Office has experienced both major strikes and, on a regular basis, unofficial work stoppages. For example, in the fiscal year 1987-88, there were 213 unofficial disputes, involving 63,500 working days. Although that represented only 0.2 percent of the total working days, it still delayed 126 million letters.[6]

The difference in methods of impasse resolution between the United States and the United Kingdom is important in understanding the comparability issue. Although the strike weapon may appear to strengthen the unions' power, in comparison to the arbitration machinery this may not be the case.

A feature of the USPS arbitration mechanism is that an arbitrator is not legally required to abide by the comparability rules. The result is attenuated accountability. If USPS management were to attempt to force wage adjustments to achieve comparability, the postal unions need only hold out in hope of a more favorable result from an arbitrator. Hence, whether comparability is achieved by the USPS may ultimately rest with the decisions of an outside arbitrator. It is at least plausible to argue that the requirement of binding arbitration to resolve bargaining impasses weakened Post Service managements' ability to attack the comparability issue during the past decade.[7] Of course, the obvious benefit of such a system is that postal customers do not face the costs of a strike.

On the other hand, a feature of the strike mechanism is that it forces the parties to come to an agreement. If British Post Office management believes that it is not meeting its public obligations to abide by the comparability standard, it can take a strike and hold firm on the issue. Strikes have helped to resolve important issues in the British Post Office, such as the right of management to pay supplements in difficult recruitment areas, to use flexibility in shifting work away from the tight labor markets in London and the southeast, and in restructuring overtime arrangements.[8]

3. Testing for Wage Comparability

In this section, we evaluate the evidence on USPS wage comparability. The primary problem in calculating the relative wage of postal workers is that there are virtually no direct counterparts to postal clerks and carriers in the private sector. Given the availability of the Bureau of the Census's Current Population Survey (CPS) in the United States, standard statistical techniques can be used to calculate comparable wages for occupations that have no direct match in the private sector.[9] The multivariate regression approach is a generally accepted method for calculating interindustry wage differentials and for answering the question as to postal wage comparability.

Table 1. Previous Empirical Studies of USPS Wage Differentials			
Study	Year of Data	Comparison Group	USPS Wage Differentials
Quinn (1979)	1969	vs. men aged 58-63 in the private sector	11-12%
Smith (1976a)	1973	postal group vs. corresponding private sector group:	
		Male nonunion:	25%
		Male union:	26%
Gyourko and Tracy (1988)	1977	vs. private sector, averaging union & nonunion	
		Ordinary least squares:	22%
		Two-stage least squares,	
		unconditional:	23%
		conditional:	48%
Perloff and Wachter (1984)	1978	vs. weighted average of the private sector:	21%
		female nonunion:	69%
		female union:	54%
		male nonunion:	25%
		male union:	10%
		weighted average of all males:	13%
Asher and Popkin (1984)	1979	vs. corresponding race/gender group in private sector:	
		white males, large firms:	3%
Perloff (1985)	1984	vs.	
		private sector:	24%
		trade:	37%
		service:	36%
Perloff (1989)	1987	vs. retail and wholesale trade:	51-57%

3.1. Brief Review of the Literature

There is broad agreement in the literature that the Postal Service pays a substantial wage premium over the private sector, with most studies concluding that the premium is around 20 percent. The results, which include our own earlier work, are summarized in table 1.[10]

One study, Gyourko and Tracy (1988), finds that if one adjusts for the differences in the people who work in the USPS (i.e., "adjust for sample selection"), that the differential is as large as 48 percent. Their analysis, however, is based on a comparison of all federal union workers, and not just union postal workers. Below, we report our sample selection results for an analysis that concentrates on only postal workers.

The one study that offers at least superficial disagreement is Asher and Popkin (1984). Their finding of approximate wage parity between the Postal Service and the private sector only emerges, however, when the comparison group is restricted from the overall private sector to white males in large firms.[11] They argue that due to discrimination in the private sector, the USPS should pay its workers comparable wages to those earned by white males in unionized large firms.[12] Their regression results, however, are compatible with the other studies, if the wage comparison had been with wages received by all workers in the private sector.

3.2. The Basis of Comparison

The exact definition of the comparison group has important effects on the wage comparison. The following econometric implementation of pay comparability involves measuring the wage differentials between otherwise identical workers in the postal sector and the private sector.[13] As in previous studies, a wage equation is estimated that controls for geographic and demographic differences between workers in the two sectors. Demographic variables, presumably reflecting worker skills, such as occupation, age, education, and experience, are held constant when calculating USPS wage differentials. Similarly, variables that reflect geographic compensating differentials (such as city size and region) also are held constant. These differences across individuals, which reflect demographic, skill, and geographical factors, are for brevity, called "individual-descriptive" or "individual-traits."

In such regression analyses, differences in jobs (called "job-descriptive" or "job-traits") are not held constant when calculating wage differentials. The two job-descriptive variables we use are union status and firm size. These variables reflect the determinants of noncompetitive wage differentials between postal and private sector workers. The coefficients on these variables, along with the industry dummy variables must be used together to identify the postal-private wage differential.

Typically, different equations are estimated for private and public sector workers, and the resulting equations are used to calculate predicted wages based on the mean values of the control variables.[14] An alternative, but conceptually similar, econometric technique imposes parameter restrictions, uses a single equation, and identifies public sector wage differentials from the coefficients on the industry dummy-variables.

3.3. Identification of Job-Descriptive Variables

With respect to the job-descriptive variables, there is a broad consensus that unions successfully bargain with employers to achieve noncompetitive wage premiums. Consequently, the union wage is higher than the nonunion wage for comparably skilled workers. Because these wage differentials correspond to the (union status of the) job rather than the skill of the workers, they serve to introduce discrepancies among workers doing comparable work.[15]

The treatment of firm size poses a somewhat more difficult question than union status. There exists robust empirical evidence that large firms pay, on average, persistently higher wages than smaller firms. The traditional explanation for this finding is that large firms are more likely than small firms to be either regulated or to possess some degree of product market power. These noncompetitive features of the large firms' product market generate rents. The empirical finding that large firms pay above market wages thus reflects rent-sharing with the workers of the firms. High wages due to rent-sharing are correctly interpreted as noncompetitive, wage premiums.[16]

Mellow (1982, 1983), on the other hand, has argued that firm size may also be a proxy for otherwise unmeasured skill factors. For example, large firms may require and successfully screen for more skilled workers. The weakness of the Mellow argument about unmeasured skills is that that interpretation is more applicable to management positions than to the nonsupervisory positions that make up the great majority of postal jobs.

A related argument is that some large firms may pay higher wages in order to reduce the costs of monitoring workers. This efficiency wage theory, developed by Akerlof (1984) and Akerlof and Yellen (1985), holds that if supervision is more costly in larger firms, those firms may decide to pay above competitive wages in order to provide workers with an incentive to self-monitor.[17]

We conclude, however, that the efficiency wage model is less applicable to the British Post Office or the USPS "firms" than is the rent-sharing model of noncompetitive equilibrium. Government firms and agencies operate in the most protected product markets in the economy, and hence may operate noncompetitively, paying above market wages without fear of entry by firms paying competitive wages. That is, they can pay wage premiums without a competitive threat to the workers they employ or the services they provide. This is the reverse of the Akerlof-Yellen argument, where higher wages are paid to meet to a competitive threat.

Hence, in the absence of empirical evidence supporting the efficiency wage concept for the government sector, we adopt the standard of treating firm size as a job-trait rather than as an individual-trait. Moreover, the empirical results that are available (discussed below) favor interpreting the high postal wage as reflecting the rent-sharing.

Estimation Methodology

To demonstrate the appropriate distinction between skill- and job-descriptive variables, we specify the wage equation as:

$$\ln(W_t) = A'S + B'I \quad (1)$$

where S is a vector of control variables, I is a vector of job-descriptive (dummy) variables (such as industry-union status, and firm size), and A' and B' are the vectors of coefficients corresponding to S and I respectively.[18]

The natural base group for the wage differential calculation is workers with the omitted, job-descriptive characteristics. Following Halvorsen and Palmquist (1980), this differential is:[19]

$$D_{i,j} = 100 e^{B'E_{i,j}} - 1 \quad (2)$$

where $E_{i,j}$ is a vector with ones where the corresponding elements of B are a characteristic of the i,j subgroup and zeroes elsewhere. The i subscript indexes industry and the j subscript indexes the elements in the cross-product space of all the job related characteristic dimensions in I.[20]

Aggregating subgroup differentials across the job-descriptive dimensions requires taking a weighted average of these pay differentials. The appropriate weights for aggregating the subgroups depend upon the conceptual thought experiment (lottery) being conducted. We are interested in the expected wage prospects of postal workers if they were to leave for the private sector. If they leave the Postal Service, these former postal workers lose the set of job-descriptive characteristics of the postal sector. In moving to a private sector job, each worker's expected value depends not only on the differential wage payoffs identified in (2), but also on the distribution of payoff probabilities in the private sector. Thus, we use own-industry weights,

$$P_{i,j} = \frac{N_{i,j}}{N_i} \quad (3)$$

where N_i and is the number of workers in the i industry. The aggregate industry wage differential is[21]

$$D_i = \sum_j P_{i,j} \times D_{i,j} \quad (4)$$

4. Comparability Results for the United States

Our basic result is that the Postal Service pays a wage premium of approximately 21.3 percent with respect to otherwise identical workers in the private sector. The premium shows a sizable discrepancy from the policy mandate of wage comparability.

The premium is calculated as (postal wage - private sector wage)/ postal wage. That is, the result shows that private sector workers are paid 21.3 percent less than postal workers. If the private sector is used as the divisor, instead of the Postal Service, the resulting premium is 28 percent. Because the results in table 1 (with the exception of our earlier studies) use this base, 28 percent is the relevant figure.

The premium is an average across industries and union status, and thus must be differentiated from the more widely studied union premium with respect to the nonunion sector. Our focus on the overall private sector is dictated by the PRA. The PRA standard is for comparability "in the private sector of the economy." Obviously the postal premium, if calculated with the nonunion sector as the base group, would be larger; that is, over 30 percent (with the nonunion sector as the divisor).

The results are based on the 1988 Current Population Survey, which contain approximately 150,000 usable observations. The premium is not a union premium in the sense that the private sector, including union and nonunion is used as the comparison group.

Table 2 displays alternate estimates of the USPS wage premium, which differ with respect to the differential treatment of firm size and union status. Our preferred estimate of the Postal Service wage premium is shown in row 1 of table 2.

Table 2. Alternative Estimates of Federal Wage Premiums	
Comparison Group	Premium
(1) **All** private sector workers	21.3
(2) **Union**, private sector workers	10.8
(3) **All** workers in similarly large-firms and establishments	18.2
(4) **Union** workers in similarly large-firms and establishments	10.1
Notes:	
1. Data are from the 1988 Current Population Survey.	
2. The premiums are calculated as the postal wage minus the private sector wage, divided by the postal wage. Dividing by the private sector wage, the more conventional approach used in table 1 would result in a premium of approximately 26 percent in row 1.	
3. See Linneman and Wachter (1990) for a full discussion of the equation specification. The sample is nonagricultural, full-time scheduled workers over age 15 with usual hours of 35 to 50, and valid responses for all the variables.	
4. Firm and establishment size effects are based on factors computed based on 1983 markups for those variables.	

Row 2 shows the premium when the comparison group is restricted to union workers; that is, it measures the differential between union postal workers and union, private sector workers. The 10.8 percent premium is approximately one-half the premium paid by the Postal Service. The premium with respect to the union sector is an average across industries; reflecting the relatively low union wages in the service and trade sectors and the higher wages in manufacturing, transportation, and public utilities.

In row 3, we show the effect of treating firm and establishment size as individual-descriptive variables. This treatment of firm and establishment size means assuming that workers of given education, job tenure, occupation, etc. in a large firm are more skilled than similar qualified workers in a small firm. (As discussed above, we disagree with this assertion except perhaps in the case of professional or managerial-type workers.) Because the Postal Service is in the largest firm category, the impact of this assumption is to restrict the comparison of postal workers to workers in other large firms. Perhaps surprisingly, little hinges on the treatment of this variable. The premium is reduced from the 21.3 level, but only three percentage points to 18.2 percent.

In row 4, we show the effect of restricting the comparison to union workers in large firms. In this case, the premium declines to 10.1 percent, but this is only slightly higher than the all union premium of 10.8 percent. The reason for the small additional affect is that, because most union workers are in large firms, comparing postal workers to union workers already has the effect of introducing much of the firm size effect.

4.1. The Private Sectors That Pay High Wage Premiums

Our results show that the Postal Service wage premium is close to that paid in the transportation and public utility sector. A two-digit decomposition of those sectors shows that postal wages are slightly higher than wages in transportation, but slightly lower than wages in public utilities. In other words, the Postal Service pays a union premium that is roughly comparable to that paid to unionized transportation and public utility workers.

These results support the rent-sharing model. Because the Postal Service and public utilities operate in highly protected product markets, and do not face entry by competitors, their wages can be set above competitive levels at little cost. On the other hand, the results also suggest that the Postal Service cannot be singled out for failure to achieve wage comparability.[22]

4.2. Sample-Selection Bias

As noted above, only the Gyourko and Tracy (1988) study controlled for sample selection bias. Because it dealt with all federal workers, it is possible that its relatively large estimate of the USPS wage premium would not be observed in a study on postal workers. To check their results, we tested the selectivity bias for postal workers alone. The results are based on the Bureau of Labor Statistic's Current Population Survey data for 1987.[23]

The reason for controlling for sample selection is that workers are not randomly assigned to work in the USPS or elsewhere. As a result, the error term in the wage equation may be correlated with the factors that determine whether the worker chooses the USPS. Such a consideration would occur, for example if Postal Service workers are unusually smart, even after controlling for education and other skill variables. If this were the case, then the large postal premium would partly reflect the impact of unmeasured skill differences.

A number of different models could be used to check for selectivity bias. The one we use is a variant of Heckman's technique using logit to control for any possible sample selection bias.[24] The usual approach to resolving this potential problem is to estimate a two-equation system. The first equation (a logit in our case) explains whether the worker is employed by the USPS or not. Let z^* be an unobserved index that reflects the tendency to work in the USPS and let

$$z = 1 \quad \text{if } z^* > 0 \text{ and}$$
$$z = 0 \quad \text{if } z^* < 0,$$

where $z = 1$ indicates that the worker is employed by the USPS and $z = 0$ indicates otherwise.

The tendency to work in the USPS is a function of various demographic characteristics and other variables, X_i:

$$z^* = X_1 B_1 + \varepsilon_1$$

where ε_1 is the error term. We estimate this equation using logit for the observed variable z.

We then regress the logarithm of the wage, w, on demographic and other variables, X_2, and z correcting for sample selection:

$$E(w \mid X_2, z) = X_2 B_2 + \delta z + E(\varepsilon_2 \mid \text{sample selection rule}).$$

The coefficient δ measures the effect of postal status on the logarithm of the wage. If $E(\varepsilon_2 \mid \text{sample selection rule}) = 0$, then the wage equation can be estimated by ordinary least squares. Thus, for example, if the assignment of workers were random, then using ordinary least squares would be correct. If the error in the wage equation is correlated with the sample selection rule, however, other techniques must be used. To test the role of sample selection, we estimate the system of equations taking into account the possibility of such a bias.

Based on the logit equation that "explains" which workers are in the USPS, only veteran status is a statistically significant determinant at the 0.05 level.[25] The equation correctly predicts most of the outcomes, but that is, in large part, because virtually everyone is a non-USPS employee.

The second equation is a regression of the logarithm of usual hourly earnings on various demographic characteristics. Unlike most previous studies that used single equation models, we have included interaction terms between USPS status and various demographic characteristics to allow a differential effect of these characteristics in the USPS compared to the rest of the economy. In addition, geographic, demographic, occupational, and industry variables are included.

We have estimated the wage equation in two ways. First, we have used the traditional ordinary least squares (OLS) estimate. Second, we have adjusted for possible sample selection bias using a maximum likelihood technique. The results show a statistically significant, positive correlation between ε_1 and ε_2—the errors in the equation that explain who works in the USPS and in the wage equation.[26] That is, unobserved factors that lead to a worker being employed by the USPS are positively correlated with unobserved factors that lead to a higher wage in the

USPS. Our results show that there is a statistically significant selection bias. Some of the coefficients differ between the OLS and the equation that adjusts for sample selection. The coefficients that affect the wage differential, however, are not affected.[27]

4.3. Other Factors that Affect the Premium

The wage differentials presented above use the standard approach of determining what a specific postal employee would earn in the private sector. If, however, the USPS hires over-qualified individuals, this differential may be larger. A widely accepted feature of union wage premiums is that the unionized firms respond by hiring more qualified workers. USPS clerks, mailhandlers, and carriers average 14.1 years of education. If they had 13.6 years, the average for their private sector equivalents (the overall average, excluding professionals and managers, in the private sector), then the wage differential would be 1 percent larger than the figures reported above. If only high school graduates were hired, the differential would be 5 percent larger.[28]

5. Employment Queues, Quit Rates, and Other Job Separations

Although our results indicate that the USPS pays a large premium over wages in the private sector, it is possible that this premium is a "compensating differential." That is, if workers viewed Postal Service jobs as unattractive, high wages would be needed to compensate them for taking the jobs. We can indirectly test this hypothesis by examining employment queues, quit rates, and other job separations in the USPS and in the private sector.

If potential employees consider the USPS an attractive employment opportunity, taking wages and other factors into account, there should be large job queues. Obviously, the attractiveness of a Postal Service job depends on the relative probability of a layoff (layoffs in the Postal Service are essentially zero), benefits, nonpecuniary job attributes, and other such factors, as well as wages.

In competitive labor markets, a firm knows to raise its relative wage when it cannot retain current employees and attract new ones. Alternatively stated, relative wages are too high if the firm hires off long employment registers or job queues. Unfortunately, Postal Service data on the number of applicants for its positions are not readily available. Although anecdotal evidence has to be used with great caution, numerous newspaper articles indicate that the Postal Service has no trouble finding new workers.[29] The Postal Service maintains an employment register for some jobs and that register is always filled. The data maintained by the Postal Service indicates that they almost never have trouble filling positions.

Related evidence on the relative attractiveness of Postal Service employment is provided by the quit rate. Perloff and Wachter (1984) show, based on Postal Service and Bureau of Labor Statistics data, that, in 1980, the monthly quit rate per 100 workers was 0.28 for the Postal Service versus 1.5 in manufacturing (1.2 in durables, and 1.8 in nondurables). In other words, approximately four times as many workers quit their jobs in the highly unionized, high wage, durable goods manufacturing industry as quit the Postal Service.

These results reinforce those of other studies based on data from earlier periods. Borjas (1980) reports that the average monthly separation rate (per 100 employees) in the USPS, for the period 1961-1976, was 1.44 compared to 1.83 for all government agencies; while the corresponding quit rates were 0.62 and 0.74. The USPS had the third lowest quit rate of the twenty-one federal government agencies Borjas studied.

Adie (1977) provides evidence that annual separations due to all causes are relatively low in the USPS. He notes that for the period 1975-76, the USPS had an average gross turnover of 17.2 percent, of which the great bulk were due to retirement and only 25 percent were due to voluntary quits. Adie also notes that, in 1972, the annual separation rate for the USPS was 15.0 percent compared to 50.1 percent in all of manufacturing.

Eck (1984) reports that the occupational separation rates of postal mail carriers and postal clerks were considerably below those exhibited by other clerical and blue-collar workers. In fact, mail carriers ranked below all but eight other occupations, all of which were professional or managerial occupations.

One reason that the quit rate is so low in the USPS is its relatively high wage. Another is its policy of not laying off workers. Seasonal spikes in demand, such as during the Christmas season, are absorbed through the employment of part-time or seasonal workers.

The USPS's collective bargaining workers obviously benefit from not being subject to cyclical or seasonal layoffs. The labor literature clearly shows that job security has a value and that high union wages in the private sector are, in part, a "compensating differential" for the higher risk of layoff. Abowd and Ashenfelter (1981), for example, estimate that compensating differentials are over 14 percent in industries that "experience substantial anticipated unemployment and unemployment risk."

For the USPS, this additional nonpecuniary feature suggests that the wage premium, based on the overall value of the job, is greater than the 21 percent reported above. We return to this issue when we evaluate the British Post Office below.

6. Evidence of the British Post Office Relative Wage Position

Unfortunately, data and time limitations prevented us from implementing a wage comparison study for the British Post Office that parallels the study for the United States. The major data gap for the United Kingdom is the lack of a large household data set that provides information on skill, location, and demographic characteristics of the workers by union status and industry. Although a small household survey does exist, there are too few postal observations to allow for statistical analysis.

We are thus forced to rely on establishment (as distinct from household) data that do not contain information on control variables. The data are available, however, for broadly defined manual and non-manual occupations by gender.

6.1. British Post Office Wage Levels in 1989

Post Office earnings were made available to us by Paul Richards of the British Post Office.[30] Most Post Office workers are in the manipulative trades, which the British Post Office compares to manual workers. Based on British Post office data, average gross weekly earnings of Post Office (manipulative grade) male workers is approximately the same as for male manual workers in the overall economy.[31] The weekly pay for Post Office workers is £216.8, which compares to £217.8 for manual workers. Hence, there is a negative postal premium of less than 1 percent.

A comparison that is restricted to male workers, however is limited.[32] Female labor force participation is the most dynamic growth area of the labor market both in the United States and in the United Kingdom. Compared to all manual workers, including females as well as male workers, the all-manual earnings of £203.2 results in a positive postal wage premium of approximately 6 percent.

A possible weakness in the above analysis is that postal, manipulative grade workers are not an occupational match to manual workers. In fact, most postal workers are classified by the Department of Labor (United States) as fitting into a white collar, clerk category. This category includes, for example, clerical workers who operate office machines.

Fortunately, given our limited data, the results are relatively robust across these alternative occupational classification. Clerical workers who are in occupations most similar to postal workers are paid wages that are relatively close to that paid to manual workers. This is not an entirely fortuitous result. In the United States, we find that such white collar workers have approximately the same human capital as the manual workers.

Another issue that could affect our conclusion are differences in hours of work. This is a difficult area to assess given the relative importance, in the United Kingdom (compared to the United States), of overtime pay, payment-by-result, and shift differentials. Also complicating the analysis is the sharp difference between males and females in the percentage of weekly wages that are received as a return to overtime, payment-by-result, or shift differentials. For private sector males, approximately 27 percent of weekly pay is a return to those three factors, while for private sector females it is 17 percent. For manipulative grade, male Post Office workers, the figure is 33 percent.

The difficulty in analyzing non-base pay, is that workers preferences with respect to these factors matter. While overtime may be a negative for some workers, others may actually prefer to work more hours than the standard. Absent the availability of overtime, such workers often moonlight, typically at lower wages than at their primary job. For these workers, the opportunity to earn premium pay only makes those hours more attractive. The same can be said for payment-by-result. To some workers, payment-by-result is a positive option to earn higher wages. To others it may only be a negative risk. The issue could be resolved if a data base were available where those factors could be treated as control variables. We could then calculate the premium, taking as given, levels of non-base pay.

Absent those variables, we can only report on alternative interpretations. If one takes the neutral view, that only average hourly earnings matter, than postal worker premiums would be higher than the figures reported above. If one assumes, on the other hand, that non-base pay does not adequately compensate for the extra hours, than the postal premium is smaller.

Regardless of how one decides the above unsettled questions, it is clear that the British Post Office premium is small compared to that paid by the USPS. The obvious question that emerges from this brief comparison of the two postal labor markets is what factors might explain the difference in the premium: large for the USPS and small for the British Post Office. Likely places to look for explanations are the differences between overall union wage premiums in the two countries and differences in the time-series of wages, particularly beginning in the early 1970s, soon after both organizations went through a governmental reorganization.

6.2. Union Density and Wage Premiums in the United Kingdom and United States

Union behavior differs considerably between the United States and the United Kingdom with respect to the degree of union representation of the work force and the size of union wage premiums. In the United States the union-nonunion wage gap is approximately 22 percent. In the United Kingdom, on the other hand, the wage gap is closer to 10 percent.[33] In other words, unions in the United States are less pervasive, but have a bigger effect on wage differentials where they are present.

To the extent that there is any pattern bargaining across union industries, we can indirectly expect that the British postal premium would be smaller than the United States postal premium. Indeed, as mentioned above, the United States postal premium is close to the premium existing in the transportation and public utilities sectors of the United States economy.

The flip-side of the union-nonunion wage differential is union employment shares. Effectively, unions in the United States have traded off employment shares in return for high premiums.[34] Not only in percentage terms, but also in absolute numbers, union membership has been declining in the United States. In the United Kingdom, unions have achieved lower premiums, but with a resulting higher degree of employment coverage. In the United States union membership is low and declining. Approximately 17 percent of the current United States work force is unionized compared to 31 percent in 1970. In the United Kingdom, on the other hand, 51 percent of wage and salary employees are currently unionized; virtually unchanged from the 51 percent recorded in 1970.

The degree of representation has an impact on the importance of the union sector in determining the comparable wage. The higher the degree of union representation, the higher the percentage of union members in the overall occupation and the comparison group. Because manual occupations in the United Kingdom are heavily unionized, union wage trends significantly affect the economy-wide trend in manual wages. In the United States, union representation is located primarily in a small group of industries, most of which are losing employment and output shares. Hence, the union sector does not bulk as large in the United States as it does in the United Kingdom in forming the comparison group.

6.3. Time Trend in Postal Wages

It is useful to analyze not only current wage levels, but also the historical time path of wages. Wage differentials that have existed for a long period of time are more likely to reflect competitive compensating differentials, which do tend to be stable over the longer run. On the other hand, wage discrepancies that balloon in a shorter period of time, absent significant changes in job content, are likely to reflect changes in the premium.

Postal and union wage trends in the United Kingdom are very different than the trends in the United States. In the "National Trends Study" of the British Post Office, it is shown that postal wages have closely tracked the weekly earnings for economy-wide manual occupations between 1974 to 1987. Whereas postal hourly wages increased by 11.2 percent annually between 1974 to 1987, manual hourly earnings increased by 11.3 percent. On the other hand, hourly earnings across the economy increased by 12.6 percent.[35]

Unfortunately, at least from the vantage point of reaching a clear-cut conclusion, 1974 may not be a valid starting point. In his study, Loveridge (1971, 123) states that "much of the financial benefit (achieved by the Post Office when it reorganized) was almost immediately passed on in a pay increase for postmen." If the

Table 3. Time Series of USPS Relative Wage (1969 = 100)	
Year	Relative Wage
1970	104.6
1971	107.3
1972	110.7
1973	114.3
1974	115.9
1975	118.8
1976	120.3
1977	120.3
1978	118.9
1979	118.3
1980	122.2
1981	121.4
1982	121.0
1983	121.9
Calculated by dividing USPS clerks'/mailhandlers' average hourly earnings by the industry-weighted average hourly earnings in the private sector, multiplying by 100, and then dividing by 123.7 (1969 total value). Source: U.S. Department of Labor, Bureau of Labor Statistics, *Employment and Earnings*, various issues; and USPS unpublished data. Table is from Perloff and Wachter (1984).	

Table 4. Economy-Wide Union Premium Series in the United States					
Year	Major Agreements/ AHE Low Union	AHE High Union/AHE Low Union	Year	Major Agreements/ AHE Low Union	AHE High Union/AHE Low Union
	(1)	(2)		(1)	(2)
1947		21.8	1971	24.0	22.3
1950		24.2	1972	24.3	24.9
1955		28.2	1973	25.7	26.3
1956		28.9	1974	27.9	26.9
1957		29.7	1975	30.1	30.4
1958		31.4	1976	32.0	33.7
1959	26.5	32.6	1977	32.7	35.3
1960	26.7	32.6	1978	32.7	35.9
1961	26.5	32.5	1979	34.6	37.2
1962	25.0	31.4	1980	36.2	38.0
1963	24.5	30.6	1981	37.3	39.9
1964	23.5	29.4	1982	37.5	40.4
1965	22.1	28.0	1983	35.1	39.3
1966	20.3	26.3	1984	35.5	39.8
1967	19.1	24.0	1985	35.6	40.1
1968	18.3	23.5	1986	34.6	38.7
1969	17.6	22.5	1987	34.7	37.0
1970	20.7	21.2	1988	32.5	35.0
			1989	31.0	32.8

Key to Table:
"Major Agreements": The Bureau of Labor Statistics series on effective wage adjustments in major collective bargaining contracts. The Major Agreements union series are effective mean or median (before 1968) wage adjustments (see table 1, note 3). Prior to 1966, construction, finance, and services were excluded from this series.
"AHE": The Bureau of Labor Statistics series on average hourly earnings by industry.
"AHE High union" is an average of the average hourly earnings in industries with high union density. Listed in descending order they are: railroad, coal mining, primary metals, transportation equipment manufacturing, paper, telephone communications, stone clay and glass, metal mining, petroleum refining, food products, fabricated metals, rubber, machinery, electrical equipment, chemicals, construction, tobacco, and electric power.
"AHE Low Union" is an average of the average hourly earnings in industries with low union density. Listed in ascending order they are: finance, insurance and real estate, service, crude and gas mining, retail trade, textile manufacturing, and wholesale trade.

British Post Office paid a large premium in 1974, then the close tracking of British Post Office wages since 1974 may have only narrowed an existing premium.

For the USPS, on the other hand, the historical record is relatively clear. Postal wages have increased much faster than overall wages, particularly since postal reorganization. Postal wages have increased approximately 20 percent faster than economy-wide wages for production and nonsupervisory workers since 1970. The results are presented in table 3.

Although the growth in the postal premium after 1970 may reflect the bargaining climate in the ten years following the Postal Reorganization Act, it does closely reflect the trend in union wages. Today's large union wage premium has increased significantly since 1970. Two union premium series are shown in table 4.[36] The series in column 3 shows a 50 percent increase in the premium from 1947 through 1959. From a low of 21.8 percent in 1947, the premium grew to 32.6 percent by 1959. Both premium series show a substantial decrease in the premium during the 1960s. The premium in column 2, our preferred series in terms of the reliability of the data, declined from 26.7 to a low of 17.6 in 1969. Between 1969 and 1974, the union wage premium increased back to and then beyond the 1959 level. Between 1974 and 1989, the series shows that the union premium in 1989 is above the level existing in 1960, prior to the 1960s decade of union wage moderation.[37]

The difficulty posed by the above data is that it shows that 1974 is not a neutral starting point, an issue that is important for drawing inferences from the British Post Office data. Both USPS wages and United States union wages increased significantly between 1969 and 1974. Hence, drawing inferences about the United Kingdom is made less reliable.

6.4. Labor Market Pressures

The final data on the British Post Office relative wage position deals with its ability to hire workers. As noted above, ultimately the test of whether a premium exists hinges on whether the firm has difficulty recruiting workers for job openings. The British Post Office data supports a difficulty in hiring workers in London and in the southeast area in general. "Even though postmen's earnings kept close to the average growth for all occupations between 1982 and 1987, this did not prevent some increase in voluntary resignation rates toward the end of the period."[38]

Their difficulty in hiring in London and the southeast, which differs sharply from the experience of the USPS, provides supporting evidence for the lack of a significant postal premium in the British Post Office.

On the other hand, the British Post Office does not have any reported difficulty in hiring workers in other regions of the country. This supports the existence of a small premium in these sectors of the economy. Alternatively, it may reflect the extra job security that goes with employment in an cyclical business.

As reported above, Abowd and Ashenfelter (1981) suggest that the value of job security, at least in the United States, may be approximately 14 percent. This factor would have to be added to both the USPS and the British Post Office, and hence would not affect their positions relative to each other. On the other hand, it would certainly add weight to a conclusion that the British Post Office pays a wage premium in regions outside of London and the southeast.

7. Conclusion

In this paper, we have presented evidence on the comparability rules guiding wage determination in the USPS and the British Post Office. Our results support the existence of a postal premium in the United States of approximately 21 percent compared to the private sector. Although available data sources are much richer for the United States than for the United Kingdom, we tentatively conclude that the British Post Office pays a slight wage premium compared to the private sector. This would include a zero premium in the London and southeast region, and a small premium in other regions.[39]

Our evidence suggests that the differences in achieving pay comparability rests on a number of factors. Most importantly, the British Post Office operates in a labor market in which the aggregate union premium is much lower than in the United States. The postal union-nonunion wage gap in the United States is approximately double the overall union-nonunion wage gap. Moreover, the postal wage is close to the high union wages in transportation and public utilities.

If the British Post Office patterned its wages on those of other United Kingdom unions, the result would be a small union-nonunion wage gap. Although our results are mixed due to data limitations, we cannot reject the possibility that the British Post Office pays a premium of approximately 6 percent, approximately one-half the aggregate wage premium of 10 percent calculated by Blanchflower and Freeman (1990).

As a consequence of the increase in the union premium in the United States over the past two decades, there has been a substantial loss in union employment shares. The losses are particularly severe in those industries where the premium has increased to historically very high levels. On the other hand, a much lower and more stable union wage premium in the United Kingdom has allowed unions to maintain their employment share.

Union employment shares have a feedback effect on the size of the premium. Our premium measures the postal wage against the entire private sector wage. That is, the premium does not take the nonunion sector as the base group. The higher the union employment share, the larger the weight of union wage scales in determining prevailing private sector wage rates. These facts alone would predict a lower union wage premium in the United Kingdom.

Union premiums in the private sectors of the United States and United Kingdom, however, cannot be the entire story. As noted above, the postal premium in the United States is greater than the overall union premium in the United States, while the postal premium in the United Kingdom appears to be smaller than the overall union premium in the United Kingdom.

The missing factor is likely to be the differences in the industrial relations and labor laws in the two countries. Although the differences are substantial in many areas, we have focused on the methods of resolving contract bargaining impasses. In the United States, where binding arbitration resolves any bargaining impasse, arbitrators have not always abided by the comparability mandate in the sense of unwinding the wage premium. The ability of postal management to implement the comparability rule has thus been missing. The result has been the large discrepancy from comparability. In the United Kingdom, where management has the ability to enforce comparability, albeit at the possible cost of a strike, the result has been wage setting that roughly achieves comparability.

Notes

The authors wish to thank William H. Carter for research assistance and Paul Richards, Frank Rodriguez, and Paul Kleindorfer for many useful suggestions.
1. Postal Reorganization Act, 39 U.S.C. paragraph 1003.
2. Our earlier work includes Perloff and Wachter (1984), Perloff (1989) and Linneman and Wachter (1990). Our results were presented to postal arbitration panels in 1981, 1982, 1984, and 1985.
3. Current postal operations in the United States and the United Kingdom can be traced to statutory changes made at approximately the same time. The British Post Office was established as a public authority by the Post Office Act of 1969. The USPS was established as an independent establishment of the executive branch of the government of the United States by the PRA of 1970.
4. Loveridge (1971).
5. Most corporations in the United Kingdom do not have a duty to bargain with the union that represents its members. The U.K. Post Office, however, does have a duty to bargain with postal unions. The U.K. Post Office is "to seek consultation with any organization appearing to it to be appropriate" with a view to the establishment of negotiating and arbitration machinery. Post Office Act 1969, sch. 1, para 11(1). In the United States, all private sector firms have a "duty to bargain" with unions that are certified by the National Labor Relations Board to represent the firm's employees.

For an excellent comparison of the right to strike under United States and United Kingdom labor law, see Katherine Van Wezel Stone, "Legal Regulation of Economic Weapons: A Comparative Perspective," presented at the NYU Conference on Labor Law, June 1990.
6. *The Post Office: Report and Accounts 1987-88.*
The great majority of strikes in the United Kingdom are "unofficial." Because "no strike" clauses cannot be enforced, there is little reason for British unions to engage in "official" strikes. The Post Office Act of 1953, section 58, which provides that any officer of the Post Office who "wilfully detains or delays" any postal packet commits an offence, primarily relates to "go-slows," "work to rule," and "overtime bans." It appears that these types of employee actions have been restricted by the union leadership (Hepple and O'Higgins 1971).

This lack of a distinction between official and unofficial actions in the United Kingdom differs sharply from labor law in the United States. In the sectors where strikes are legal, most collective bargaining contracts contain "no strike" clauses which are enforced to the letter. In addition, strikes are permissible only over "mandatory topics of bargaining," a term which covers "wages, hours and other terms and conditions of employment" (Cox, Bok, and Gorman 1989).
7. This loss of power at least occurred in the 1980s and 1990s, a time when union power waned in the United States. See Tierney (1981) for a discussion of postal negotiations and arbitrations during the 1970s.
8. *The Post Office: Report and Accounts 1988-89.*
9. The CPS is a large household data base for the entire United States population with observations across individuals, including a set of demographic, skill, and regional variables for each observation. Sampling is by household location.
10. Other empirical studies which indirectly support a substantial USPS premium, by examining quit rates and employment queues are discussed in section 5.
11. They also appear to restrict their comparison to unionized firms. This occurs because of the presence of a "union density" variable in the equation. Since the average union membership is approximately 80 percent, and because union density is a control variable, the implicit comparison is to industries with similarly high union densities.
12. Their argument for also restricting the sample to large firms is based on the work of Mellow (1982; 1983), which is discussed below.
13. This discussion is based on Linneman and Wachter (1990) but uses new empirical results.
14. The technique was used by Ronald Oaxaca (1973) to study wage differentials by gender and by Smith (1977) to study wage differentials between the government and private sectors.

15. A separate question can be raised as to whether labor law, in protecting collective bargaining, should also be interpreted as protecting union wage premiums. In other words, once the federal law allows for collective bargaining, does it also protect any resulting union wage premium for government workers? The law and economics literature in labor law does not support this contention. Labor law only protects the bargaining process and not the bargaining outcomes. See Wachter and Cohen (1988).

Alternatively, one might choose to compare only skill-adjusted government wages to wages in the non-union private sector. This perspective implicitly argues that Congress mandated federal wages to be comparable to "competitive" wages in the private sector. We believe that this interpretation of Congressional intent is too narrow because a worker losing a federal government job has a positive probability of obtaining a unionized job in the private sector. Thus, the comparable wage opportunity for federal workers is a weighted average of union and non-union wages in the private sector, where the weights reflect the probabilities of finding employment in these respective sectors.

16. A separate issue is the wage gap between large and small firms in the union sector is smaller than in the nonunion sector. The difference, in part, can be attributed to the greater "threat effect" of unionization in the large firms in the nonunion sector compared to smaller nonunion firms. To the extent that these wage differentials are related to such competitive factors, they should be treated as job-descriptive. For a discussion of this issue, see Pearce (1990) and Podgursky (1986).

17. This model rests on competitive equilibrium properties of the economy and does not require the introduction of non-competitive sectors. This model is more reasonable when applied to the private rather than to a government agency. The large private sector firms in the equilibrium wage model reflect realized economies-of-scale. The government agency, however, is large for political, not for economic, reasons. That is, there can be no presumption that the large size of the federal firm is driven by the competitive need to reduce costs by realizing economies-of-scale in the production of government services.

18. After estimating (1), the first step in calculating an industry premium is to obtain wage differentials for each of the subgroups in the cross-product space of the job-related dimensions. This space has dimension equal to the number of characteristics to be treated as job-related. If firm size, union status, and industry constitute I, for example, the dimension is 3. The number of elements in the space is given by the product of the number of (mutually exclusive) categories in each dimension. Continuing the example, one might have 2 union statuses multiplied by 5 firm size categories multiplied by 10 industries for a total of 100 subgroups. Interactions between job-related dimensions do not increase the size of the space, although they do add independent variables.

19. The exponentiation is required because a simple coefficient sum is not the correct estimate of the percentage impacts of dummy variables in a log-linear regression. This formula is an approximation that assumes the relevant variance-covariance matrix is "small."

20. For example, if union is the only job descriptive dimension, then j is either union or nonunion. Alternatively, if there were two establishment size categories, each interacted with union status, then there would be four values, for example, one for nonunion-small establishment, one for nonunion large establishment, one for union large establishment and one for union small establishment.

21. The differential in (4) is relative to the omitted set of job-related traits. A similar aggregate differential is then constructed for the desired base industry, and the industry premiums are renormalized to be relative to this base.

22. The difficulties in controlling costs in regulated industries is stressed by Posner (1985).

23. In this study, professionals, managers, and technicians are excluded (although including them makes little quantitative difference) on the grounds that their job decisions are different than most of those workers in the USPS. To keep the number of observations manageable, we use all the USPS workers but only a one-in-ten random sample of other workers. Appropriate weights reflecting this sampling scheme are used in the estimates reported below.

24. Variants of the approach used by Gyourko and Tracy (1988) were also tried with limited success. Their estimation procedure is an application of Heckman's technique in which he controls for sample selection in either industry (government) choice or union status. Based on both Heckman and Hausman type tests, we did not find that union status mattered in the sense that treating it as an exogenous variable was likely to lead to sample selection bias. Moreover, we were unable to estimate the union status and USPS status equations simultaneously using a joint bivariate probit routine. We also experimented with using government status (as opposed to USPS status) with little difference in our results. For these reasons, we only consider USPS status in the equations reported here.

25. The selection equation reported here was also estimated using probit rather than logit, and the wage differential results were quantitatively very close as were the various measures of goodness of fit. See Perloff (1989).

26. The correlation between the logit equation and the wage equation was statistically significant (asymptotic t-statistic of 2.93), whereas the correlation between the probit equation and the corresponding wage equation was not. Other than that difference, the results are virtually the same in the two models.

27. For the specific equation results, see Perloff (1989).

28. These calculations are from Perloff (1989).

29. At the time of the Mail Handlers' arbitration hearing in 1981, for example, newspapers reported how a handful of New York City openings brought in more than 100,000 applications and that police had to be called in Baltimore to control a crowd of 7,000 people that formed after word got out that some postal jobs were being filled. See, *San Francisco Chronicle*, May 10, 1981, "This World," p. 5. The *New York Times*, April 2, 1981, p. A24, reported that when the Postal Service listed 20 positions (paying more than $17,000 per year) at the main post office in Baltimore, 15,000 people picked up applications. Potential employees waited in block-long lines for the application for examinations for jobs that might open up later that year or early in 1982.

30. The data and analysis are in "National Trends in Earnings Since the Mid 1970s. A data limitation for our purposes is that the postal earnings are only for male workers.

31. Although postal workers are not a direct match for manual workers, this comparison is obviously more relevant in terms of market forces than is the all-occupation comparison. Non-manual occupations include professional and managerial occupations. In both countries, these occupations have received much higher salary increases than have lower skilled occupations. However, the manual category does have its limitations. Postal workers work at an unusual blend of blue-and white collar tasks. In the United States, for example, postal workers are included in a broadly defined clerical group that includes office machine operators, communications operators, and material recording, scheduling and distributing clerks.

32. This is true even though approximately 95 percent of postmen/women grade workers are males. Unless the Post Office were attempting to recruit mostly male workers or, if male characteristics were a necessary feature of the job, average private sector wages should be the basis of a wage comparison.

33. The statistics used in this section on United Kingdom unions are from Blanchflower and Freeman (1990). Beenstock and Whitbread (1988), however, using the methodology of Layard, Metcalf, and Nickell (1978) find a rising premium.

34. See Linneman, Wachter, and Carter (1990).

35. Non-manual earnings increased 15.5 percent, which reflects the more favorable excess demand conditions for the highest skilled occupations.

36. The construction of the series is explained in Wachter and Carter (1990).

37. The gains in the union premium, however, have come at the cost of a substantial decline in union employment shares. As discussed in Linneman, Wachter, and Carter (1990), union employment has fallen from close to 30 to under 20 percent of the civilian work force between 1973 and 1987. In the heavily unionized industries have declined from close to 50 percent, to below 30 percent.

38. "National Trends," p. 14. Since this study was written in 1987, postal wages have increased faster than male manual wages.

39. Lacking a data set comparable to the CPS, any conclusions comparing the United States and United Kingdom postal premiums must be viewed as tentative. This is especially the case given the disagreement as to the union premium in the United Kingdom between Blanchflower and Freeman (1990) versus Beenstock and Whitbread (1988).

References

Abowd, John M., and Orley Ashenfelter. 1981. "Unemployment, Layoffs, and Wage Differentials." In *Studies in Labor Markets*, edited by Sherwin Rosen. Chicago: University of Chicago Press.

Adie, Douglas K. 1977. *An Evaluation of Postal Sector Wages*. Washington, DC: American

Enterprise Institute.

Akerlof, George A. 1984. "Gift Exchange and Efficiency Wages: Four Views." *American Economic Review* 74 (no. 2, May): 79-83.

Akerlof, George A., and Janet Yellen. 1985. "A Near Rational Model of the Business Cycle with Wage and Price Inertia." *Quarterly Journal of Economics* 74 (no. 3, August): 823-838.

Asher, Martin, and Joel Popkin. 1984. "The Effect of Gender and Race Differentials on Public-Private Wage Comparisons: A Study of Postal Workers." *Industrial and Labor Relations Review* 38 (no. 1, October): 16-26.

Beenstock, Michael, and Chris Whitbread. 1988. "Explaining Changes in the Union Mark-Up for Mail Manual Workers in Great Britain, 1953-1983." *British Journal of Industrial Relations* 26 (no. 3, November): 327-338.

Blanchflower, David G., and Richard B. Freeman. 1990. "Going Different Ways: Unionism in the U.S. and other Advanced O.E.C.D. Countries." National Bureau of Economics Research, Working Paper #3342, April.

Borjas, George J. 1980a. *Wage Policy in the Federal Bureaucracy*. Washington, DC: American Enterprise Institute.

Borjas, George J. 1980b. "Wage Determination in the Federal Government: The Role of Constituents and Bureaucrats." *Journal of Political Economy* 88 (no. 6, December): 1110-1147.

Cox, Archibald, Derek Curtis Bok, and Robert A. Gorman. 1988. *Cases and Materials on Labor Law*, 10th ed. New York: The Foundation Press.

Eck, Alan. 1984. "New Occupational Separation Data Improve Estimates of Job Replacement Needs." *Monthly Labor Review* 107 (no. 3, March): 3-10.

Gyourko, Joseph, and Joseph Tracy. 1988. "An Analysis of Public- and Private-Sector Wages Allowing for Endogenous Choices of Both Government and Union Status." *Journal of Labor Economics* 6 (no 2, April): 229-253.

Halvorsen, Robert and Raymond Palmquist. 1980. "The Interpretation of Dummy Variables in Semilogarithmic Equations." *American Economic Review* 70 (no. 3, June): 474-475.

Hepple, B.A., and Paul O'Higgins. 1971. *Public Employee Trade Unionism in the United Kingdom: The Legal Framework*. Ann Arbor: Institute of Labor and Industrial Relations, University of Michigan—Wayne State University.

Kennedy, Peter E. 1981. "Estimation with Correctly Interpreted Dummy Variables in Semilogarithmic Equations." *American Economic Review* 71 (no. 4, September).

Layard, R., D. Metcalf, and S. Nickell. 1978. "The Effects of Collective Bargaining on Relative and Absolute Wages." *British Journal of Industrial Relations* 16 (no. 3, November): 287-302.

Linneman, Peter D., and Michael L. Wachter. 1990. "The Economics of Federal Compensation." *Industrial Relations* 29 (no. 1, Winter): 58-76.

Linneman, Peter D., Michael L. Wachter, and William H. Carter. 1990. "Evaluating the Evidence on Union Employment and Wages." *Industrial Labor Relations Review* (forthcoming).

Loveridge, Raymond. 1971. *Collective Bargaining by National Employees in the United Kingdom*. Ann Arbor: Institute of Labor and Industrial Relations, University of Michigan—Wayne State University.

Mellow, Wesley. 1982. "Employer Size and Wages." *Review of Economics and Statistics* 64 (no. 3, August): 495-501.

Mellow, Wesley. 1983. "Employer Size, Unionism, and Wages." In *New Approaches to Labor Unions*, edited by Joseph D. Reid, Jr., Research in Labor Economics. 2 Supple-

ment. Greenwich, CT: JAI Press. 253-282.
Pearce, James E. 1990. "Tenure, Unions, and the Relationship between Employer Size and Wages." *Journal of Labor Economics* 8 (2, April): 251-269.
Perloff, Jeffrey M. and Michael L. Wachter. 1984. "Wage Comparability in the U. S. Postal Service." *Industrial and Labor Relations Review* 38 (1, October): 26-35.
Perloff, Jeffrey M. 1989. "U. S. Postal Service Labor Issues," University of California, Berkeley. March.
Podgursky, Michael. 1986. "Unions, Establishment Size, and Intra-industry Threat Effects." *Industrial and Labor Relations Review* 39 (1, January): 277-284.
Posner, Richard A. 1985. "Some Economics of Labor Law." in *Labor Law and the Employment Market*, edited by Richard A. Epstein and Jeffrey Paul. New Brunswick, NJ: Transaction Inc.
Quinn, Joseph F. 1979. "Postal Sector Wages." *Industrial Relations* 18 (no. 1, Winter): 92-95.
Smith, Sharon P. 1976. "Are Postal Workers Over- or Underpaid?" *Industrial Relations* 15 (no. 2, May): 168-176.
Smith, Sharon P. 1977. *Equal Pay in the Public Sector: Fact or Fantasy*. Princeton, NJ: Industrial Relations Section, Department of Economics, Princeton University.
Tierney, John T. 1981. *Postal Reorganization: Managing the Public's Business*. Boston: Auburn House.
Wachter, Michael L., and William H. Carter. 1990. "Norm Shifts in Union Wages: Will 1989 be a Replay of 1969?" *Brookings Papers on Economic Activity*. (no. 1): 272-302.
Wachter, Michael L., and George M. Cohen. 1988. "The Law and Economics of Collective Bargaining: An Introduction and Application to the Problems of Subcontracting, Partial Closure, and Relocation." *University of Pennsylvania Law Review* 136 (no. 5, May): 1349-1417.

COMMENTS
Frank Rodriguez

At the risk of oversimplification, the main points in the Wachter and Perloff (WP) paper can be summed up as follows—
(i) In the United States, there is a postal wage premium relative to all private sector workers of between 20% and 30%, the figure depending on how precisely the premium is measured (the WP preferred estimate is 21.3% in table 2, row 1).
(ii) In the United Kingdom, the premium is much smaller, and, although WP cannot apply the same estimation methods as they do for the United States, they "cannot reject the possibility... [that the premium is] approximately 6 percent".
(iii) The main reasons for the difference are stated to be a larger union wage premium in the United States (due to a combination of rent-sharing and United States unions' preference functions) and the United States arbitration system's role in postal wage determination, which has failed to eliminate these premia.

The comments below are organized under these three heads, emphasizing United Kingdom issues.

The basis used for comparability is individualistic and applies regression analysis to estimate "wage differentials between otherwise identical workers in the postal service and private sector." Looked at slightly differently, these estimates imply "expected wage prospects of postal workers if they were to leave for the private sector." In a wage determination context, when comparability has been applied in the United Kingdom, it has tended to rest not on this individualistic perspective. Instead, it has depended on the characteristics of occupations, so that it has been job content and profiles rather than the characteristics of individuals that have mattered. For example, jobs would be judged comparable in terms of whether they carried equivalent degrees of responsibility or pattern of hours worked and so on.

WP suggest that the United Kingdom postal wage premium is lower than the United States, and, although this may well be so, they cannot show this from the measure of comparability they are able to use on United Kingdom data. As they indicate clearly, to estimate a premium satisfactorily requires disaggregated data on individuals' earnings, their characteristics or "traits", and job-specific variables. The only United Kingdom source which potentially can provide data covering these areas is the New Earnings Survey (NES, an annual 1% sample of employees in employment). But data from the NES have not been used in that way here.

Of necessity, the United Kingdom comparisons in the paper are much simpler, though they have the same objective as those for the United States, namely an individualistically-based measure of a premium. The United Kingdom comparisons just look at the level of earnings of postal workers in the NES (male, manipulative grades) against possible comparator groups outside, with the 6% figure quoted above showing the "premium" in this sense against all manual workers. Given that the premium is an estimate of how much less the "expected wage prospects of postal workers (would be) if they were to leave" for a job in the comparator set, but that the postal earnings data quoted are for males only, then the comparator set should also be male. This would reduce the "premium" measured on this basis to roughly zero but, in any case, any estimate along these lines shows very little. To estimate a premium (or discount for that matter) would require an application of the methodology applied to the United States. However, data on quits, some of which are covered in the paper, suggest that the general proposition that the United States premium is higher than the United Kingdom's is valid. The United Kingdom is prone to much higher and cyclically variable quit rates which would be difficult to square with a view that postal wages are relatively high and that some premium exists.

Why then should there be such large differences? From a United Kingdom perspective, the most puzzling feature in the United States is the role of the arbitrator there and their interpretation/application of comparability rules. Differences in institutions and practice between the countries seem to be of importance. For the United Kingdom, WP fail to include a consideration of government's role. The postal wage setting process takes place against a background of control exerted by government over the United Kingdom Post Office as a nationalized industry. These controls are principally a financial or profit target and a real unit cost target, where the pressure is to reduce real costs year on year. The combined effect of these controls is to squeeze the wage bill. Periodically, particularly towards the top of the business cycle, relative pay deteriorates as outside pay races ahead and quits rise significantly.

In this context, notions of comparability and "premia" or otherwise are not of direct relevance. Rather it is competitiveness which matters and these things differ, inter alia, because of compensating differentials, as pointed out by WP, and regional factors, if comparability can only be estimated nationally. In the United Kingdom, bargaining needs to satisfy recruitment and retention objectives, and in this it seems closer to the market than the United States system. Indeed, the issue of postal wage competitiveness in the United Kingdom is much more immediate than appears to be the case in the United States.

7
PRODUCTIVITY AND COST MEASUREMENT FOR THE UNITED STATES POSTAL SERVICE: Variations Among Regions

J.R. Norsworthy
Show-Ling Jang
Wei-Ming Shi

1. Introduction

This paper extends the application of cost function-based analysis of productivity to the complex service sector, where it is generally believed that the influence of worker attitudes on productivity is greater than in manufacturing sectors. Also introduced is an explicit model of worker attitude formation, based on measures of workload, supervision, and the organization of production. The data base for the study is a cross-section of 200 Management Sectional Centers for the United States Postal Service (USPS) for 1984. These Management Sectional Centers (MSCs) have responsibility for mail collection, forwarding, and delivering for geographic regions that completely cover all 50 states. The resulting cost model is used to estimate productivity at these 200 MSCs, as well as the cost of serving the particular geographic areas, characterized in terms of the number of delivery points, population, and areas served in square miles.

The form for the production model is the translog variable cost function with eight output categories of delivered and collected mail, three descriptors of the geographic area (hereafter abbreviated "network") served, five labor input categories, materials input, and three quasi-fixed capital inputs. The worker attitude formation submodel, which uses absenteeism as an indicator of worker attitude, has measures of workload, supervision, and the organization and mechanization of delivery.

The results are very interesting. The model shows a large fixed cost associated with the network served and generally declining marginal costs of delivery on the network. Negative worker attitudes have a very large cost elasticity compared with manufacturing sectors studied earlier (Norsworthy and Zabala 1985a; 1985b). The shadow costs of capital inputs are very near zero, although they interact significantly with the output and network elements of the model. Substantial productivity differences are found to exist among MSCs within regions and size classes, even after appropriate measurement of output (pieces of mail weighted by marginal costs and inclusion of network as a dimension of output). These productivity differences suggest scope for improvement in particular MSCs and hence of overall system performance.

The paper also demonstrates the versatility of the translog cost function model for describing complex production processes. The t-statistics for most of the estimated coefficients are significant, which indicates that two hundred observations at the cost center level suffice to define the production process in services reasonably well. Further, examination of individual model coefficients in section 3. gives results that are generally plausible when interpreted in the light of the functioning of the USPS and refutes the often-heard (but never published) criticism that "... all those coefficients [in translog models of production] mean nothing to anyone."

Productivity measurement for the system as a whole requires parametric estimates of the system's marginal cost for each type of mail processed by the system, because postal rates are determined administratively and may, therefore, differ substantially from marginal costs. There are at least two good reasons to believe that the conventional equilibrium condition, "marginal cost equals marginal revenue," does not hold for the postal service: the charges for mail collection and delivery do not vary with the volume of mail processed (and there is evidence that the costs *do* vary), and internal efforts to attribute costs inevitably respond to administrative as well as measurement objectives.[1]

Without adjustment for the effects of worker attitude, the cost function model exhibited nonconcavity in most of the labor inputs and somewhat unstable weights for the mail classes and network measures comprising the workload of the system. Consequently, an indicator of worker attitude has been included in the basic model specification, and there is no credible base case that omits it. For the attitude formation submodel, we have simply used a "second-order reduced form"—a translog approximation to the function determining worker attitude based on nine variables reflecting management decisions and partial workload descriptions. The principal focus of this paper is to develop productivity measures for MSCs from the estimated production model; more prescriptive results of the worker attitude model are discussed in Norsworthy, Jang, and Rebne (1989).

The framework of the paper is as follows. Section 2 outlines the econometric cost function model. The empirical results of the estimation are discussed in section 3. Productivity and network costs by region and classes are presented in section 4. Section 5 presents conclusions and implications for future research. The data on which the study is based are described in Appendix A. The five administrative regions for the United States are defined in Appendix B.

2. The Choice of the Variable Cost Function Model for the USPS[2]

The restricted variable cost function (VCF) model that is estimated for the panel of MSCs for 1984 is the least restrictive model that can be applied which results in estimates of marginal costs by class of service, economies of scale, and economies of scope. These, of course, are chief among the variables to be considered in appraising the prospects for privatization of postal services. The VCF model requires the assumption that variable costs of production are minimized and that the prices of the variable inputs are not influenced by how much of each is used by the MSC. The latter assumption is likely to be fulfilled. The former, treated at greater length below, can certainly be debated, but not, with present modeling techniques, improved upon. The VCF model does not require the assumption that capital is adjusted to its long-run equilibrium value at each observation point, nor does it require any particular assumption about competition in the markets for outputs.

Alternative models that lead to estimates of marginal costs and economies of scale and scope include the total cost function, the production function, and the total and variable profit functions.

The profit functions require the additional assumption that profit is maximized, as well as knowledge (or joint estimation) of the elasticities of output demands on the relevant range. The production function treats input quantities as externally fixed or exogenous. It is generally considered, however, that input prices are more likely to be externally fixed and the input quantities model-determined or endogenous, and, therefore, the cost function is preferred to the production function.[3]

In the USPS as in most enterprises, capital input is not quickly adjusted. Treatment of capital as exogenously fixed in the short-run is likewise realistic: capital spending and its allocation to particular MSCs is determined with considerable external (to the MSC) guidance. Consequently, the cost function or profit function (which includes a cost function) has been the model of choice in most recent work. The assumptions of profit maximization and endogenous determination of the prices of outputs, which characterize the profit function models, are inappropriate for the USPS. Rather, output prices are predetermined in the ratemaking process, and the service must serve all comers at those prices; thus, exogenous determination of output is the appropriate assumption. Given the comparative information requirements and stringency of assumptions of the other production models, the variable cost function is clearly the most appropriate and most realistic for applications to the USPS.

The point is then made that such variation as *does* occur among the prices of labor inputs across MSCs is due to variations in the mix of seniority and occupational subgroups, and that the associated wage differentials do not measure "true" productivity differences. An advantage of the demand equation estimation scheme applied here is that such errors in variables are forced into the residuals of the input demand equations and do not affect the estimated structural parameters to the same degree that they would in estimation of the cost share equations.[4]

There may be no cost minimizing adjustment in the USPS, or so little that its effects do not emerge through the noise of errors in measurement. To understand the effects of this possibility, consider three cases that would be expected to engender cost minimizing responses in the quantities demanded of variable inputs: changes in input prices, changes in output quantities, and changes in other factors affecting the technology of production.

Production theory requires that the production technology exhibit homogeneity of the first degree in prices of inputs and that the function be non-convex (downward) in input prices and monotonically nondecreasing in output quantities (Nadiri 1986; Diewert 1982). Violation of either of these conditions could be interpreted as evidence against cost minimization.

If a change in an input price occurs, the primary effect should be a move in the input quantity demanded of opposite sign or no move at all; i.e., the demand elasticity should be non-positive. That is the case for all variable inputs in the model at all MSCs. In the case of the demand for other workers, where that condition is imposed, the response was perverse before imposition of the parameter restriction at about 20% of the MSCs. Even after restraining the parameter value, however, the estimated demand equation explains 99% of the variation in the demand for other workers. And because the composition of the "other workers category" varies considerably among MSCs, it is not surprising that the price response before restraining the parameter was perverse in many cases.

If a change in output occurs, then, in general, the input quantity demanded will move in the same direction. This can be seen intuitively by replacing C in equation (3) by the exponential of its estimation expression based on equation (1) to separate mail volumes and network from other factors affecting the technology of production. The first-order terms are then seen to be

$$\hat{C} = a_o \, \Pi_i \, p_i \, a_i \, \Pi_m \, y_m \, b_m \, \Pi_d \, Q^{dk}$$

(The second order terms are constrained so that there are zero average effects in the neighborhood of the approximation and need not enter this part of the analysis.) $\hat{C}$, the first-order component of variable cost may then be seen to increase unambiguously with an increase in any output, since the a_i and b_m coefficients are positive: thus, C in equation (3) below will rise. Correspondingly, the input demand quantity in equation (3) will rise because its cost share $\partial \ln C / \partial \ln P_i$ is also positive. Second-order terms appearing in the estimated form of C and in the cost share expression modify the increase in the use of the input depending upon other inputs, the output mix, the quantities applied of various types of capital, and other factors influencing the technology of production. (The translog cost function even accommodates the case where an increase in some output would actually reduce the demand for an input through strong economies of scope, but that did not occur in this application.) If an input is specialized to particular outputs, it is well within the scope of the translog variable cost function for a zero or negligible net response to occur when some other output is increased. In short, cost minimization requires no particular response in variable input demand when a particular output is increased; thus, there is no unambiguous test for a cost-minimizing response to increases in output in the multiproduct case.

3. The Econometric Model

The mail collection and forwarding and delivery activities of the USPS were modeled using a translog restricted variable cost function based on Brown and Christensen (1981). The translog restricted variable cost function is a second order approximation to a general cost function with multiple outputs, variable inputs, and quasi-fixed inputs:

$$CV = f(P, Q, Y),$$

where P,Q,Y are vectors of the prices of variable inputs, quantities of quasi-fixed inputs, and quantities of outputs (including the network served), respectively. In extended form, the translog approximation is written

$$lnCV = a_o + \sum_i a_i \, lnP_i + \frac{1}{2} \sum_i \sum_j a_{ij} \, lnP_i \, lnP_j + \sum_m b_m \, lnY_m$$

$$+ \frac{1}{2} \sum_m \sum_n b_m \, lnY_m \, lnY_n + \sum_i \sum_m c_{im} \, lnP_i \, lnY_n + \sum_K d_K \, lnQ_K$$

$$+ \frac{1}{2} \sum_K \sum_l d_K \, lnQ_K \, lnQ_l + \sum_i \sum_K l_{im} \, lnP_i \, lnQ_K + \sum_n \sum_K f_{iK} \, lnY_m \, lnQ_K. \quad (1)$$

This general form of the model has an unmanageably large number of parameters for ready estimation, given the numbers of outputs and variable and quasi-fixed inputs that we wish to represent. Consequently, for purposes of interaction with the inputs and each other, the mail output types are grouped into delivered *(D)* and collected mail, network into a single group *(N)*, and capital into a single group *(K)*, each of the last two groups having three members. Second-order interactions were also limited among components within these groups. This procedure results in a kind of separability similar to that imposed by Norsworthy and Zabala (1985a; 1985b) in earlier studies of worker attitudes and productivity.

The resulting translog restricted VCF is written

$$lnCV = a_o + \sum_i a_i \, lnP_i + \frac{1}{2} \sum_i \sum_j a_{ij} \, lnP_i \, lnP_j + \sum_r y_r Z_r$$

$$+ \frac{1}{2} \sum_r \sum_s y_{rs} Z_r Z_s + \sum_i \sum_r c_{ir} \, lnP_i \, Z_r \quad (2)$$

where $i, j = c, d, t, o, p, m$; c = customer service worker; d = mail carriers; t = materials; o = other workers; p = postmasters and supervisors; m = mailhandlers; $r, s = d, c, n, k, x$; d = delivered mail; c = collected mail; n = network; k = capital; x = worker attitude, and

$$Z_c = \sum_m b_m \ln Y_m \sum_m b_m = 1, m = f, t, o,$$

where f = first class mail, t = third class mail, and o = other mail, is the *collected mail* subfunction.

$$Z_d = \sum_n b_n \ln Y_n, d_n b_n = 1, n = f, t, o$$

is the *delivered mail* subfunction, wher

$$e \ln Y_f = \ln Y_o - a_{Pl} \times P_l,$$

$$\ln Y_t = \ln Y_{ot} - a_{P3} \times P_3,$$

$\ln Y_{of}$ is the log of first class delivered mail, P_l is the proportion of first class mail that is presorted, and a_{Pl} is an estimated parameter for the effect of presorting. $\ln Y_{ot}$, P_3, and a_P are defined analogously for third class mail. Z_n is the *network* subfunction,

$$Z_n = \sum_o b_o \ln N_o, \sum_o b_o = 1, o = n, p, a$$

where n = number of delivery points, p = population, and a = area served in square miles.

Z_K is the *capital* subfunction,

$$Z_K = \sum_c b_l \ln K_l, \sum_K b_K = 1, K = b, m, v$$

where b = buildings, m = mail processing, and v = vehicles, customer service, and other equipment.

Z_x is the worker attitude indicator, $Z_x = q(T)$, where T is a set of supervisory ratios, workload, and organizational characteristics that affect worker attitude, and Z_x is a measure of absenteeism based on excess sick leave and leave without pay.

Within each of the subfunctions, the coefficients are restricted to sum to unity; thus the b coefficients may be thought of as distributing the y_r and c_{ir} coefficients to the components of the subfunctions.

Homogeneity of first degree in prices of variable inputs is imposed by

$$\sum_i a_i = 1; \quad \sum_i a_{ij} = \sum_j a_{ij} = \sum_i c_{ir} = 0$$

for $i, j = c, d, t, o, p, m$, $r = d, c, n, k, x$.

Homogeneity in the Z subfunctions is also imposed by

$$\sum_r y_{rs} = \sum_s y_{rs} = 0, \quad r, s = d, c, n, k, x$$

The latter restrictions are not required, but they simplify estimation. It is desirable and may be possible to test these restrictions in subsequent research.

The y_{rs} coefficients measure second-order interactions among the output, network, and capital subfunctions, and between those subfunctions and the indicator of worker attitude. The second-order terms for individual subfunctions, y_{rr} denote economies or diseconomies of scale for the delivered and collected mail and network activities according to whether they are negative or positive, respectively. The cross terms, y_{rs} for $r \neq s$, denote economies or diseconomies of scope for y_{rs} negative or positive respectively.

First-order restrictions are also imposed such that the coefficients are nonnegative for first and third mail classes, delivered and collected, and for all components of network.

Thus for the delivered mail subfunction Z_d, $y_d > 0$ and $b_n > 0$, $n = f, t, o$; for the collected mail subfunction Z_c, $y_c > 0$ and $b_m > 0$, $m = f, t, o$; for the network subfunction Z_n, $y_n > 0$ and $b_o > 0$, $o = n, p, a$; and for the capital subfunction Z_k, $y_K M < 0$ and $b_l > 0$, $l = b, m, v$.

The resulting model of USPS production had 73 free parameters in the cost function and 55 free parameters in the worker attitude formation model.

Demand equations were estimated for the inputs jointly with the cost function, based on the additive general error model (AGEM) discussed and illustrated for the translog total cost function by McElroy (1987).[5] This specification proved superior to the conventional approach, estimating the share equations jointly with the cost function.

The AGEM is formulated as follows.

Let $CV = C(p,Z,e)$ be the cost expression, with $h(p,Z)$ the translog variable cost function. Then

$$C = \exp[h(p,Z)] + \sum_i p_i e_i$$

is the stochastic form of the cost function, where $h(p,Z)$ is the translog restricted variable cost function in (2) above and e_i is the error term in (3) below.

Estimable demand equations for variable inputs are then derived simply by

$$\frac{\partial C}{\partial p_i} = q_i = \left(\frac{C}{p_i}\right) \times \left(\frac{\partial \ln C}{\partial \ln p_i}\right) + e_i, \quad i = c, d, t, o, p, m, \quad (3)$$

where, by Shephard's Lemma and the assumptions of cost minimization, $\dfrac{\partial \ln C}{\partial \ln p_i}$ is simply the conventional share expression

$$s_i = a_i + \sum_j a_{ij} \ln P_j + \sum_r c_{ir} Z_r, \quad i = c, d, t, o, p, m. \quad (4)$$

All demand equations are stochastically independent, whereas in the conventional approach, one share equation is redundant. The demand equations, cost function, and the worker attitude subfunction were simultaneously estimated using the full information maximum likelihood method (FIML) in the SORITEC econometric software package. The AGEM approach proved superior to the cost shares approach in that far fewer (about half) the number of iterations to solution were required compared to the conventional approach, and the parameter estimates were more stable in the face of small changes in model specification.

The criticism has been made that the prices show little variation from one MSC to another, and that the model will therefore (somehow) be underidentified. In fact, the model requires no variation whatsoever in prices of variable inputs; the variable input demand function in equation (3) is a function not only of input prices but of the various output quantities, the network served, and the capital applied in the MSC. The major sources of variation in input demand among MSCs may indeed lie elsewhere than in the input prices. If there is insufficient variation in all the determinants of input demand to explain the movements in input quantities demanded, then the estimated demand equations will show large unexplained variation. If the estimated input demand quantities in this model were poorly explained by the independent variables in the demand equations, the properties of explained total variation in quantities demanded, the R^2, would be low. Quite to the contrary, they are relatively high, particularly for a cross-section model. There is nothing in the theory of production generally nor in the conditions for estimation of a cost function-based model of production that requires any particular degree of variation in the variable input prices. The prices may in fact be identical across MSCs as long as other variables show sufficient variation to identify the demand equations. But both require that those prices appear in the cost function and in the input demand equations.

4. Empirical Results of the Cost Function Estimation

The model is large and complex, so discussion of the results is separated into several parts: the overall model results and the estimated coefficients of variable inputs, delivered mail, collected mail, network, and capital. The worker attitude formation function results are discussed in section 4.

Interpretation of the empirical findings from a large econometric model such as we report here is not a simple matter; correct interpretation often depends upon knowing how the postal system operates. For example, a large coefficient for interaction of collected mail with mailhandlers is easily interpreted only if one knows that the sorting and routing of unpresorted mail is carried out primarily by mailhandlers. However, many of the effects are so clear that even those without detailed knowledge of the USPS may correctly interpret the results.

4.1. Overall Model Results

Table 1 shows equation statistics for the seven equations simultaneously estimated. The adjusted R-squared statistics for the demand equations all indicate that a large fraction of the variation in demand for each input is explained by the model.[6] The poorest fit is for postmasters and supervisors (q_p), but even in that case, more than three-fourths of the variation in demand for the input is accounted for by the model.

Table 1. Equation Statistics

Dependent Variable	Equation Type	Adjusted R-squared
lncv	VCF	0.9617
q_c	demand	0.9270
q_d	demand	0.9833
q_t	demand	0.9727
q_o	demand	0.9887
q_p	demand	0.7622
q_m	demand	0.9737
x	attitude formation	0.6265
Log of Likelihood Function		5305.6

4.2. Variable Inputs

Table 2 shows estimated and inferred parameters for the first order and interaction effects among variable inputs. The first-order parameters, a_c, a_d, etc., are just average cost shares for the variable inputs, ranging from about 37 percent for mail carriers, a_d, down to less than 8 percent for other workers, a_o.

Own price elasticities of demand are negative for all variable inputs except at four data points (out of 1200). However, concavity in its price is imposed on the demand function for other workers (which has one remaining nonconcave data

Table 2. Estimated Coefficients of Variable Inputs and Their Interactions

Parameter Name	Estimated Value	T-statistic	Parameter Name	Estimated Value	T-statistic
a_o	0.0202	5.3352	a_{cd}	-0.0047	-1.1923
a_c	0.1323	64.8151	a_{ct}	0.0056	1.6142
a_d	0.3689	129.2270	a_{co}	-0.0041	-1.1228
a_t	0.0873	80.3892	a_{cp}	0.0239	6.8509
a_o	0.0782	76.1555	a_{dt}	-0.0309	-5.6921
a_p	0.1108	58.0114	a_{do}	-0.0804	-17.4308
a_{cc}	0.0008	0.2176	a_{dp}	0.0277	5.0510
a_{dd}	0.1382	9.6623	a_{to}	0.0029	0.8727
a_{tt}	-0.0039	-0.9396	a_{tp}	0.0405	13.9440
a_{pp}	-0.1704	-29.6105	a_{op}	0.0358	7.8322
a_{oo}	0.0200	Restricted Value			
Inferred Parameters					
a_m	0.2225	78.3209	a_{om}	0.0257	4.3587
a_{cm}	-0.0216	-3.0204	a_{pm}	0.0425	6.2166
a_{dm}	-0.0499	-5.8991	a_{mm}	0.0175	1.4368
a_{tm}	-0.0143	-1.7576			

point). No other restrictions were imposed to obtain concavity in prices. There are two instances of non-concavity in price for mail carriers and one for materials inputs. Nonconcavity in "other workers" price is not terribly surprising since this residual category varies considerably in occupational composition across MCSs. The variation in composition leads to price variations that probably lead to violations of concavity.

Interaction coefficients among the variable inputs ("share elasticities" in Jorgenson, Gollop, and Fraumeni (1987)) are strongly negative for delivery workers with other workers, a_{do} and materials, a_{dt}, denoting complementarily. The smaller MSCs have larger proportions of their costs in delivery because some other functions are performed for them by larger MCSs, such as vehicle maintenance (whose personnel are included in the "other workers" category). The opposite effect is captured in the positive relationships between the share of postmasters and supervisors on the one hand with other workers, a_{op}, and materials, a_{tp}, on the other.

4.3. Cost Effects of Delivered and Collected Mail, Network, and Capital

Table 3 shows the coefficients and their respective T-statistics for direct cost effects and interactions among delivered and collected mail, the delivery network served, and capital inputs. Returns to scale for the restricted variable cost function is based on

$$r = \frac{1 - y_K}{\sum_r y_r}.$$

For the system as a whole, the scale coefficient r is about 1.099, denoting returns to scale of about 10%.[7]

| Table 3. Output and Capital Weights for Categories and Components ||||||
Parameter Name	Estimated Value	T-statistic	Parameter Name	Estimated Value	T-statistic
y_d	0.1659	21.7006	Collected Mail		
y_c	0.3004	36.3328	m_f	0.2706	49.2819
y_n	0.4458	62.2487	m_k	0.0112	14.1039
y_k	-0.0001	8.5366	m_o	0.0186	36.3328
Delivered Mail			Network		
m_f	0.0343	62.1062	m_n	0.1832	49.2801
m_t	0.0633	26.0592	m_p	0.1044	27.3703
m_o	0.0683	21.7006	m_a	0.1582	47.9451
			Capital		
			m_m	0.000006	8.2849
			m_c	0.00006	8.3588
			m_v	0.00006	8.5366

Delivered mail has a much smaller weight, y_d, than originated mail. After adjustment for scale economies, it contributes about 18 percent of total variable cost compared with 33 percent for originating mail. The network itself has the largest cost value, about 49 percent of total variable cost. More of the network cost is probably associated with mail delivery, although it does not vary sufficiently with delivered mail to be directly attributed. Capital, whose overall coefficient y_K was constrained to be nonnegative, is nonetheless quite small at -.0001, although its t-statistic shows that it is significantly different from zero.

Interaction effects among output categories, network and capital are analyzed in detail in the following sections.

4.4. Delivered Mail[8]

A layman's view of the functions of the postal service is typically conditioned strongly by the most visible element, the mail carrier, who delivers mail on a local route. The delivery function depends upon considerable prior sorting and transporting of mail pieces. When mail is pre-sorted to the sequence of addresses on the carrier's route, the carrier's job is much easier; mail that is not sorted by the mailer must be sorted by the carrier himself. Further, the increase in output that comes about due to increasing delivery volume on a given network is expected to be less costly than an increase in volume based on an increase in the size of the network served.

4.4.1. Cost Weights and Interactions with Other Aggregates. Table 4 shows the coefficients associated with delivered mail. The overall cost weight of delivered mail as a whole, y_d, is .166. The second order term for delivered mail, y_{dd}, is small and negative, but significant, indicating that economies of scale are realized as the volume of delivered mail increases. Interaction with collected mail, y_{dc}, is positive, which indicates a tendency toward cost-raising interference between delivered and collected mail: that is, diseconomies of scope. However, the interaction term with network, y_{dn}, is rather large and negative, -.26, which shows strong economies for expansion of the volume of delivered mail on a given network. Interaction with capital has a small effect and is cost-increasing; the coefficient may simply reflect the requirement for more vehicles as the volume of delivered mail rises.

4.4.2. Interactions with Inputs. Increasing volume of delivered mail is associated with increasing costs of customer service workers, c_{cd}, and mail carriers, c_{dd}. The latter effect is easily interpreted; the former is not. Negative interactions, denoting economies associated with increasing volume, occur with other inputs, particularly mailhandlers, c_{md}, and other workers, c_{od}. The materials and postmasters and supervisors effects, c_{td} and c_{pd}, are insignificant.

4.4.3. Weights Within Delivered Mail Aggregate. The b coefficients in table 4 show the distribution of costs within the delivered mail aggregate, where the third class mail has the largest weight, b_t, about .41 percent. The first class mail

Table 4. Coefficients Associated with Delivered Mail					
Parameter Name	Estimated Value	T-statistic	Parameter Name	Estimated Value	T-statistic
Weight of Delivered Aggregate and Interactions with Collected Mail, Network and Capital			Weights within Delivered Mail Aggregate		
y_d	0.1659	21.7006	b_f	0.2066	24.9747
y_{dd}	-0.0113	-3.2245	b_o	0.3814	98.1133
y_{dc}	0.0869	28.8013	b_t	0.4119	35.1909
y_{dn}	-0.2613	-31.2761	Effects of Presorting		
y_{dk}	0.0871	10.9094	a_p	-0.3923	-52.3474
Delivered Aggregate's Interactions with Inputs			Direct Cost Weights		
c_{cd}	0.0318	7.5704	m_f	0.0343	62.1062
c_{dd}	0.0325	5.6116	m_o	0.0633	26.0592
c_{td}	-0.0025	-1.0221	m_t	0.0683	21.7006
c_{od}	-0.0103	-4.3762			
c_{pd}	-0.0058	-1.4145			
c_{md}	-0.0457	-6.8856			

coefficient, b_f, is 21 percent and other mail, b_o, about 38 percent. These results are somewhat puzzling. First class mail was expected to show the largest weight; however, delivered mail effects are partially picked up in the network costs, and that may account for much of the "missing" first class mail effect.

4.4.4. Effects of Presorted Mail. The coefficients associated with first class and third class presorted mail were constrained to be equal and are denoted a_p. The large size of a_p is not surprising; it indicates approximately 40 percent saving in total delivery cost from presorting, which is probably reasonably accurate.

4.4.5. Direct Cost Weights. The direct cost weights, m_f, m_o, and m_t, represent the distribution of the overall weight for delivered mail, y_d, to the three categories, first and third class and other mail, based on the b coefficients discussed above. As noted above, the largest weights, m_t and m_o, are associated with third class and other mail, and the smallest with first class.

4.5. Collected Mail

Mail in a local area is received by the USPS in several ways. Some first class mail is collected by delivery personnel, particularly in business areas. Parcels sent by individuals (part of "other" mail) are typically received at the local post office, as are most second and third class mail. Except in business areas, the number of points where mail is collected is far smaller than the number of delivery points.

Hence the "network" served by mail collection activities is effectively smaller than that served by delivery. A major part of the cost of processing collected mail is sorting, a task generally performed by mailhandlers.

4.5.1. Cost Weights and Interactions with Other Aggregates. Table 5 shows that coefficients that are associated with collected mail. The overall weight for collected mail, y_c, is 0.3, nearly twice the value for delivered mail. The second order term, y_{cc}, is fairly large at -0.086, indicating economies of scale in processing collected mail. The interaction of collected with delivered mail, y_{cd}, is 0.087, indicating cost-increasing interference between the two activities. This coefficient probably reflects the collection activities of mail carriers. There is a large positive coefficient, 0.122, for the interaction of collected mail with the network served, y_{cn}, which reflects congestion or interference effects with delivery activities. The interaction with capital, y_{ck}, is rather small and negative.

4.5.2. Interactions with Inputs. Increasing volume of collected mail is as-

Table 5. Coefficients Associated with Collected Mail

Parameter Name	Estimated Value	T-statistic	Parameter Name	Estimated Value	T-statistic
Weight of Collected Aggregate and Interactions with Delivered Mail, Network and Capital			Collected Aggregate's Interactions with Inputs		
y_c	0.3004	36.3328	c_{cc}	-0.0339	-7.3739
y_{cc}	-0.0855	-31.1182	c_{dc}	-0.0631	-11.8785
y_{cd}	0.0870	28.8013	c_{tc}	-0.0011	-0.3867
y_{cn}	0.1220	20.9432	c_{oc}	0.0058	2.1847
y_{ck}	-0.0053	-0.9065	c_{pc}	0.0193	3.8980
			c_{mc}	0.0730	10.8186
Weights within Collected Mail Aggregate			Direct Cost Weights		
b_f	0.9007	102.3200	m_f	0.2706	49.2819
b_o	0.0373	22.1407	m_o	0.0112	14.1039
b_t	0.0619	0	m_t	0.0186	36.3328

sociated with decreasing expenditures for customer service workers, c_{cc}, and mail carriers, c_{dc}, for which the coefficients are all negative. The effect is relatively large with mail carriers, -0.0631. There is substantial increasing cost of mailhandlers, c_{mc}, associated with collected mail, about 0.073, which reflects the sorting and routing activities largely associated with first and second class mail. Interaction with postmasters and supervisors, c_{pc}, is resource-using, indicating that substantially greater expenditures for management and supervision are associated with larger volumes of collected mail. The resource-using interaction with other workers, c_{ow}, is small but significant.

4.5.3. Weights Within Collected Mail Aggregate. The b_m coefficients show the distribution of cost weights within the collected mail aggregate; about 90% of the weight goes to first class mail collection, b_f; about 6.2% to third class mail, b_t: and the remainder, 3.7%, to other mail, b_o. The small weights for third class and other mail derives from two practices: most of these types of mail are delivered to the post office by the sender, and most of third class mail is presorted, thereby eliminating much of the cost of processing these types of collected mail.

4.5.4. Direct Cost Weights. The m coefficients measure the direct cost impacts of components of the collected mail aggregate and are computed as the product of the overall collected mail category weight, y_c, with the b distribution coefficients. Thus, the greatest weight, 0.271, is for first class mail, m_f, with other weights correspondingly smaller as their distribution coefficients dictate.

4.6. The Mail Delivery and Collection Network

Similar to other communication industries, the postal service consists of rendering the service on a network of points. The service consists of collection and delivery of mail, with significant collection activity "short circuited" because a great deal of the total volume of mail is brought to post offices by the originating person or enterprise; that is, the delivery and collection networks are not symmetric in either extent, usage, or mix of mail types. The network itself is described in terms of the number of delivery points, the population served by the network, and the geographic area served (in square miles).[9] The delivery and collection aspects of the network are distinguished as they interact with delivered and collected mail.

4.6.1 Weight of Network Aggregate and Interactions with Collected and Delivered Mail and Capital Input. Table 6 shows the estimated coefficients associated with the mail collection and delivery network. The overall cost weight of the network is 0.446 as measured by the coefficient y_n, about half of the variable cost of overall mail service. The cost of network expansion, measured by the second-order coefficient, y_{nn}, is quite high at 0.345, signifying decreasing returns to scale in network expansion. Interaction with delivered mail, y_{dn}, is negative, as noted in discussion of that category above, and quite large, denoting economies of scale in expansion of delivery volume on a given network. Interaction with collected mail, y_{cn}, is positive, denoting increasing costs of rising mail collection volume on the network. Capital input interacts with the network to reduce costs, as measured by y_{nk}, with a value of -0.1. Considering the very small direct cost effect of capital, this cost-reducing effect is important and probably arises from the capability of vehicles and mail sorting machinery to accommodate larger loads as mail volume increases.

4.6.2 Network Interactions with Inputs. The interaction of the network with customer service workers, c_{cn}, is insignificantly small, which is entirely plausible.

Table 6. Coefficients Associated with Network

Parameter Name	Estimated Value	T-statistic	Parameter Name	Estimated Value	T-statistic
Weight of Network Aggregate and Interactions with Collected and Delivered Mail and Capital			*Network Aggregate Interactions with Inputs*		
y_n	0.4458	62.2487	c_{cn}	0.0001	0.0309
y_{nn}	0.3450	36.2964	c_{dn}	0.0297	5.0419
y_{dn}	-0.2613	-31.2761	c_{tn}	0.0112	4.6697
y_{cn}	0.1220	20.9432	c_{on}	-0.0087	-3.6988
y_{nk}	-0.1001	-12.1401	c_{pn}	0.0236	5.7334
			c_{mn}	-0.0559	-9.1043
Weights within Network Aggregate			*Direct Cost Weights*		
b_n	0.4111	84.9682	m_n	0.1832	49.2801
b_p	0.2341	40.1324	m_p	0.1044	27.3703
b_a	0.3548	41.5129	m_a	0.1582	47.9451

Customer service workers are located in the post offices and have no duties involving the network. Substantial coefficients denoting resource using are the interactions with mail carriers, c_{dn}, at 0.030 and with postmasters and supervisors, c_{pn}, with a value of 0.024. Clearly these coefficients represent specific requirements for mail carriers and their supervision to service the network: to deliver (primarily) and collect mail. There is a small materials-using effect, c_{tn}, which may reflect the greater requirements for gasoline and nonlabor vehicle maintenance costs on larger networks. There is a substantial resource saving effect, c_{mn}, with a value of -0.059, for the interaction of network with mailhandlers, which suggests economies of scale in processing collected mail. There is also a small but significant saving in other workers measured by c_{on}.

4.6.3 Weights within the Network Aggregate. The components of the partially separable network aggregate are delivery points, population, and area, with respective relative weights b_n, b_p, and b_a. The number of delivery points, b_n, and area, b_a, are the dominant components, with respective weights 0.411 and 0.355. The remaining component, population, b_p, at 0.234 is still reasonably large. That the number of delivery points should dominate the network measure is not surprising; however, the values of the other components are larger than expected. It is quite clear that a single-dimensional measure of network would omit or misspecify much of its cost-generating character.

4.6.4. Direct Cost Weights. The direct cost weights of the network components are simply the distribution of the total network weight across the relative component weights. Thus, the largest direct cost effect is the direct cost elasticity of delivery points, m_n, at 0.183, followed by m_a, at 0.158, the cost for the area served in square miles. The total network costs are not quite as high as the costs of both collecting and delivering mail, but it exceeds the cost of either alone.

This finding is important for the USPS because it argues that about 40 percent of the systems' variable costs (which are about 95% of total costs) are not readily allocable among the mail classes. The high cost supporting of the network itself, however, permits economies, particularly in the distribution of mail on the network—recall that y_{dn} is large and negative at -0.261. Much of the network-related scale economies are in sorting the mail, as attested by the negative interaction coefficient of network with mailhandlers, c_{mn}.

4.7. Capital Inputs

Capital inputs as aggregated from detailed asset information include buildings, mail processing equipment, and an "all other" category including vehicles, customer service equipment, and other equipment.

Capital expenditures in the USPS are a very small part of total costs, averaging less than 5 percent. The restricted variable cost function model that we have used gives a shadow price for the (fixed) capital input with a very specific interpretation: it is the value of variable resources that would be saved by one additional unit of capital input. Throughout the investigation, this shadow cost has been quite small. Tierney (1988) points out that considerable investment took place in 1984, and it is likely its effects were not realized immediately. In other terms, capital has no substantial net cost reducing effects, at least in 1984.

Table 7. Coefficients Associated with Capital					
Parameter Name	Estimated Value	T-statistic	Parameter Name	Estimated Value	T-statistic
Weight of Capital Aggregate and Interactions with Delivered and Collected Mail and Network			Capital Aggregates' Interactions with Inputs		
y_k	0.0001	8.5366	c_{ck}	-0.0019	-0.4840
y_{kk}	-0.0149	-2.3615	c_{dk}	-0.0009	-0.1721
y_{dk}	0.0871	10.9094	c_{tk}	0.0076	3.7421
y_{ck}	-0.0053	-0.9065	c_{ok}	-0.0132	-6.8429
y_{nk}	-0.1001	-12.1401	c_{pk}	0.0371	10.2417
			c_{mk}	-0.0287	-5.5664
Weights within Capital Aggregate			Direct Cost Effects		
b_b	0.0480	42.4490	m_b	0.000006	8.2849
b_m	0.4923	40.0130	m_m	0.00006	8.3588
b_v	0.4597	34.3982	m_v	0.00006	8.5366

4.7.1. Weight of Capital Aggregate and Interactions with Delivered and Collected Mail and Network. The shadow cost of capital, y_k, is quite small, -0.0001, although the coefficient is significant. Most of the effect of the capital input in fact comes through interactions with other aggregates. The second order effect of capital, y_{kk} with a value of -0.015, is cost reducing. This issue can be investigated in future research by disaggregating the partially separable aggregate of capital inputs. Interaction of the capital stock with the delivered mail aggregate, y_{dk}, is large and positive, which probably reflects the use of the small electric powered vehicles by mail carriers. Substantial resource saving is associated with the network, measured by the coefficient y_{nk}. This interpretation is consistent with the weights for mail processing equipment and vehicles and other equipment, which dominate the capital aggregate as noted below.

4.7.2 Capital's Interaction with Inputs. The interaction of the capital aggregate with inputs is insignificant for customer service workers, c_{ck}, and mail carriers, c_{dk}. The other coefficients are significant. Capital input exhibits a small resource-using effect with materials, c_{tk}, and a substantial using effect with postmasters and supervisors, c_{pk}. The reason for the materials effect is unclear, but it is not very large. The effect of capital on supervision suggests that use of automation requires greater supervision which may partly result from the incomplete assimilation of the technology introduced in 1984, and perhaps from worker resistance as noted by Baxter (1987). The cost reducing effect with mailhandlers, c_{mk}, probably reflects greater use of mail processing equipment in large MSCs with major responsibilities for mail sorting for their regions. The same effect may explain the saving of other workers, c_{ok}.

4.7.3. Weights within the Capital Aggregate. The distribution of weights within the capital aggregate shows the dominance of mail processing equipment, b_m, with a value of 49% and of vehicles and other equipment, b_v, with a value of 46%. Buildings get a very small weight, b_b, at about 5%. The dominance of mail processing equipment and vehicles is consistent with the patterns of cost saving in interactions of capital with the mail aggregates and network, and with the labor and materials inputs as noted above.

4.7.4. Direct Cost Effects. The direct cost effects of the capital components are quite small, but surprisingly significant in view of their small values. They are negative, but are constrained to be so, as noted above.

Overall, the capital story is promising, in spite of small direct weight for the aggregate, y. Future investigations should include disaggregation of the components, and perhaps elimination of the buildings and structures component altogether.[10] Since the interaction coefficients are in many cases significant and seem to apply to different components of the capital aggregate, disaggregation in subsequent models may clarify the role of capital.

5. Distribution of Productivity Performance Among Regions and Classes of MSCs

The estimates of productivity levels at the MSCs can be computed from the estimated cost function model. Point estimates of total factor productivity (TFP) at individual MSCs are subject to estimation error and will not be reported here. However, the distributions of productivity by region that result from the estimated model can be useful in two ways. The range of productivity differences within a region suggests the potential for productivity improvement that can be achieved by raising productivity in the lagging plants. Systematic productivity differences between regions indicate the presence of cost-raising factors not incorporated in the model-factors which may range from inadequate specification of the network served by MSCs, the use of capital, or the workload, to the omission from the model of crucial management practices or labor-management relations.

In this section, distributions are reported for three variables for the five administrative regions of the USPS: total factor productivity computed in two ways (TFPAV, TFPOWN) and the marginal cost of serving a larger network (MCNET).

Total factor productivity is computed conventionally:

$$TFP = \sum_i mc_i \times \frac{Z_i}{\sum_j s_i Q_i}$$

where i ranges over all outputs and network, j ranges over all variable inputs and capital, mc_i is the marginal cost of output i, Z_i is the quantity of output i, s_j is the share in total cost of input j, and Q_j is the quantity of input j.

The TFP measures are based on all measured inputs, capital as well as labor and materials. Capital input is aggregated by service prices of the three asset classes derived from Christensen, Christensen, Degen, and Schoech (1989). The total cost of capital is computed as the sum of service prices for each asset class multiplied by capital input for that class. Labor and materials inputs are aggregated by unit cost measures developed for this study to a total variable input. Capital and variable inputs are aggregated to a measure of total factor input based on their respective shares in total cost, which is defined as total variable cost plus the total capital cost.

For an enterprise operating with administered prices, aggregation of multiple outputs by revenue weights is inappropriate; marginal cost weights should be used (Diewert 1980). Accordingly, we have aggregated the various components of output by estimated marginal costs, using average marginal costs for the region (TFPAV) and for the individual MSC (TFPOWN). The marginal costs of the network component is also reported. These marginal variable costs are computed from the definition

$$\frac{\partial C}{\partial Z_n} = \frac{\partial \ln C}{\partial \ln Z_n} \times \frac{C}{Z_n},$$

where Z_n is the network aggregate noted above.

Results are also reported by class, which corresponds roughly to size. Some internally provided services are often not performed in MSCs of classes 5 and 6, but are supplied by larger MSCs.

5.1. Distribution of Productivity Performance Among Regions

Tables 8.a and 8.b show the mean, median, and range for total factor productivity computed using average marginal costs for the region (table 8.a) and marginal costs for the individual MSC (table 8.b). In each case, the overall mean for all regions together is 1.00. Roughly speaking, differences among means and medians may be interpreted as percentages when multiplied by 100.

Based on regional average and own marginal costs, the North Central region, Region 4, shows the highest average productivity. The Western region, Region 5, is clearly an outlier with lowest productivity when regional average weights are used; it is still lowest, but much closer to the other regions when own weights are used. The reason for this divergence becomes clear on inspection of table 8.c showing the distribution of network costs, which are high in the West. The *value* of the network area element is also much greater for Western MSCs, raising the network contribution to total cost. This result no doubt derives from the larger

Table 8.a. Distribution of Total Factor Productivity by Region Weighted by Average Marginal Costs

Regional	Median	Mean	Range	Observations
1	1.034	1.103	1.716	32
2	0.987	1.088	1.822	26
3	0.793	0.824	1.198	43
4	1.070	1.2l2	2.805	60
5	0.591	0.552	0.742	29

Table 8.b. Distribution of Total Factor Productivity by Region Weighted by Own Marginal Costs

Regional	Median	Mean	Range	Observations
1	1.133	1.180	1.190	32
2	1.080	1.131	1.854	26
3	1.058	1.085	1.085	43
4	1.135	1.355	3.727	60
5	1.106	1.015	1.362	39

Table 8.c. Distribution of Cost of Network Services by Region Weighted by Average Marginal Costs

Regional	Median	Mean	Range	Observations
1	0.221	0.303	3.523	32
2	0.478	0.533	2.891	26
3	0.641	0.876	3.233	43
4	0.416	0.630	l.864	60
5	0.504	0.622	2.037	39

geographic areas served by MSCs in the Western region and the generally lower density of delivery points. The range of TFP results is far greater within than among regions; and the North Central region, which has the best productivity performance, also shows the largest range *and* has the largest number of MSCs.

The ranges of productivity performance within each region, based on regional average marginal costs, show that there is great scope for improvement within each region; the means and medians also show that there are examples of MSCs with good productivity performances within each region.

To place the ranges of productivity performance in some context, Klotz (1970) finds productivity ranges of about 100% from top to bottom among manufacturing plants in the same four digit industry, when no adjustment is made for product differences. By contrast, *after* adjustment for product differences among MSCs in the same region, productivity differences show ranges in the area of 200-300%. The West shows a much smaller range (but systematically lower productivity), when average marginal cost weights are used to compute its productivity; with the MSCs' own weights, the productivity range in the West region is more typical, but still on the low side. Based on own marginal cost weights, the range of measured productivity is smallest in the Northeast region, where network has the lowest cost, as shown in table 8.c.

Based on the intra-regional dispersions of productivity performance, it appears that there is considerable scope for raising productivity in many MSCs, especially since productivity measures here are adjusted for workload differences. Because capital shows up rather poorly in this model, however, it may be that differences in the use of capital equipment explain some differences in productivity that the model does not capture. In particular, there may be interactions of particular types of equipment, e.g., small delivery vehicles, with particular occupations, e.g., mail carriers, that would explain much of the observed productivity differences. Indeed, some of the results of analyzing the formation of worker attitudes (Norsworthy, Jang, and Rebne 1989) suggest that such forces are at work. Disaggregation of the worker behavior variables by occupation would permit this issue to be explored.

It also appears that the model and resulting productivity measures could be improved by separating the size of the area served from delivery points and population, to capture the costs of dispersion better. (This point is elaborated below.)

5.2. Performance Among Classes of MSCs

Tables 9.a, 9.b, and 9.c show the distributions of total factor productivity and network costs among MSCs by class of MSC. Roughly, MSC class is inversely related to size, with the largest MSCs in classes 1 and 2 and the smallest in class 6. The number of observations in each class is reported in the tables. As noted, some administrative and service functions are performed for the smaller MSCs by the larger ones. Thus, unlike region, except in the case of network, there are *a priori* reasons to expect systematic productivity differences among classes of MSCs. Dummy variables permitting intercept shifts in the cost function were

Table 9.a. Distribution of Total Factor Productivity by Class Weighted by Average Marginal Costs

Class	Median	Mean	Range	Observations
1&2	0.632	0.918	2.184	5
3	2.404	2.714	6.092	42
4	1.261	1.307	3.955	80
5	0.523	0.551	1.050	58
6	0.296	0.279	0.296	15

Table 9.b. Distribution of Total Factor Productivity by Class Weighted by Own Marginal Costs

Class	Median	Mean	Range	Observations
1&2	1.186	1.705	4.023	5
3	0.879	0.997	2.201	42
4	0.991	1.034	3.154	80
5	1.012	1.047	2.070	58
6	1.119	1.044	1.330	15

Table 9.c. Distribution of Cost of Network Services by Class Weighted by Average Marginal Costs

Class	Median	Mean	Range	Observations
1&2	0.215	0.323	2.757	5
3	0.154	0.219	1.361	42
4	0.416	0.439	1.765	80
5	0.890	0.945	2.563	58
6	1.634	1.505	4.658	15

introduced to allow for these effects.

Productivity based on average weights shows a low mean for class 1 and class 2 MSCs and very high productivity for class 3, with productivity declining for further decreases in size. Some of the explanation for this result can be obtained from table 8.c. The cost of the network rises rapidly as the class (size) of the MSC declines (although there is a slight reversal between the first two categories). This is not surprising, because the smallest MSCs often serve the largest geographical areas. The size of the network effect moving down the class gradient is somewhat surprising and suggestive for further analysis.

Given the results, it is not at all surprising that interclass productivity differences are narrowed considerably when the marginal costs at each MSC are used to compute productivity.

5.3. Network Service and Productivity at MSCs

The cost of serving the distribution network, as specified in this model, can be thought of as the costs that are associated with the measures of network introduced into the model that do not vary systematically with outputs as well.

We have found that the network component of costs is quite large (larger than delivered or collected mail alone) and that it plays a major role in determining productivity at the MSC level. In view of this finding, it is desirable to add more detail to the model describing the interaction of the network served and the measures of pieces of mail, particularly pieces of delivered mail. In such a case, we might expect the network cost to be reduced, somewhat, and the cost of delivered mail to be increased.

Recall that at present all delivered mail interacts as an aggregate with network, also specified as an aggregate. (The same is true of collected mail, but there is less reason to believe that the network cost may be overstated and the cost of collected mail correspondingly understated.)

This modification might be expected to result in little change in productivity performance of the system as a whole but could raise measured productivity in the Western region and perhaps in smaller MSCs.

It is also likely that the effect of the area component of the cost of network service is nonlinear. If mail volume per delivery point is constant throughout the system,

| Table 10. Worker Attitude Formation Model ||||||
Parameter	Coefficient Estimate	T-Statistic	Parameter Name	Estimated Value	T-statistic
w_0	0.1062	41.2629	w_{oo}	-0.0164	-6.9713
w_o	0.1290	43.4241	w_{or}	-0.1023	-12.7982
w_r	-0.0937	-24.2790	w_{oc}	-0.0701	-21.7983
w_c	0.1257	32.0705	w_{os}	0.1124	89.2887
w_s	-0.0496	-30.4830	w_{od}	0.0078	4.9349
w_d	0.1168	64.1460	w_{of}	-0.0207	-7.0627
w_f	0.1553	25.0573	w_{op}	0.0166	3.9265
w_p	-0.0417	-13.5199	w_{oa}	-0.0321	-4.9935
w_a	-0.0338	-13.0974	w_{ou}	-0.0225	-7.7524
w_u	0.1630	38.7575	w_{rr}	0.0488	16.7995
w_{cc}	0.0072	2.3662	w_{rc}	-0.0154	-6.9549
w_{cs}	0.2533	90.8861	w_{rs}	0.2436	118.6940
w_{cd}	-0.0965	-15.1937	w_{rd}	0.0547	7.3893
w_{cf}	-0.0328	-2.9968	w_{rf}	-0.0700	-15.6432
w_{cp}	0.0862	-11.6959	w_{rp}	0.0542	8.5194
w_{ca}	-0.0378	-10.1051	w_{ra}	0.0093	1.8534
w_{cu}	-0.0617	-11.3307	w_{ru}	-0.0450	-11.3485
w_{ss}	-0.3442	-512.161	w_{ff}	0.0377	4.9372
w_{sd}	-0.4234	-290.274	w_{fp}	-0.0709	-13.4181
w_{sf}	0.2829	192.594	w_{fa}	0.0695	17.2644
w_{sp}	0.0957	38.778	w_{fu}	0.0215	4.1858
w_{sa}	-0.1629	-261.317	w_{pp}	0.0823	34.9006
w_{su}	-0.1890	-107.469	w_{pa}	-0.0867	-13.7131
w_{dd}	0.0459	9.4753	w_{pu}	-0.0628	-12.9018
w_{df}	-0.0811	-14.4282	w_{aa}	0.0008	1.2476
w_{dp}	0.0361	22.8641	w_{au}	0.0373	10.0684
w_{da}	-0.0286	-4.2080	w_{uu}	0.0503	13.4489
w_{du}	0.0691	26.9461			

then, in large geographic areas, the cost per piece of mail delivered will rise as delivery points are more widely dispersed, because travel time between delivery points must rise, resulting in higher costs of carrier time and higher energy costs per piece of mail delivered. Lower productivity that results from this circumstance is spurious; greater weight should properly be assigned to mail delivery under these circumstances, resulting in greater measured output and productivity.

5.4. Worker Attitudes and Productivity at MSCs

Productivity measures tend to be correlated with measures of negative worker attitudes; the correlation coefficient between negative attitudes and total factor productivity, based on the MSCs own marginal cost weights, is -0.545 across all regions and classes. See tables 10 and 11 for specific results.

Table 11. Worker Attitude Parameters in Cost Function

Parameter	Estimated Coefficient	T-Statistic	Parameter	Estimated Coefficient	T-statistic
Direct Effects on Costs					
Worker Attitudes' Interactions with Variable Inputs			Interactions with Delivered and Collected Mail, Network and Capital		
M_x	0.2773	32.4823	a_{xx}	0.0040	0.4906
C_{xxu}	-0.0040	0.4906	a_{ydx}	-0.1941	-57.49
C_{cx}	0.0011	0.7294	a_{ycx}	-0.0097	-1.567
C_{dx}	-0.0204	-10.0642	a_{ynx}	0.0707	15.87
C_{tx}	0.0013	1.5826	a_{kx}	0.0760	10.21
C_{ox}	0.0045	5.7673			
C_{px}	0.0117	7.9391			

Table 12 shows the cost effects of negative worker attitudes found in other studies; these effects are high in the USPS, but comparable in size to the effects found in the United States automobile industry. In this paper, we do not show the worker attitude effects by MSC because we were unsuccessful in developing a reliable measure of MSC productivity adjusted for attitude effects to provide a check on the measured effects.

Table 12. Cost Elasticity of Negative Worker Behavior in Various Sectors

U.S. Auto Industry, 1959-76	.24	Norsworthy & Zabala (1985a)
U.S. Manufacturing, 1959-81	.11	Norsworthy & Zabala (1985)
Japanese Manufacturing, 1965-78	.03	Lam, Norsworthy & Zabala (1985)
U.S. Postal Service, 1984	.28	Study from this paper

6. Implications of Productivity and Network Costs for Privatization: A Geographic Perspective

Most discussions of privatization of postal services have examined the prospects in terms of particular classes of service: first class, third class, etc. The concept of privatization through geographic franchising can be examined in a preliminary way based on the information developed here.

It is generally realized in discussions on the introduction of competition into postal services that the skimming phenomenon must be controlled in some way. Our results concerning the geographic distribution of productivity and costs, particularly network costs, illustrate the potential for skimming on the geographic dimension.

Even though the measures of network costs are less accurate than we would like, it is clear that unstructured competition or franchising would be drawn to areas— MSCs—of high density, leaving the low-density, dispersed network MSCs to be served by a vestigial "carrier of last resort." The unit cost of serving the residual MSCs would be quite high. An estimate of how much higher the costs would be could be obtained by experimenting with various partitioning or "gerrymandering" schemes based on the MSC as the elemental unit, with cost of service estimated for packages of MSCs assembled according to different algorithms.

Clearly, if packages were franchised corresponding to existing UPSP regions, the Western region would be the least desirable from the perspective of a potential franchisee. If franchises were defined along state boundaries—certainly a threat in the United States political system—the states of the West other than California would be highly undesirable. If franchises were defined at the MSC level, then the unit cost of service in Western MSCs outside the major population centers would be very high indeed. The policymaker must deal, therefore, not with the question of whether there should be a subsidy for the MSCs whose low density makes them "basket cases," but with the questions associated with how the size of subsidy should be determined and how it should be financed.

In addressing these issues related to privatization, estimates of productivity and costs at the MSC level, based on pooled cross-sections of data for multiple years, can play a major role.

7. Conclusions

In this paper, a model of productivity at the level of United States Postal Service Management Sectional Centers is presented. The general implications of that model are discussed, regarding the costs of delivered and collected (and forwarded) mail, of serving the network of delivery and collection points in the geographic area of the MSC, of negative attitudes and related behaviors on the part of workers, and of the effects of capital inputs on costs.

This model is used to compute total factor productivity and the cost of network service for 200 MSCs. The results are analyzed and reported by region and class. There clearly is scope for substantial productivity improvement, because the dispersions of productivity by region and class are quite large compared to comparable measures for manufacturing plants in the same industry. Part of that dispersion appears to be related to inadequate adjustment for dispersion of delivery points in the geographic area served by the MSC. Future modeling efforts will be required to deal with this shortcoming; however, it is reasonable to expect that large productivity differences among MSCs will persist even after adjustment.

We expect that partitioning the regions and more numerous classes into high, low, and medium productivity performers can add insight to productivity—enhancing initiatives concerning labor management relations, perhaps automation, and other practices.

Appendix A. Data Sources and Development

The major dimensions of mail volume by class that we use in the econometric model are from the Origin-Destination Information System (ODIS) which is a sample survey of mail by type at the destination. The origin of each piece of mail sampled is determined by the return address, which may not appear. Thus, there is a quality difference between the measures of originating and "destinating" mail. Origins are imputed for the unallocated originating mail by class in proportion to measured mail.

A weakness in the mail output measures is that second class mail is not measured in the ODIS survey. Second class mail originations are approximated by second class revenues; we judged that no reasonable imputation could be made for destinations of this mail. Consequently, the mail destination and origination estimates include only first class, third class, and other mail estimates from the ODIS survey.

A final dimension to the volume of mail handled is presorted mail. Two mail classes, first and third, offer substantially lower rates for presorted mail. Presorted mail is less costly to process because it does not need sorting by USPS, a very labor-intensive part of overall operations. We thus modify the delivered mail in first and third class categories by the proportion of mail that is presorted, and parametrically determine its effect on costs.

An important dimension in recent studies of output and productivity growth has been to distinguish the volume of goods or services from the network on which they are delivered. This results in an output measure with two major components, volume and network. Landmark studies of this type include Christensen, Cummings, and Schoech (1981); Gollop and Roberts (1981); Denny, Fuss, and Waverman (1981). These studies distinguish output growth based on volume delivered on a given network from network expansion, on the sensible principle that the scale effects associated with the different types of output expansion almost certainly differ in magnitude, and may also differ in sign. We characterize the network served by each MSC with three measures: number of delivery points, population served, and area in square miles.

Similarly, the labor input data (labor costs comprise about 80 percent of total cost) are very good. There is detailed information on hours worked, hours paid, and leave experience for more than sixty categories of employees by occupational type. These are aggregated into five categories of labor input: mail carriers (d), mailhandlers (m), postmasters and supervisors (p), customer service workers (c), and other workers (o).

Capital equipment and structures are annually appraised by the USPS with considerable detail. Christensen Associates (1984) have compiled the USPS statistics into estimates of more than 30 types of equipment by MSC and have included structures as well. The equipment estimates appear to be excellent, while the structures data are essentially book values based on acquisition costs and are probably rather weak. The capital data are aggregated into three categories, building and other structures (b), mail handling and processing equipment (m), and vehicles, customer service, and other equipment (v). We use a restricted variable cost function model of production as applied in Brown and Christensen (1981), treating these three categories of capital as fixed in the short run; consequently, capital service prices are not required for the estimations. For input aggregation to compute total factor productivity, depreciation rates are used as capital service prices for each category of capital, based on Hulten and Wykoff (1981).

Other purchased inputs at the MSC level include leased vehicles and purchases of gasoline and other supplies. These inputs are reported on USPS survey form 1655. There was no satisfactory way to obtain price estimates for materials by MSC. Gasoline prices from the Bureau of Labor Statistics' Consumer Price Index for a cross-section of 20 areas were assigned to materials (T) for the 200 MSCs.

Thus, the input, output, and capital stocks for the 200 MSCs included in the study vary in quality by variable, although quality does not vary systematically across MSCs. One potentially important result of our econometric modeling effort will be to identify, from the standard errors of parameter estimates, the data elements which are weakest and, from the parameter estimates themselves, the data elements whose refinements would add most to the quality of the resulting output and productivity measures.

Appendix B. Regions of the USPS

Region 1. Northeast. Maine, New Hampshire, Vermont, Massachusetts, Rhode Island, Connecticut, New York City area, Newark area in New Jersey (Puerto Rico).

Region 2. Atlantic. Rest of New York, rest of New Jersey, Pennsylvania, Delaware, Maryland, West Virginia, Virginia, Washington, DC.

Region 3. Southern. North and South Carolina, Georgia, Florida, Tennessee, Alabama, Mississippi, Louisiana, Arkansas, Texas, Oklahoma, Missouri.

Region 4. North Central. Kentucky, Ohio, Indiana, Illinois, Michigan, Iowa, Minnesota, Wisconsin, North and South Dakota, Nebraska, Kansas.

Region 5. Western. California, Arizona, New Mexico, Colorado, Nevada, Utah, Wyoming, Montana, Idaho, Oregon, Washington (Alaska, Hawaii).

MSCs in Alaska, Hawaii, Puerto Rico, and the United States Pacific islands were deleted, because they were highly atypical.

Notes

This research was partially supported by NSF research grant (SES-8713585). The opinions and conclusions expressed here are those of the authors alone and do not reflect the positions or policies of the United States Postal Service or any other institution. The authors are more than grateful for detailed comments at the conference from the designated discussants, Thomas Abbott and Donald O'Hara. It is generally difficult to get knowledgeable suggestions on a project of this scale and scope.

1. Present system-wide measures of productivity growth through time are based on aggregation of mail categories weighted by internally-attributed costs system. It is very much an open question, however, as to how good the internal measures are. Comparison with econometrically-determined marginal cost benchmarks for major mail categories may, in fact, demonstrate that the internally-determined cost attribution methods perform reasonably well, particularly when contrasted with revenue weights, which are the chief alternatives. Marginal cost weights determined from aggregate time series data have been unstable and are thus unsatisfactory for productivity measurement. Whether marginal cost estimates from cross-section data confirm or challenge the system-wide imputed costs for various classes of mail service, there is a solid information gain from the comparison.

Another major objective of cross-section measurement of marginal costs (not pursued in this paper) is to permit geographically disaggregated measurement of performance. There appear to be major differences in the costs of mail collection, handling, and delivery across geographic areas. However, the differences in the volume and composition of output among MSCs are great, with large local variations in the mail class composition of mail collected and delivered, as well as large differences in the "network" served and the degree of automation. Also, some functions, such as major vehicle service and repair, are assigned administratively only to MSCs of certain classes. Consequently sorting out the varied and interrelated factors influencing the marginal cost of mail processing is a complex task, requiring a model sufficiently detailed to account for much of the complexity.

2. This section clarifies the factors concerned with the choice of modeling framework raised by Professor Abbott.

3. Binswanger (1974) makes this point clearly.

4. See McElroy (1987).

5. In our current studies of technology (Norsworthy and Jang 1988) we have also applied the AGEM approach and extended it to appraise the intertemporal effects of technological change. In this application, the AGEM has properties that improve the quantitative interpretation of technological change.

6. While the R-squared statistics for individual equations do not have the same meaning for individual equations in a simultaneously estimated set that they have for separately estimated equations, it is nevertheless encouraging to see these results, especially in a cross-section model.

7. Second-class mail is not represented, however. Its inclusion could reduce measured returns to scale.

8. It is argued that the measures of presorted mail represent originating mail rather than mail at its destination, in contradiction of information earlier supplied by the USPS. Reestimation of the model omitting the presort measures altogether result in slightly lower overall costs for delivered mail and higher costs for collected mail. The network cost component is essentially unchanged; there is no appreciable effect on other inferences from the model. Regrettably, time did not permit reporting of the revised model, but those results are available on request.

9. We have not included in the network description several variables that represent the technological or organizational response to the network served, such as the numbers of city routes and rural routes, the proportion of city routes that are motorized (the others are walked on foot), the supervisory ratio for mail carriers, etc. Some of these variables enter the function describing the formation of worker attitudes and will be considered as technological variables in the cost function itself in subsequent studies.

10. Recall that the measure is based on book values which vary enormously in their relevance according to when the assets were purchased and where they are located.

References

Baxter, Vern 1987. "Technological Change and Labor Relations in the United States Postal Service." In *Workers, Managers and Technical Change: Emerging Patterns of Labor Relations,*" Plenum: 91-110, edited by Daniel B. Cornfeld.

Brown, R.S., and L.R. Christensen. 1981. "Estimating Elasticities of Substitution in a Model of Partial Static Equilibrium: An Application to United States Agriculture 1947 to 1974." In *Measuring and Modeling Natural Resources Substitution*: 208-229, edited by E.R. Berndt and B.C. Field. Cambridge, MA: MIT Press.

Christensen, D.C., L.R. Christensen, R. Degan, and P. Schoech. 1980. "Capital Formation in the United States Postal Service." In *Technology and Capital Formation*, edited by D.W. Jorgensen and R. Landan. Cambrige, MA: MIT Press.

Christensen, L.R., D. Cummings, and P.E. Schoech. 1983. "Econometric Estimation of Scale Economics in Telecommunications," In *Telecommunications in Canada*, edited by L. Courville, A. DeFontenay, and R. Dobell.

L.R. Christensen Associates, Inc. 1984. *United States Postal Service, Real Output, Input and Total Factor Productivity, 1963-1982.*

Cowing, T.G., and R.E. Stevenson. (eds.) 1981. *Productivity Measurement in Regulated Industries.* Academic Press.

Denny, M., M. Fuss, and L. Waverman. 1981. "The Measurement and Interpretation of Total Factor Productivity in Regulated Industries, with an Application to Canadian Telecommunication." In *Productivity Measurement in Regulated Industries* edited by T.G. Cowing and R.E. Stevenson, pages 179-217. Academic Press.

Gollop, F.M., and M.J. Roberts. 1981. "The Sources of Economic Growth in the United States Electric Power Industry." In *Productivity Measurement in Regulated Industries*, edited by T.G. Cowing and R. E. Stevenson, pages 107-163.

Hulten, C.R., and F.C. Wykoff. 1981. "The Measurement of Economic Depreciation." In *Depreciation, Inflation and the Taxation of Income Capital*, edited by C.R. Hulten, pages 81-132. The Urban Institute.

Klotz, B.P. 1970. *Productivity Measurement in Manufacturing Plants*, Staff Paper #50, Bureau of Labor Statistics.

Lam, Alice, J.R. Norsworthy, and C. Zabala. (forthcoming). In *Productivity in Japan and the United States*, edited by C.R. Hulten. National Bureau of Economic Research volume.

McElroy, Marjorie B. 1987. "Additive General Error Models for Production, Cost, and Derived Demand or Shared System." *Journal of Political Economy* 95(4): 737-757.

Norsworthy, J.R., and C.A. Zabala. 1985a. "Effects of Worker Attitudes on Production Costs and Value of Capital Input." *The Economic Journal* 95:992-1002.

Norsworthy, J.R., and C.A. Zabala. 1985b. "Worker Behavior and Productivity in the U.S. Automobile Industry, 1959-1976." *Industrial and Labor Relations Review* 38:544-58.

Norsworthy, J.R., and Show-Ling Jang. 1988. "Quantity-Based Measurement of Technological Change in Economic Models." Working paper, Center for Science and Technology Policy, School of Management, Rensselaer Polytechnic Institute (RPI).

Norsworthy, J.R., Show-Ling Jang, and D.S. Rebne. 1989. "Worker Attitudes, Supervision and Productivity in Service Industries: A Study of the United States Postal Service." Technical Report No. 01-89, Center for Science and Technology Policy, RPI.

Rebne, D.S., and J.R. Norsworthy. 1989. "A Sociotechnical Model of Production Systems and Worker Attitude Formation." Working paper, School of Management, RPI.

Tierney, John T. 1988. *The United States Postal Service: Status and Prospects of a Public Enterprise.* Auburn House.

COMMENTS
Thomas A. Abbott

Let me begin by commending the authors for the massive undertaking that this paper represents and for providing some of the empirical analysis needed to address the natural monopoly and productive efficiency issues that are central to this conference. Moreover, it is only through conscientious empirical work like this, that someday we may be able to evaluate the consequences of opening postal service to competitive forces without living through the experience. Despite this praise, there are two issues which must be addressed before accepting the empirical results.

The first issue is using the restricted variable cost function (RVCF) to model the behavior of the United States Postal Service (USPS). The authors discuss this choice in section 2, arguing that the RVCF is the least restrictive alternative available. This, however, is not sufficient justification for accepting the model—simply because you don't have a screwdriver doesn't make a hammer the right tool. The key is that in order for the cost function to correctly describe the underlying technology, one must assume cost minimization. Were the USPS a private firm, one could appeal to the profit motive and the market for managerial control as incentives for managers to minimize costs; however this is not the case. In fact, it is precisely because of the lack of competitive forces that the issue of breaking up the postal monopoly arises.

The USPS is currently a public corporation with a set of competing objectives—e.g., universal daily service, convenient locations, speedy delivery, and low cost. Postal management is thus faced with several priorities and may not pursue cost minimization to the extent needed to justify the RVCF. Moreover, if, as we are led to believe by postal authorities, there is a lack of detailed information on day-to-day operations, it is difficult to believe that managers have sufficient information to support cost minimizing decisions, even if they were so inclined.

In response, the authors point out that their estimated cost function is, as predicted by cost minimization, quasi-concave in input prices—i.e., the factor demand equations are downward-sloped. This, however, in no sense "proves" cost minimization. There could be a large difference between downward-sloped and having the optimal slope. Thus, quasi-concavity is a necessary, but not sufficient, condition for cost minimization.

The implications of this issue are crucial for the interpretation of the empirical results. If the USPS is not minimizing costs, what behavior does the estimated model capture? Figure 1 illuminates the situation; it shows a factor price frontier (i.e., those input prices which lead to the same total costs for a fixed level of output). If the postal service were minimizing costs, all of the observations would lie on this frontier—however, if the postal service is inefficient, the observations would

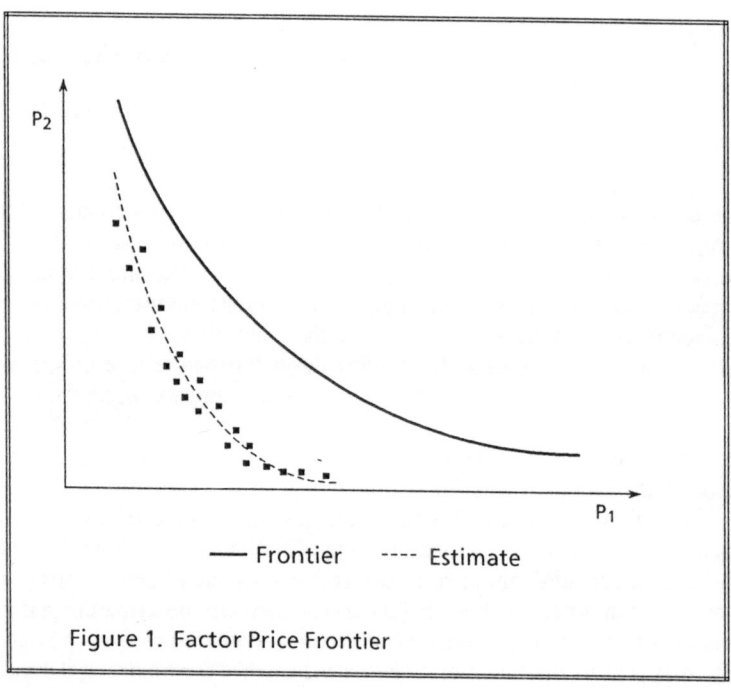

Figure 1. Factor Price Frontier

lie below the frontier, as shown. Econometric estimates using observed data result in estimates of the dashed line. As illustrated, there need not be any relationship between the estimated function and the feasible price frontier. Thus, the estimated RVCF would only provide a convenient way of expressing current practices, that is, it is an "institutional" cost function. The current practices of the USPS might be established through union rules, standardized business practices, or other managerial guidelines.[1] Thus, the estimates might not provide any information on how the USPS would react if the environment suddenly changed and it was forced to compete with profit seeking firms. Moreover, since the estimates of relative productivity are based on the estimated model, they may not reflect economic efficiency—although they would reflect different efficiencies in implementing current practices and are thus still interesting.

The second issue deals with the construction of several key variables. As expected, labor is a very important part of the model. Despite this, the authors provide little discussion of the construction of the labor variables—specifically, the wage rate and quantity variables for each of the five labor categories.[2] This issue arises in part because most postal employees are paid a national wage on the basis of job classification and seniority. Thus, the average wage for a particular group of workers depends on the distribution of seniority of workers, not on local labor conditions, and the idea that MSCs face different (quality adjusted) wage rates seems incorrect—even assuming that seniority leads to differences in marginal productivity. Moreover, with the high retention rates, the ability of managers to adjust labor in response to changes in relative prices seems limited. As a result, it is not clear in what sense the model is able to estimate "factor" demand equations using the cross sectional data—a problem which the heterogeneity of the "other worker" category seems to have exacerbated. In addition, because of the way the data is constructed, errors in measuring the real wage rate would lead to corresponding errors in the measured quantities.

In response, the authors make two points. First, they argue that because of the non-linearity of the model, they do not require variation in labor prices to identify the parameters of the model—although it seems hard to believe that one can obtain accurate estimates of the factor price elasticities without variation in prices. Second, they argue that the Additive General Error Model (AGEM) is designed to handle the measurement problems, citing McElroy (1987). Unfortunately, that paper doesn't really apply. The McElroy AGEM model assumes classical errors in measurement, i.e., the errors in input quantities are independent of the real inputs, the level of output, and factor prices.[3] In this case, however, because of the factor reversal property of the Fisher Index, errors in measuring quality adjusted labor quantity must be negatively correlated with errors in the real wage rates. Such correlated errors lead to biased estimates of the factor demand equations for the usual reasons. To see this problem more clearly, simply replace their price variable by the total cost for each category of labor (C_i) divided by their measured input quantity (q_i) in equation 3 and observe that the authors regress q_i against itself—albeit in a non-linear framework.

Subsequently, the authors argue that if there were significant errors in the measurement of the input quantities, then they would not be able to explain such a high proportion of the observed variation. While this would be true for the classic errors in variables case, in the case of correlated errors the measurement problems could actually lead to higher "predictability," since the same error appears on both sides of the equation. Thus, the fact that they obtain a high R^2 may actually indicate a measurement problem. Moreover, it is not clear to what extent the predictability of the factor demand equations is driven by the factor prices rather the measures of real output (which vary by an order of magnitude across the MSCs).

Having raised these issues, one must question the validity of the empirical results, even though, as the authors adeptly point out, many of the parameters conform to prior beliefs about postal service operations. The primary results of interest are the estimated returns to scale, the marginal cost output, and the measures of relative productivity. Overall, the first objection seems most damaging; it suggests that the estimates conform to managerial practice rather that technical feasibility and it is these practices which shape our prior beliefs—thus the "reasonability" test cannot be used to overturn the objection. As outside researchers, we have no way of determining to what extent current managerial practice conforms to cost minimization without comparing estimates over time or (preferably) across postal systems with varying competitive environments.

The measurement error problem is harder to assess. If there is no useful variation in factor prices, it would suggest that one could use total expenditures as a proxy for labor quantity (assuming that wage differentials reflect differences in marginal productivity) or total hours (assuming that there are no differences in marginal productivity). Since both variables are available in the data set, it would be interesting to know how sensitive the results are to alternative methods of measuring real labor inputs.

Overall, the Norsworthy-Jang-Shi paper provides an admirable start to the comprehensive empirical analysis needed on the questions of natural monopoly and productive efficiency in the postal service. Additional analysis, particularly using cross temporal and international data as well as alternative methodologies is needed before these results can be used as a basis for policy.

Notes

1. While I don't have the specific institutional knowledge necessary to provide examples of these institutional guidelines, I imagine that there are guidelines such as: the normal delivery route should be between $x1$ and $x2$ households; if a route is more than y miles, a motor vehicle should be provided; or in sorting facilities, there should be one supervisor for every z mail handlers. Without competitive market pressures to reward the firms with the best rules, there is no way to insure that these guidelines conform to cost minimizing behavior—even in the long run.

2. Subsequent conversations with the authors revealed that the labor quantity and wage rates for each category were computed using Fisher quantity and price indices which, they explained, have the desirable property that the product of the price and quantity index equals total expenditures.

3. McElroy, M. "Additive General Error Models for Production, Cost and Derived Demand or Share Systems." *Journal of Political Economy*. August 1987. p. 741.

COMMENTS
Donald J. O'Hara

This paper attacks an important problem—measuring and explaining productivity differences among Management Sectional Centers (MSCs), the roughly 200 local operating units of the United States Postal Service (USPS). Unfortunately, it is also a very difficult problem, and the conceptual issues and data limitations are so great that the complex, multi-equation approach embodied in this paper does not appear to yield any useful information about postal costs or productivity.

Productivity measurement requires data on both input and output. At the aggregate or national level, the USPS has good measures of both, and, as a consequence, it has been able to measure system-wide productivity with a high degree of accuracy.[1] At the MSC level, however, data are much less satisfactory, especially with respect to output. These data issues must be given careful attention, even in fairly simple investigations of MSC cost and productivity, and they significantly constrain the kinds of analysis that can be carried out.

The present paper attempts an enormously complex analysis of the structure of Postal Service costs at the MSC level, with correspondingly severe data requirements. Notwithstanding the ability of the econometric software to generate parameter estimates, there is an enormous gap between the data used and those that would be required to produce meaningful results. My comments will be directed first to a single data issue—labor prices—that by itself presents a formidable barrier to the approach taken in this paper. Briefer comments will then be devoted to other issues.

This paper employs "state-of-the-art" econometric techniques to estimate simultaneously cost and factor-demand equations for MSCs. Estimation of this system of equations, however, depends critically on the variables representing the prices of the various labor inputs. In both the cost function itself and the labor input demand functions, labor prices play a central role dictated by the underlying cost-minimization theory. This approach requires that each labor price variable reflect the marginal cost of using additional labor of that type. Of course, without variation in this marginal cost across MSCs, estimation of meaningful price-related parameters will not be feasible.

In fact, the three largest categories of labor (carriers, "mailhandlers" including clerks, and customer service workers) are hired under nationally uniform contracts, with nationally uniform starting wages, step increases, and time between step increases.[2] Thus, the marginal cost of labor, at least on the extensive margin (additional workers), is uniform across MSCs.

However, the variable used in the estimation is not this marginal cost, but an average wage for the labor category in the MSC.[3] Most of the observed variation in this average is due to variation in the seniority profile of workers across MSCs.

MSCs with lower than average "wage rates" simply have more of their workers on the lower steps of the salary schedule. Lower average wages will thus be correlated with recent growth in the workload for that labor category, which in turn may be correlated with unmeasured aspects of the MSC's cost structure. This variation permits coefficient estimates to be calculated, but the estimates cannot realistically be viewed as having much relationship to the true cost function parameters that they are supposed to represent.

Neither high R^2s nor large t-statistics on the first-order coefficients for labor prices are evidence for meaningful variation in those prices. Although this is a cross-section, it is a cross-section in which the largest MSC is about 50 times the size of the smallest; most of the variation in cost and input usage is explained by this variation in scale and R^2s in the mid-90s can be obtained with a single explanatory variable such as mail volume delivered. The first-order coefficients on input prices represent average expenditure shares, and, since the expenditures are observed directly, high t-statistics are to be expected.

Because labor prices⁴ are so central to the approach adopted in this paper and because the barriers to estimation posed by national wage schedules are so significant, there is little prospect of successfully implementing this approach using Postal data. Since all the coefficients are estimated simultaneously, difficulties with the labor price variable may well contaminate estimates of other parameters; discussion of individual parameter estimates thus seems pointless. However, a few other data and specification problems deserve mention.

1. The Origin/Destination Information System (ODIS) volume data used to represent an MSC's "collected" and delivered mail volume by major class (First-Class, third-class, and other) have fairly large sampling errors, and these errors are (inversely) correlated with the size of the MSC. Sampling errors range from about 3% for delivered mail in the largest MSCs to 15% for "collected" mail from small MSCs. This will produce errors-in-variables biases for their coefficients and may possibly affect other coefficients as well.

2. The nature of cost reductions from presorted mail is improperly represented in the model. The paper talks about presorted mail being presented to the Postal Service already arranged in the sequence in which carriers walk their routes. The presort variable is thus included in the delivered mail aggregate. This misrepresents presort-related cost reductions with respect to both the stage-of-processing and the location of the MSCs at which the cost reductions occur:

    (a) Stage-of-processing: In fact, relatively little presorted mail is walk-sequenced—mailers receive no discount for doing this. All presorted mail is presorted at least to the first three digits of the ZIP Code, most is presorted at least to the five-digit ZIP Code, but only in third-class is a substantial portion presorted to the carrier route (although not to walk-sequence). Thus, all presorted mail reduces costs at the initial (or "collected" mail) stage of processing, with successively smaller cost reductions on average as processing proceeds toward the delivered mail stage. The presort variable would therefore be more appropriately included in the "collected" mail aggregate than the delivered mail aggregate.

(b) Location: The presort data for each MSC in fact refer to mail originating in the MSC, not to mail delivered there. Since a large fraction of mail originating in an MSC is delivered by other MSCs, those presort-related cost reductions that do arise at the delivered mail stage-of-processing will occur largely in MSCs other than the one to which the data point refers.

Moving the presort variable to the "collected" mail aggregate would appear to alleviate both of these problems. Unfortunately, subsequent investigation of this source of data for presorted mail has revealed very large inconsistencies in the accuracy and coverage of this variable across MSCs, so that not much information can be expected from this variable even with a conceptually correct specification.

3. Since the above data and specification problems prevent any meaningful analysis of costs at the MSC level, it is redundant to observe that this model can tell us nothing about the costs or productivity of the system as a whole (despite passing remarks about marginal costs, economies-of-scale, etc). However, there is an additional barrier to system-wide inferences: MSC expenditures represent only about 75% of total USPS expenditures. In particular, MSC expenditures do not include either Bulk Mail Centers or mail transportation between MSCs, both of which are largely attributable to specific classes of mail. For the system as a whole, the standard data systems used for accounting and rate-making produce information that is much more accurate (and more detailed with respect to the classes of mail identified) than any data available at the MSC level.

Notes

In the interests of full disclosure, it should be noted that the U.S. Postal Service Office of Economic Analysis funded Professor Norsworthy's initial research in this area but has had no role whatever in the current paper.

1. See Christensen Associates (1990) for a description of the data and its use in productivity measurement.

2. Things are not quite so mechanical for the other two labor categories, but they both have nationally uniform wage schedules and promotion policies.

3. The available data are expenditures on each labor category and hours-worked by employees in that category. The labor "price" variable is an average cost per workhour calculated as the ratio of these two numbers.

4. The materials price variable is also highly unsatisfactory. For materials, only expenditure data are available. Gasoline prices from the Consumer Price Index for 20 areas were assigned to the 200 MSCs and used to compute each MSC's quantity of materials input. Gasoline accounts for less than 5% of MSC materials expenditures, much of it purchased through bulk contracts whose geographic price variation may not correspond to retail price variation, especially since the latter is affected by state excise taxes. Many other materials inputs are purchased through national contracts, with no price variation across MSCs.

Reference

Laurits R. Christensen Associates, Inc. 1990. "United States Postal Service Annual Total Factor Productivity." Available from the Office of Economic Analysis, U.S. Postal Service (March).

8
POSTAL NEWSPAPER DELIVERY AND DIVERSITY OF OPINIONS
Ulrich Stumpf

1. Introduction

In West Germany, prices of postal newspaper delivery (also encompassing periodicals) have traditionally been lower than for comparable large-volume mailings. Postal pricing with regard to the press has been justified by two arguments, the first being related to the demand side and the second to the supply side of press markets. First, consumption of journals would create external benefits to society, notably the informed public vital to a democracy. External benefits would justify lowering prices below marginal costs to induce further consumption. Second, the supply of distribution services would be marked by economies of scale. Large publishers would have an incentive to vertically integrate into distribution and drive smaller competitors out of the market by denying them access to distribution services, thereby reducing diversity of opinion. The danger of restrained access to distribution would justify a subsidized postal service operating as a common carrier.

The Deutsche Bundespost Constitution Act passed in 1989 requires that statutory obligations for postal services provided in competition with private firms are to be reviewed and, if considered as socially beneficial, explicitly defined. As postal newspaper delivery is a competitive service, an evaluation of the preferential treatment of the press is needed. This paper will not try to draw a complete picture of all the questions involved.[1] Rather, it will concentrate on a prominent aspect of the second of the above mentioned arguments: the relationship between postal prices, the structure of press distribution, and access to distribution services. Free access to distribution services may be considered as a structural pre-condition for diversity of opinions transmitted by the press.[2]

I will not deal with all journals admitted to postal distribution at reduced rates. Journals of associations and public institutions will not be taken into account. I will rather concentrate on newspapers, consumer periodicals, and trade (technical, professional, academic) periodicals, whose share of total volume delivered by the

Bundespost was roughly 62% in 1988.

2. Postal Pricing of Newspapers and Periodicals

At present, the price *level* of postal newspaper and periodical delivery is the result of a political bargaining process. The Bundespost and the publishers' associations negotiate on a long-term target share, by which postal revenues should cover fully allocated costs. The rate having been agreed upon, the Bundespost may adjust the price level in order to create a sufficient revenue. Table 1 shows the actual rate at which costs are covered since 1970, which reached an all-time low in 1971 (26.6%). In 1977, the Bundespost and the publishers' associations agreed on a target rate of 50% to be reached by 1985. A series of price increases enabled the Bundespost to reach this rate practically by the year 1982; in 1985, revenues already covered fully allocated cost by 54.1%. In 1988, a new agreement followed on a target rate of 60% to be reached in the year 1994.

Table 1. Revenues and Fully Allocated Costs of Bundespost Distribution of Newspapers and Periodicals, 1970-1988

Year	Revenue (Mio. DM)	Fully Allocated Cost (Mio. DM)	Deficit (Mio. DM)	Rate of Cost Coverage (%)
1970	186.7	602.4	415.7	31.0
1971	187.6	705.3	517.7	26.6
1972*	241.9	709.9	468.0	34.1
1973	245.1	781.6	536.5	31.4
1974	236.3	845.4	609.1	28.0
1975*	305.6	879.7	574.2	34.7
1976	312.0	926.9	615.0	33.7
1977	323.2	930.5	607.4	34.7
1978*	377.1	953.8	576.6	39.5
1979*†	405.6	893.6	488.0	45.4
1980*	445.5	937.3	491.9	47.5
1981*	487.6	1 019.2	531.6	47.8
1982*	516.6	1 038.7	522.1	49.7
1983*	569.1	1 055.2	486.1	53.9
1984	581.4	1 062.2	480.8	54.7
1985	584.3	1 079.1	494.9	54.1
1986*	630.3	1 151.0	520.7	54.8
1987	639.8	1 209.5	570.3	52.9
1988*	690.7	1 233.3	542.7	56.0,

*Price increase at the beginning of the year.
†At the beginning of the year 1979 all packaging, addressing, and cashing-in of subscription fees was transferred from the Bundespost to the publishers resulting in a significant decrease in costs.
Source: Statistical Yearbook of the Deutsche Bundespost

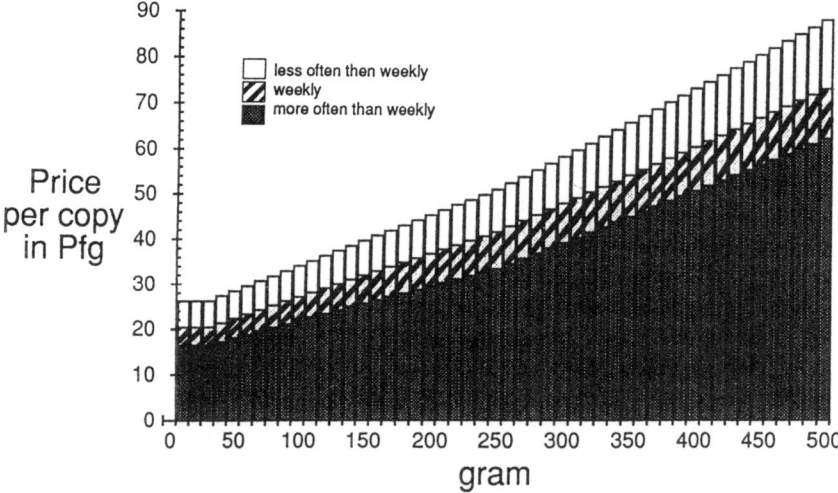

Figure 1. Bundespost Tariffs for Newspapers and Periodicals 1990(a)

(a) Tariff for Postvertriebsstuecke; Journals admitted to reduced tariffs may have a weight up to 1000 g. The overwhelming share of journals distributed by the Bundespost (more than 95 %) has a weight lower than 500 g.

If the Bundespost would be freed from such a constraint on its price level, in the long run, it would try to cover at least its incremental costs of newspaper and periodical delivery. Depending on the degree of competition with alternative delivery services and with the wholesale/retail system, prices could of course be increased above the level necessary to cover incremental costs.In order to cover costs common to newspaper and periodical delivery and the letter and parcel services, some deviation of the price level from average incremental costs is warranted. A welfare-optimal solution requires that the services with a lower price elasticity of demand for the postal service carry a higher mark-up.

The current postal price *structure*, shown in figure 1, has historically been based on frequency of publishing. Three categories are distinguished: journals published more often than weekly, journals published weekly, and journals published less often than weekly. The more frequently published journals bear a lower tariff. Prices are also based on the weight of a journal. For a given frequency of publishing, price increases with weight in steps of 10 gram, as indicated in figure 1.

If the Bundespost were freed from any statutory obligations on newspaper and periodical delivery, the price structure would be fundamentally changed. The price of delivering a certain title would have to cover at least the marginal costs incurred by the Bundespost. Prices could also reflect, to some extent, differing degrees of competition with alternative delivery services and the wholesale/retail system, categories of journals with a less price-elastic demand for postal delivery carrying a higher mark up on marginal costs.

A more cost-based pricing structure necessitates the following changes: first, marginal costs increase with frequency of publishing. Daily or weekly publications require a higher speed of delivery than less frequently published journals. As daily and weekly journals are targeted for delivery the next day after posting, they must be handled at peak-load times associated with higher marginal costs. Other things constant, postal prices for daily or weekly publications should be higher than prices for less frequently published journals.

Second, the rate at which marginal costs increase with weight is probably lower than the current rate at which prices increase with weight, at least in the region of up to 250 g (Most journals have a weight of less than 250 g.) Other things equal, this should be reflected in postal pricing.

Third, publishers with a large postal delivery volume are legally obliged to presort the journals, but receive no discount. As presortation leads to a reduction of postal costs, it should be reflected in lower postal prices. Increasing the postal price level without introducing discounts for presortation would give an advantage to alternative delivery services.

Forth, postal prices are geographically uniform and do not reflect the transport and delivery costs actually incurred.[3] Some publishers use the Bundespost only for local delivery, and transportation to the local destination areas is carried out by private transport firms. There are also publishers who use the Bundespost only for delivery to less densely populated rural areas. Statutory obligations (and cross subsidization) absent, competition with alternative delivery services would force the Bundespost to reflect actual transport and delivery costs to a greater extent in its price structure. Increasing the postal price level without geographically differentiating prices could create profitable opportunities for entry of alternative home delivery services in urban areas.[4]

3. Postal Pricing and the Structure of Newspaper and Periodical Distribution

How would the structure of distribution be changed if postal journal delivery were a competitive service without any statutory obligations? The structure would then be determined by relative consumer valuation and the relative costs of the different modes of distribution. I will briefly sketch these factors before analyzing the probable effect of an increase in postal prices on the structure of journal distribution.

3.1. Consumer Valuation of Different Modes of Distribution

Home delivery services may differ with regard to speed of delivery. A journal may be distributed at the day of publishing with early or late morning delivery rounds or it may be delivered at a later date. Consumer valuation of speed of delivery varies with frequency of publication. A newspaper published six days a week is most highly valued in Germany if it is available by 7 a.m. and will quickly loose its value to most consumers during course of the day. In contrast, valuation of a weekly periodical will not differ between early and late morning delivery at the day of publication. Less frequently published periodicals may loose their value to consumers only slowly during the days following publication.

Compared to home delivery, acquiring a journal regularly at a retail outlet of course causes opportunity costs to a consumer which reduce the net value of a journal. The opportunity costs vary, first, with the density of retail outlets in a particular area, as the time necessary to go to a newsstand decreases with increasing density. Second, opportunity costs increase with increasing frequency of publication of a journal. Purchasing a daily newspaper when its value to most consumers is highest, i.e., at around 7 a.m., entails relatively high opportunity costs. In contrast, acquiring a less frequently published periodical may be postponed, without loss of value, to a time when opportunity costs are low, e.g., when passing by a newsstand returning from work. Third, opportunity costs of acquiring a low-circulation journal might be prohibitive, because there would be high search costs. However, for regular consumers, search costs could be evaded by an explicit or implicit long-term contract between consumer and a retailer.

Home delivery is competing with the wholesale/retail network, but only with respect to regular readers. For occasional readers, transactions costs associated with home delivery are very high or even prohibitive. It is for this reason, that home delivery is normally based on a long term contract, a subscription.

3.2. Costs of Different Modes of Distribution

Distributing journals to homes or retail outlets encompasses essentially two stages.[5] (a) at a national level, sorting the circulation to local/regional destination areas and transporting the bundles to these areas; (b) at a local/regional level, sorting the local/regional circulation to delivery addresses (which may be individual home addresses or retail outlets), and delivering the journals to home addresses by carriers or postmen or to retail outlets by car/truck. We may skip the question of economies of scale at level (a). First, transport costs make up the smaller part of total distribution costs. Second, home delivery firms (or wholesalers) must not be vertically integrated into long-distance transport. If transport volume is too low to exploit economies of scale, transport services might easily be purchased in the market place, as there are a number of suppliers.

Local area delivery of journals to *individual* homes by carriers or postmen is subject to economies of scale, because the time effort per address decreases with an increasing number of addresses on a given delivery route. However, extending local delivery areas by additional delivery routes will be possible only at a rising marginal cost.

In less densely populated areas with a low number of journals to be delivered, newspaper and periodical distribution will be a natural monopoly. In competing for this monopoly, the Bundespost has an advantage because of its legal monopoly on letters, which are jointly delivered with journals. (Joint delivery is associated with economies of scope.) In the more densely populated areas, more than one delivery service can exist. In these areas, there is also room for entry at a smaller scale, if delivery is confined to a few journals with a high enough circulation. If only a few journals are to be delivered, the capital-intensive preaddressing necessary for multiple-journal delivery can be replaced by the less costly alternative of using an address list when delivering the journal.[6] As a delivery route takes two or three hours, this process can use part-time employees. Small scale delivery is also warranted if speed of delivery becomes important, as it is the case for daily newspapers, which have to be delivered to homes within a few hours (4 to 7 a.m.).

Local delivery markets are natural monopolies or oligopolies, depending on the density of population in the area, but local delivery markets seem to be contestable. As delivery is not very capital-intensive and sunk costs are low, entry barriers to local delivery markets should be low.

Delivering a journal to *retail outlets* by a wholesaler also is subject to economies of scale. Serving a geographical area might be a natural monopoly. However there is no market test for this, as West Germany (and West-Berlin) is partitioned into 81 territories with wholesalers protected by monopoly franchises.[7]

The costs of distributing a journal to retail outlets should be lower than the costs of distributing a journal to individual home addresses. Purchasing a journal at a retail outlet implies a transfer of distribution activities to the consumer. Distribution costs are transformed into opportunity costs born by the consumer.

Nevertheless, the costs of distributing a journal to retail outlets may rise above the costs of distribution to home addresses, even if all consumers were regular readers. Demand for a journal at a given retail outlet fluctuates. If the supply of the journal at retail outlets is determined to satisfy maximal demand, periodically a stock of unsold journals will be created. It is essentially the costs associated with the excess supply which may increase the costs of distributing a journal to retail outlets above the level of costs associated with home delivery. Demand fluctuation at individual retail outlets increases for a journal as total demand decreases. The volume supplied of a journal at a retail outlet is larger if the retailer may return unsold stock (sale or return system, as applied in West Germany); it is lower if the retailer must bear the costs of excess supply (firm sale system, as partially applied in the United Kingdom). Consequently, the costs of distributing a low-circulation journal to retail outlets should be higher than the costs of home distribution, in particular if the sale or return system is applied.

3.3. The Structure of Daily Newspaper Distribution

The current postal price structure based on frequency of publication and weight seems to particularly favor the relatively light daily newspapers. Nevertheless, the Bundespost distributed in 1987 only 4.8% of total circulation sold per edition (compare table 2).We can distinguish two groups of daily newspapers. The first group is predominantly sold at retail outlets. It consists of papers with a high share of irregular or impulse purchasers which might only be caught when passing by a newsstand. Circulation sold per edition is also high enough to make home delivery to regular readers more costly than using the wholesale/retail network (including the associated consumers' opportunity costs). Consequently, the share of home delivery is negligible.

The second group of papers is predominantly home delivered to subscribers.

Table 2: Circulation Sold of Daily Newspapers by Mode of Distribution, West Germany 1987

	Number of Titles	Circulation Sold per Edition (1000 Copies)	Average Circulation per Title (1000 Copies)	Share of Circulation Sold			
				Retail (%)	Home Delivery		
					Bundespost (%)	Publisher (%)	Others (%)
Dailies predominantly sold at retail outlets[a]	13	6,389	491	98.6	0.2	0.3	0.9
Dailies with a predominant share of subscribers[b]	305	14,715	48	9.3	6.7	73.2	10.8
All Dailies	318	21,104	66	36.3	4.8	51.1	7.8

[a] Straßenverkaufszeitungen
[b] Abbonnementzeitungen
Source: Statistisches Bundesamt, Bildung und Kultur, Fachserie 11, Reihe 5, Presse 1987, Wiesbaden

Most of them are local/regional newspapers with a high "brand loyalty." Especially for the low-circulation papers, the costs of using the wholesale/retail network seem to be higher than the costs of home delivery. The Bundespost share is nevertheless quite small, and alternative home delivery services are preferred. The reasons are twofold. First, the Bundespost does not provide the speed of delivery most valued by regular readers, which is early morning delivery until 7 a.m. Second, in the more densely populated areas, small-scale delivery of a large-circulation local/regional newspaper with part-time employed carriers using address lists is a low-cost alternative to large-scale delivery.

Taking into account the low Bundespost share of total distribution of daily newspapers, an increase in postal prices for newspapers will only have a small impact on most publishers. An increase in subscription prices for newspapers delivered by the Bundespost would only affect subscribers in areas where publishers have not established home delivery services. Depending on their valuation of the newspaper and their opportunity costs of purchasing the paper at a retail outlet, some of these subscribers might cancel their subscription and become regular or occasional purchasers at the newsstand. A greater competitiveness of the Bundespost could only be achieved if postal early morning delivery rounds would be offered.

3.4. The Structure of Distribution of Weekly Newspapers and Periodicals

At current postal prices, weekly newspapers, as well as consumer and trade periodicals, seem to be subsidized to a smaller extent than daily newspapers, as they are published less frequently and have a higher weight. The Bundespost share of circulation sold per edition varies between 11.5 % for weekly newspapers and 90.4 % for trade periodicals (compare table 3).

Table 3: Circulation Sold of Periodicals and Weekly Newspapers by Mode of Distribution, West Germany 1987

	Number of Titles	Circulation Sold per Edition (1000 Copies)	Average Circulation per Title (1000 Copies)	Share of Circulation Sold			
				Retail (%)	Home Delivery		
					Bundespost (%)	Publisher (%)	Others[a] (%)
Weekly Newspapers	9	4,276	475	67.8	11.5	0.8	19.9
Weekly Political Journals	108	1,693	16	51.4	30.4	12.9	5.2
Consumer Periodicals							
Weeklies[b]	108	39,633	367	78.1	10.9	0.4	10.5
Monthlies[c]	776	50,577	65	45.4	47.4	1.2	6.0
Quaterlies[d]	556	9,928	18	65.7	28.5	1.7	4.1
All	1440	100,139	70	60.4	31.1	0.9	7.6
Trade Periodicals	3168	46,330	15	4.4	90.4	1.4	3.8

[a] Retail (Werbender Buch- und Zeitschriftenhandel) and leasing of periodicals (Lesezirkel)
[b] Including consumer periodicals published more often than weekly
[c] Including consumer periodicals published fortnightly.
[d] Including consumer periodicals published 6 - 8 times/year
Source: See Table 2.

Journals predominantly sold at retail outlets are weekly newspapers (67.8%) and weekly consumer periodicals (78.1%). These are journals which address a general public and which have a high circulation and a high share of irregular readers. Distributing these journals by the wholesale/retail system should be associated with a lower cost than delivering them to individual home addresses. Because circulation is high and frequency of publication is weekly, consumers' opportunity costs of purchasing the journals at retail outlets should also be relatively low.

In contrast, trade periodicals are predominantly home delivered (95.6%). These are journals serving specialized interests of a small number of regular readers. Distributing them by the wholesale/retail system would only be an alternative if consumers and retailers would agree on a regular provision of a journal at a particular newsstand. In West Germany, there are vertical restraints on retailers to sell subscription contracts to consumers, so a contract might only be implicitly formulated. Moreover, unlike weekly newspapers and consumer magazines, a larger share of subscribers to trade magazines consists of firms for which post box delivery is the preferred mode of distribution.

The Bundespost is the preferred delivery service for all periodicals and weekly newspapers. In contrast to daily newspapers, the subsidization of postal rates has a larger impact. First, periodicals and weekly newspapers are less time-sensitive. Consumers would not place a higher value on a journal if a competitor would deliver it earlier than the Bundespost. Second, because of low postal prices, only small-scale alternative delivery confined to a few large-circulation consumer magazines is profitable. The geographical scope of these services is also fairly limited. Extending these services into less densely populated areas would rapidly

lead to marginal delivery costs rising above the Bundespost price.
Increasing postal prices for weekly newspapers and periodicals will not increase the share of alternative delivery to a large extent. First, small-scale delivery services confined to a few journals will face rapidly increasing marginal costs of delivery if extended into less densely populated areas. Marginal costs will quickly rise to the increased Bundespost price level, making further extension unprofitable.Second, entry of large-scale multiple-periodical delivery services will be confined to some urban areas, where a number of competitors can exist. Rural areas are natural monopolies. The Bundespost has an advantage in competing for these monopolies, because it can deliver journals together with letters and large-volume mailings on which it has a legal monopoly.

Rather than inducing entry of alternative home delivery services, the main effect of a postal price increase seems to be that consumers will substitute purchasing at retail outlets for postal home delivery. Particularly, if subscription prices rise above retail prices, retail purchasing will be an alternative for readers of high-circulation weekly newspapers and consumer magazines. In contrast, low-circulation trade periodicals might not be purchased at the newsstand, unless consumer and retailer implicitly or explicitly agree on regular provision of the journal.

4. Postal Prices and Access to Distribution

Opinions can only be freely expressed in the press if access to the distribution stage is free. As local/regional wholesaling and home delivery is marked by economies of scale, distributive services will not be produced by each publisher. Local/regional wholesaling and home delivery will be a natural monopoly or an oligopoly, depending on the density of population in the area. Freedom of access to the distribution stage then has two normative implications: the incumbent distributors (a) earn no supranormal profits and (b) offer their services at non-discriminatory prices to all publishers.

In West Germany, freedom of access to wholesale distribution cannot be achieved by competitive forces. Wholesaling is geographically monopolized and the territorial wholesaler monopolists are protected by exclusive arrangements with all publishers. The volume distributed to retail outlets is determined according to a demand estimation model agreed upon by the publisher, wholesaler, and retailer associations. Wholesalers (and retailers) receive a margin of the cover price of the journals sold, which is also based on an agreement between the respective associations.This system of vertical and horizontal restraints, which has been exempted from the cartel ban, prevents wholesale markets from being competitive or contestable. Therefore, free access to wholesale distribution cannot be guaranteed by competitive forces. The extent to which the horizontal and vertical restraints discriminate against smaller publishers is a question which cannot be answered in this paper.

In contrast to wholesaling, home delivery is not cartellized. Freedom of access to delivery might be seen endangered by two factors. First, the monopolist or oligopolist suppliers of delivery services may be able to reap monopoly rents. The consumers would have to pay higher prices, and journals with a price elastic demand may no longer be financially viable. Market power on the delivery stage may also be used for political purposes, e.g., for cross-subsidizing journals, which consumers would not want to purchase at a price covering the costs of the journal. Second, publishers may have an incentive to vertically integrate into delivery, in order to squeeze out smaller rivals competing in the same relevant journal markets by denying them access to delivery services at a non-discriminatory price.

The proposition that concentration on the delivery stage leads to monopoly power is unfounded. As sunk costs associated with local/regional home delivery are relatively low, potential competition would discipline the incumbent distributors. The price level could not be raised above the stand alone costs of journal delivery, and the scope for supranormal profits or for a discriminatory price structure would be small.

A problem may arise with vertical integration of publishers into delivery. If their own circulation is large enough to arrive at lower average delivery costs than competing delivery services, including the Bundespost, they may be able to squeeze smaller publishers out of the market. They will simply have to deny competing smaller publishers access to their delivery services.

The necessary conditions for such a situation are:

(1) in the local delivery area, the delivery volume of the vertically integrated publisher is larger than that of competing delivery services;

(2) readers of small circulation journals (which serve a differentiated taste) are prepared to switch to the high circulation journal (which serves a more general taste) if the price advantage of the latter is high enough, but not vice versa;

(3) there are barriers-to-entry, in particular introducing a journal into the market is associated with sunk costs.

Figure 2 illustrates the proposition. For simplification suppose that there are only two publishers with a circulation of q_1 and q_2. Assume that the long-run average costs of production curve of the incumbent publishers is downward sloping and that the larger publisher has a cost advantage of $(\overline{q_1 A_1} - \overline{q_2 A_2})$. Suppose also that delivery is marked by economies of scale and that initially both publishers purchase delivery services from an independent supplier at a price of $\overline{A_3 C_3}$ (equal to the average cost of delivery at a delivery volume of $q_1 + q_2$). The two journals are therefore produced and distributed at average costs of $\overline{q_1 A'_1}$ and $\overline{q_2 A'_2}$, respectively. Finally, assume that some consumers are willing to pay a higher price for the small circulation journal because they find that their preferences are better served.

Vertical integration of the larger publisher into delivery would increase its average costs from $\overline{q_2 A'_2}$ to $\overline{q_2 C_2}$, whereas the average costs of the smaller publisher would increase from $\overline{q_1 A'_1}$ to $\overline{q_1 C_1}$. (Because the delivery volume of the independent producer would fall to q_1, average costs of delivery and, therefore, the price to be paid to the independent delivery service would rise from $\overline{A_3 C_3}$ to $\overline{A_1 C_1}$). Vertical integration would increase the cost advantage of the larger publish-

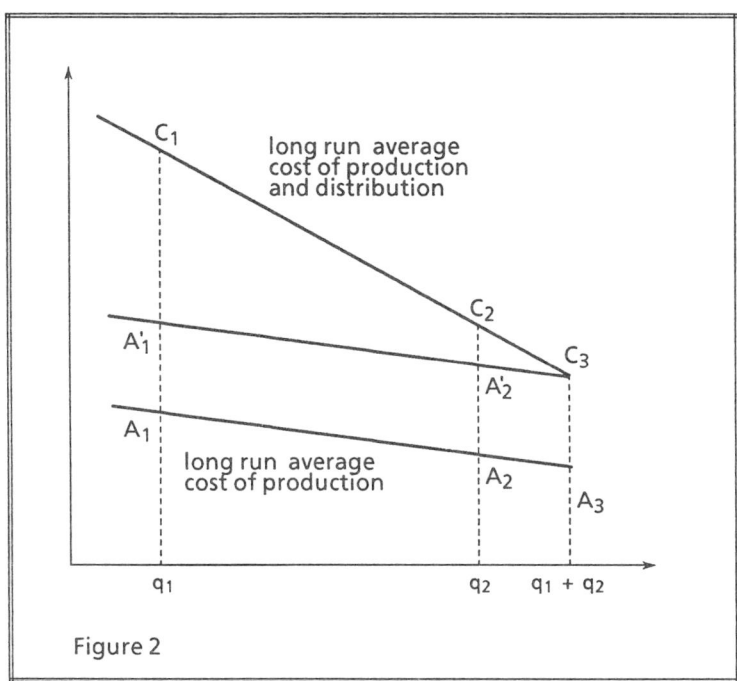

Figure 2

er. The price of the large circulation journal will have to rise, but the price of the small circulation journal will have to rise even more, so that the price differential will increase. A situation might occur where some or all readers of the small circulation journal might find the price advantage of the large circulation paper attractive enough to compensate for the loss of value associated with a substitution. As a result, the smaller publisher would be squeezed out of the market by the larger, vertically integrated publisher. Society is worse off as the number of journals (and opinions) has decreased.

However, although the above-made assumptions of entry barriers and asymmetric substitutability are quite realistic, it is currently unlikely that vertical integration of publishers of *periodicals and weekly* newspapers into delivery would cause a problem. First, total delivery volume will encompass all periodicals, as well as large volume mailings, letters, and other small items which might be jointly delivered with periodicals. Local circulation of a single publisher will only make up for a small part of total local delivery volume. Second, regularly purchasing a periodical at the newsstand will be an alternative to many consumers. Publishers vertically integrated into delivery cannot gain market power as long as access to the wholesale/retail system is free.

In contrast, early morning home delivery is specific to a certain class of *daily newspapers*. Bundespost late morning delivery and the retail network are only partial substitutes for it. Total early morning delivery volume is small. The leading local newspaper publisher in the area may easily arrive at a lower average delivery cost than his competitors due to his larger circulation and may therefore be able to squeeze them out in the way described above.

5. Conclusion

The preservation of a greater number of competing publishers and of diversity of opinion does not require a postal subsidization of *periodicals* and *weekly newspapers*. Only with regard to *daily newspapers* the argument has some merit, although subsidization of postal prices would not be sufficient. Preserving diversity of opinion in the local/regional newspaper markets would require in the first place the introduction of postal early morning delivery rounds. Subsidization might be warranted if the postal volume of daily newspapers (and other time-sensitive items delivered together with newspapers) would not be high enough to arrive at the level of unit delivery costs of the leading local/regional newspaper publisher's delivery service. Finally, it should be noted that an overall subsidization of postal journal delivery might still be grounded on positive externalities associated with the consumption of journals, an argument which I did not deal with in this paper.

Notes

1. A Wissenschaftliches Institut für Kommunikationsdienste (WIK) research project on postal newspaper delivery will complete a full theoretical and empirical analysis until mid 1991.
2. Hypothetically, a monopolist publisher vertically integrated into distribution may have an economic incentive to transmit diversity of opinions in his journals, but I do not consider the alternative as compatible with democratic principles.
3. If postal circulation of a publication is more than 200,000 copies and if the average number of copies delivered per post code area is more than 75, the Bundespost offers a (negligible) discount, which might be interpreted as a discount for nationwide delivery.
4. Alternatively, geographical uniformity of prices could be defined as a statutory obligation. In this case, postal delivery in rural areas would have to be internally subsidized out of profits made in sectors where the Bundespost has a legal monopoly. The 1989 Deutsche Bundespost Constitution Act offers such a possibility.
5. There may be intermediate stages of sorting and conveyance.
6. The delivering personnel might also cash in the subscription fees.
7. In five territories, the spectrum of journals is split between two wholesalers.

COMMENTS
Frank A. Scott, Jr.

How should postal rates be set, for newspapers, or for any other category of mail? The seemingly easy answer is: Set prices equal to long-run marginal cost. If long-run marginal cost is less than long-run average cost and a break-even constraint must be satisfied, then some second-best solution must be reached. If multiple products are offered by the monopolist and there are economies of scope, we are led into some scheme like Ramsey pricing. We add the stipulation that revenues should cover incremental costs but not exceed stand-alone costs.

All this implies that the first order of business in postal ratemaking is good cost data. It is crucial to know how different functions affect postal costs. Without such information, we are operating in the dark. The reluctance of postal services like the USPS and the Bundespost to come up with such data does not lead one to be optimistic about their ability to survive if they are ever thrown to the competitive wolves.

Now, given that we know next to nothing about the Bundespost's costs of delivering newspapers, let us turn first to their rates and then to the vertical structure of the periodicals industry. Stumpf points out four ways in which the Bundespost would have to adjust rates if faced with open competition. Prices would have to reflect differences in quality of service, weight, presorting, and point of delivery into the system. If current deliberations over postal policy in the European Economic Community lead to greater competition in areas like newspaper and periodical delivery, then I think that his predictions will be soon realized.

As for the vertical structure of the industry, Stumpf raises a number of concerns. I must admit that I do not share all of his concerns. When it comes to delivery of the newspaper or periodical to the customer, producers and consumers will arrive at the solution that is efficient, if they are left to work it out themselves. To the extent that consumers are willing to pay for the convenience of home delivery, publishers will provide for it. Consumers who regularly pass newsstands at convenient times will likely take care of final delivery of the product themselves.

Home delivery of newspapers may display some aspects of natural monopoly. It is entirely plausible that average delivery costs decline with increasing density of customers. As delivery points change from being a quarter-mile apart to twenty yards apart to five feet apart, one can imagine decreasing average costs. Beyond that, however, it is hard to see how costs could decline much more, since such a small portion of the deliverer's time and effort is spent on moving from one point to another. In fact, the congestion that goes with greater density may cause unit costs to rise. Mr. Rogers of the United Parcel Service has indicated that delivery in midtown Manhattan, with a density rivalling that of uranium, is more costly than in more sparsely populated areas.

Stumpf addresses the issue of who bears the cost of variability in demand. These costs do not disappear if a magazine publisher adopts a return system rather than a firm sale system in dealing with its retail outlets. Suppose consumers desire to read a magazine some weeks and do not want to read it other weeks. The publisher will find it profitable to publish only if consumer willingness to pay on those occasions when a magazine is desired covers the total publication and distribution cost. Consumers ultimately bear the cost of their uncertain demand, if magazine publishing is competitive. Allowing a newsstand to return unsold copies does not alter this principle. Retailers who are asked to bear the risk of unsold copies will respond by reducing the wholesale price they are willing to pay for the periodical. A better way to view low-circulation journals is in the same way as letters from one's grandmother. Infrequently delivered items are more efficiently distributed if they are grouped with other infrequently delivered items.

Another worry of Stumpf's is that a large newspaper may create market power by vertically integrating into delivery. In figure 2, he analyzes a scenario where there are scale economies both in production and delivery of the periodical. I do not see why it makes a difference whether the economies come from production or delivery—the situation described is a natural monopoly. The expressed concern is that diversity of opinion may be stifled; however, consumers are depicted as not valuing such diversity enough to make publication of a second newspaper profitable. The monopolist in this example could lower its own costs by delivering a rival's product along with its own, so squelching diversity has a price attached to it. Apparently, the monopoly newspaper values lack of diversity more than readers value a second option in newspapers.

From this argument Stumpf concludes that society is worse off. To reach such a conclusion one must posit a social welfare function that has diversity of opinion as its only argument. Newspapers in the United States do seem to display natural monopoly tendencies. This may be as much due to declining demand as consumers shift to alternative media as to anything else. I think that the scenario created in this example is a bit stretched. I certainly am not comfortable justifying the subsidization of newspaper delivery on this line of argument.

9

COMPETITION IN POSTAL SERVICE
Roger Sherman

The post office "...will be a source of eternal scramble among the members (of Congress), (to see) who can get the most money wasted in their states."
Thomas Jefferson (in letter to Madison, March 6, 1796)

The largest public enterprise in the United States is the United States Postal Service (USPS), which claims to handle over 40% of the world's mail. Revenues of USPS in fiscal 1989 totaled almost $40 billion, and the workforce numbered about 800,000. In its original department-of-government form, postal service allowed political representatives to satisfy their constituents so thoroughly as to confirm the prediction by Thomas Jefferson quoted above. Postal service has passed through remarkable changes since then, moving from reliance on equestrian skills to the use of high-tech optical sorting and from a department of government to a public enterprise form of organization. But further dramatic changes are now in prospect, and, for speeding the delivery of important messages, the daring of the pony express rider from the 1800s may be giving way to the cleverness of electronics engineers as we approach the twenty-first century.

Today's rapid technological change favors new means of communicating the written word. To be sure, there now are simple means of coding, and thereby cheaply sorting, regular mail items. But there also are more ways to transmit messages immediately from one point to another, without any need for physically sorting and moving an original hard copy. And there are effective alternative movers of some hard-copy materials, where the purpose is narrow and the movers have tailored their service carefully to meet users' needs. Traditional mail thus is surrounded by a growing number of alternative ways for users to accomplish their written communication purposes.

In many countries, traditional ways of organizing many economic activities are being reconsidered, and, given the changes in technology that are occurring, it is not surprising that postal service should be included among them. One country,

New Zealand, has seemed to turn postal service over to market forces, although the postal organization there is really close to a public enterprise form, in that it is government-owned. What is unusual about the New Zealand arrangement is that the enterprise is charged with returning a profit as a taxpaying entity, and it is limited in its price increases to the change in consumer prices, less a percentage for productivity improvement (2% for the first price increase and 1% for any additional increase in the three-year term of the arrangement). Perhaps aided by its relatively small scale, the New Zealand Post has responded vigorously to this organizational change, and the consequences are worth careful observation. Postal service remains almost solely a government-provided service, however, and any change from this status will require thoughtful consideration. To consider a change in this status, we shall focus on the United States, where calls for competition and privatization have occurred recently.

One of the major features of the economic reorganization that is sweeping through many countries is the growing role being given to market competition. It provides a basis for both evaluating consumer satisfaction with the goods and services that are provided and for motivating their efficient provision. Postal service has rarely been subject to competition in the modern age, mainly because government authority has given protection from it. Without an opportunity to observe competition in postal service, it is difficult to gauge the role that it might play.

Our approach is to evaluate the limited degree of competition that exists and very crudely to observe its consequences, and also to evaluate the soundness of USPS arguments over the past twenty years about its need for protection from competition. We begin by describing the organization of the USPS and examining the basis and scope of its protection from competition. Next, we consider the forms of competition that now exist, and the recent experience of USPS in light of these elements of competition. We then consider some theoretical aspects of competition and monopoly, giving special emphasis to the role of the uniform price in the USPS argument for protection from competition. Finally, we shall raise the questions of how and whether competition should be considered for postal service in the United States.

1. Organization of the USPS and Its Monopoly Status

1.1. Current Organization

The USPS was created as a public enterprise in 1970, to replace a predecessor organization that had operated as a cabinet-level government department essentially since two hundred years ago, 1790. The original Post Office Department's spending had been from Congressional appropriation, while postal revenues had gone into the Treasury. Political influences controlled activities, from the levels of postal rates to the appointments of village postmasters. The organization was widely regarded as inefficient, and was even the butt of jokes on the subject. Indeed, service problems in the 1960s, combined with billion dollar deficits,[1] led to organizational reform in 1970 through the Postal Reorganization Act.[2]

The Postal Reorganization Act created a public corporation, the USPS, in order to remove the postal agency from politics, so that it could operate with modern management methods. The USPS was a responsible unit that would meet its expenses out of its own revenues, with a transition level of explicit overall subsidy and limited borrowing and investment decision powers. Employees of the USPS were taken out of the United States Civil Service system and allowed to bargain collectively. Resulting wages were expected to match those in the private sector. To oversee the establishment of mail classes and rates, a Postal Rate Commission (PRC) was created by the Act. This commission was to ensure that rates were justified, with each service covering its costs so there was no cross subsidization among the services. However, the PRC was not a regulatory commission in the ordinary sense; its decisions were advisory to the Board of Governors of the USPS in that the Board could overturn them if it acted unanimously to do so.

Collective bargaining seems to have led to handsome wages for postal workers. Queues for job openings are long, turnover rates are remarkably low, and the premium earned by USPS workers over their private sector counterparts may even be growing.[3] In agencies that compete with USPS (where that is allowed), wages appear to be lower.[4] It is possible, therefore, that some USPS monopoly power has been converted to wages for postal employees beyond those appropriate for comparable work in the private sector, which is certainly an unfair and inefficient outcome of a grant of monopoly power. If it would be accomplished, the introduction of competition should limit conversion of monopoly power into excessive wage payments, and thereby achieve one of the purposes of the Postal Reorganization Act.

Although the USPS was organized very differently from its predecessor, the Post Office Department, many old pricing policies were continued, seemingly in violation of the 1970 Act. Indeed, in deciding an appeal by the Association of American Publishers to the first rate decision of the Postal Rate Commission, the District of Columbia Court of Appeals found cost allocation methods inadequate. And in deciding an appeal of the next Commission decision in 1974 (by the National Association of Greeting Card Publishers) the court said:

> We conclude that the Commission's present method for assigning unattributable costs proceeds from a faulty premise in contravention of the Act and therefore must be rejected.[5]

The main problem courts saw in USPS pricing could be traced to inadequate determination of costs. The USPS initially argued that most of its costs were fixed and independent of the volume of mail it handled; it claimed it could assign or attribute less than half its total costs to individual mail services, with the result that the fractions of costs that varied with the volumes of those services were very low. When used as a basis for setting welfare-maximizing Ramsey prices, these cost representations would lead to a relatively high rate for first class mail, where the postal monopoly resulted in the lowest elasticity of demand, and low rates for other classes, where there was more competition. This result followed from the application to lower marginal costs of mark ups that had to recover a large portion of total cost, since, according to the Ramsey rule, the markups were inversely proportional to demand elasticities. Those for whom first-class rates were important, such as greeting card publishers, objected that resulting rates were too high. Competitors in high elasticity mail classes, such as United Parcel service which contended for parcel post business, argued on the other hand that USPS rates there were lower than marginal costs would be if costs were properly calculated.

Cross subsidization among the mail classes was a major issue of the 1970s. The response by regulators at the Postal Rate Commission was not to focus on the cost determination problem, as one might expect, but rather to temper its sympathy for Ramsey pricing. For its part, the USPS presented cost analyses at rate hearings that quite obviously were designed to sustain the long existing rate structure, to keep the rate high where monopoly power was greatest, on first-class mail, and to offer relatively low rates on other classes of mail. The interests that historically had benefitted from this sort of rate structure included newspapers, magazines, book and record clubs, churches, and many others, and they continued to work their will. Indeed, legislation was even introduced in Congress to limit arbitrarily the percentage of total cost that could be traced to mail classes,[6] but fortunately this effort to control the facts of the world by legislating them did not pass. Of course, elimination of cross subsidization had been one of the aims of the Postal Reorganization Act, so questions about accounting for costs to see whether cross subsidization existed were important. And since cross subsidization requires monopoly power, the monopoly question also is important to pricing soundness.

1.2. Origin of the Postal Monopoly

The United States postal monopoly primarily covers letter mail, and its origin has been traced by Priest (1975) back to English rule of the colonies. The original postal monopoly in England was political, not economic, to "compel all writers to use the royal post so that government officials, by reading the letters, could discover and suppress communication of treason and sedition."[7] When Parliament took control of postal service in the 17th century, it used monopoly power to raise revenue, by awarding the contract to provide service on specified terms to the highest bidder. This practice was nominally continued under the restoration Parliament, except that profit would go to the crown and Charles II would choose the contractor. The result was management either by leaders too busy to handle the task properly or by incompetents, and one consequence was inattention to postal service in the colonies. The Continental Congress established its own mail delivery organization, primarily because secure communication was needed as war threatened. Monopoly was claimed for the service, perhaps to create revenue for a financially weak government, but the service connected only state capitals and major cities, and some states still had to provide delivery within their territories and even assist the national delivery. The political advantages of an effective mail service soon became evident to early leaders of the new country, though, including George Washington, and that is why the decade from 1790 to 1800 saw great expansion of the service, even to southern and western frontiers. At that time, the fundamental reasons for monopoly arose: to raise sufficient revenues from eastern cities to cover the cost of delivering mail to remote frontiers, to carry newspapers and magazines for less than they cost, and to carry governmental mail free (franked mail). Monopoly was needed to support a policy of cross subsidization, from thriving cities to developing frontier areas, for newspaper and magazine delivery, and for government mail.

The postal monopoly was strengthened and redefined repeatedly in early United States history,[8] mainly to eliminate loopholes, but a crisis developed after about 50 years. Revenues needed to support service to the frontiers required postal rates so high that private express services, while illegal, could be very profitable. Even though greater speed and security were also advantages of private services and their rates in eastern cities were much lower, for years most citizens continued to respect the laws against private express services. When reform of postal service in England was initiated in 1839 and 1840, however, with a reduction in postage to a uniform rate of one penny regardless of distance, similar reform was thought by many to be appropriate in the United States. After the United States Congress refused to undertake reform, mailers lost their respect for the statutes, and private express services flourished.

The loss of Post Office revenues to private express services became serious in the early 1840s. In response, the strongest law against private express was passed in 1845,[9] and it remains essentially the law against private express service today. It prohibited privately sending a letter, carrying a letter, transporting a person carrying a letter, and carriage of letters by employees, managers, or owners of transport companies.[10] The Act exempted carriage of newspapers and periodicals, and, while the Postal Service has since claimed it can prohibit private carriage of them, it also has said that it will suspend this right.[11]

It is worth noting that the aim of Sir Rowland Hill, who led the 1939-40 postal reform in England that brought the uniform one-penny post, was primarily to have postal rates reflect postal costs, so that mailers would pay the cost consequences of their actions. Before the reform, rates had been based on a complicated formula, including distance, and the recipient could pay for the mail rather than the sender. Sir Rowland Hill found that, for mail service among main towns, transportation was a fairly small part of total cost (.28 of a penny out of .84 of a penny (Coase 1947)). Since distance was not a crucial determinant of cost, he argued against making distance a crucial determinant of price. Distribution to other, secondary, communities from the main "post-towns" was more costly, and he suggested a number of ways to pay the added cost. His main proposal was to have recipients in secondary communities pay an added charge to cover that cost on delivery, though he also thought communities might shoulder the added cost in a variety of ways (Hill and Hill 1880, Vol. I, 251-57). In the end, he embraced the uniform rate because it was a way politically to win improved rates through adoption of reform, and not because he found the principle of a uniform rate important for its own sake.

No one doubts that a mail monopoly was created in the United States to foster cross subsidization, mainly to have eastern cities support mail service to the nation's frontiers. So when cross subsidization was rejected in the Postal Reorganization Act, the need for monopoly was wisely questioned; the 1970 Act ordered the Postal Service Governors to reevaluate the prohibition of private letter carriage.[12] Their reevaluation supported continuation of the monopoly, but on grounds that Priest (1975) has shown to be unconvincing. For instance, they appealed to natural monopoly as a reason, yet they seemed to acknowledge also that a true natural monopoly would need no protection through legislation because cost advantages alone would provide it. They argued that the requirement of a uniform rate, which they defended, justified protection from entry, since some services would cost much less than that rate and some more and without protection the low-cost services would be skimmed away. It was also claimed that some services that are provided, such as window service in post offices, could not recover compensation without the presence of monopoly. Finally, although the Postal Service was to be compensated for providing services, such as those in small communities, that would otherwise not be self supporting, the Postal Service Governors feared that such compensation might not be adequate. Then self sufficiency could require higher rates on other services where, without monopoly protection, entry could occur. The latter two claims could be overcome by proper government payment for the services involved. The possibility of "cream skimming" under uniform rates appears to be the only substantive point raised by the Board of Governors as basis for postal monopoly. It should be noted in passing that no consideration was given by the Board of Governors to the incentives for efficiency that might be created by weakening the monopoly statutes.

The Postal Service Governors are like many others who make arguments about postal service—their claims lack a basis in fact. The accounting system is not able to reveal how much different letters cost within the uniform price class. The problem of accounting for such costs is a very difficult one, to be sure, but it also has not been seriously attempted. In the twenty years since postal reorganization, there has been no convincing demonstration of correctly allocated postal costs. Costs are imputed to broad historical mail classes, rather than to the various functions performed, and subsequent overhead allocations are sometimes nonsensical. Simply because a uniform rate is required for first-class mail is not reason enough to ignore cost differences within that class. If USPS is going to argue that important cost differences exist, it should demonstrate them. Essentially, the best argument for monopoly by the Postal Service Board of Governors is an admission that the Postal Service does not know the costs of its services reliably enough to set prices with the precision needed to protect itself from entry.

2. Growing Sources of Competition and Their Effects

2.1. Sources of Competition

The telephone, along with radio and television, transformed the way that we communicate. The importance to politicians of these communication media today is quite obvious and helps us to understand how, in the absence of modern communications media during the first fifty years of United States history, politicians were so keen to promote postal service. In addition to these audio and visual media, the electronic age has fostered written communication through telex, facsimile machine, and computer connections that allow a variety of modern marvels such as instantaneous transfer of funds. A host of organizations also move hard copy missives outside the government postal service. A brief review of some of these alternative means of communication is useful just to remind us of how different our environment is from the ones where postal service was established or protected so strongly as a monopoly.

Facsimile (Fax) Machines. Last year about 1.4 million fax machines were sold in the United States, raising the total number in use to about 3 million. Roughly half are commercial machines, currently doing about $5 billion annual turnover. First brought to the mass market by the Japanese, whose language can be transmitted more efficiently when no keyboard is involved, fax machines send written messages immediately as data over telephone lines so other machines can receive the messages and produce copies. Although such a copy is not legally an original document, the speed of its transmission gives fax an advantage over the mail.

Present day fax machines use regular rather than thermal paper, can deal with color, and can store messages to be transmitted at night, saving telephone costs and/or reaching people conveniently in other time zones. They can even work with cellular phones in vehicles. Perhaps the greatest advantage of fax machines is that they can connect with personal computers, which for want of standardization are often unable otherwise to communicate with each other. This computer interface allows effective management of information, a function that goes beyond the mere transmission of written messages. Here, in addition to speed, is another potential advantage of the fax machine over the mail.

E-mail Services. In the United States, AT&T Mail, MCI Mail, U.S. Sprint Telemail, Western Union Telegraph's Easy Link, and others provide the equivalent of mail boxes for individual subscribers to whom they provide electronic mail (E-mail). [13] These subscribers are able to communicate electronically with other subscribers in the same system. Some of the public systems are also affiliated with data sources such as CompuServe, which is accessible from MCI Mail. Recent international agreement on protocols promises interconnection among different systems, although details that would control aspects such as the sharing of revenues have yet to be worked out. In the meantime, there exist organizations that can translate messages across systems, at some added cost. Mailbox systems built around local area networks usually are not easily connected to the public carriers, but that might change in the future and have considerable effect.

The simplest E-mail communication within one system is cheaper than fax transmission (by 10% to 40%) for one page, and much cheaper for a longer report. Different addresses and routings can cause major differences in costs, however, so economies on that order cannot be expected across a wide range of addresses. E-mail and fax are usually cheaper than long-established telex communications systems. Express mail service, which is slower but carries originals, can be less expensive than telex or even fax, if a long report is involved, but will seldom match the low cost of E-mail within a single system.

Within a single company, communication by E-mail through a computer network is even cheaper, once the network is in place, and roughly 70% of current electronic mailboxes are on such private systems. In many cases, software allows messages to be converted to the fax medium, thereby overcoming the lack of standardization that keeps private networks from connecting with one another. A large coordinated effort among business, government, and universities is underway to transfer information from one computer to another at far greater speeds than are presently available. AT&T, IBM, and more than ten other companies are participating, along with the National Science Foundation, and the effectiveness of E-mail might improve enormously from the effort.

Express Mail. Many express-mail services have been introduced in recent years, such as Federal Express, Purolator Courier, Emery, DHL, TNT, UPS, or the USPS's Express Mail. They deliver original hard-copy messages as rapidly as overnight. The largest, Federal Express, takes in more than $5 billion a year, while Express Mail at USPS takes in a little more than 10% of that, over $500 million a year. Although, in protecting its monopoly, the Postal Service has regarded as letter mail such items as "payroll checks, fishing licenses, Mickey Mouse posters, San Francisco Forty-niners tickets, punch cards, blueprints, data processing tapes, computer programs, credit cards" and more, it now does not oppose express mail services.[14] One reason is that they are point-to-point courier services, and perhaps another is that the users of these services would complain so much if they were ended.

Express mail services may draw away some business that would otherwise go to first-class mail, and so be seen as a competitor. But it can also be seen as a way to extend mail service into the high-speed realm of electronic services, and thereby enlarge the market for mail. To the extent it is an extension, however, it is dominated by private suppliers of express mail rather than by USPS.

Newspapers, Magazines, Radio, and Television. All of the print and electronic media carry advertisements to potential consumers. The USPS carries these advertising messages, too, in third-class and direct mail forms and also in newspapers and magazines, when those are delivered as mail. Third-class direct mail is clearly in competition with the other forms of advertising, which have grown enormously in this century. Advertising messages can be delivered to homes by private agencies if the messages are unaddressed. Such agencies are prevented by USPS from using the recipients' mailboxes, however, so the messages are often left in plastic sacks hanging from doorknobs. USPS claims a monopoly right to deliver addressed third-class advertising.

This range of alternative communication means has greatly diminished USPS activities relative to what they might have been, especially those that lacked monopoly protection. And it has eroded the power of the monopolized areas as well. Of course, communication is also growing in volume and importance, but the share going to means other than postal service appears to be growing at the same time. Adie (1989) estimates that about half of today's mail, mainly first-class, could be shifted to an electronic form of communication. There now is no way to reach every household by electronic communications, but that may come, for Japan is currently considering a fiberoptic network for households. With such a network, there would be little need for postal service as we know it today. Considerable change in postal revenue patterns can be seen over the past ten years as a result of alternative means of communication.

2.2. The Pattern of Postal Revenues

Revenues from major classes of mail in the 1980s are shown in table 1. Table 2 presents the same data in constant 1989 dollars. Table 3 compares the classes' shares in total revenue at the beginning and end of the period. Although changes in reporting require minor adjustments to allow comparison across the period,[15] table 3 shows that First-Class and Priority mail have changed little in the proportion of mail revenue represented. Another area with some monopoly protection, Third-Class Mail, was a major source of growth as it increased its share of total revenue by 50% (from 14.42% in 1981 to 21.60% in 1989). The competitive field of express mail saw growth in revenue share of 5.4% from a very low starting point just after the service was introduced, so the dollar volumes are not large. Moreover, the service has had almost no growth in revenue since 1984. As a portion of total revenue, the classes that have faced long standing competition have declined. In share of total revenue, Second-Class mail fell 15% over the decade (from 4.86% in 1981 to 4.15% in 1989), and Fourth-Class mail share fell 42% (from 4.31% in 1981 to 2.48% in 1989).

Table 1. Fiscal Year Revenues by Major Mail Classes (in Current $ Billions)

Mail	1989a*	1988	1987	1986	1985	1984	1983	1982	1981
First-Class and Priority	23.81	21.96	19.87	19.05	17.70	16.14	15.10	14.57	12.22
Express	.55	.51	.50	.49	.54	.49	.42	.34	.27
Second-Class	1.51	1.39	1.28	1.22	1.09	1.03	.96	.96	.89
Third-Class	7.73	7.13	6.15	5.61	4.89	4.24	3.68	3.30	2.64
Fourth-Class	.85	.87	.82	.81	.76	.77	.75	.79	.79
All Mail	36.66	33.92	30.50	29.12	26.82	24.45	22.72	21.78	18.31

Source: Annual Reports of the Postmaster General of the United States Postal Service.
*Revenues were reported differently from other years in 1989, when franked and penalty mail volumes were distributed among mail classes rather than being separately reported. Column 1989a has been adjusted to make the 1989 data consistent with earlier years following a procedure that is described in note to table 3.

Table 2. Fiscal Year Revenues by Major Mail Classes (in 1989 $ Billions)									
Mail	1989a*	1988	1987	1986	1985	1984	1983	1982	1981
First-Class and Priority	23.81	22.87	21.38	21.14	20.16	18.93	18.36	18.40	16.42
Express	.55	.53	.54	.54	.61	.57	.51	.43	.36
Second-Class	1.51	1.45	1.38	1.35	1.24	1.21	1.17	1.21	1.20
Third-Class	7.73	7.42	6.62	6.23	5.57	4.97	4.47	4.17	3.55
Fourth-Class	.85	.91	.88	.90	.87	.90	.91	1.00	1.06
All Mail	36.69	35.31	32.81	32.32	30.54	28.67	27.62	27.51	24.60

Source: Data in table 1, adjusted to constant 1989 dollars by GNP deflator.
*Revenues were reported differently from other years in 1989, when franked and penalty mail volumes were distributed among mail classes rather than being separately reported. Column 1989a has been adjusted to make the 1989 data consistent with earlier years, following a procedure that is described in note to table 3.

The pattern of change over the 1980s is also apparent from table 2, which gives revenue by mail classes in constant dollars, and from table 4, which reports the number of pieces and the weight of each class of mail by year. Even in constant dollars, First-Class mail revenue per piece grew by 7% from 1981 to 1989, while Express Mail revenue per piece fell 29% over the same period. In Second-, Third-, and Fourth-Class mail, where weight is more important, constant-dollar revenue per pound rose by 10.5% in Third-Class and 5.4% in Second-Class, but fell 4.1% in Fourth-Class mail.

Thus the areas of lower relative revenue gain for USPS are areas where there is competition, Express Mail, Second-Class mail (comprising mainly newspapers and magazines), and Fourth-Class mail (mainly parcels). Third-Class mail has grown enormously in the 1980s, to the point where there are common complaints about the volume of "junk mail" we find in our mailboxes. The USPS has enjoyed

Table 3. Percentage of Total Revenue by Major Mail Classes			
Mail	1989*	1989a	1981
First-Class and Priority	67.24	64.96	66.74
Express	1.55	1.50	1.47
Second-Class	4.15	4.13	4.86
Third-Class	21.60	21.10	14.42
Fourth-Class	2.48	2.31	4.31
Total These Classes	97.02	94.00	91.80
Total All Classes	100.00	100.00	100.00

*As reported in 1989, two mail classes that formerly were identified separately, Penalty and Franked, which accounted for 4.15% of revenue in 1981, were allocated to actual classes where they were processed. The additional column, 1989a, has been reconstructed to reduce revenues in these classes, to make them comparable with earlier years, according to the distribution of Penalty and Franked mail among the classes that is available for 1988. See note 15 for this distribution.

Table 4. Weight and Number of Pieces in Major Mail Classes by Fiscal Years									
Mail (millions)	1989a*	1988	1987	1986	1985	1984	1983	1982	1981
First-Class and Priority									
Pounds	3942	3889	3734	3516	3335	3168	1929	2811	2859
Pieces	83391	82721	79224	76517	72748	69722	64518	62459	61679
Express									
Pounds	96	82	77	125	144	146	109	107	93
Pieces	52	44	42	40	45	44	37	28	24
Second-Class									
Pounds	4159	4108	4012	3972	3966	3852	3526	3482	3483
Pieces	10488	10448	10324	10588	10380	9522	9220	9527	9956
Third-Class									
Pounds	7408	7579	7155	6544	6453	5787	5062	4296	3758
Pieces	61509	61970	59733	55049	52170	48249	40735	36719	33607
Fourth-Class									
Pounds	2074	2205	2179	2254	2156	2289	2248	2446	2480
Pieces (millions)	603	649	615	602	576	599	568	597	590
Source: Annual Reports of the Postmaster General of the United States Postal Service. *Quantities are adjusted for 1989 in column 1989a to make them comparable with earlier years. The adjustment used percentage effects from data for 1988, which were reported under both new and old procedures in Postmaster General's Annual Report for 1989.									

substantial revenue growth from the surge in direct mail advertising and solicitation. At the same time, it has not shared greatly in the impressive growth of Express Mail, and the portion of its revenue from Second-Class and Fourth-Class mail, where it faces competition, have declined. Indeed, the mail classes with some monopoly protection, First-Class (and Priority) and Third-Class, have gone from representing 80% of revenues in 1981 to nearly 90% today.

3. The Economic Theory of Monopoly and Competition

3.1. Contestable Market Theory

In the last 15 years, much precision has been brought to the definition of monopoly in terms both of the conditions that make it suitable for market organization and of the conditions that make entry limitation an appropriate policy to ensure monopoly.[16] Persistent economies of scale and scope make monopoly suitable for a market, because under those technological conditions one firm can achieve the lowest possible cost. Exact definitions of those conditions, plus limitations on demands for the monopolist's products (weak gross substitutability),[17] determine whether the firm can set prices, called sustainable prices, that alone will prevent entry by inefficient firms. When prices are sustainable, it is possible to forego any statutory limitation on entry. Then the threat of entry can serve to discipline the monopoly, provided that there are no sunk costs so that entry and exit are so easy that the monopoly cannot act strategically to discourage entry. Markets satisfying such conditions are called contestable markets, since there is always someone ready to contest for sales in the market if the current supplier's price is high enough to make that profitable.

To apply these contestable market ideas requires information that is rarely available for postal service, such as the exact relations between all possible levels of outputs and total cost or the ease of entry and exit. In the case of postal service, we can expect that entry and exit are easy in principle, since sunk costs are relatively low, with more than 80% of total cost being accounted for by labor. Whether there are economies of scale or economies of scope is an awkward question that has been disputed for years, for want of a sound and persuasive cost analysis system at USPS. To complicate matters, the cost patterns themselves can be influenced very much by choices and policies of USPS management. For instance, if, as a matter of policy, temporary employees are seldom used, then a large portion of total cost may appear fixed in the form of obligatory payments to permanent employees. Work rules, which in principle are subject to change, may also be so rigid as to create the appearance that many costs are fixed independently of work loads.[18] If excess capacity is maintained, that too will give the impression that scale economies exist, since greater volumes can be handled at low marginal cost. Empirical evidence suggests that costs actually do vary with mail volume, since there is virtually no evidence of scale economies.[19]

Arguments for economies of scale tend to be anecdotal, not empirical. For example, in their 1973 rationale for monopoly protection, the Board of Governors of USPS described window service as one of the fixed costs that could not be self-supporting without monopoly protection. It is interesting that today one can see thriving, ancillary private services which earn a profit by elaborating on postal window service, offering packing, wrapping, shipping, facsimile and photocopying services, mail forwarding assistance, and even—in conjunction with the Internal Revenue Service—electronic tax return filing. Two of the largest companies in the United States are called Mail Boxes and Pak Mail. In 1989, Mail Boxes had sales of $285 million. At the British Post Office, a Counters Division was created as a profit center, aiming to offer writing materials, theater tickets, and a range of financial and other services.

Whether there are economies of scope in postal service is a harder question. On the accounting side, it requires attention to joint cost situations that historically have not been well analyzed by USPS.[20] Statistical analysis so far has not been definitive on the question. Gupta (1982) found some support for economies of scope, through a limited test across aggregated mail classes. But no full-fledged analysis has been carried out by USPS, even though techniques for such analysis were developed ten years ago.

Aspects of postal service complicate the cost determination and pricing problems beyond contestable market ideas. To begin with, almost every item of mail—and more than 160 billion of them are processed in a year—is in some respects a separate product or service. How much each one costs, and would therefore raise in revenue in a perfect (indeed, magical) system, depends on the shape of a complex network of collection, sorting, transporting and delivery functions. The mail recipient influences the cost by the form of mail receptacle used (and whether USPS or the recipient pays for it), how secure it is, and where it is located. And the sender influences the cost by presorting or precoding the mail or by the amount of postman or window clerk time taken up by queries. So, within existing classes of mail, there are cost and service differences, and some missives cost more than others to collect, sort, transport, and deliver.

3.2. The Uniform Price

It would be hard to improve on Coase's (1947) four-decade old analysis of the drawbacks in uniform pricing. He showed, first of all, how a uniform price policy is ambiguous, since many different levels of service and of average costs can be selected under a uniform price system. Proper social control requires more specification of the purposes to be served, because many different levels can be set for a uniform price. He also pointed out how a uniform price tends to lead to uniform service with only one quality level. Those willing to pay for better quality are not satisfied, because there is no option through which they can demonstrate their interest, and those preferring lower quality are not satisfied because the uniform service is too costly for them. Uniform service was an evident effect of Civil Aeronautics Board uniform price regulation of airlines, of course, as revealed by the proliferation of service prices and qualities that became available after airline deregulation.

A uniform price is presently required throughout the United States for first-class mail, under terms of the Postal Reorganization Act of 1970. [21] In the case of first-class mail, there are substantial differences in the amount of service provided—like the difference between a letter mailed to a neighbor and one sent across the country—that are deliberately not distinguished under a uniform rate. Because such differences exist, the USPS Board of Governors argued that under a uniform price, and without monopoly and its entry limitations, private suppliers could "skim the cream."[22] Private suppliers might win the low-cost portion of that mail with a lower price, for example, and even make profit. To succeed in this way, however, any private supplier would have to describe the low-cost mail so precisely that the high-cost mail could be excluded, or otherwise a lower price offer would bring in all the forms of mail to the private supplier. Of course, a high-quality service might also be identified and sold at a high price, as was the case originally for express mail. The main point is that so-called cream skimming requires careful definition of service to ensure that only the targeted business can be included, which means that, in principle, all potential providers of a defined service should be able to compete for it on fair terms.

In 1973, the USPS Board of Governors not only argued that the uniform postage rate made monopoly necessary, because without it private firms would "skim the cream," but they also defended the uniform rate on grounds that transaction costs for consumers would be too great if a range of alternative prices had to be deciphered. If the transaction cost basis for a uniform price is correct, however, the "cream skimming" argument seems wrong, since the transaction costs should also keep people from responding to small price differences in a relatively inexpensive service. A uniform postal rate cannot be justified by asserting that transaction costs are large relative to subtle differences in cost, because that question of the importance of cost or price differences is an empirical one which only the mailers can decide once they are informed of the cost differences.

What reason is there, then, for a uniform letter-mail rate? The historic rationale for a uniform rate in the United States was to "bind the nation together." Avoiding rate differences due to location was expected to discourage isolation of frontier communities. Such a rationale is not persuasive today. As Waverman (1980) has pointed out, invoices, which constitute over 80% of first-class mail, do not bind the nation together.[23] Too many alternative means of communication exist today for the extent of our community feeling to be greatly affected by whether first-class mail has a uniform rate everywhere in the country. To the extent that it is a significant influence on decisions, the uniform rate probably should be abandoned, so we make decisions about where we locate and with whom we deal based on the true costs of doing so.

The uniform rate is the prime rationale for protection from competition today. Yet there is little examination of cost differences among the various services that are included in the uniform rate to see how serious is cross subsidization within those services. In order to attract customers, a supplier of alternative mail service must commit to some well defined scope of service, which brings with it a necessary level of cost. If it turns out that confining the scope of service to one city lowers cost considerably below the current uniform first-class postage rate, for instance, then without private express statutes USPS business might be lost to one-city mail networks. If enough is known about costs to allow such precise definition, however, and if cost differences are significant, then it may be wise to abandon the uniform price requirement as it presently exists and allow the USPS to reflect the cost differences in its prices. In this way, USPS should be able to protect itself from "cream skimming" entry. The uniform rate is the cause of cross subsidization among mailers that no longer is justified if the cost differences that are not now considered really matter to mailers. Sale of local postal service in this case will better align prices of services with their costs, which is clearly a desirable aim if decentralized economic activity is to function effectively. Nonuniform mail service networks would thus allow more precise description of each service and more precise pricing.

3.3. Nonuniform Mail Service

We still collect, transport, sort, and deliver the same hand-addressed mail, in a range of envelope sizes, as when postal service started. Some coding is used, but possibilities for standardization have not really been pursued.[24] The requirement of a uniform price is part of the reason, since it gives the Postal Service an excuse for not distinguishing carefully among the different kinds of mail it processes at the uniform price and tracing their separate costs. A standardized envelope printed at some position with simple outlines, where users could indicate 5-digit or 9-digit zip codes in ways that could easily be recognized, would allow rapid and detailed sorting at low cost. Instead of developing such a vehicle to exploit sorting technology, USPS has attempted to handle at one price—with costly devices like optical character recognition—whatever letters users submit.[25] This approach may be popular, since it requires of consumers no change in behavior, but it also fails to exploit low cost sorting technology and therefore causes higher costs and prices. With a better-designed system, the same variety of letters we have today could still be processed, but, if we gave up the uniform price, the standardized ones could be processed at lower cost and therefore served at lower rates. As mailers responded to such a choice, the variety of letters might narrow, and we should expect postal costs to decline as a result.

The Postal Rate Commission's Office of the Consumer Advocate has estimated costs of the mail processing operation as part of the current postal rate case.[26] The lowest-cost mail to process was courtesy envelope mail, used for example by credit-card customers to return payment for invoices they receive. These reply envelopes are economical to process because they are barcoded in advance to allow low-cost sorting and sometimes are even picked up at the post office by the receiving company, thus saving sorting-to-carrier and delivery costs. Depending on the possible sorting combinations, these items fall mainly in the 2 cents to 3 cents range of processing cost, without sorting for delivery (which is estimated to cost less than 3 cents). Among the highest cost items to process are handwritten nonlocal letters with no coding, which by the time they are sorted to carriers for delivery can cost 18 cents apiece or even more with complicated routings. Only processing costs are included in these estimates, which are based on studies of sorting operations and should reflect relative costs of the different combinations of tasks reasonably well. And they indicate two things. First, it is feasible to identify cost differences among items processed at the uniform first-class rate. Second, large differences exist in the cost of processing mail within the uniform price category.

The Office of Consumer Advocate has proposed, in the current rate case, a conservative price discount of 3 cents for courtesy envelope mail, and also the introduction of a standard, automation-compatible envelope which has features that make it easier to process than letters with diverse handwritten addresses.[27] Similar in principle to stamped envelopes now sold by USPS, the automation-compatible envelope would designate the location of the address information and require that it be typed or printed. A 2 cent discount is proposed for the envelope, based on cost savings in its processing, which should encourage its use and thereby take fuller advantage of modern sorting technology. That is a major reason for departing from uniform prices: to give customers incentive to act in ways that will lower the costs of services they receive.

We should keep in mind the virtue of contestable market forces, which might be created for postal service if uniform pricing was abandoned and private services were permitted. The vigilance of alternative suppliers can bring innovation in method and service design, as well as incentive to control cost. Even a nonuniform rate structure may not guarantee USPS freedom from entry in a regime without statutes preventing private express services, for a supplier might hit on a new way to organize mail delivery and a new rate structure reflecting that method might win a portion of the mail class. Such a result would be a benefit of free entry, not a drawback. If USPS is protected from entry while being allowed to set a nonuniform price, it might tie that price to costs that follow its chosen way to organize service, which means a certain sorting pattern for each piece of mail. If its choices of methods are not ideal, and without entry there really is no way to tell, prices will reflect them anyway. With free entry, we would know more about the quality of such choices by USPS, because entry might occur where they had been poor and had caused costs and prices to be high. At the same time, the threat of entry would motivate USPS to make those choices very carefully. We can refer again to airline deregulation, where entry brought benefits through the greater range of more efficient services it fostered.

Thus, the original rationale for monopoly protection of postal service, to allow cross subsidization primarily in favor of remote frontier regions, no longer exists. Nor does the original reason for a uniform price—"to bind the nation together"—still hold. Without uniform pricing, monopoly protection of USPS should no longer be necessary. Alternative providers of mail service might enrich mailers' choices, lower postal rates, and force USPS to operate efficiently. At the same time, it is true that there might be advantages in having a network of governmental offices, and removal of private express statutes could bring enormous upheaval to USPS. It is therefore useful to consider the politics of postal monopoly and competition.

4. The Politics of Monopoly and Competition

All sellers would prefer to have a monopoly position in their markets. It is safer and easier to be a monopolist, and, in any interesting case, potentially much more profitable as well. Thus, it is not surprising that USPS argues for preservation of every aspect of monopoly it possesses. What might be surprising is that the Congress essentially has allowed USPS great influence in deciding disputes over the extent of its monopoly position. As we have seen, the arguments offered in support of monopoly have been weak and have lacked a foundation in facts, yet they have prevailed, probably in part because of the political support that exists for the USPS positions. It would therefore be desirable, and wise, to find ways to experiment with less extreme forms of monopoly, in order that facts could be obtained and brought into play in considering the postal monopoly question.

The simple question, "should postal services compete?," is neither apt nor useful. It is not apt, because alternative services already force a degree of competition on postal services. It is not useful because Postal Service can be organized in many different ways, some of which may be more amenable to competition than others. The useful question therefore is "can postal service be organized so that competition can function better and, if so, is that form of organization desirable?" The best approach to this question is through experimentation, which would involve new rules and new possible practices to develop more facts about postal service and its costs.

Terrible consequences can be imagined from removal of the mail monopoly in a choice between either the present monopoly or no monopoly protection at all. But many opportunities exist for modest experiments to test for consequences. A most promising experiment in moderating the force of the postal monopoly can be seen in addressed third-class mail. A hearing was held by the Postal Rate Commission in October 1989 on the question of monopoly protection for this class of mail.[28] Arguments to retain the monopoly were presented by users of other mail classes,[29] who might have feared that competition in addressed third-class mail could result in higher rates for the classes they use. Testimony favoring elimination of the monopoly protection for addressed third class mail came from users of that mail, Direct Marketing Association, Inc. and Third Class Mail Association, and also from Citizens for a Sound Economy.[30] United Parcel Service called generally for narrow interpretation of any postal monopoly, to be rendered by a party other than USPS.[31] The Bureau of Economics Staff of the Federal Trade Commission described information needs for any decision.[32] No action was taken on the question, nor is it entirely clear procedurally what steps are needed to modify current practice under which USPS enjoys a monopoly over third class mail pieces if they are individually addressed.

In the last decade, third-class mail has grown substantially, to where it accounts for one-fifth of mail volume and revenue. Television has become very expensive in the same period, as it has grown to deliver advertising mainly for mass markets (Gilder 1990). Direct mail serves well for the carefully targeted and focused campaigns that have claimed a growing share of media budgets in the 1980s, when the share going to standard media (TV, radio, newspapers, billboards, etc.) declined (Farhi 1990). Postal rates have risen during the same period. Cost comparisons that were presented by Third Class Mail Association showed considerable savings, more than a billion dollars annually, to be possible through greater reliance on private third-class mail processors. The question is important if USPS is able to make money on third-class addressed mail because of its monopoly advantage and not because its service is better.

It is surely possible to question whether advertising pieces which are identical for every recipient should be regarded as letters, to be protected from private express carriage. It seems unlikely that without such protection genuine letters will be sent as addressed third class mail, in violation of private express statutes. Such illegal actions would not seem to be greatly motivated if competition was allowed in addressed third-class mail. Allowing competition in addressed third-class mail is another area where the effectiveness of USPS relative to private suppliers could be examined at little risk to the overall postal system.

Several possibilities could moderate the extreme monopoly protection that is accorded to first-class mail in the United States. The users of monopolized first-class mail are numerous but poorly organized, being represented only by a few lobbying groups, such as the American Greeting Card Association. Thus, little lobbying supports first-class mailers. On the other side, an enormous voting workforce, plus bastions of well-organized mail users, who benefit through lower rates on other mail classes, support the first-class mail monopoly. Religious denominations, for example, are remarkably unified in their views about mail matters. Thus, the political power of its beneficiaries is probably an important reason why monopoly has been retained for the mail.

In response to USPS claims that no private service will bring mail to rural areas if private express statutes are repealed, Miller (1990a) has proposed that the private express statute might be suspended solely for rural areas, to see whether private services would arise there.[33] Rural areas are less densely populated, so more delivery time may be needed to handle the typical piece of mail. This situation can raise costs, especially for USPS which pays the same wages in all locations. Private suppliers of mail service that pay local wage rates in rural areas might operate at substantially lower cost, however, and, if so, a valuable lesson would be learned through this proposed experiment. Although the proposal is one that USPS should not resist, given its claims, there could be much argument over which rural areas would receive such treatment. One possibility would be to identify areas where post offices are subsidized and allow private service alternatives there. Even then, there would be considerable difficulty framing legislation to suspend private express statutes in a form that would not be regretted later, as communities grew and declined.

Another possible experiment could be pursued by abandoning the uniform first-class pricing policy. Without mandatory uniform pricing, USPS could develop a lower-price standardized service, perhaps using courtesy envelopes that facilitate precoding, and also automation-compatible envelopes of the general kind proposed by the Postal Rate Commission's Office of the Consumer Advocate in the current postal rate case. It would also be reasonable to ask a higher price for handling letters without zip codes or of odd sizes. Other distinctions might be made wherever cost differences would warrant, possibly including lower prices for letters mailed within a local area. The advantage of this change would simply be the identification of costs more carefully with differences in services as needed to justify price differences. With such service varieties, it should be possible at a later time to evaluate consumers' interests in price differences, as well as USPS claims about costs. It is interesting to note that price distinctions were approved by the Postal Rate Commission in an earlier postal case, but were denied by the Postal Service Board of Governors.[34]

One other modification of the mail monopoly has been introduced in several countries. Alternative providers of mail service can exist if they charge higher prices. In New Zealand, for example, there is a declining schedule of minimum prices for alternative suppliers that reaches $.80 (New Zealand) in 1991; the uniform New Zealand Post first-class rate is $.40 (New Zealand). An advantage of this pricing-limit policy is that it can be set at any desired distance from current prices, and so can allow gradual implementation. Of course, it could be set at a level below current rates, especially if the uniform rate is abandoned. The entry price is regarded as the "degree of protection" in New Zealand, and is expected by many to be set equal to the New Zealand Post price before long. In this circumstance, only the same or higher quality suppliers can be expected to provide service, but at least all entry is not foreclosed. In a public enterprise organization like the USPS, that is supposed to break even rather than earn profit, pressure from the direction of higher quality services could be desirable.

Obviously there is an advantage in allowing entry at higher prices, if the monopoly provider skimps on service quality. A profit-seeking monopoly often is motivated to provide quality levels consumers desire, because that will maximize profit. There are exceptions, as when a low-profit service that is a substitute for a high-profit service is not offered, or when high monopoly prices reduce quantities demanded and can make fewer levels of quality profitable. If the monopoly cannot recognize consumers according to their quality preference and must allow the consumers to select their own preferred price-quality categories, then qualities may be distorted, usually to make the lower qualities lower than optimal, to keep them from attracting custom away from higher quality, higher profit items.[35] If no profit is allowed, however, the motivation to choose quality in an optimal way will be seriously reduced. And without profit motivation, the quality a monopoly will provide is apt to be lower, because lower quality service requires less managerial energy or worker effort. So allowing entry on the high price, and presumably high quality, side of current offerings might serve the useful purpose of creating pressure for good quality service. It is another example of a feasible change from present policy that could generate new information about postal service effectiveness.

One topic raised by the PRC at the monopoly theory hearing on addressed third-class mail is the limitation that present law imposes on USPS. The PRC's Office of Consumer Advocate pointed out that USPS serves national markets and prices accordingly. Without the monopoly protection, it could be disadvantaged in local markets and lose business, with the result that costs to other classes might be raised (of course users of mail in those local markets could benefit). Another problem emphasized was that the law limits how USPS can respond in the market, say in price or service features, and with competition such a disadvantage could be serious. With competition permitted even on an experimental basis it will probably be necessary to change these rules in the law, perhaps to allow USPS some flexibility in prices comparable to the ranges that were introduced in other industries during their deregulation.

Miller (1990b) has pointed out difficulties that simple repeal of private express statutes would causes USPS. Not only would USPS be woefully handicapped by its inability to alter prices quickly, but it could also face an angry Congress if it proposed to depart from politically popular pricing policies or to alter work rules against the wishes of influential postal unions. In part for these reasons, he favors privatization of postal service rather than continued government operation under less-complete monopoly.[36] Based largely on European experience with what made privatization more successful, he has proposed granting postal employees an ownership interest in the private postal undertaking, in an amount he estimates to be worth over $30,000 per postal employee. This is a more extreme proposal than the smaller, more experimental, steps we are urging. But it raises the ownership incentive problem squarely and also illustrates the magnitude of the vested interests that influence postal policy.

5. Conclusion

Cross subsidization, which motivated the original monopoly protection for postal service in the United States, is no longer a social goal. Yet the main argument for monopoly within first-class mail today is essentially to preserve cross subsidization, which results from a mandated uniform rate. But the rationale for a uniform rate, to "bind the nation together," also no longer exists. So there really is no persuasive social rationale for postal monopoly. What data are available give no general support to an economic rationale for monopoly, either. Looking at USPS revenues in recent years reveals a poor showing in mail classes that lack monopoly protection, so there is reason to question the motivation and efficiency of the monopoly enterprise.

Whether competition could actually work effectively in postal service is presently difficult to know. The USPS would clearly have some advantages over rivals, in operating such a large network and possibly having some economies of scale or scope. The rigidities of regulation create disadvantages, but the law could be changed to reduce the advantages in flexibility that rivals might otherwise have over USPS. The record shows that alternative servers have performed very effectively in any situation where they were allowed, and also that they have rarely been allowed. Monopoly protection for USPS is extremely strong and is enforced vigorously by USPS. The appropriate policy step quite obviously is to experiment further with competition.

The most promising actions would yield information about the effectiveness of competition. One entirely feasible step is to allow competition in addressed third class mail. There is no compelling reason why USPS needs monopoly protection to deliver impersonal standardized messages, even to specific addresses. Another step is to suspend private express statutes in rural areas, to see whether alternative services come into existence and if they do how effective they are. A third possible step would be to abandon the requirement for uniform pricing of first-class mail, and indeed to require that some distinctions be made. This step is necessary to induce greater use of low-cost sorting technology. Finally, a fourth possibility is to allow alternative suppliers of first-class mail, but to require that they set prices above current USPS levels. This would tend to elicit high quality services from private suppliers.

Allowing such experiments would yield information on the effectiveness of alternatives to USPS. It would also reveal much about postal technology and efficiency and could lead to less costly means of controlling USPS. The many arguments that develop now at Postal Rate Commission hearings are wasteful, as when newspaper publishers argue about rates with deliverers of consolidated third-class advertisements because they are competing carriers of advertising messages. If these services were provided by profit seeking enterprises such arguments would be inessential, because the survival of firms would ensure that services covered costs. Since USPS cannot convince observers as to its costs, no such assurance is available, and rate cases are seen as opportunities for argument and even for resort to political influence. Experiments with competition would provide evidence about USPS costs and effectiveness and could thereby improve postal performance.

Notes

For helpful discussion I am grateful to Rand Costich of the United States Postal Rate Commission.
1. In fiscal 1967, the deficit was $1.17 billion, which was then almost 20 percent of the total postal budget. See *Towards Postal Excellence: The Report of the President's Commission on Postal Organization*, Washington, DC, 1968.
2. 84 Stat. 719 (August 12, 1970), 39 U.S. Code.
3. See Adie (1977; 1989), Perloff and Wachter (1984), Quinn (1979), and Smith (1976, 1980).
4. See U.S. Postal Rate Commission Monopoly Theory Inquiry, Docket No. RM89-4, pp. 178-180, testimony of Thomas M. Lenard for the Third Class Mail Association.
5. *National Association of Greeting Card Publishers v. U.S. Postal Service*, 569 F 2nd 570 (D.C. Cir., December 28, 1976).
6. S. 3229, which was introduced in 1977 would have limited to 60% the proportion of total cost that could be attributed to all the individual mail classes. Sherman (1983) showed that by understating the marginal costs of services, a budget-constrained public enterprise could maximize its sales revenue.
7. Priest (1975, 35).
8. Legislation with this purpose was passed in 1794, 1825, 1827, 1836, and 1838, but was not totally effective until the Act of 1845.
9. March 3, 1845, ch. 43, 9-12, 5 Stat. 732.
10. Priest (1975, 68).
11. Priest (1975, 68).
12. Postal Reorganization Act, section 7 (1970).
13. See Simone (1989) for a description of E-mail services.
14. See Robinson (1980) on efforts by the Postal Service to protect its monopoly through its definition of a letter. See Priest (1975, 79-80) on whether the Postal Service can suspend statutory prohibitions.
15. In 1989, Penalty and Franked mail were no longer reported as separate classes, but were included instead in the classes where they were actually carried. In 1988, a year for which data are available under both procedures, Penalty and Franked mail accounted for 3.12% of total revenue. Under the new procedure, this mail was distributed to other classes as follows: First-Class and Priority 2.28%, Express Mail 0.05%, Second-Class 0.02%, Third Class 0.5%, and Fourth Class 0.17%.
16. See in particular Faulhaber (1975), Panzar and Willig (1977), and Baumol, Panzar, and Willig (1982).
17. See Mirman, Tauman, and Zang (1985).
18. See Priest and Havemann (1989).
19. See, for examples, Christensen (1985), Dziadek (1959), Gupta (1982), Merewitz (1971), Stevenson (1973), and Wattles (1963). The Christensen (1985) study might suggest some economies of scale if the mail network (number of addresses) was fixed, but no scale economies were found by Stevenson (1973). At the post office level, Merewitz (1971) found scale economies in small post offices

and diseconomies in large post offices.

20. One of the USPS accounting practices for some years was to avoid dealing with such questions. If a particular cost could be traced to two or more classes of mail, for example, it would not be imputed to those classes in any way; it would simply be placed in a large category called "institutional cost," and spread over all mail classes. That is why the billion dollar bulk mail system, which was designed primarily for third-class and fourth-class mail, was originally classified as an institutional cost and supported largely by first-class mailers.

21. 84 Stat. 719 (August 12, 1970), 39 U.S. Code, Subsection 3623(d).

22. See U.S. Postal Service, Statutes Restricting Private Carriage of Mail and Their Administration, House Committee on Post Office and Civil Service, 93rd Congress, 1st Sess. Comm. Print, 1973.

23. Waverman (1980, 18-19).

24. See Jacob Rabinow, "Commentary," in Sherman (1980).

25. Jacob Rabinow, an inventor and developer of mail sorting machines, has argued this point, ibid.

26. See testimony of W. Gail Willette on behalf of the Office of the Consumer Advocate, Docket R-90-1, July 1990.

27. See testimony of Pamela A. Thompson of the Office of the Consumer Advocate, Docket R-90-1, July 1990.

28. See U.S. Postal Rate Commission Monopoly Theory Inquiry, Docket No. RM 89-4, November 1989.

29. In particular, see submissions by American Bankers Association, American Newspaper Publishers Association, and Independent Bankers Association of America in U.S.P.R.C. Docket No. RM 89-4, ibid.

30. ibid.

31. ibid.

32. ibid.

33. See Miller (1990a).

34. See Decision of the Governors of the United States Postal Service on the Recommended Decision of the Postal Rate Commission on Mail Classification Changes, May 2, 1988, pp. 2-4.

35. See Mussa and Rosen (1978) and Srinagesh and Bradburd (1989).

36. For this argument see Miller (1990b).

References

Adie, Douglas K. 1977. *An Evaluation of Postal Service Wage Rates.* Washington, DC: American Enterprise Institute.

Adie, Douglas K. 1989. *Monopoly Mail: Privatizing the U.S. Postal Service.* New Brunswick, NJ: Transaction Publishers.

Baumol, William J., John C. Panzar, and Robert D. Willig. 1988. *Contestable Markets and the Theory of Industry Structure*, rev. ed. San Diego, CA: Harcourt, Brace Jovanovich.

Christensen, Laurits R. and Associates, Inc. 1985. *United States Postal Service Real Output, Input and Total Factor Productivity, 1963-1984.* Report to the U.S. Postal Service.

Coase, Ronald H. 1939. "Rowland Hill and the Penny Post." *Economica* (November): 423-35.

Coase, Ronald H. Coase. 1947. "The Economics of Uniform Pricing Systems." *Manchester School of Economic and Social Studies* 15: 139-56.

Collier, Earl M., Jr., and George H. Bostick. 1972. "The Postal Reorganization Act: A Case Study of Regulated Industry Reform." *Virginia Law Review* (September): 1030-98.

Dziadek, Fred. 1959. "The Productivity of the U.S. Post Office." Ph.D. dissertation, Johns Hopkins University.

Farhi, Paul. 1990. "Cost-Conscious Marketers Try Honing the Hype." *Washington Post* (June 10).

Faulhaber, Gerald R. 1975. "Cross Subsidization: Pricing in Public Enterprises." *American*

Economic Review 65: 966-77.
Ferrara, Peter J., ed. 1989. *Free the Mail*. Washington, DC: Cato Institute.
Fleishman, Joel L., ed. 1983. *The Future of the Postal Service*. New York: Praeger.
Gilder, George. 1990. *Life after Television*. New York: Whittle.
Gupta, Satinder Nath. 1982. "Production and Cost Functions of the United States Postal Service." Ph.D. dissertation, George Washington University.
Hill, Sir Rowland, and George B. Hill. 1880. *Life of Sir Rowland Hill and History of Penny Postage*. I and II. London: Thos. De La Rue and Co.
Merewitz, Leonard. 1971. "Costs and Returns to Scale in U.S. Post Offices." *Journal of the American Statistical Association*. (September): 504-509.
Miller, James C., III. 1990a. "A Critique of the Case Against Privatization of the U. S. Postal Service." George Mason University Discussion Paper (April 2).
Miller, James C., III. 1990b. "Free the Mail, Part I." In Ferraro (1989).
Mirman, Leonard J., Y. Tauman, and I. Zang. 1985. "Supportability, Sustainability, and Subsidy-Free Prices." *Rand Journal of Economics*. 16: 114-26.
Mussa, Michael, and Sherwood Rosen. 1978. "Monopoly and Product Quality," *Journal of Economic Theory*. 18:301-17.
Panzar, John C., and Robert D. Willig. 1977. "Free Entry and the Sustainability of Natural Monopoly." *Bell Journal of Economics*. 8:1-22.
Perloff, Jeffrey M., and Michael L. Wachter. 1984. "Wage Comparability in the U.S. Postal Service." *Industrial and Labor Relations Review* 38:26-35.
Priest, Dana, and Judith Haveman. 1989. "Mail Reform Languishes By the Book." *Washington Post* (November 27): A1 and A10.
Priest, George L. 1975. "The History of the Postal Monopoly in the United States." *Journal of Law and Economics*. 18:33-80.
Quinn, Joseph F. 1979. "Postal Sector Wages." *Industrial Relations* 18.
Rich, Wesley Everett. 1924. *The History of the United States Post Office to the Year 1829*. Cambridge, MA: Harvard University Press.
Robinson, Kenneth. 1980. "The Postal Service and Electronic Communications: Various Legal Issues and Sundry Open Questions." In Sherman (1980).
Sherman, Roger. 1980. "Pricing Behavior of the Budget-Constrained Public Enterprise." *Journal of Economic Behavior and Organization*. 4:381-93.
Sherman, Roger, ed. 1980. *Perspectives on Postal Service Issues*. Washington, DC: American Enterprise Institute.
Simone, Luisa. 1989. "E-mail, the Global Handshake." *PC Magazine*. 8:175-202.
Smith, Sharon P. 1980. "Are Postal Workers Over or Underpaid?." *Industrial Relations*. 15:168-76.
Smith, Sharon P. 1980. "Commentary on 'How Have Postal Workers Fared Since the 1970 Act?.'" In Sherman (1980).
Srinagesh, Padmanabhan, and Ralph M. Bradburd. 1989. "Quality Distortion by a Discriminating Monopolist." *American Economic Review* 79:96-105.
Stevenson, Rodney E. 1973. "Postal Pricing Problems and Production Functions." Ph.D. dissertation, Michigan State University.
U.S. Postal Service. 1973. "Statutes Restricting Private Carriage of Mail and Their Administration." House Committee on Post Office and Civil Service, 93rd Congress, 1st session, Committee Print.
Wattles, George M. 1973. "The Rates and Costs of the United States Postal Service." *Journal of Law and Economics* (April): 89-117.
Waverman, Leonard. 1980. "Pricing Principles: How Should Postal Rates be Set." In

Sherman (1980).
Willig, Robert D. 1980. "What Can Markets Control?." In Sherman (1980).

COMMENTS:
Marginal Experiments, Unintended Results
Michael R. Frierman

In his article "Competition in Postal Service," Sherman considers whether competition in place of the current monopoly provision of postal services would work to increase the efficiency and scope of such services. He suggests that there is currently not enough information to permit the determination of such a proposition and so provides four experiments designed to provide the necessary information. However, because of the nature of a multi-product monopoly like the United States Postal Service (USPS), I would argue that it is unlikely that the experiments described would provide the information thought to be required. Indeed, several of the experiments suggested would be expected, rather, to have no observable impact on the current provision of services and so provide no information whatever. In any case, if the USPS's monopoly power arises from its legal protection rather than from fundamental economic forces as Sherman implies, then economic theory would argue for the elimination of that protection. The relevant question, then, is not, as put forward in this article, whether the USPS can be organized to allow competition to function better, but rather, how the political agreement necessary to assure a competitive market structure can be achieved.

Sherman's article begins with an interesting presentation and discussion of the institutional aspects of the USPS. The history of the organization is described with particular attention to the rationale for the Postal Service's monopoly power. Current forms of competition, including FAX machines, electronic-mail and express mail, are then described, with an assesment of their impact on USPS services. This is followed by some general theoretical considerations of monopoly power with their implications for cross subsidizations between mail classes by the Postal Service. Attention is focused on the way uniform pricing of first class mail leads to a reduction in the array of different quality services provided.

In his application of the concept of contestable markets, described in the theoretical section, Sherman confronts the question of whether the USPS derives its monopoly power from underlying economic forces. He suggests that the monopoly power of the Postal Service stems not from its economic structure, but rather, from its legal status. Sherman argues that the existing evidence does not support the claim that the Postal Service exhibits any economies of scale. Nor does he appear to believe that the evidence is strong enough to suggest that economies of scope exist. Hence, throughout the paper, the impression is given that the ability to cross subsidize both across and within mail classes arises from the legal monopoly granted the USPS and not from its natural economic strengths.

If, as this paper argues, legal protection is all that provides the Postal Service with its monopoly power, economic theory would recommend eliminating that protection to obtain the benefits associated with competitive markets. As there seem to be no externalities associated with the provision of mail services, straightforward micro-economic theory would argue that competition in such services would: (1) increase the efficiency of the provision of all services, (2) increase the quality of all services, and (3) provide a greater array of services. Considering only the economic aspects of the situation, economic theory would argue for the repeal of all laws which confer monopoly status on a firm which would otherwise face competition in the provision of its services.

However, from the article's discussion concerning the opening of the Postal Service's markets to competitors, it is clear that such an attempt is politically very difficult. Sherman appears to argue that a form of "Congressional Capture Theory" is at work. There are enough pressure groups benefiting from the Postal Service's existing arrangements that Congress is unable or unwilling to alter the Postal Service's monopoly protection.

Confronted with this kind of Congressional behavior, he proposes that the most *useful* question to be asked about the USPS's monopoly status is: "Can the Postal Service be organized so that competition can function better and, if so, is that form of organization desirable?" He seems to be arguing that in the face of Congressional obstruction to deregulation or privatization, a more limited goal might prove attainable, namely, a reorganized, more "competitive" Postal Service.

It is this political reality which motivates Sherman's suggested experiments. The "new" facts regarding the benefits of competition obtained from the experiments could then be used in an attempt to persuade Congress to, if not eliminate the Postal Service's protection, at least reduce it. In addition, it is possible that new interest groups who would support the goals of greater competition in postal service might arise in the process and counter those groups already in opposition. In this reading of the article, the article is seen to be concerned not only with the "pure" economics of the problem, but also with its politically feasibility.

To generate the facts Sherman believes would be useful, he suggests four experiments in competition. These experiments are to be tried at the margins of postal service. The experiments are to: (1) allow entry into the service of rural areas; (2) allow entry into third class mail provision; (3) allow entry into first class mail provision, provided the new entrants' price above the existing uniform postal rate; and (4) eliminate the uniform rate on first class mail.

The difficulty with each of these experiments is that the piecemeal elimination of monopoly protection is not likely to work in the way intended. In some cases, no observable differences will occur as a result of the experiment. While in other cases, a "push-down pop-up" phenomenon is likely to occur. That is, pushing-down on one portion of an integrated system, such as the USPS, typically results in an unexpected result popping-up somewhere else in the system. This phenomenon has serious negative implications for several of Sherman's suggested experiments. To see the difficulties which can arise in this setting, look at each of the proposed experiments in turn.

Consider the Rural Service Experiment. In this experiment, competitors are allowed to enter the market for mail services provided to (appropriately defined) rural areas. However, in the paper it is noted that rural service is cross subsidized by urban service. If this is the case, then few potential entrants would likely be able to compete with the USPS in the provision of these services. Hence, we would not expect to see much competition develop on this margin. In order to observe competition for rural customers, it would be necessary to ensure the elimination of most, if not all cross subsidies. In light of the problems associated with the identification and enforcement of subsidy elimination, this would seem to be a very difficult proposition to guarantee.

Next, consider the Third Class Mail Experiment. This experiment is similar to the previous one except now with respect to third class mail. In this case, first class mail appears to subsidize third class mail. To the extent that this is the case, this experiment is subject to the same kind of criticism as the preceding one. Again, without guaranteed elimination of the subsidies, we would not expect to observe entry into this market.[1]

The difficulty with the first two experiments is that they allow entry into markets in which the Postal Service has an advantage due to the cross subsidies provided by the profits on other, still protected services. Nothing in the design of the two experiments prevents the USPS from exploiting its statutory monopoly advantage to prevent entry. Hence, with little or no entry observed, little or no "new" information will be gained from these experiments.

The third experiment present a different problem. It results in a version of the push-down pop-up phenomenon. In this experiment, entry into first class mail provision is allowed. However, new entrants must charge a higher rate than does the USPS for its first class service. This form of restricted entry is meant to provide a wider variety of higher quality services in the provision of first class mail. In contrast to the two prior experiments, we would expect to observe new firms entering the market during this experiment. Indeed, the greater the Postal Service's profits are perceived to be, the more vigorous the competition we would expect to arise in an attempt to compete away those profits at this "high end" of service. However, the resulting reduction in the Postal Service's profits from this service, must of course lead to a reduction in the level of subsidization previously bestowed upon its other services. This reduction or elimination of the cross subsidy would naturally lead to either a deterioration in the quality of the provision of the beneficiary services or a rise in their prices, or both. It would be infeasible to allow competition in the Postal Service's profit centers *without* also altering the organization of the other services of the USPS.

Finally, consider the last experiment, which calls for the elimination of uniform pricing in first class mail service. It is not clear whether Sherman means to permit entry into this service as well as eliminating the uniform price. Suppose entry is not allowed. Then, all that occurs is that the Postal Service is no longer required to have a single rate for first class service. It is not clear, however, that without some form of incentive or disciplinary mechanism the Postal Service would provide a scheduled rate structure and supply the array of services Sherman hopes would evolve. After all, he states that in the past the Postal Service itself had argued for a uniform rate. Hence, it may be inferred that, for whatever reason, the USPS seems to believe that it is in their best interest to have a single rate. Acting on their own then, they do not appear to have an incentive to alter the uniform rate structure. On the other hand, if entry is also permitted, this experiment is subject to the same push-down pop-up problem as in the previous experiment.

The problems arising in each of the four experiments indicates the general difficulties which can occur when a protected monopoly is opened piecemeal to competition. When competition is permitted in a subsidized service, one would not expect to observe many firms entering the market. On the other hand, if cross subsidies are present among various services, it is not possible to permit competition in the profit center's market without also affecting the provision of the beneficiary service.

On considerations of economic efficiency criteria alone, to the extent that the Postal Service derives its monopoly power from government protection, the legal structure confering that status on the USPS should be repealed. Only then can the benefits arising from competition be obtained. Such a conclusion can be arrived at without the need for further experimentation. Moreover, if it were determined that, for whatever reason, a particular service deserved subsidization, then economic effeciency would require the subsidy be provided directly to that service rather than having the subsidy mediated through a monopoly profit center on some other service, as is the case with the USPS.

Of course, the economically efficient method of subsidization often times is the less politically astute method. For one thing, direct subsidization of a service would require that service be openly designated as such, thereby providing an opportunity for public debate and possible opposition. The question then becomes: "How to get political agreement for such a move?" Hence, the focus is shifted from economic to political feasibility.

Not withstanding Sherman's proposed experiments, it is the unstated political aspects surrounding the issues of the USPS monopoly which lie at the core of his article. Consequently, it might be more useful for Professor Sherman's purposes to investigate the way in which a consensus in the United States Congress was achieved concerning the privatization of the rail system (Amtrak) or the deregulation of the airline or trucking industries. In addition, it might be useful to examine the privatization and deregulation programs instituted in England over the last decade or so. Research into these areas would be of great help in determining the future organizational structure of the Postal Service.

Note

1. If, on the other hand, Third Class mail provision is a profit generating service and entry is permitted, then the difficulties encountered by the remaining two experiments described below will also develop here.

10
IS POSTAL SERVICE A NATURAL MONOPOLY?
John C. Panzar

1. Introduction

The title of this paper raises what is perhaps the most pressing empirical question facing policy makers interested in postal reform. For if postal service is a technological natural monopoly, competition should be introduced into the system with extreme caution, if at all. Unfortunately, I have nothing to contribute to the empirical debate. Indeed, I shall argue that it is unlikely that the question will ever be satisfactorily resolved by econometric research. Nevertheless, I am convinced that postal service is a natural monopoly. Yet that "fact" in no way exempts the industry from competitive reform. This apparent paradox is resolved by appealing to the network structure of postal service and to carefully drawn analogies to recent United States experience in telecommunications, another network industry.

2. The Policy Relevance of Economies of Scale and Scope

Postal service has been provided as a governmental monopoly since ancient times, so there is ample historical tradition on which to base current practice. However most *rational* arguments for a monopoly postal service use the appeal to technological natural monopoly as one of their primary supporting pillars. Let us briefly examine the strength of this prop before discussing whether or not it is truly present.

Most simply, if an industry is a technological natural monopoly, it is less costly for it to be served by a single firm rather than by two or more firms.[1] In such a circumstance, allowing competition could only result in industry costs which were greater than the minimum possible. It would be better to develop institutions which act to control the prices and profits of a single firm. In most times, and in most places, the institution chosen to deal with the natural monopoly problem has been government enterprise, especially in the case of postal service.

Recently, however, traditional institutions for dealing with natural monopoly—

public enterprise and economic regulation—have lost favor among economists and, eventually, policy makers as well. From treasured islands of stability amidst chaotic competitive seas, government controlled monopolies became objects of great skepticism. The postwar academic attitude toward monopoly was best expressed by Alfred E. Kahn:

> If a natural monopoly is producing and pricing as efficiently as possible, there is no need to bar competitive entry: it is economically unnecessary and will not take place anyway.[2]

Notice that the presumption of natural monopoly cost advantages has been turned from a reason to shield the enterprise from competition to an excuse to challenge it whenever possible.

The philosophical attraction of this view is quite strong. For, if true, it offered a way to have the "best of both [competitive and monopolistic] worlds." Industries which were truly natural monopolies would be invulnerable to competitive entry, thereby preserving the cost advantages of single firm production. Yet these efficiencies could be obtained without sacrificing the dynamic incentive effects promised by Schumpeterian competition. Academics took this position seriously, even though it ignored some awkward political facts of life and, later, was proven incorrect as a matter of logic. Thus when entrants were attracted into long distance telephone markets in the United States during the 1960s, this was seen as evidence of Bell System inefficiency rather than the inevitable result of decades of politically motivated cost shifting from local to interstate jurisdictions. Of course one could argue that part of the import of the Kahn quote is to admonish the regulated or public enterprise to assume *economic* responsibility for its *politically* influenced rate structure. However, dominant firm efforts to adjust rates toward costs were met with accusations of predation.

In any event, about the time that academic conventional wisdom began to penetrate into the policy-making process, economic researchers began to uncover some of the many complexities underlying the theory of multi product natural monopoly.[3] In particular, Faulhaber (1975) discovered that the problem of cross-subsidization was much more complicated than had hitherto been recognized. He demonstrated that a multi service monopoly may be fundamentally unable to quote prices that are subsidy free. That is, cross-subsidization may be the inevitable result of the cost and demand conditions facing the firm, rather than the outcome of some conspiratorial pricing scheme. By definition, a cross-subsidy exists whenever any service (or group of services) pays more to the monopoly firm in revenues than it would cost to provide only the service(s) in questions. This means that there is the incentive for the service(s) providing the subsidy to have an entrant come in and serve only it. Thus there will always be incentives for wasteful entry when subsidy free prices do not exist. In such situations, the advantages of single firm production might need to be defended using state-imposed restrictions on entry.

Panzar and Willig (1977a) showed that the problem was even more serious. Even if the monopolist's current prices were subsidy free, wasteful entry might still be attracted into the market. This can occur if, for example, one of the monopoly services is characterized by strong product-specific economies of scale,[4] but is only weakly bound to the remainder of the enterprise by economies of scope. In such cases, a non innovative entrant might anticipate earning a positive profit by undercutting the monopolist's price and greatly expanding output. Thus, monopoly prices and services may be *unsustainable* even if they are subsidy free.

These considerations argue for a case-by-case consideration of the available evidence before adopting a blanket open entry policy for the markets of a regulated monopolist or public enterprise. Ideally, the evidence in question should include (at least) the following:
(1) Econometric and engineering cost studies.
(2) Econometric demand studies.
(3) Examination of the appropriateness of the various rate and service categories employed.

With the above information in hand, it is possible, at least in theory, to determine whether or not postal service is a natural monopoly. It would then be necessary to determine what policies are needed to ensure that a postal service monopolist provides efficient, reliable service at socially desirable rates. If it is found that cost and demand conditions are such that socially desirable rates are likely to be unsustainable, then an appropriate public policy might include legal barriers to entry.[5]

3. Good Empirical Evidence is Extremely Hard to Come By

Unfortunately, it is extremely unlikely that the above ideal evidence can ever be assembled for postal service or any historically monopoly industry. The reason is quite simple: too few degrees of freedom. When service has always been provided by a single firm, there is no cross-section of enterprises to work with, and the available time-series is far too short and much too collinear to be of much use. This is not to say that it is not possible to do sophisticated studies of multi product postal cost functions. International data might be used in order to construct a meaningful cross-section. Internal data might make it possible to analyze the cost structure of the firm at the micro level, etc. My purpose in this section is not to make concrete suggestions about how to carry out such studies, but rather to argue that, even with the best of intentions and abundant resources, the results are destined to be less than satisfactory.

There is ample basis for this pessimistic assessment of our scientific capabilities. In 1974, the United States Department of Justice (DOJ) filed an antitrust suit against AT&T, seeking divestiture of the Bell Operating Companies, A.T.&T. Long Lines, Western Electric, and Bell Telephone Laboratories. Although it was not the main focus of the legal case raised by the DOJ, a part of AT&T's initial defensive position was that the break up of the Bell System's "natural monopoly" would result in a loss of economic efficiency. This issue was also at least implicit in the policy debate concerning the entry of MCI and others into AT&T's long distance monopoly markets. The Bell System's position was that these long distance markets were natural monopolies and that wasteful duplication of facilities would result if competitive entry were permitted and protected.

Thus, empirically determining the extent of economies of scale in the telecommunications industry became more than a mere academic exercise. As in the case of railroads and trucking, the presence or absence of empirically estimated economies of scale was thought to be vitally important for public policy purposes. And, in the case of telecommunications, it was recognized rather early on that the multi product nature of the technology should play an important role in the empirical work. A great amount of interest, academic talent, and money rose to the challenge of uncovering the "true" cost structure of the telecommunications industry. It is doubtful that an equivalent agglomeration of resources would ever be marshalled for the study of postal service costs.

Yet this outburst of activity yielded relatively little that was useful for policy analysis. There are many reasons why this was so.[6] Some of the difficulties, having been recognized, perhaps may be avoided in the future. However, there are others which I think will inevitably resurface in postal cost studies.

First, of necessity, any such study will be highly aggregative. Thus, the multi product nature of postal service will be captured by, at most, two or three classes of mail at the national level. (In the telecommunications case, the output of national telecommunications networks was often measured by "value added." In some cases, two categories output measures, "local" and "toll," were used.) Second, it is unlikely that the "distance dimension" of postal costs could be addressed at all in an aggregative study. Yet the "postalization" of the rate structure, the invariance of postal rates to mileage, is a major pricing and policy issue. (In telecommunications, which does have mileage band categories and rates, the analogous complaint is the "hi-lo" averaging over high density, low cost routes and low density, high cost routes.) A third, and related problem, is that important cost-causative services (e.g., delivery) are not "unbundled." This makes it difficult to attempt to measure the associated costs. (Again, a telecommunications analogy can be found in the case of local usage.) To summarize, enterprise level postal cost studies are unlikely to be useful for policy analysis because they are highly aggregative and tend to employ service categories which do not adequately reflect cost causality.

4. Postal Service *is* a Natural Monopoly!

Despite the pessimistic methodological musing of the preceding section, I am quite convinced that postal service would be found to be a natural monopoly in the provision of its currently defined services. After explaining the basis of this confidence, I shall go on to explain why I think this fact is largely irrelevant for policy purposes.

Consider the stylized "postal network." It consists of: (1) local communities and their post office and postal delivery routes; (2) centralized sorting facilities; and (3) a long distance transportation network. For simplicity, let us assume that there is only one class of mail.[7] Then the two *services* provided by the postal network are *local* mail delivery (*L*) and *national* mail delivery (*N*). There are three types of cost causation in the postal network: *delivery costs*, $D(L+N)$, which are a function of the total volume of mail; *sorting costs*, $S(N)$, which are a function of the volume of national mail;[8]. and *transportation costs*, $T(N)$, which also depend only on the volume of national mail.

First notice that, even in this simple network, there is a discrepancy between the number of traditional classes of service (1) and the true number of services with distinct cost-causative impacts (2). But, in the spirit of the previous section, let us assume that this problem has been rectified so that we may focus our attention on postal costs viewed as a function of the levels of cost-causative services. Further, let us assume that there is enough symmetry in the network so that postal costs depend only on the total volumes of local and national mail, and not on how each is divided up among communities.[9]

I think it is safe to assume that there are significant economies of scale in delivery services. It would surely be wasteful to have two or more carriers making daily visits to all the mail boxes in a given neighborhood. Similarly, it would be counterproductive to have multiple local post offices performing route-level sorting chores. (Inter post office local mail would be sorted twice instead of only once.) Therefore, I shall assume that the delivery cost function exhibits increasing returns to scale: i.e., $D'(x) < D(x)/x$ for all $x>0$. For sake of argument, suppose that economies of scale have been exhausted in the sorting and transportation functions of the postal network. This is almost certainly true for transportation, since much of the transportation function is subcontracted to competitive transportation sector, at least in the United States. While there may (or may not) be unexploited economies of scale in the sorting function, positing their absence will only sharpen the point I am attempting to make. Therefore, assume henceforth that $S(N) = sN$, and that $T(N) = tN$.

Now, let us consider the properties of the multi product cost function $C(L,N) = D(L+N) + (s+t)N$. Economies of scope are present if the total costs of providing local and national mail services over two separate networks is greater than the costs of providing them together. Since $C(L,0) + C(0,N) = D(L) + D(N) + (s+t)N$, the postal network exhibits economies of scope if $D(L+N) < D(L) + D(N)$. But this condition is an immediate implication of the assumption of economies of scale in delivery services.[10] Next, let us examine returns to scale in the postal network. The formula for S, the degree of multi product returns to scale[11], is given by

$$S = C(L, \frac{N)}{LC_L + NC_N} = \frac{D(L+N) + (s+t)N}{(L+N)D' + (s+t)N},$$

where subscripts indicate partial differentiation. Clearly, the assumption of increasing returns to scale in delivery will ensure that the postal network enjoys overall economies of scale.[12]

Thus, we have seen how economies of scale in delivery will impart economies of scale and economies of scope to any postal network cost function. Somewhat surprisingly, economies of scale and economies of scope, taken together, are *not* sufficient to guarantee that the postal network is a natural monopoly.[13] However, in the present example, it is easy to show that the multi product cost function is also transray convex, which, when combined with economies of scale, suffices for natural monopoly.

Hence, should the practical difficulties discussed in the previous section ever be overcome, I am convinced that the evidence would clearly show that postal service is a natural monopoly. Does this mean that it should be provided by a single firm, shielded from entry? That is the subject of the next section.

5. Postal Service is a Network Industry

The stylized postal network of the previous section is very like the typical stylization of telecommunications networks. The local post office is analogous to the local distribution system of the local exchange carrier; sorting is analogous to switching; and transportation is the postal counterpart of long distance transmission. Thus, the recent history of the United States telecommunications industry may offer useful insights for the role competition in markets for postal services. There, the network structure also "transmitted" the undeniable scale economies of local exchange service to the system wide level. Yet the end result was that the Bell System was broken up, with manufacturing and long distance transmission going one way and local exchange service another.

The Department of Justice argued that the local exchange was a "monopoly bottleneck" that was being used to thwart entry into the potentially competitive long distance market. By structurally separating the monopoly facilities and making access to the local exchange take place as a market transaction, the breakup of the Bell System has facilitated competition and altered traditional pricing arrangements in the telecommunications industry. Given the parallels between postal and telecommunications networks, can one expect or recommend similar developments for the future of postal service?

Before addressing this question in greater detail, it is necessary to bring up an important difference between postal and telecommunications networks. Unlike telecommunications (electric power and transportation) networks, the postal network requires relatively little in the way of *sunk costs*. That is, there is not much capital investment that is both specialized and irrevocably committed to any particular market. First, the bulk of postal costs are labor costs, rather than equipment costs.[14] Second, much of the capital investment is in rather general purpose buildings and motor vehicles. Thus, unlike a telephone company's local loop or an electric power company's local distribution system, postal assets can probably be redeployed into another market, or even another industry, at a relatively low cost.

This fact has important implications for the design of public policy toward the natural monopoly elements of postal service. While the absence of significant sunk costs doesn't mean that it is any less wasteful to have several enterprises competing in local delivery markets, it does mean that alternative mechanisms such as Demsetzian competition *for* the market might prove to be a workable alternative to monopoly regulation or public provision. Similarly, while the transportation component of the postal network may topologically resemble its telecommunications counterpart, it also exhibits little of the sunk costs. As noted earlier, in the United States much of the transportation of mail is contracted to private firms, who themselves often rely on a government-supported transportation infrastructure. As suggested by Bailey (1981) and Bailey and Baumol (1984), when sunk facilities are largely absent or provided by the public sector, competition can be workable even in natural monopoly industries. Indeed, the most successful competitors of the U.S. Postal Service, United Parcel Service and express mail carriers, exploit the flexibility of the transport network in their success. A key ingredient has been these carriers' use of the excess capacity of the airways during the overnight hours. This has enabled them to design and operate innovative and efficient transportation and sorting networks.[15] Their ability to successfully undercut USPS for parcel post and express mail business casts serious doubts on the natural monopoly position of the Postal Service and/or its efficiency.

6. Concluding Thoughts on Introducing Competitive Forces into the Provision of Postal Services

The network structure of postal service and the relative lack of sunk costs convince me that competition can be more aggressively injected into postal service. What could consumers expect to gain from such a policy, and how would it be implemented?

First, when competition is introduced into the marketplace, even in a rather limited way, suddenly it somehow becomes possible to charge for services that had never been separately priced before! In telecommunications, the classic example is *access* (*to* the network of the local exchange carrier) and *usage* (*of* said network). Traditionally, access and usage had been bundled together for consumers under one monthly flat rate. But when competitive long distance firms entered the picture, it no longer made sense to provide either at a marginal price of zero. With some difficulty, regulators and Bell Operating Companies learned the importance of "unbundling" access and usage prices.

The most obvious unpriced postal service is delivery service. It consistently accounts for about 40% of postal costs,[16] costs which must be allocated to the various classes of mail service, since delivery itself is not a service. This serves to increase the wedge between price and marginal cost for mail (especially first class), since, as argued above, there are likely to be substantial fixed costs associated with delivery service. Some might argue that, since delivery service is the mechanism that "binds a nation together," it cannot or should not be priced. However Owen and Willig (1983) point out that, although delivery service may have characteristics of a nonexcludable public good[17] and exhibit network externalities,[18] these difficulties can be dealt with (internalized) at the community level along with other local public goods. This would make it possible for individual communities to choose (and pay for) high or low frequency delivery service, or no delivery service at all! Consumers would add the quality of postal service to the list of attributes they consider when selecting their domicile. One might argue that this proposal is in the spirit of Rowland Hill, since his original "penny post" proposal was based on delivery to centralized locations rather than to each individual's residence.[19]

The principle advantage of the Owen and Willig proposal is that it would make the community level the focal point of postal decision making. Here is where competition could be introduced into the system without foregoing the advantages of governmental monopoly. For example, the city council could contract with the USPS over the terms of its delivery service, or it could hire its own civil service employees to deliver the mail. It could even ask for bids from private contractors! Garbage collection is a good analogy. The nature of the function and the equipment used are quite similar. Perhaps most importantly, the lack of fixed investment means that incumbents are not likely to have an insuperable advantage. Many communities contract with private scavenger companies to get their garbage collected, and many maintain city crews of sanitation workers. But I'm not aware of any country which maintains a national army of garbage collectors.

Local responsibility for delivery service would also make it easier to uncover subsidies imbedded in existing postal rate structures. For example, if rural communities needed financial assistance in providing the (socially agreed upon) minimal level of delivery service, targeted subsidies could be enacted, just as they are in the case of rural electricity and telecommunications in the United States. Since the local post office would be a logical point of entry into the postal network, this structure would stimulate the unbundling of prices for transportation and sorting.

For example, if a business wished to distribute an advert to, say, left-handed sports car fanatics all over the nation, it would have several options. It could let the postal service do it. It could pre-sort its adverts (to the local P.O. level or the carrier route level) and "bypass" the centralized sorting facility, but make use of the postal service's transportation and delivery networks.[20] Alternatively, it could arrange for transport and sorting itself, delivering bundles to the loading docks of local post offices around the country, which it would pay for delivery services. (This could be a source of revenue for local postal authorities. Businesses generate the vast majority of postal volume, most of which nobody wants.) Finally, given the elimination of statutory restrictions, businesses could take their messages directly to the consumers mail boxes. However, I hope the discussion has made clear that substantial competition can be introduced into the provision of postal services *without* taking this last controversial step.

I shall close by mentioning, but not elaborating on, what I suspect will be the most dramatic effect of the introduction of competitive forces: the reduction in postal wage rates. I am not qualified to explain why postal wage rates are high all over the world, or, indeed, even to pass judgment on whether they are, in fact, "too high" in some well-defined sense. However, governments and regulated firms are notoriously inept at limiting the wage demands of their employees. A major effect of competition and deregulation in the United States has been a decline in the real wage rates of employees in the airline, trucking, and telecommunications industries.

Notes

1. See Panzar (1989) for a rigorous definition of natural monopoly and its determinants.
2. Kahn (1970-71) Vol. 2, page 223.
3. See, for example, Faulhaber (1975), Panzar and Willig (1977a: 1977b; 1981), Baumol (1977), and Baumol, Bailey, and Willig (1977).
4. Product specific economies of scale occur when the average incremental costs of a service decline when output is increased while holding constant the output of other services. See Panzar (1989) for a complete discussion.
5. See Chapter 15 of Baumol, Panzar, and Willig (1982) for a thorough discussion of this type of idealized empirical implementation of natural monopoly theory.
6. See Panzar (1989) and Fuss (1983) for discussions of the accomplishments and shortcomings of this literature.
7. The analysis would go through unaltered if the full set of mail classes were maintained. However, the vector notation might get a bit tedious.
8. Thus, this component does not refer to the sorting that goes on at the level of the local post office: e.g., assigning letters to the appropriate carrier route and differentiating between local and out of town destinations. Rather, it represents the cost of specialized regional sorting facilities used to aggregate mail for optimal routing over the transportation network.
9. Spady (1985) has developed a methodology for dealing with aggregation of this type in network industries. He posits a common cost function applicable to each node and link in the network. Costs are assumed to differ over links and nodes not only due to differing traffic volumes, but also due to differing technological and demographic characteristics, which are entered as parameters of the cost function. Remarkably, through clever choice of functional form, it is possible to estimate the parameters of the node and link-level cost functions without disaggregate data: only the means and variances of node and link-level variables are required.
10. Proof: First note that $d[D(x)/x]/dx = [xD' - D]/x2$, so that average delivery costs are falling when there are economies of scale. Thus $D(N+L)/(N+L) < D(N)/N$, or $ND(N+L)/(N+L) < D(N)$. Similarly, $LD(N+L)/(N+L) < D(L)$. Adding these two inequalities yields the desired result.
11. See Panzar and Willig (1977b) or Panzar (1989) for a complete discussion of this concept.
12. Of course, it is possible that these scale economies might be offset by sufficiently strong decreasing returns to scale in sorting and transportation. While certainly possible, such a circumstance doesn't seem likely.
13. See Panzar (1989).
14. According to Sorkin (1980), 85% of the costs of the United States Postal Service are wages and salaries.
15. For example, Federal Express flies *all* intercity packages (even, say, New York to Philadelphia packages) to its Memphis hub in the middle of the night. There, the packages are sorted and the planes return to their origins.
16. See Owen and Willig (1983) and Report of the United States Postmaster General 1985.
17. That is, it may be too costly to direct mailpersons *not* to stop at particular addresses.
18. An individual cannot appropriate all of the social benefits resulting from his subscribing to delivery service, because other individuals (especially businesses) value the ability to communicate with him. He does not take this external benefit into account when making his subscription decision. Therefore socially optimal prices should be set below marginal cost. Since I have already argued that marginal costs are themselves below average costs for delivery services, this effect aggravates the natural monopoly problem.
19. See Crew and Kleindorfer (1991).
20. This option is currently available to some extent in the United States via the USPS's differen-

tiated rates for bulk mail.

References

Bailey,E. E. 1981. "Contestability and the Design of Regulatory and Antitrust Policy," *American Economic Review*, (May): 178-183.
Bailey, E. E., and W. J. Baumol. 1984. "Deregulation and the Theory of Contestable Markets," *Yale Journal of Regulation*: 111-137.
Baumol, W.J. 1977. "On the Proper Cost Tests for Natural Monopoly," *American Economic Review* (December): 809-822.
Baumol, W.J., E. E. Bailey, and R. D. Willig. 1977. "Weak Invisible Hand Theorems on the Sustainability of Prices in a Multiproduct Monopoly," *American Economic Review* (June): 350-365.
Baumol, W.J., J. C. Panzar, and R. D. Willig. 1982. *Contestable Markets and the Theory of Industry Structure*. New York: Harcourt Brace Jovanovic.
Crew, M.A., and P. R. Kleindorfer. 1991. "Rowland Hill's Contribution as an Economist". (In this volume).
Faulhaber, G.R. 1975. "Cross-Subsidization: Pricing in Public Enterprise," *American Economic Review* (December) 966-977.
Fuss, M.A. 1983. "A Survey of Recent Results in the Analysis of Production Conditions in Telecommunications." In *Economic Analysis of Telecommunications: Theory and Applications*, edited by L. Courville, A. de Fontenay and R. Dobell. Amsterdam: North-Holland.
Kahn, A.E. 1971. *The Economics of Regulation: Principles and Institutions*, Volume 2. New York: Wiley.
Owen, B.M., and R. D. Willig. 1983. "Economics and Postal Pricing." In *The Future of the Postal Service*, edited by Joel Fleishmanin. Aspen: Aspen Institute.
Panzar, J.C. 1989. "Theoretical Determinants of Firm and Industry Structure." In *Handbook of Industrial Organization*, edited by R. Schmalensee and R. Willig. Amsterdam: North Holland.
Panzar, J.C., and R. D. Willig. 1977a "Free Entry and the Sustainability of Natural Monopoly." *Bell Journal of Economics* (Spring): 1-22.
Panzar, J.C., and R. D. Willig. 1977b. "Economies of Scale in Multi-Output Production." *Quarterly Journal of Economics* (August): pp. 481-494.
Sorkin, A.L. 1980. *The Economics of the Postal System*. Lexington, MA: Heath.
Spady, R.S. 1985 "Using Indexed Quadratic Cost Functions to Model Network Technologies." In *Analytical Studies in Transport Economics*, edited by A. F. Daughety. Cambridge, UK: University Press.
U.S. Postal Service. 1985. Annual Report of the Postmaster General.

COMMENTS
Michael Waterson

In commenting on this paper, I will confine myself mainly to the earlier sections. The paper ranges fairly widely, but I do not want to pre-empt later papers and discussants' comments, so I shall very largely focus on the issues posed in the title's question.

I must first welcome the general idea of simplifying the determination of scale economies. Central to this is the formula for overall scale economies. In fact, it can be written in what I believe is a slightly more useful form:

$$S = \frac{1+y}{\frac{1}{s_d}+y},$$

where y = sorting + transport costs/delivery costs, s_d = economies of scale in delivery, and S is overall economies of scale, that is it represents the relationship between output of all products and costs. Then for the United Kingdom, if we take, for example, Pryke's (1981) figures for $1/s_d$ (.875) and proxy the ratio y by the ratio of labor costs in the two areas (≤ 1), S turns out around 1.05; modest though significant overall economies of scale. The fact that it is so easy to get an estimate from comparatively little information demonstrates the power of this a priori approach.

But of course this is not a true empirical estimate because of the assumptions underlying the formula, and various alternative views have been put forward. For example, Estrin and de Meza's (1990) aggregative work suggests a higher value as do the United Kingdom Post Office's internal studies. On the other hand, Albon (1987), for example, has argued that there are not scale economies in delivery and, therefore, not overall scale economies. Multiple deliveries of milk in a typical street in urban Britain would be an example consistent with his view.

More pertinent are the multiple suppliers of essentially parcels service. If we take it for the moment that parcels service is a natural monopoly because of economies of scale in delivery, further that the Post Office is obliged to provide a parcels service but that it is relatively inefficient in doing so, what structure would this imply? I suggest a dominant low cost competitor to the Post Office would emerge, with little other competition. Yet this is not, so far as I am aware, a very accurate description of that industry's structure in the United Kingdom, since a number of operators are present. At the same time, there are observations consistent with the hypothesis that, if anywhere, there are economies of scale in the delivery aspect of postal operations. An example is provided by the phenomenon of "remail," whereby letters arrive in Britain from Australia postmarked

"Hounslow" with TNT's logo along the top—TNT are in effect subcontracting delivery to the Royal Mail.

What this points to, I think, is that rather more care has to be invested in examining what it is about delivery of some goods (letter post but also others) which gives rise to substantial economies of scale in delivery. Panzar is in fact talking about the economies available when density of service increases. Generally speaking, output volume can increase either through increased density on the existing network or through an extension of the network, and the latter is likely to be subject to diseconomies, if anything (Hay and Morris 1979, ch.2). But since postal operators engage in universal service, the former is the relevant concept to them and to the natural monopoly debate on efficiency. Nevertheless, the industry may be vulnerable to entry into a dense part of the network, if there are diseconomies in network size.

It is interesting to examine some of the implications of Panzar's a priori argument regarding natural monopoly. Normally, nowadays, one teaches that whether or not an industry is a natural monopoly depends upon the relationship between scale economies and demand. But the argument made in the paper is independent of demand. The labels "local" and "national" can in principle apply at any level. Thus, the same argument could be made to support the case for New Zealand post or for the United States Postal Service being a natural monopoly. Indeed, by suitable redefinition, it could be used to support the case for the *world's* postal service being a natural monopoly. This could, in part, explain the existence of the Universal Postal Union. But it does also reinforce the point I made just now about the need to be clearer about what one actually means by delivery, "local," "national," etc.

Still remaining within the area of costs, I note the remark in the paper that the postal network requires relatively little in the way of *sunk costs*. This is contrasted with telecommunications, electric power, and transportation. But in an earlier era (ten to fifteen years ago), we were being told that the remarkable thing about airline routes was that they provided a prime example of a natural monopoly without sunk costs or entry barriers. This turned out to be far too sweeping a statement. The availability of slots and the investment in booking systems has proven of considerable importance for some airlines in retaining powerful market positions. This is of relevance because it is fairly generally expected that there is the possibility of substantial investment in automated sorting facilities in the postal service over the medium term. But as the impending reorganization of electricity generation in the United Kingdom teaches us, the effect of allowing entry is to make everyone go for investments with a quick payback, plant with a relatively high marginal cost as long as it has a low fixed cost. Thus, any policy decisions made about entry may well have an effect on technical change in the industry.

Since I am now moving into the more policy-oriented areas of the paper, I cannot resist one final comment. The comments made towards the end of the paper concerning payment for delivery are interesting. However, the proposals regarding individual communities being able to choose levels of postal service could, I fear, only come from a country with a rather more vibrant tradition of local democracy than currently exists in the United Kingdom. Here, local communities are being allowed by central government to make fewer and fewer decisions for themselves. Thus, it is hard to imagine the suggestions being taken up in practice.

References

Albon, R. 1987. *Privatize the Post*. London: Center for Policy Studies.
Estrin, S., and D. De Meza. 1990. "The Postal Monopoly: A Case Study." *Economic Review* (January): 2-7.
Hay, D.A., and D.J. Morris. 1979. *Industrial Economics: Theory and Evidence*. Oxford: Oxford University Press.
Pryke, R. 1981. *The Nationalized Industries*. Oxford: Martin Robertson.

11
POSTAL RATE-MAKING PROCEDURES AND OUTCOMES IN VARIOUS COUNTRIES
Robert Albon

1. Introduction

In all major countries, postal services are government-owned and, at least on standard mail, have statutory monopoly power. Courier and parcel operations are usually competitive. Administrative procedures for determining rates vary across countries with some (e.g., the United Kingdom) apparently leaving it mainly to the postal service; while others (e.g., the United States) have a formal rate-making body. Outcomes in all cases appear to reflect political influences and often cannot be given a rationale on the basis of public utility pricing principles.

Before considering the evidence on postal pricing efficiency, we review (section 2) the administrative procedures for determining postal rates in various countries. The countries considered are the United States, Canada, the United Kingdom, the Federal Republic of Germany, Japan, Australia, and New Zealand. Other countries (e.g., South Africa and Spain) receive incidental mention. As already noted, procedures differ between these countries, and our sample covers the spectrum of practices.

Questions of efficiency of postal pricing are considered in section 3. Examples of deviations from efficient pricing (in the Ramsey-Boiteux tradition) include the following:

1. Telecommunications profits still support postal losses in some countries (e.g., Federal Republic of Germany).
2. In some countries, loss-making postal services are supported by profits on other postal operations.
3. The uniform price on internal letters, a feature in all countries considered except Spain, cannot readily be justified on conventional efficiency grounds.
4. The first-class/second-class price differential in the United Kingdom cannot be supported on Ramsey-Boiteux grounds.

5. Peak-load pricing problems are not properly addressed.

Section 4 of the paper contains a consideration of the ways that postal pricing could be made more efficient, including use of: (1) separation of telecommunications from postal services (where applicable); (2) direct subsidies rather than uniform price subsidies on rural services and other community service obligations (CSOs); (3) direct regulations on pricing; (4) less intrusive regulations such as "RPI-X" revenue constraints; and (5) free market forces.

As it is beyond my brief—and as it is dealt with in other papers—the last of these policy options only receives incidental attention.

2. Postal Pricing Practices in Various Countries

In all countries reviewed, the role of the free market in determining postal prices is limited, and, accordingly, administrative procedures must play a major role. The actual procedures range from effectively leaving the decision-making to the postal administration, to heavy involvement of the government in price-setting. It is illuminating to compare and contrast these procedures in a number of countries.

2.1. Federal Republic of Germany

West Germany has only recently (1989) gone through the process of splitting its 'Bundespost' (DBP) into three independent, government-owned corporations—telecom, post, and post bank. Within Bundespost, the postal service was heavily subsidized from telecommunications profits, and this continues for a limited period (but in a more explicit form) under the new arrangements. The new postal corporation will eventually be required, through cost-cutting and substantial rises in rates, to cover its costs of operations.

The restructuring of the Deutsche Bundespost was aimed at separating the regulatory from the entrepreneurial tasks and at establishing a market-oriented and efficient corporate structure. The law concerning the Constitution of the Deutsche Bundespost (*Deutsche Bundespost Constitution Act* 1989) forms the legal basis of the new arrangements. The management board runs the enterprise in accordance with this law. Before the restructuring of Deutsche Bundespost, it had responsibilities in two general areas. Firstly, it was the government authority empowered to grant to third parties rights allocated to the Federal level in the posts and telecommunications field, in accordance with the respective legal provisions and, where applicable, to issue licences. Second, it was the provider of a comprehensive range of services in the market.

Regulation of pricing is assumed by the Ministry. The main features of this regulation are as follows: The Federal Minister of Posts and Telecommunications is responsible for overseeing the management of the Deutsche Bundespost. There are three categories of services for post and telecommunication services: (1) monopoly services where pricing is subject to approval by the Ministry; (2) mandatory services, where decisions may be vetoed by the Ministry; and (3) free services with no regulation. There is an obligation for DBP Postdienst to maintain a uniform rate for ordinary letters. There is a ban on cross-subsidization from monopoly to competitive services. The extra cost of infrastructural and political obligations for mandatory services may, however, be subsidized to counterbalance competitive disadvantages.

2.2. The United States

Posts and telecommunications have always been independent in the United States. In 1970, the Government passed the *Postal Reorganization Act* which established the Postal Rates Commission (PRC) specifically to "regulate" the pricing of the United States Postal Service (USPS), which had been created out of the previous service operated by a government department (the Post Office Department). The new arrangements had the following features: (1) the USPS was, as previously, obliged to maintain a uniform price for all first-class letter mail; (2) the overall level of postal rates had to be framed so as to generate sufficient revenue to cover total costs of the operation; and (3) there was a requirement that, in all services, prices had to at least cover marginal costs so as to avoid cross-subsidization. This has led to considerable controversy over the identification of marginal costs, with USPS allegedly tending to "understate" marginal costs, preferring to view the bulk of costs as common rather than specific to particular services. The history of the conflict between USPS and the PRC has been traced in Sherman (1989, 264-268) and discussed in the detailed analysis of Scott (1986). We return to this interesting case in the next section. Finally, (4) postal rates had to be approved by the PRC, but the initiative on prices lies with the USPS.

2.3. Australia

In Australia, the Postal Corporation operates separately from the telecommunications body (Telecom) under the *Australian Postal Corporation Act* of 1989. It is obliged to cover its costs of operation and meet a financial target and has considerable discretion in how it does this. However, it is obliged to apply a single uniform rate of postage on standard articles carried within Australia by ordinary post. The Corporation's Corporate Plan requires it to keep the increase in the basic postage rate at no faster than the rise in the Consumer Price Index (CPI) over the three years 1989-90 to 1991-92. Further, since 1984, the Prices Surveillance Authority (PSA) has had a role in regard to pricing of standard articles and registered publications. The Corporation must notify the PSA of proposed price changes for these items, and the PSA may then accept the proposals or recommend to the Treasurer that a public inquiry be held on the Corporation's proposals; supporting them or suggesting variations. Following release of the PSA's report, the Minister for Transport and Communications has the power to disapprove the proposals. In practice, the PSA's procedures initially resulted in reductions in the increases for registered publications and once in a short delay on the date of implementation of the price increase for standard articles. These expectations seem to have come to be built-in to the Corporation's notification. However, the PSA's attitude to registered publications changed with the advent of a new Chairman, and major steps towards cost recovery have occurred.

2.4. Canada

The government-owned Canada Postal Corporation has traditionally been quite separate from the country's private and public telecommunications system. Unlike the United States, Canada does not have an explicit regulatory body overseeing Canada Post's pricing decisions. Draft legislation to establish such a rates commission was not passed by the legislature. Under the *Canada Post Corporation Act* of 1981, the postal operator is required to achieve overall financial self-sufficiency and to set "fair and reasonable" prices. There is an approval mechanism for rates on basic letters and third-class addressed mail, whereby Canada Post must gazette its intentions sixty days in advance. Interested parties react to the proposals and Cabinet makes the final decision. All other rates are decided under either generic or specific contracts. There is no requirement to have a uniform geographical price.

Canada Post is also constrained under the terms of the corporate plan entered into with the Government. This involves keeping the increase in the basic letter rate below the rise in the CPI, maximizing the contribution from competitive products, and the pricing of social services consistent with explicit funding. Canada Post receives direct subsidies for four categories: newspapers, periodicals and books; parliamentary mail; literature for the blind; and transport of foodstuffs to native communities. Very large amounts are involved in these subsidies.

2.5. Japan

Japan's postal administration has long been separate from telecommunications, even though they both come under the same Ministry of Posts and Telecommunications. The *Postal Law* states three principles for setting postal rates—they should be economical, lead to the entire postal service being self-supporting, and implicitly that they be based on "process costing." First and second class mail rates are set "by law," while others are set by ministerial ordinance, following consultation with the Postal Services Council. There are four classes of letter post and a parcel post. Third and fourth class mail rates are set by ministerial ordinance but must be "set low by law since such mail furthers social policies and programs" (Ad Hoc Commission on Fundamental Issues Facing the Postal Services 1988, 27). The Government does not provide explicit subsidies to cover the losses consequently sustained on third and fourth class mail. All other services at least cover their avoidable costs. Postal rates (except for ordinary parcels) apply uniformly throughout the country and, while the Commission describes this as "an inherent flaw" (p. 29), the uniform price is justified on other bases. However, there is no explicit statutory requirement for a uniform rate under the legislation.

2.6. New Zealand

In New Zealand, the postal and telecommunications services have only recently (1987) been separated and corporatized. The changes to each service have been dramatic, especially in telecommunications (i.e., corporatization, virtual total demonopolization and privatization). New Zealand Post Limited has basic responsibility for pricing without government intervention. However, there are some effective constraints, the first two of which are established by a Deed of Understanding (New Zealand 1989). Firstly, New Zealand Post must maintain a uniform price nationwide for the basic letter post. Secondly, price increases on basic postage must be kept to no greater than the rise in the CPI less, at first, two percentage points and thereafter one percentage point (after the first price increase). Thirdly, the provisions of the *Commerce Act* apply to New Zealand Post and could be invoked if pricing were deemed anti-competitive. Further information on the New Zealand case are included in Toime's paper in this volume.

2.7. The United Kingdom

The Post Office in Britain has operated separately from the telecommunications body since 1981, the year of the *British Telecommunications Act*. To a large extent, postal prices are, at least explicitly, a matter for the Post Office, but there is a requirement to be profitable overall, and there have been indications of what the Government requires. Perhaps the most pointed comments came in 1986 from the then Secretary of State for Trade and Industry (Channon 1986). This was in a letter to the then-Chairman of the Post Office, Sir Ronald Dearing. The first requirement was that the Post Office "should make a profit in each year in each of its constituent businesses." Second, the Secretary required that the Post Office "ensure that the main elements of its price structure are sensibly related to the costs of supply and the market situation." Third, the Post Office was told it "should avoid cross-subsidy, particularly from monopoly to competitive activities". The Royal Mail is not required to maintain a uniform price for ordinary inland letters. However, in practice, there may be substantial informal interference in the pricing process.

3. Efficiency Aspects of Postal Pricing

The efficiency of postal pricing has various aspects, not all of which are incorporated into rate-making procedures and criteria. It is now nearly always a requirement to cover costs overall, usually with a profit target as well. The phenomenon of telecommunications profits supporting postal losses is now a thing of the past except in a few cases like the Federal Republic of Germany and South Africa. In contrast, there are many instances where there is no requirement for the different services of a postal administration to be individually profitable. That is, profitable areas of postal operation sometimes support loss-making ones. Further, there can be problems within particular services, especially standard mail, where the uniform price exists in the face of cost differences. Not only is this tolerated, often a uniform geographical price is required by statute.

3.1. The Ramsey-Boiteux Pricing Principle

In reviewing the efficiency aspects of postal pricing practices, we consistently have in mind the Ramsey-Boiteux public utility pricing principle. This approach involves deviating from marginal cost prices in a manner which causes the least overall distortion of the pattern of usage prevailing at marginal cost prices. To do this involves mark-ups on marginal cost which vary inversely with the own-price elasticity of demand of the service. This is the famous "inverse-elasticity rule." As Crew and Kleindorfer note in their first paper in this volume, a rudimentary form of this approach can be found in the writings of Rowland Hill.

The Ramsey-Boiteux approach is more formally set-out in general terms by Brown and Sibley (1986) and Sherman (1989), and specifically with regard to postal pricing by Scott (1986), Sherman and George (1979), and others. Given the difficulties (although not the impossibility) of access charging in the postal industry, Ramsey-Boiteux pricing suggests itself as the appropriate approach to pricing.

3.2. Subsidization of Postal Losses by Telecommunications Profits

There are now very few major countries which still have posts and telecommunications under one administration. Some European countries still have this arrangement, as does South Africa. The Federal Republic of Germany has only recently (1990) split its Bundespost, and New Zealand is also a quite recent (1987) addition to the list of those that have split. Significant reorganization (or "corporatization") usually occurs at the time of the separation.[1]

Where telecommunications and post are together, the result is almost always one where telecommunications profits support postal losses. This practice results in efficiency losses at the points of both implicit taxation (i.e., telecommunications) and implicit subsidization (i.e., posts). These losses could be very substantial.

In Australia, for example, there were very heavy postal losses in the old (pre-1975) Australian Post Office. In 1973-74, for example, reported losses reached $54.5million. on a total earnings of only $245million.[2] These were more than offset by telecommunications profits of $59.2million. In June 1974, the rate for standard articles stood at 7c, but two years later it was 18c, a rise in real terms of nearly 100 per cent. The extent of the price rise necessary to make the postal service profitable is also indicative of a very large subsidy to posts. On the other side, the proportionate tax on telecommunications, which mostly fell on Subscriber Trunk Dialling, was very much less. This was because of the larger base on which it fell. Given that, at that time, the STD elasticity was probably larger than the letter elasticity, the overall deadweight loss may not have been all that great.

The pattern of prices produced by this type of subsidy and tax arrangement probably could not be given an efficiency rationale, even if telecommunications services were more inelastic in demand. This is because the Ramsey-Boiteux rule will always require that each service at least covers its marginal cost and that average variable costs are probably quite close to marginal costs. As such, the rule is highly unlikely to throw up a mark-up producing a deficit on variable costs on any service. Given that postal demand is probably more inelastic than telecommunications demand, a loss is very difficult, if not impossible, to justify.

3.3. Pricing Across Mail Categories

Postal administrations provide many services other than standard mail, including (in all countries) overseas mail and parcels and (in many countries) courier services and electronic mail. It is interesting to review the efficiency with which pricing across categories is practised, especially in the light of the possibility of cross-subsidizing from areas protected by statutory monopoly (e.g., standard mail in all countries) to those that are competitive with other service providers (e.g., parcels in most countries).

In the United States, years of wrangling between the PRC and the USPS seem to have resulted in a tolerably efficient outcome, loosely-based on Ramsey-Boiteux principles. The Postal Service has had to be forced to attribute more of its costs to particular services, the proportion rising from less than 50 percent to over 70 percent during the 1970s. Costs that are not attributed are distributed over services on the basis of 'demand factors' or, as Scott (1986, 280) describes it, the "inverse elasticity rule." Scott estimates the extent to which the rate structure reflects Ramsey-Boiteux prices. His overall conclusion is that the PRC "sets rates that turn out to be fairly consistent with general Ramsey pricing principles" (p. 288). One category where this is not true is the second-class regular rate covering educational, scientific, cultural, and informational items. In spite of an inelastic demand, this has a very low mark-up on marginal cost.

In the Australian context, "second-class regular" corresponds to the category "registered publications" which have traditionally attracted a substantial concession. Australia Post, partly on the basis of its attribution of overhead costs, has estimated a large loss on this category of mail. However, recently it has been successful in raising registered publications rates relative to other rates. This was initially resisted by the PSA, but the process of cost recovery is now almost complete, especially when viewed in the light of Australia Post's probable overstatement of costs of this service. The recent reorganization in New Zealand has produced the complete elimination of registered publications concessions.

Postal administrations have tended to resist the pressure to offer explicit concessions, but have been more amenable to less obvious ones (e.g., the uniform price). Often it is very difficult to get information on the performance of particular areas. In other cases, rather odd allocations of common costs make assessment of service profitability difficult. "Commercial-in-confidence" is sometimes claimed for particular services.

The United Kingdom Post Office has generally been fairly open about its internal finances with detailed information about the costs and revenues of its major operations. These data reveal that all areas have been profitable in recent years, although parcels (including Expresspost) only became profitable during the 1980s and are now only marginally profitable. With the possible exception of the parcels area, the United Kingdom does not display any major difficulties with its pricing between services, but there are problems within categories, including in the parcels area. Competition has recently forced the parcels business of the Post Office to move towards non-uniform geographical pricing.

In Australia, there has been a suspicion that two areas—courier services and electronic mail—have been subsidized by other operations. This support cannot be verified because of a dearth of cost information provided by the Corporation. This illustrates the possibility that information requirements alone could act as an inducement to more efficient pricing. It also illustrates the power of the criteria in many countries requiring all areas to cover their costs.

3.4. The Uniform Price[3]

In all countries reviewed, there is a uniform geographical price on standard domestic letters in the face of what are, in some cases, very substantial cost differences. In some cases, a uniform price is a statutory obligation. Discussions of the uniform price involve questions of efficiency, equity, and the national interest. The focus here is narrower, with concentration on the efficiency implications of this practice. It is highly unlikely that a uniform geographical price could be given a Ramsey-Boiteux justification. If this is the case, we should seek the rationale in terms of the higher administrative and compliance costs that would be associated with a non-uniform price. This is the argument usually given by postal administrations. Tabor (1987) exemplifies this approach in a defence of the uniform price in the United Kingdom.

There are three major concerns in this sub-section. First, we present a simple model of the uniform price which highlights the dual nature of the efficiency costs and serves as a background to the discussion, later in the paper, of replacing implicit taxes with direct subsidies. Second, there is a brief discussion of whether a Ramsey-Boiteux justification of the uniform price can be mounted. Third, there is a review of the collection and compliance costs that might arise if the uniform price were abandoned.

Suppose there are two markets, urban (u) and rural (r), with different but constant marginal costs C_u and C_u, where $C_r > C_u$. Overhead costs are assumed zero but could be incorporated in the analysis without affecting the broad conclusions regarding uniform pricing. Demands in each market, D_u and D_r, are downward-sloping and independent of each other.

The optimal quantity in the urban area is Q_u^* with price P_u^*. In the rural area, the quantity $\overline{Q}_r$ and price P_r^* are socially-efficient. A uniform price, $\overline{P}$, can be found which lies between P_r^* and P_u^* and just covers costs. The setting of a uniform price of $\overline{P}$ results in a fall in urban quantity to $\overline{Q}_u$ and a rise in rural quantity to Q_r^*, representing a tax on urban users of $\overline{Q}_u (\overline{P} - C_u)$ equal to the subsidy to rural users of $\overline{Q}_r (C_r - \overline{P})$. When a subsidy is financed in this way, it is usually known as a "cross-subsidy." The cross-subsidy through the uniform price results in two dead-weight losses: one from the tax, equal to $\frac{1}{2} (Q_u^* - \overline{Q}_u)(\overline{P} - C_u)$, and one from the subsidy, equal to $\frac{1}{2} (\overline{Q}_r - Q_r^*)(C_r - \overline{P})$. These are shaded in figure 1.

The value placed on the subsidy by rural users is less than its dollar amount. The

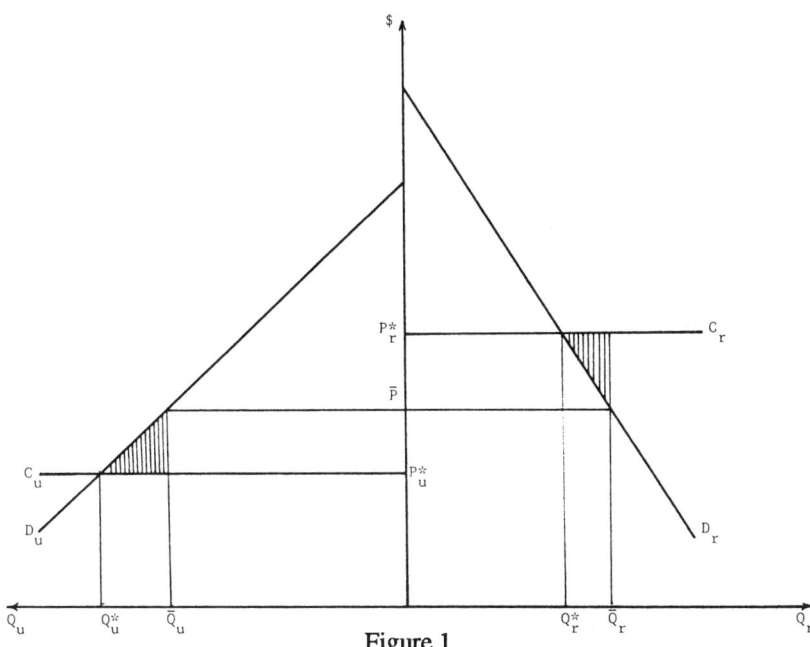

Figure 1

equivalent income variation of the subsidy is the area to the left of D_r between P_r^* and $\overline{P}$, or the amount of the subsidy less the deadweight loss. The equivalent variation will deviate more from the amount of the subsidy the greater is the elasticity of demand. The deviation could be quite substantial, approaching one-half of the subsidy amount with a linear demand and more than one-half, given a constant elasticity demand.

Now consider whether there is likely to be a Ramsey-Boiteux justification for the uniform geographical price. In the face of cost differences, differences in mark-ups would have to spring from differences in own-price elasticities such that rural demand was more elastic than urban demand. We need to examine data on both rural-urban cost differentials and on urban and rural price elasticities. There is no empirical evidence, for any country, that throws any light on the elasticities of demand for urban as against rural postal services. However, one suspects that, if anything, rural demand is more inelastic than urban demand. There are some data on urban-rural cost differentials, and these can be substantial, especially in countries like Australia, but also in more surprising cases like the United Kingdom. Tabor (1987) notes that "before allocating overheads and profit, it costs about half as much again as the average to deliver a letter in a rural area. This would mean about 6p to 7p on a letter to the country" (p. 44). This appears to be something of an overstatement based on earlier data (Post Office 1979), but all available data suggest a large cost differential. These data do not support a uniform price on a geographical basis.

The third aspect of the uniform price is the issue of administrative costs to the service provider and of compliance costs to the user. Would these be raised substantially if prices were differentiated on a geographical basis?

In the context of the conference on which this volume is based, it is interesting to review the position of Rowland Hill on the uniform price question. Hill was not, as commonly represented, an unqualified supporter of the uniform price. This point has been made by a number of writers including Daunton (1985) and Coase (1939). Hill only justified uniformity of price by uniformity of cost. The original penny post scheme proposed was confined to "primary distribution" within and between post-towns. Other inland letters (the "secondary distribution") would either be subject to a surcharge or be subsidized by local authorities. Hill dropped this plan in order to get support for the penny post idea; a decision he later regretted.

If a two-tier structure were introduced there would be additional costs; in particular some initial setting-up costs (for the service provider and users) and continuing costs of additional sorting for the postal administration and of compliance for users. It is difficult to envisage that these costs would be substantial, but they would have to be carefully considered. The survey here is very brief.

The new system would require a change to the postcode system. This could probably be achieved by adding a suffix to all rural postcodes. This would appear to be a relatively simple move, certainly far less difficult than introducing the postcode system in the first place. This would be unlikely to be difficult for the vast majority of users, i.e., those in the business sector. In most cases, these users already have sophisticated mailing systems that could be easily modified to incorporate the new requirements. Some personal users (especially the aged) may have trouble adjusting to the new system, just as they did in conforming with the postcode system itself.

Sorting systems already have the capacity automatically to 'face' and separate mail according to its stamped value reflecting weight differences, destination (inland or overseas) and (in the United Kingdom) its class. This could probably be easily modified to differentiate on the basis of urban and rural destinations, but there may be minor difficulties at first. Over time, this would become routine as the system evolved around the new rate structure.

Of course, some mistakes would be made, especially where rural letters were placed in the system with only the urban postage. This could be handled by pursuit (on a random basis) of the additional postage from either the receiver or the sender of the mail. As an alternative, rural mail with an urban stamp could be given 'second-class' treatment (or, in the United Kingdom, 'third-class' treatment) which was especially slow. This would act as a disincentive to both deliberate abuse and careless use of the system.

In Australia, the question of a multiple rate structure was considered by the 1982 Committee of Inquiry. While it did not advocate a non-uniform rate structure, this was not because it envisaged high administrative costs. A two-tier tariff would not be a problem, but if there "were more than say two ....tariffs, the additional administrative costs involved would outweigh the benefits" (p. 47). The Post Office in the United Kingdom was, in 1979, pessimistic about the prospects for a two-tier system. They thought it could work for mail within post-towns, but not for other mail—"Application of different price rates requiring customers to identify an address as e.g. 'town' or 'rural' will probably not work." (1979, 12.3). Tabor (1987) was also very negative about the prospects of a two-tier system.

In spite of this official pessimism, multiple-tier pricing structures for ordinary letters have operated in the past and there is at least one existing case. A two-tier structure worked in two Australian colonies prior to the formation of a national postal system after Federation. More recently, in Canada, a lower local rate was available for many years until 1968. When airmail was first introduced in Canada, it was at a higher rate than for ordinary domestic letters. When the two rates were combined, local mail was kept at the surface rate, opening-up a local/long-distance price differential. The two-tier structure was ostensibly removed because of administrative difficulties with the two-tier structure, but was more likely the casualty of a quest for greater revenue through a rate increase.

A current case of a two-tier structure is that of Spain. Local letters (i.e., those posted within a territory to an address in the territory) are cheaper than all other letters. A "territory" is an administrative area which can be as large as greater Madrid. Local letters are 8 pesetas, compared with 20 pesetas for those posted to outside the territory. Wrongly-stamped letters are subject to a penalty of twice the difference, payable by the receiver.

3.5. The First-/Second-Class Price Differential in Britain[4]

A distinction between first- and second-class mail was established in Britain in 1968. The second-class service is slower and cheaper than first-class, supposedly reflecting a cost differential between the two services. First-class mail tends to be sorted at night when costs are higher. However, it is worth asking whether the extent of the price differential can be justified on efficiency grounds?

In 1976, the Post Office reported that the cost differential was nearly 0.5p, a figure reported by the Post Office Review Committee (1977, 30). The price differential at this stage was 2p. By 1985-86, the cost differential would have risen to about 1p (if it had risen at the same rate as postal prices), and the price differential was 5p. By 1990, the cost differential would have reached a little over 1p with a price differential of 5p. The price differential has, therefore, narrowed somewhat in proportional terms since the mid-1980s.

The Monopolies and Mergers Commission (1984) looked at this question and reported a Post Office rationalization of the disparity between the price and cost differentials. The claim was that the Ramsey principle was being applied in that the first-class service is more price inelastic than the second-class one. There was no detailed evidence on this, but the Post Office reasoned that this was the case because the ratio of first-class mail volume to second-class had risen at the same time as the ratio of the first-class price to the second-class price had risen. Given the presence of other determinants of postal demand, this conclusion does not necessarily follow.

The multiple-regression analysis of postal demand reported in Albon (1989) does not support the contention that first-class mail is more price-inelastic.[5] Using annual data for the period 1969-70 to 1985-86, an attempt was made to explain first- and second-class mail volumes in terms of their prices, a telephone price variable, income variables, and delivery standards. Both equations were satisfactory from both statistical and economic viewpoints, although the second-class price was insignificant in the first-class equation. Two aspects of the results require highlighting.

First, the variable gross domestic product (GDP) is significant in both equations, but positive for first-class mail and negative for second-class. This could be an alternative explanation for the observed movement in the volume ratio. At the very least it stands as a warning against casual empiricism of the kind conducted by the Post Office.

Second, the estimated own-price elasticities, calculated at the mean volumes of each category, are remarkably similar at -0.86 for first-class and -0.89 for second-class. This result is even more damaging to the Post Office's Ramsey rationalization of the price differential.

The difference between the Ramsey-Boiteux prices for first- and second-class mail would, then, be about 2p, a little more than the cost differential. This is based on the slight difference in the elasticity and, more particularly, because of the fact that the first-class mark-up is on a higher base. In 1985-86, the reduction in the first-class rate of 2p and a decision not to reduce the second-class rate by 1p, would have kept revenue constant and been consistent with minimizing deadweight losses. The net efficiency gain would have been about £17 million, comprising a loss on second-class of £19 million and a gain on first-class of £36 million. The data on which these calculations are based are set-out in Albon (1989, table 1).

In spite of the price differential, the proportion of mail that is first-class is rising. This creates a considerable problem. It seems to suggest that the differential should be widened even further, a result inconsistent with the Ramsey-Boiteux conclusion. The bottom line is that there is something fundamentally wrong with the structure of letter mail. One area that may need to be developed is the usage of pre-sorting by customers.

4. Improving the Efficiency of Postal Pricing

Postal pricing practices in all countries are, to greater or lesser extents, inefficient. The inefficiency can arise within mail categories (e.g., the uniform price) and between categories (e.g., loss-making activities like electronic mail being supported by profits from other categories). Various means of reducing these inefficiencies are available, even working within the current institutional frameworks of substantial statutory monopoly and government ownership. This section contains several suggestions for the improvement of postal rate-making. More radical solutions (involving greater competition) are also possible, but these are beyond the scope of this paper.

4.1. Separation of Posts and Telecommunications

Many countries have now reformed their "post offices" by taking them from direct departmental control and separating their postal and telecommunications services into independent administrations. This has always been true in the United States, Japan, and Canada and has been a more recent phenomenon in other countries—Australia (1975), United Kingdom (1981), New Zealand (1987), and the Federal Republic of Germany (1990). In other countries (e.g., South Africa) this change has not yet occurred. This reform must be seen as essential to providing a basis for an efficient postal pricing structure.

We argued earlier that the existence of postal losses financed from telecommunications profits is an inefficient arrangement with deadweight losses at both ends of the tax-subsidy exchange. Removal of the telecommunications subsidy to posts will, thus, produce efficiency gains at both ends. The extent of the gains from cost recovery in posts will depend on how the composition of prices changes. The objective would be to move to overall cost recovery with individual prices being adjusted in ways that most enhance efficiency. Exploitation of relative demand elasticities will ensure an overall efficiency gain in keeping with the Ramsey-Boiteux principle. This is, in broad terms, the likely outcome when a postal administration is forced to seek cost-recovery. However some mechanism(s) may be necessary to ensure this outcome.

4.2. Direct Subsidies

Where postal pricing is inefficient as a consequence of inbuilt cross-subsidies (especially the uniform price and pricing of newspaper and magazine deliveries below cost), there is the alternative of unshackling the postal administration from the "community service obligation" and replacing the implicit tax/subsidy arrangement with a direct subsidy.[6] This will have the definite advantage of greater transparency and a possible efficiency bonus. As efficiency is our major concern, we concentrate on the second of these.

A possible argument in favor of direct subsidies is that additional tax revenues to finance these subsidies will cause deadweight losses that may, on the margin, be less than those from the implicit taxes on other postal users. That is, in the case of the uniform price, we must compare the deadweight loss of the tax on urban users (figure 1) with the deadweight loss from raising the revenue for the subsidy from explicit taxes.

For many countries, we have estimates of the marginal deadweight losses from raising revenue through major taxes such as the income tax. In Australia, for example, Findlay and Jones (1982) estimated the marginal deadweight loss from personal income taxation at somewhere in the region of 25 cents per dollar. What is the corresponding marginal deadweight loss from the "tax" on, say, intrametropolitan mail users? The "marginal cost" of an intra-metropolitan letter in Australia is probably about 20 cents compared with a price of 41 cents. If the elasticity is about -0.3 (a figure that must be regarded as about the most inelastic it could be),[7] the marginal deadweight loss is about 21 cents. However, with an elasticity of -0.9, the marginal deadweight loss is about $1.09. The true figure is probably within these bounds, but towards the upper end. If so, there would be a substantial efficiency gain from moving to a direct subsidy financed by an income tax increase. A similar conclusion would probably be reached if the same sort of calculation were made for other countries in the sample.

4.3. Direct Regulations on Prices

No country has particularly heavy-handed regulations on postal prices, although some have regulatory structures that approach this. While it is unfashionable to recommend the use of direct price regulations, there is some scope for moving in this direction, while postal administrations remain public and monopolistic. However, as argued in the next sub-section, more subtle regulations are preferred.

As we noted in section 2, the usual type of regulation is one which requires overall cost-recovery and an approval process for prices suggested by the postal administration. Ministerial approval is required in most countries, sometimes after deliberation by a pricing review body. The United States PRC and the PSA in Australia exemplify such review bodies. Would it be desirable for countries without such bodies to adopt them? If so, what is the best form that the body could take?

The PRC is, perhaps, a good model to follow. It is comprehensive in its coverage of mail categories, an attribute which has forced it to be interested in questions of common cost allocation and identification of marginal costs. As noted by Scott (1986), it has explicitly pursued the Ramsey-Boiteux principle and has been broadly successful in inducing the United States Postal Service to price on this basis. The nature of the conflicts between the PRC and the USPS (see Sherman (1989)) indicate that the postal administration would not have adopted a rational pricing structure of its own volition.

The procedures used by Australia's PSA are, in contrast, not to be recommended. The Authority is not a specialist postal regulatory body, covering as it does a wide variety of industries. It has not developed specific postal pricing criteria and acts mainly to confirm that claimed cost increases will, in fact, eventuate. It does not take much interest in the structure of Australia Post's prices. Indeed, to some extent, the PSA in its first two inquiries acted to thwart Australia Post's attempts to move the prices of registered publications so as to generate cost recovery. In short, they acted to prevent a move to Ramsey-Boiteux prices.

4.4. Regulatory Mechanisms Inducing Efficiency Indirectly

In recent years there has been considerable academic and practical interest in rather subtle regulatory mechanisms which induce the firm to price efficiently. Theoretical research began in the late 1970s with papers by Loeb and Magat (1979) and Vogelsang and Finsinger (1979) which set-out regulatory schemes of this type. Berg and Tschirhart (1989) provide a good survey of this work. The practical work has been led in the United Kingdom by Stephen Littlechild (1983) in his report on telecommunications pricing regulation for the Department of Trade and Industry. Littlechild advocated a scheme where British Telecom's prices for its major services must be kept such that the quantity-weighted average increases at no more than the RPI less an agreed percentage (X). X is supposed to reflect both increases in total factor productivity and, if applicable, any excess profits. *"RPI-X"* pricing regulation allows adjustments across individual prices, presumably in a Ramsey-Boiteux direction, if overall profit is a consideration to the regulated firm.

It is possible that profit may not be an important objective for postal management under some circumstances. Many postal administrations have recently undergone a form of "corporatization" resulting in, *inter alia*, an improved incentive structure and a requirement to meet profit targets. While this is not a complete substitute for market forces, corporatization appears to be producing a far more commercial approach from postal managements and may be sufficient to drive appropriate price adjustments under *RPI-X*.

The influence of these mechanisms has largely been absent in postal pricing regulations, although New Zealand (through its Deed of Understanding) and Canada and Australia (agreed in their Corporate Plans) have versions of *"CPI-X"* for standard mail. While this is commendable, it does not employ these mechanisms to do what they do best—that is, influence the structure of pricing towards a Ramsey-Boiteux pattern. This can be illustrated in the Australian context.

In Australia, standard mail and registered publications must go through the PSA notification procedures. Overall, the standard mail has consistently been profitable (although this masks a large loss on rural services) and registered publications have made large losses (although these tend to have been over-stated by Australia Post). Australia Post has attempted, by stealth, to move registered publications prices upwards towards commercial levels. This has been extremely difficult within the current institutional framework where sectional interests have used PSA inquiries as a venue to oppose adjustments to these prices. If Australia Post had been regulated by *CPI-X* across the relevant services, it would have been able to achieve an allowed profit target with a lesser overall deadweight loss.

5. Conclusions

Postal rate-making in many countries has been moving towards greater efficiency in recent years, especially as postal operations have been taken out of government departments and disentangled from telecommunications operations. With corporatization has come the requirement to recover costs, a more private-like incentive structure, and less bureaucratic and political interference in pricing. Regulations that remain tend to be more-or-less unobtrusive, but there has been little appeal to the recent developments of mechanisms to induce efficient pricing.

It is a strong recommendation of this paper that the *"V-F"* or *"RPI-X"* mechanisms be investigated for the control of overall postal price levels and their structures. However, there are three major caveats to this recommendation. First, great care must be taken in selecting X so as to account for total factor productivity growth and achieve a reasonable profit. Other measures may be necessary to ensure that potential profits are not taken out in cost-inefficiency. Second, this regulatory approach works best where profits are a major objective of management. Such a profit mentality is not always obviously present in the public postal industry. Third, these mechanisms have a role only in the absence of competition. Littlechild (1983) proposed *RPI-X* for the newly-privatized British Telecom as an interim measure in the lead-up to a competitive environment. In the postal industry, many countries are forcing their postal administrations to be more commercially-oriented. In addition, there is an increasing trend towards greater competition, especially in the peripheral areas. Competition could ultimately be the main price regulator in many countries. Both the United Kingdom and New Zealand have mechanisms in place which respectively, may and will, ultimately, result in complete demonopolization. Further consideration of this trend to greater competition is, however, beyond my brief in this paper.

Notes

I am grateful to many conference participants and others for valuable information, comments, and suggestions. In particular, I would like to thank Maurice Castro, Fernando Gomez, John Haldi, William Price, Paul Richards, Walter Simpson, Walpurga Speckbacher, Elmar Toime, and Toshio Yamashina.

1. Corporatization often involves the removal of cost advantages (e.g., tax exemptions) and disadvantages. Financial targets are also usually part of the reform package. These reforms are necessary (although not sufficient) for an efficient pricing outcome is to be achieved.

2. The extent of reported losses depends on the way that common costs are allocated over the different services. This is usually not reported, and certainly was not in this case. Our main interest is, in this context, whether variable costs are covered or not.

3. Uniform geographical pricing of standard mail is the only concern in this sub-section. Other areas may also share the same problems, albeit on a small scale. The parcel service in Britain has traditionally been left with loss-making long-distance traffic because of its uniform price.

4. This question has been dealt with by Albon (1989) and, in a slightly different context, by Crew, Kleindorfer, and Smith (1990) and by Crew and Kleindorfer in their second paper in this volume.

5. Cuthbertson and Richards (1990) have undertaken a more recent and more sophisticated analysis of United Kingdom letter demand and find that second-class demand is more elastic, but only slightly so. The difference is certainly not enough to justify the price differential.

6. The question of whether any subsidy is justifiable on grounds of fairness or public interest is not pursued. Some would dispute that a uniform price is a "fair" arrangement. Other implicit subsidies (e.g., to books, magazines, and newspapers in many countries) could similarly be questioned.

7. Having made this assertion, I have discovered a study of United States postal demand by Tolley (1988) which estimates the first-class mail elasticity at -0.21.

References

Ad Hoc Commission on Fundamental Issues Facing the Postal Service. 1988. *A New Era for the Postal Service—Outlook and Issues.* Tokyo: Postal Bureau, Japanese Ministry of Posts and Telecommunications.

Albon, R.P. 1989. "Some Observations on the Efficiency of British Postal Pricing." *Applied Economics* 21: 461-473.

Berg, S.V., and J. Tschirhart. 1989. *Natural Monopoly Regulation: Principles and Practice.* Cambridge: Cambridge University Press.

Brown, S.J. and D.S. Sibley. 1986. *The Theory of Public Utility Pricing.* Cambridge: Cambridge University Press.

Channon, P. 1986. "Letter to Sir Ronald Dearing, Chairman of the Post Office." Written Answers, House of Commons Hansard, 21 July, 17-18.

Coase, R.H. (1939). "Rowland Hill and the Penny Post." *Economica* 6, 423-435.

Committee of Inquiry into the Monopoly Position of the Australian Postal Commission (Bradley Committee) 1982. *Report.* Canberra: AGPS.

Crew, M.A., P.R. Kleindorfer and M.A. Smith. 1990. "Peak-Load Pricing in Postal Services." *Economic Journal* forthcoming.

Cuthbertson, R. and P. Richards. 1990. "An Econometric Study of the Demand for UK Inland Letters." *Review of Economics and Statistics* forthcoming.

Daunton, M.J. 1985. *Royal Mail: The Post Office Since 1840.* London: Athlone Press.

Findlay, C.C. and R.L. Jones. 1982. "The Marginal Cost of Australian Income Taxation." *Economic Record* 58 253-262.

Littlechild, S.C. 1983. *Regulation of British Telecommunications Profitability: A Report to the Secretary of State of Trade and Industry* London.

Loeb, M. and W.A. Magat. 1979. "A Decentralized Method for Utility Regulation." *Journal of Law and Economics* 22, 399-404.

Monopolies and Mergers Commission. 1984. *The Post Office Letter Service* Cmnd. 9332, London: HMSO.

New Zealand (1989), Deed of Understanding between the Government of New Zealand and New Zealand Post Limited, 7 September, Wellington.

Post Office. 1979. *The Letter Monopoly - A Review* London, October.

Post Office Review Committee (C.F. Carter, Chairman). 1977. *Report of the Post Office Review Committee.* London: HMSO.

Scott, F.A. 1986. "Assessing USA Postal Ratemaking: An Application of Ramsey Prices," *Journal of Industrial Economics* 34, 278-290.

Sherman, R. 1989. *The Regulation of Monopoly.* Cambridge: Cambridge University Press.

Sherman, R. and A. George. 1979. "Second-Best Pricing for the U.S. Postal Service," *Southern Economic Journal* 45, 685-695.

Tabor, R. 1987. "Who Benefits from "One Price for Everywhere"?" *Public Finance and Accountancy* 12, 44-49.

Tolley, G.S. 1988. "Mail Volume Forecasting in the United States." A Report on the work of the US Postal Service Staff and RCF Inc., under contract to the Postal Service.

Vogelsang, I., and J. Finsinger. 1979. "A Regulatory Adjustment Process for Optimal Pricing by Multiproduct Firms." *Bell Journal of Economics* 10, 157-171.

COMMENTS
John Haldi

Albon has done an admirable job of comparing postal rate-making procedures and outcomes over a widely dispersed group of countries with differing traditions and political systems. The trend to eliminate subsidies from other sources, such as telecommunications, and to have rates cover the full cost of providing postal services appears not only to be irreversible, but also to represent an improvement in consumer welfare.

The following comments, which relate chiefly to experience in the United States, concern the issue of efficient pricing. As an initial point, prices are signals, not only to consumers, but also to suppliers. A full analysis thus requires an examination of whether competition and competitive pricing would induce greater efficiency in the provision of postal services. Although an analysis of free market forces is beyond the scope of Albon's paper, a "middle ground" is fast developing in the United States. Pricing signals are now being used to encourage privatization of certain traditional postal functions in a manner that is complementary to the Postal Service, rather than competitive with it. In this way, pricing signals now relate importantly to efficiency in supply, as well as consumer welfare.

By way of illustration, the United States Postal Service now offers substantial discounts, up to 25 percent, for letter mail that has been prepared in ways that reduce the Postal Service's processing costs. These discounts apply to all letter mail (i) that has been presorted or (ii) that includes in the address certain optional information that facilitates processing on high speed automation equipment. For volume mailers, these discounts provide a substantial inducement to presort or print optional address information, work that the Postal Service would otherwise have to do. As a result of these discounts, by 1992 as much as 50 percent of all letter mail in the United States will pay less than the nominal, or "uniform," rate for letter mail. At least one country, Great Britain, also gives significant discounts to mailers that presort their letter mail. Preparation discounts, such as those described here, thus represent significant moves in the direction of cost-based pricing and deserve to be recognized in any discussion concerned with efficiency in pricing.

The United States gives the Postal Service a statutory monopoly on letter mail and requires a uniform geographical rate for letter mail, as in all other countries surveyed by Albon. For reasons discussed below, however, it is far from clear whether nonuniform geographical rates would in fact be sustainable in a competitive delivery market. In competitive markets, it is axiomatic that prices are set by firms so as to maximize profits. Competitive firms do not need to justify their rates in terms of Ramsey-Boiteux pricing principles. With this in mind, it may be instructive to examine briefly the evolution of prevailing pricing patterns in certain highly competitive delivery markets that are not too different from letter mail.

The United States now has well-developed and rather competitive markets for (1) overnight delivery (the "express" market) and (2) second-day air delivery. Although private enterprise competitors publish slightly different rates for overnight delivery, all of them, including the Postal Service, have established uniform geographical rates for next-day delivery anywhere within the contiguous 48 states, which span a distance of some 3000 miles. Private enterprise competitors are free to price as they see fit, yet no competitor has attempted to "cream-skim" by offering lower rates for delivery to urban areas and higher rates for delivery to non-urban areas.

In the closely-related market for second-day air delivery, rates are somewhat lower than for overnight delivery. Here, every delivery firm except the Postal Service has also published a uniform rate that is applicable to the contiguous 48 states. The Postal Service also charges a uniform geographical rate for second-day delivery of packages that weigh up to two pounds. In 1991 it is planning to extend uniform rates to packages that weigh up to five pounds. The fundamental economic reasons that would explain such uniform geographical prices have not been studied or documented. In light of the observed tendency to abandon zoned rates in favor of uniform pricing, however, there is reason to believe that nonuniform pricing of lighter-weight items, such as letters, might not be sustainable in a competitive delivery market.

To sum up, the overnight and second-day delivery markets are marked by free entry and keen competition. In light of pricing experience in those markets, the policy of uniform geographical rates established by Sir Rowland Hill in 1840 may, in fact, have a strong market logic, which is masked by the statutory monopoly over letter mail found in virtually every country.

12

POSTAL SERVICE AND LESS DEVELOPED COUNTRIES

David E. Treworgy
James A. Waddell

> The Post is a place for all business, for all negotiations. Through it, those who are away become near. It is the consolidation of life.
>
> —Voltaire

1. Introduction to the International Postal Network

Within a single nation, the same postal organization that collects revenue for a particular piece of mail performs all services associated with delivering that piece. When a piece of mail is bound for a foreign country, however, a different postal administration performs final processing and delivery services from the postal administration that collected revenue and initiated processing. The postal administration of the destinating country provides services for which it does not directly receive revenue.

Historically, the question of international revenues collected not being returned to the party performing final delivery services has not been an issue. Traditionally, it was assumed that for every letter sent, a reply was made, resulting in fairly even flows of mail between nations. As Great Britain and other countries granted independence to colonies after World War II, however, imbalances that were formerly hidden became apparent and the old assumption discredited.

The Universal Postal Union (UPU) was founded in the nineteenth century as a forum for nations to discuss and resolve international postal issues. Its members, who meet every five years, first initiated debate on the question on mail imbalances at the Vienna Congress of 1964. Deliberations resulted in the institution of a system of *terminal dues* at the Tokyo Congress of 1969. Under this system, each postal administration responsible for originating foreign mail reimburses the appropriate recipient foreign postal administrations. So that massive sums of money are not needlessly exchanged, terminal dues are paid only on the imbalance of bilateral mail flows between countries.

The precise level at which terminal dues should be set, however, has been a source of disagreement. Some argue that terminal dues for a letter should equal precisely the cost of handling that letter from the time it crosses the border to the time final delivery is made to the recipient. For example, consider an international postal world with only three countries: Britain, France, and Spain. In this world, there exists only one class of mail, First-Class. For each country, there is a cost to collecting and processing outgoing international mail and a cost to processing and delivering incoming international mail. For each pair of countries there is an international transportation charge. Table 1 outlines a hypothetical schedule of costs for the three countries.

Table 1. Hypothetical Postage Costs (SDR's)				
Country	Outgoing	Incoming		
France	0.20	0.28		
Spain	0.03	0.05		
United Kingdom	0.14	0.18		
Country Pair	Outgoing	Incoming	Int. Trans.	Total
France → Spain	0.20	0.05	0.01	0.26
France → United Kingdom	0.20	0.18	0.02	0.40
Spain → France	0.03	0.28	0.01	0.34
Spain → United Kingdom	0.03	0.18	0.03	0.24
United Kingdom → France	0.14	0.28	0.02	0.34
United Kingdom → Spain	0.14	0.05	0.03	0.22

Cost-based pricing of international rates would build rates as the sum of the domestic costs plus international transportation and handling charges. For example, as outlined in table 1 and figure 1, the international rate from France to the United Kingdom would be 0.20 (France outgoing cost) + 0.02 (international transportation cost) + 0.18 (United Kingdom incoming cost) = 0.40. With these rates, terminal dues of exactly the incoming postage costs apply. Such a cost-based system of terminal dues would reimburse each nation for precisely the amount of expense it incurs for foreign inbound mail; all nations cover their costs.

If France, Spain, and the United Kingdom were the only three countries in the world, the six prices of international postage for First-Class letters could be equitably set and maintained as just described. However, more than three nations comprise the UPU, and terminal dues are not so easily settled upon. In the interest of simplicity, the UPU determined that terminal dues should be calculated by weight, with a single rate for all countries and all classes of mail. The UPU calculates the rate as an average of the delivery costs of all countries. This decision is understandable; to have a different terminal dues rate for each class and country

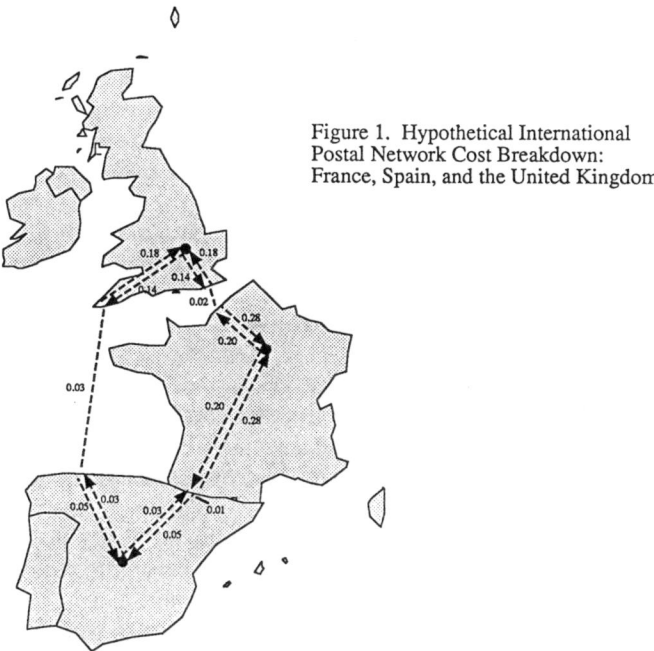

Figure 1. Hypothetical International Postal Network Cost Breakdown: France, Spain, and the United Kingdom

would leave each postal service facing a large number of terminal dues rates:

(175 countries * 30 subclasses of mail) = 5,250 terminal dues rates

Historically, such a large number of rates has been impractical.[1] However, adopting a uniform rate regardless of destination creates difficulties of its own, both in terms of subclasses of mail and destinating countries. Table 2 lists terminal dues rates since their institution.

Table 2. Terminal Dues Rates Since Introduction		
Year	Congress	Terminal Dues
1969	Tokyo	0.50 gold francs/kg
1974	Lausanne	1.50 gold francs/kg
1979	Rio de Janeiro	5.50 gold francs/kg
1984	Hamburg	8.00 gold francs/kg
1989	Washington	9.00 gold francs/kg
Note: In the 1989 Washington Congress, a dual system of terminal dues rates was introduced: 22.84 gold francs/kg of LC, 6.3 gold francs/kg of AO. These dual rates, however, apply only to bilateral mail flows exceeding 150 tons. A relatively small proportion of the 170 UPU member nations are required to use this rate; developing countries are almost always completely exempted, except for several high-volume bilateral flows, such as the United Kingdom to India.		

A uniform terminal dues rate causes revenues to diverge from costs in two distinct manners. The first results from the failure of the terminal dues system to account for variations in pieces of mail per pound and the corresponding different delivery costs. The second is a function of the averaging mechanism by which terminal dues are calculated, causing countries whose costs are not near the average to find financial compensation out of line with costs.

1.1. Effect of Variations in Pieces per Pound on Terminal Dues Receipts

By charging all classes of mail the same amount of terminal dues by weight, the system fails to consider the fact that different classes of mail require varying amounts of effort to process, transport, and deliver. A one-pound parcel is charged the same terminal dues as sixteen one-ounce letters. The sixteen letters, however, are more expensive to a postal service to process and deliver, because the sixteen letters require roughly sixteen times the sorting effort as the single package and require delivery to sixteen different addresses instead of one. If terminal dues are set based on average costs per unit of weight, the lighter letters will be undercharged and the heavier parcel overcharged.

Postal administrations generally divide international mail into two general categories: LC (letters and cards) and AO (other objects, primarily parcels and published material). The phenomenon of undercharging LC and overcharging AO disadvantages mailers of heavy items, such as publishers, whose postage rates reflect the steep terminal dues; the recipients of the windfall are the nations collecting the high terminal dues relative to domestic rates. Assistant Postmaster General of Rates and Classifications of the United States Postal Service (USPS) Frank Heselton recently testified before the United States Congress:

> The terminal dues fee represents an averaging of costs to deliver lighter and heavier weight mail pieces. This terminal dues structure badly disadvantages countries like the United States, where the Postal Service transmits to foreign countries many more heavier-weight pieces than it receives, and receives many more lighter-weight pieces than it sends. (United States Congress 1988)

While the terminal dues structure may disadvantage nations such as the United States, it often benefits developing countries.[2] Lacking their own publishing industries, developing countries tend to import AO to a greater extent than industrialized nations. The difference between the terminal dues charged for AO and the cost of delivery amounts to a windfall for LDCs.

1.2. Effect of Variations in Processing and Delivery Costs on Terminal Dues Receipts

Failure to distinguish between costs of processing and delivery in different countries, which can vary tremendously, when setting terminal dues also produces interesting effects. Information on the cost of mail delivery, while highly advanced and available for administrations such as the USPS, is scarce in general.[3] For most countries, costs are best approximated by domestic postage prices. Table 3 lists

Table 3. Internal Postal Rates for Printed Papers		
Country	50 Gram Item (SDRs)	200 Gram Item (SDRs)
China (People's Republic)	0.006	0.012
El Salvador	0.030	0.030
Egypt	0.016	0.032
Sri Lanka	0.012	0.039
Polish People's Republic	0.026	0.053
Pakistan	0.030	0.054
Lesotho	0.045	0.056
Thailand	0.044	0.059
Bangladesh	0.024	0.061
Singapore	0.037	0.073
Korea (Republic)	0.038	0.076
Chile	0.065	0.081
Liberia	0.038	0.091
Kenya	0.061	0.102
Equatorial Guinea	0.051	0.103
Yemem Arab Republic	0.079	0.118
Kuwait	0.068	0.151
Bahamas	0.038	0.151
United Arab Emirates	0.103	0.155
Zambia	0.066	0.156
Cyprus	0.113	0.161
Argentina	0.141	0.162
Costa Rica	0.080	0.171
Nepal	0.103	0.172
Belize	0.095	0.189
Venezuela	0.078	0.209
Portugal	0.092	0.233
Switzerland	0.184	0.237
Morocco	0.092	0.277
Greece	0.190	0.279
Canada	0.098	0.282
Rwanda	0.195	0.292
Syrian Arab Republic	0.199	0.299
Japan	0.218	0.300
Jordan	0.232	0.309
Cape Verde	0.154	0.357
Panama (Rupublic)	0.114	0.363
Great Britain	0.169	0.389
Spain	0.144	0.412
Belgium	0.270	0.416
Papua New Guinea	0.124	0.498
Luxembourg	0.208	0.520 below*
Italy	0.296	0.533 above*
Australia	0.297	0.538
Finland	0.248	0.567
Senegal	0.372	0.590
Germany, Fed. Republic	0.348	0.609
Qatar	0.156	0.624
Sweden	0.340	0.668
Denmark	0.394	0.676
Norway	0.345	0.690
United States	0.295	0.742
France	0.346	0.949
Netherlands	0.677	0.967
Mean	0.153	0.302
Terminal Dues	0.131	0.523
Source: Universal Postal Union, Terminal Dues Round Table (1989)		
* Below/above terminal dues rate.		

domestic postage prices for printed matter in various countries; for example, prices ranged in 1988 from 0.006 Special Drawing Rights (SDRs) for a 50 gram item in El Salvador to 0.667 SDRs for the same item in the Netherlands. The terminal dues rate for such a piece is 0.131 SDRs. Thus, El Salvador reaps a windfall of 0.125 SDRs on each 50 gram item received from foreign countries; the Netherlands loses 0.536 SDRs on the same items it receives.

As may be inferred from table 3, LDCs tend to have lower domestic postage prices than their more industrialized counterparts, and, as a result, are likely to accrue terminal dues surpluses. Such a situation is intuitive, since domestic postage rates are largely a function of local average wages,[4] which tend to be lowest in the developing nations of the world. Terminal dues deficits, on the other hand, tend to accrue to the industrialized nations.

1.3. Lower Service Standards in LDCs

Service standards (usually measured by time for delivery) in LDCs are lower than those of developed countries. This is the direct or indirect result of lower national income and resources combined with special situations, unique to developing countries, which complicate most aspects of postal operations, including mail processing, city delivery, rural delivery, and transportation.

In industrialized nations, automation has reduced the time required for mail processing. Conveyor belts, canceling machines, and bundlers have all improved productivity.[5] Mail processing in LDCs, by contrast, is primarily a manual operation, largely resulting from a combination of plentiful, cheap labor and a shortage of capital. In addition, mechanization is impeded by operational and maintenance issues, including erratic electricity supplies, dependence on foreign spare parts, and the absence of standardized letter shapes and thicknesses generally found in industrialized countries. As a result of these conditions, mechanization has failed to take hold in LDCs, leaving mail processing dependent upon traditional slow, tedious manual operations and resulting in long intervals between initial posting and final delivery of letters.

City delivery in developing nations presents problems unheard of in most industrialized nations. Population migration from rural areas to cities, prevalent in most developing countries, outpaces government efforts to plan and build permanent housing and results in unorganized urban shantytowns. In these neighborhoods, unnamed streets and unnumbered houses complicate the task of the letter carrier. Instead of delivering to straightforward, uniform addresses, the letter carrier must learn the layout of streets and alleys and match names, faces, and dwellings. High rates of illiteracy found in many LDCs also complicate delivery of mail. Poorly addressed or difficult-to-read writing is commonplace; these letters require a great deal of time to interpret and locate the proper recipient, adding further to delivery time.

Rural mail delivery poses its own set of problems. Delivery to rural addresses requires greater effort than city delivery in all countries; however, the problems of rural delivery in LDCs are more difficult, due primarily to light mail volumes combined with dispersed populations. Motorized transportation for letter carriers is expensive and scarce; 82 percent of 60 developing countries contributing to a recent UPU study had *not* yet introduced motorized vehicles in rural mail delivery (CCPS 1984). A city postman is fairly efficient on foot, able to service dozens, possibly hundreds, of households in a day. His rural counterpart, on the other hand, may walk twenty miles in a day and deliver only five letters.[6]

Transportation of mail between origin and destination towns in LDCs presents additional difficulties. Though LDC postal services utilize, to the extent available, modes such as passenger rail and air, they normally serve only major cities and towns, leaving smaller towns and remote villages to be serviced by other types of transportation. Other modes, however, are problematic. Motorized vehicles are out of reach to many financially strapped LDC postal administrations. Even when trucks and jeeps are not prohibitively expensive, roads often are not passable. Roads in rural areas are mostly unpaved and, consequently, unusable for lengthy periods during the year as a result of rain, snow, or flooding. In these situations, mail must accumulate until the climate becomes more favorable.

All these difficulties with mail delivery in LDCs result in slower processing, transportation, and delivery, producing low service performance relative to industrialized nations. In developing countries, postage rates are lower and are matched by lower service. High terminal dues rates for developing countries, the result of averaging different nations' costs, coupled with low postage rates, result in revenues for inbound international mail in excess of costs. In many cases, funds received from foreign governments greatly exceed domestic delivery charges on a per piece basis and account for inordinately large percentages of total operating budgets.

Often cited as the reason for this phenomenon is the structure of the UPU, the legislative body responsible for determining compensation rates. The membership of the UPU comprises most of the countries in the world with postal services. As in the United Nations General Assembly, each country in the UPU receives one vote, giving greater electoral power to the developing countries of the world, who hold a numerical majority.

Though the apparent overcompensation of LDC postal administrations may be due to the political structure of the UPU, the end result is not necessarily economically inefficient. At first glance, this departure from cost-based pricing of international postal products would not appear optimal. Traditional economic theory holds that to maximize welfare, price should be set equal to marginal cost, which clearly is not the case here. Industrialized countries, however, value speedy mail service; their international mail destinating in nations with poor mail service receives high quality service during only the first portion of its time in the postal system. Nations placing high value on high quality mail service would accrue greater economic surplus if mail received consistently high quality service.

LDCs will not, however, unilaterally upgrade service standards to please industrialized country mailers. Industrialized country mailers, moreover, cannot pay the marginal cost of providing high quality service for their mail only. For some mail to receive good service, the entire system must be upgraded. Thus, industrialized country mailers must pay for upgraded service not only for their own mail, but also for the domestic mail of the LDC. Essentially, inbound international mailers of industrialized countries finance the higher service level, upon which domestic mail piggybacks. As a result, the price paid by the international mailers would be above marginal cost, with the premium supporting a higher service level for domestic LDC mail than the country can afford.

In most industries, attempts to deviate from marginal cost pricing do not last indefinitely. Firms exhibiting rent-seeking behavior devise methods to take advantage of cross-subsidization and other departures from marginal cost pricing by offering the high priced (relative to marginal cost) goods or services at a price lower than that set by the incumbent organization. Price falls as rent-seekers compete with each other, eventually reaching marginal cost. Meanwhile, the original cross-subsidizer is forced to raise the price of products priced below marginal cost as it loses market share for products priced above marginal cost.

To date, the international postal system has maintained, with respect to developing countries, its ability to set terminal dues at rates which depart from marginal cost. Unfair competition by remail firms, however, could pose a threat to developing country postal administrations. The proceedings of the 1989 UPU Congress summarized the problem as follows:

> International mail forms a very big proportion of [developing countries'] mail and revenue from terminal dues finances a large proportion of their postal infrastructure... when remail firms post their items in these countries they deprive them of the terminal dues they need for maintaining and improving their infrastructure. (UPU 1989b)

Remail firms may avoid paying terminal dues by shipping mail to a developing country as freight, pay domestic postage, and deposit the letters into the mailstream as domestic pieces. This practice hurts the postal administration; not only does the remailer deprive the administration of the terminal dues premium over cost, but because rates usually are set below cost, the administration actually loses money on each piece. To preserve the terminal dues subsidy, the developing country postal administration must guard against this practice.

As long as the terminal dues subsidy is maintained, mail delivered to LDCs priced above marginal cost may increase the economic surplus accruing to industrialized nations and developing countries, and increase overall welfare. In the next section, we detail our suggestion that subsidization of certain postal administrations through the terminal dues mechanism may not cause a departure from maximum welfare, but rather could have the effect of improving efficiency.

2. International Postal Network Model

In this section, we develop a model of the international postal system as a network. The model finds its roots in a body of network theory literature dealing primarily with telecommunications, the principles of which are adapted to appropriately model the international postal system. The result provides an understanding of the consumption externalities inherent in the world postal network, and thus, may help to explain why subsidies may not necessarily be inefficient.

Traditional network theory values the node of any given network as a function of the number of nodes on the network. For example, a subway system with a single station is worthless. When a second station is added, however, the first station becomes valuable to the extent that people wish to travel between the two points. As more stations are added, the first station experiences additional increases in value. Similar principles apply to a telephone network; the more people an individual can call, the more he or she will wish to join the network. Unlike a subway system, however, the number of nodes of which is carefully planned, a telephone network involves encouraging individual consumers to join and use the system through price signals. Squire (1973) describes the consumption externalities present in a telephone network; Littlechild (1975) refines and extends Squire's work.

The post, like a telephone system, also qualifies as a network. A mailer depends upon other people belonging to the postal network; otherwise the mailer would have nobody with whom to correspond and hence, derive no value from the network. The model developed here reworks the principles detailed by Squire and Littlechild to reflect the features of the international postal network. The first part of this section explains the nature of consumption externalities; the second part formalizes these principles in the model.

2.1. Principles of Consumption Externalities

Consider, as an example, an international telephone network whose members are individual nations. Thus, the total potential of the network is in the range of 170 countries or so. For simplification, assume only the United States and the United Kingdom belong to the international telephone network, exchanging calls with only each other. Each has a demand function for calling the other, D_{US} and D_{UK} (figure 2). The horizontal summation of these two demand curves, D' represents total market demand for international calls.

Now, assume Japan decides to join the network, with its own demand for international calls, D_{Japan} (figure 3). D' now shifts out to D'' to reflect the addition of D_{Japan}, but another effect takes place: because the United States and the United Kingdom may now make calls to Japan as well as to each other, their demand functions shift outward. D'' shifts out a bit more, to D'''. The amount of additional surplus accruing to the United States and the United Kingdom as a result of Japan's joining the network (shaded in graph) is considered a positive externality. Because an additional country has joined the network, the United States and the United Kingdom have, at no cost to them, gained a substantial amount of surplus. If Japan were reluctant to join the network, the United States and the United Kingdom might find it in their interest to actually compensate Japan by some amount less than or equal to their combined consumer surplus.

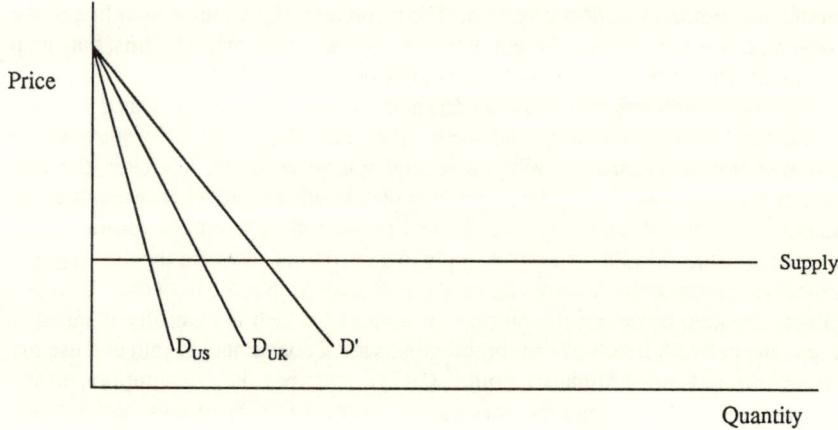

Figure 2

If a fourth country were to join the network, consumption externalities would accrue to Japan, and additional consumption externalities would accrue to the United States and the United Kingdom. As the network grows larger with the addition of more countries, the incentive for non-subscribers to join becomes more compelling. Discussions of network theory usually refer to a required "critical mass" of subscribers, at which point many non-subscribers find that the network

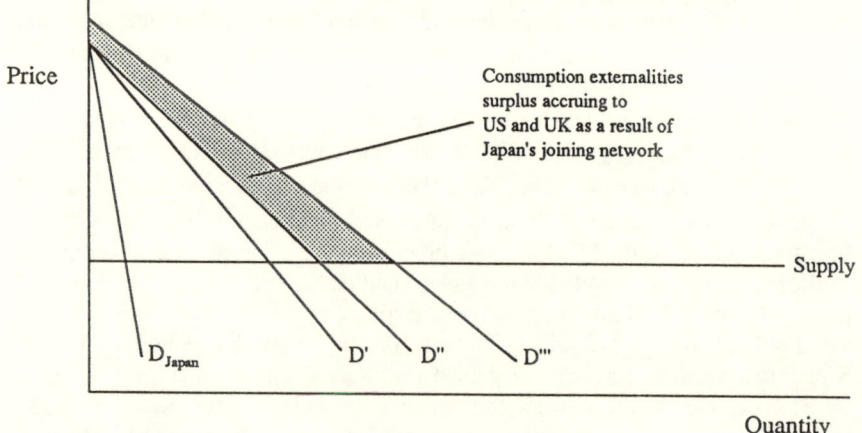

Figure 3

offers the minimum number of subscribers with whom to communicate to make their joining worthwhile.

2.2. The International Postal Network Model

In this section, we develop a model of the role played by network externalities in the international postal market. The model departs from earlier telecommunications work by including the most important aspects of the postal market. Some simplifying assumptions are made for clarity of analysis, but these may be relaxed with little change in the results.

Unlike telecommunications, international postal service is not provided by a single firm. All countries in the world independently operate domestic postal systems, each regarded as a member of an international postal network. The maximum number of members of the network is approximately 170, one for each country. These domestic postal services normally are regulated monopolies which set price equal to marginal cost.[7] Since postal services presumably act as public enterprises, the objective of the model that we present is to maximize total system welfare.

The earlier, simple discussion of consumption externalities of the United States, the United Kingdom, and Japan considers a traditional telephone network in which customers are either "on" or "off" the network. Potential customers "off" the network chose that status due to fixed costs of joining. While accurate for analyses of the telecommunications market, such an approach does not reflect the structure of the postal network. Unlike most other networks, the "fixed" cost involved in joining the international postal network is minimal to nonexistent. Most costs are purely volume variable. As a result, all nations have always and currently continue to exchange international mail. Hence, a non-subscriber cannot be financially induced to join the postal network by reducing the fixed subscriber cost, since these costs are not significant.

In the telecommunications model, all customers are serviced by the same firm, and consequently receive service of uniformly high quality. In the international postal network, however, a letter is handled by a minimum of two postal administrations and one international air freight carrier.[8] The quality of postal services around the world varies greatly in terms of service standards; some nations have high service standards, some low, and some none at all. The quality of domestic service, though not necessarily, is generally a function of per capita income (figure 4). For purposes of simplification, our model assumes the existence of only two levels of domestic service which nations may choose to offer: high and low (figure 5). An individual customer of a domestic postal system must accept the single level of service offered. Nations with per capita incomes exceeding a critical level will maintain postal systems offering a high level of service; nations with per capita incomes below that level will offer a low level of service.

Industrialized nations generally operate modern, efficient postal services with high service standards. Developing countries, as discussed earlier, are beset by a host of problems that result in their assigning postal service standards a relatively

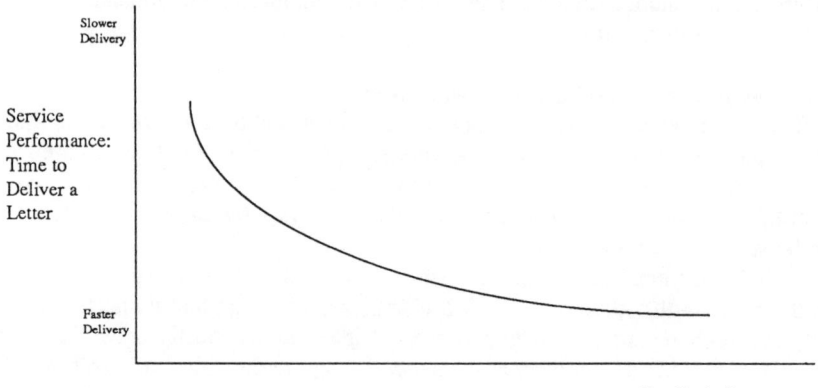

Figure 4

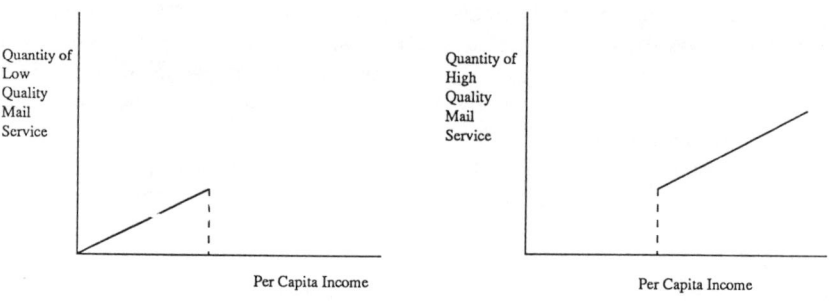

Figure 5

low priority in their nationwide agendas. An international letter or parcel traveling from a developed to a developing country, therefore, receives two different grades of service: high followed by low. Mailers in developed nations, accustomed to and willing to pay for high service standards, may find their mail subjected to unacceptable levels of service once it reaches the border of a destination developing country. Developing countries, however, with their low incomes and low demand for high quality postal services, are unable to maintain a domestic distribution system at the level of those of industrialized postal services. Hence, there exists a situation in which a subsidy of developing countries' postal services by those of industrialized countries may improve economic efficiency.

Consider a British mailer sending a letter to a developing country. The level of service in Britain is high; depending on the quality of service in the developing country, the total service received by the British mailer will be either high → low or high → high. Table 4 illustrates a hypothetical set of postal costs involved in collecting, processing, and delivering the letter. As shown, the mailer derives a consumer surplus of 0.20 when the level of service in the developing country is low, and 0.55 when the level is high. The marginal cost per letter to the developing country of providing a high level of service is 0.15. However, a higher domestic service level must apply to all mail, both domestic and international inbound. Local rates must not rise above the low service level price, so the British mailer must cover these costs as well as his own. In the example given in the table, if the British mailer were to pay the developing country this amount to offer the high level of service, the mailer would still derive a surplus of 0.30, greater than the 0.20 that would accrue if the developing country provided the low level of service.

This phenomenon may be modelled graphically in the following manner. Figure 6 represents the market for international mail from industrialized countries (with high mail service) to developing countries (with low mail service). Demand curve D' represents demand by industrialized countries to send mail to developing

Table 4. Consumer Surplus to British Mailer Under Different Service Levels			
Case 1: High → Low		Case 2: High → High	
Cost of processing at origin	.20	Cost of processing at origin	.20
Cost of international transport	.05	Cost of international transport	.05
Cost of processing at destination	.05	Cost of processing at destination	.20
Total	.30	Total	.45
Value to mailer	.50	Value to mailer	.90
Consumer surplus	.20	Consumer surplus	.45
Case 3: High → High, British Mailer Pays to Upgrade Service in Destination Country			
Assume total international inbound mail accounts for half of developing country's mailstream. To upgrade the entire postal system to the high service level and maintain low rates for domestic mail, the international mailer must pay to upgrade service for all domestic customers as well as international, amounting to an additional charge of .15.			
Cost of processing at origin	.20		
Cost of international transport	.05		
Cost of processing at destination	.35		
Total	.60		
Value to mailer	.90		
Consumer surplus	.30		

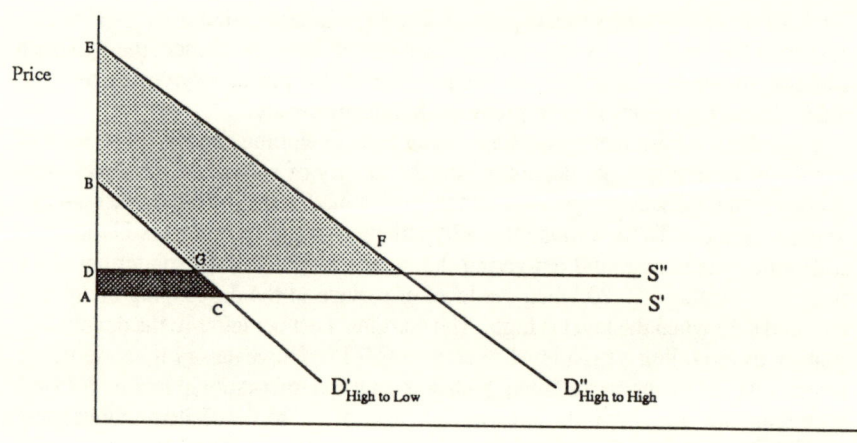

Figure 6

countries. Supply curve S' includes costs of high service incurred at the origin country, international transport costs, and cost of low service incurred at the destination country. If mail service in developing countries is upgraded to a high level, the demand curve shifts out to D''. This upgrade in service comes at the price of the supply curve moving up to S''. The amount of system surplus accrued by industrialized nations whose mail receives a high followed by low level of service is represented the area ABC. The surplus accrued when mail is given consistently high treatment is represented by area DEF. The difference $DEF - ABC$, or $BGFE - ACGD$ as depicted in figure 6, is the net increase in consumption externalities accrued by industrialized nations as a result of developing countries upgrading their service from high to low.

The principles of this model may be formalized with the following variables:

k = critical income level at which a country upgrades its postal service to the high service level

h = number of countries with critical income > or = k

l = income of countries with critical income < k

hp = number of countries offering high level postal service

lp = number of countries offering low level postal service

P_{high} = price or variable charge per unit in high service level market, same as marginal cost

P_{low} = price or variable charge per unit in low service level market, same as marginal cost

$x_{high}(P_{high}, hp, lp)$ = demand per unit of time for postal service for a high service level country, where x is a decreasing function with respect to price, an increasing function with respect to hp, and a decreasing function with respect to lp

$x_{low}(P_{low})$ = demand per unit of time for postal service for a low service level country, where x is a decreasing function with respect to price

$s_{high}(P_{high}, hp, lp)$ = consumer surplus for a high service level country, which is given by the integral:

$$s_{high}(P_{high}, hp, lp) = \int_{P_{high}}^{\infty} x(P_{high}, hp, lp)\, dp \qquad (1)$$

$s_{low}(P_{low})$ = consumer surplus for a low service level country, which is given by the integral:

$$s_{low}(P_{low}) = \int_{P_{low}}^{\infty} x(P_{low})\, dp \qquad (2)$$

From these equations, we can derive system demand and surplus functions for international postal services for both high and low level service countries. Total system demand and total system surplus are given by $X(P_{high}, P_{low})$ and $S(P_{high}, P_{low})$, respectively:

$$X(P_{high}, P_{low}, hp, lp) = \int_{0}^{\infty} x_{high}(P_{high}, hp, lp)\, h\, dp + \int_{0}^{\infty} x_{low}(P_{low})\, l\, dp \text{ and}$$
$$\qquad (3)$$

$$S(P_{high}, P_{low}, hp, lp) = \int_{0}^{\infty} s_{high}(P_{high}, hp, lp)\, h\, dp + \int_{0}^{\infty} s_{low}(P_{low})\, l\, dp \qquad (4)$$

Note that producer surplus is not part of the equation, since we have assumed that postal administrations act in the public interest by setting price equal to marginal cost.

The complement of the market to deliver mail from industrialized to developing nations is the reverse, from developing to industrialized countries. The analysis for the former market, however, has little impact on the latter. Hence demand and surplus for low level service countries is not a function of hp and lp, but only of P_{low}. Outbound developing country international mail faces the same rates as before. Quantity may rise somewhat, since a higher quality good is being offered at the price of a lower.

The ideal international postal system maximizes equation (4), total system surplus. Surplus may be increased by increasing hp, the number of members of the international postal network offering high level service (reducing at the same time lp, assuming all nations in the world belong to the network). Increasing hp produces an upward movement in the supply curve, due to higher costs of moving mail in developing countries, but also results in an outward shift in demand for sending mail. If, as shown in figure 6, the increase in surplus gained as a result of low service countries upgrading offsets the loss due to higher prices, net total welfare will rise. The use of cost-based terminal dues, by ignoring the elements of hp and lp in this surplus maximization equation, may result in failure to maximize total welfare.

2.3. Evaluating the Hypothesis

Littlechild concludes, in his analysis of network externalities, that to maximize total system surplus in a telephone network, the fixed price of joining should be set equal to the fixed cost less the increase in consumer surplus to existing subscribers as a result of the newest member joining the network.[9] This result implies for the international postal network that terminal dues subsidies should be targeted more toward those countries from which industrialized country mailers derive greater benefit from receiving higher quality service. The terminal dues system produces this effect to some extent, in that the countries with the lowest real wages and the lowest service standards receive the greatest subsidies (on a per piece basis). The terminal dues system does not, however, produce the desired effect from a network externality standpoint to the extent that the terminal dues system fails to distinguish between countries to which there is a relatively high demand to send mail (and from which mailers would accrue relatively larger consumption externalities by raising service levels) and countries to which there is a relatively low demand to send mail (and from which mailers would accrue relatively smaller consumption externalities by raising service levels).

Regression analysis verified this expected result. A cross-sectional analysis of selected countries showed that, while the per piece terminal dues subsidy is strongly correlated with per capita income, there is no correlation with demand for inbound international mail. The inability of the terminal dues system to target countries in this manner limits somewhat the potential welfare gains outlined by the model.

Moreover, the analysis relies upon two important assumptions, each of which may not be true in an undetermined number of countries. First, terminal dues revenues must be received by the postal administration itself. In many developing countries, terminal dues receipts represent a significant source of scarce hard currency. The government, rather than allow the postal administration to receive the terminal dues revenues, may deposit them in the treasury for other purposes. Without access to these funds, postal administrations cannot upgrade service.

Second, even if they do control their own finances and receive terminal dues revenues, postal administrations must spend the receipts on improved service, rather than for some other use. For example, the administration may cut postage rates for the existing lower service level. Alternatively, in many countries post and telephone operations are combined as a single administration; postal terminal dues revenues may be diverted to subsidize the telephone side of the organization. The more countries in which surplus terminal dues are not spent for the purpose of upgrading service, due either to the government retaining the funds or the postal administration using them for other purposes, the more limited the potential consumption externality welfare gains suggested by our model.

3. Conclusion

The terminal dues system, with a single rate (for developing countries) for all mail regardless of actual costs, causes departures from marginal cost pricing and may seem to produce economically suboptimal results. We propose that the system may not be as inefficient as it might appear, however, given the positive consumption externalities accruing to mailers in industrialized countries as a result of the ability of developing countries to upgrade their postal services to a higher level than would otherwise be possible.

All developing countries will join a postal network requiring a minimum level of service, since the marginal cost of doing so is extremely low, and the benefits of being able to send and receive mail internationally are substantial. These developing countries will not, however, upgrade their postal service to the level of the industrialized world on their own volition, since demand for higher service does not exist. Industrialized nations may accrue positive consumption externalities by providing developing countries to which they send mail with the financial means of bringing their postal systems up to higher standards.

Empirical consideration of the model, however, reveals certain weaknesses. The nature of the terminal dues system limits the potential to target subsidies to countries in a manner that produces the maximum welfare effect. Additionally, failure of developing countries to employ the terminal dues surplus for the purpose of raising postal service standards additionally limits welfare maximization as outlined in the network externality model. Assessing the model beyond these observations would require a detailed examination of exactly the manner in which individual developing countries handle their terminal dues subsidies. If they are, in fact, used primarily to upgrade service, this research could then be followed by estimations of supply and demand functions for international mail destined for developing countries under lower and higher levels of service standards in an effort to measure the size of consumption externalities.

Notes

1. Technology has been a limiting factor. With such a large array of terminal dues rates, price lists quickly would become outdated; retail clerks would have to spend time paging through a catalog to determine price. International telecommunications, by contrast, is priced on a country-by-country basis. In the future, with the continued development of automated postal functions such as Integrated Retail Terminals (IRTs) in the United States, different postage rates for each country ultimately may become practical.

2. As noted in table 2, the UPU redesigned the terminal dues system to distinguish, for industrialized countries, between lighter and heavier pieces. The new system, which takes effect in 1991, should relieve the problem Heselton addresses. Developing countries, under the new system, will continue to employ a single rate of terminal dues for all types of pieces.

3. The United States conducted a study of terminal dues in 1988 which included a survey of cost data for different countries, but considered the results highly unreliable (UPU 1989). It should be emphasized, however, that postage prices may not always be a reliable approximation of costs. Some countries, for example, explicitly subsidize certain classes of mail to achieve social or cultural goals; in such cases, prices will bear little or no relation to costs.

4. In the USPS, for example, which is among the most automated post offices in the world, labor costs account for 85 percent of total outlays.

5. More recently, of course, the post has witnessed even more state-of-the-art breakthroughs, such as optical character scanners (OCRs), barcoding, and other technologies.

6. The economics of rural delivery comprises an entire body of literature in itself. The variables to be balanced include: mode of delivery (formal postal employees versus village officials or other travelers between remote villages and more developed areas), frequency of delivery (many LDCs strive for daily delivery), number and placement of post offices, and capital to be expended on transportation for the letter carrier (usually bicycles or light motorcycles). Data on the volume of mail delivered by rural carriers are sparse.

7. This is not entirely accurate to the extent that (1) postal administrations may not know their costs and price arbitrarily, and (2) the postal administration and/or the government may purposely price below marginal cost by employing a social agenda in determining postage prices. These situations, however, are becoming less common as prices are set closer to marginal cost. In any event, virtually no postal administration sets prices with a deliberate profit motive in mind.

8. This situation raises an accountability problem in the case of lost or delayed correspondence. The origin postal administration may blame the destination postal administration for the missing or delayed item and vice-versa. Because postal administrations do not have to accept responsibility for late mail, they frequently assign international mail lowest priority, which only makes the problem worse.

9. Littlechild's optimization of welfare in a telephone network in which consumption externalities exist is reflected in the following equation:

$$f = g - \frac{\partial S}{\partial M},$$

where f is the fixed charge of joining the network, g is fixed cost of joining the network, and $\partial S/\partial M$ is the increase in consumer surplus to existing subscribers as a result of the newest member joining the network. In order to maximize welfare, then, the fixed price charged to a new member of the network should be below fixed cost, to the extent that existing members derive consumption externalities by virtue of the newcomer's membership.

References

Consultative Council for Postal Studies (CCPS). 1984. "Postal Mechanization in Young Countries."

Littlechild, S. C. 1975. "Two-part Tariffs and Consumption Externalities." *Bell Journal of Economics* 6 (no. 2, Autumn): 661-670.

Squire, L. 1973. "Some Aspects of Optimal Pricing for Telecommunications." *Bell Journal of Economics and Management Science* 4 (no. 2, Autumn): 515-25.

United States Congress, Subcommittee on Postal Operations and Services of the Committee on Post Office and Civil Service. 1988. *Review of Rate Setting Process of International Postage Rates.* U.S. Government Printing Office.

Universal Postal Union. 1989. *Terminal Dues Round Table* (April).

Universal Postal Union. 1989. *Documents of the 20th Congress of the Universal Postal Union.*

COMMENTS
Robert M. Pike

As a sociologist who is interested in the socio-historical development of postal systems, as well as their role in contemporary communications, I feel slightly at sea amidst the strange language codes and symbols with which many of the distinguished economists attending this conference have garnished their presentations. More to the point, my particular disciplinary focus means that I must leave an appraisal of the appropriateness of the economic model presented in Treworgy and Waddell's paper to others and concentrate my attention on the paper's broad social implications. Current policies and concerns over terminal dues subsidization might not seem like very promising material on which to hang sociological insights. But I find that there is plenty to talk about.

Before dealing with more specific matters, let me acknowl edge an intellectual debt of gratitude to the authors. I had not been aware, prior to undertaking some general background reading in preparation for my role as discussant, that research on the linkages between postal communications and socio-economic devel opment in LDC's is, outside of Universal Postal Union reports, almost non-existent. It seems to have been forgotten—amidst the myriad studies of the diverse impacts of radio, films, TV, and satellite transmission on third-world development projects—that, during the nineteenth century, postal systems played a vital part in facilitating the processes of settlement, economic growth, and national integration in countries with huge land masses and scattered rural populations, such as Canada and Australia. The geographical and socio-demographic characteristics of these countries, their transportation and communication needs, had something in common with those of many LDC's today. What a scholarly lacuna, therefore, that mail, which is vital in linking people to political and economic organisations as well as to each other (albeit dependent upon literacy), should have slipped by the development theorists as a topic for research.

Turning directly to the paper itself, one recognizes that its central argument is based upon a series of broadly valid, but quite general, propositions. A major one of these is that LDC's have poorer mail service standards, born partly of lack of mechanization and often severe delivery problems, than is generally the case in industrialized countries. Coming from an industrialized country which suffered a severe deterioration in service standards for a couple of decades despite the introduction of large-scale mechanization, this generalization makes me cringe a little. Nonetheless, it is acceptable if one recognizes that further detailed research on the subsidisation impact of terminal dues rates would do well to distinguish between the postal systems of the "less developed" countries and the group of countries which is sometimes called "least developed" by international agencies. Certainly, by the standards of the industrialized nations, the per capita mail flow and domestic postal receipts of all LDC's are small. Yet, there remains a significant difference between the role of the Post Office in, say, India which provides 18.8 post offices per 100,000 inhabitants and processes 14.2 domestic letters per inhabitant per year (UNESCO 1989), and the postal systems of some of the least developed nations which have only 2-3 post offices per 100,000 inhabitants and a miniscule flow of domestic mail (UN 1989).

But back to the authors' main argument. Since the relatively poor postal service of many LDC's tends to be combined with low internal postage rates, and since these countries usually receive more international mail than they send, the argument that the present rates of terminal dues could be considered a form of hard currency subsidization of the LDC's postal systems is an important one; especially since such subsidization is held also to yield benefits to the industrialized nations. It is important, I believe, for two main reasons. First, as a World Bank report recently noted (reported in The Independent, 16 July 1990), during the 1980s many countries suffered macroeconomic shocks as debt crisis and international recession exposed their structural weaknesses. Ghana is a case in point: the structural weaknesses of that country's postal system led to such a dramatic fall in quality of service, that the resulting loss of consumer confidence was associated with a fall in mail flow from 199 million items in 1970 to 49 million in 1986 (based on Huq (1989, 70- 71)). Whilst we do not know how many (if any) other LDC's postal systems faced such extreme conditions, it is fairly evident that debt-ridden nations need all the financial help that they can get in order to bolster their postal communications infrastructures. There are probably better ways to provide such help than through the apparently somewhat illogical schedule of terminal dues rates—but rather this illogical schedule than no help at all.

Secondly, Treworgy and Waddell's argument suggests that apparently logical shifts in economic policy, backed by apparently sound economic theories, may have some deleterious consequences when viewed from within the framework of the international postal network. A move towards cost-based pricing of international postal products appears rational—but, especially if combined with increased remailing, could be one more nail in the collective economic coffin of the least developed nations. Parenthetically, a similar line of argument when used against the continuation of uniform first-class domestic letter rates does not jibe with the view—still valid, I think, in Canada—that cross-subsidization in support of the uniform rate can be considered part of a logical policy aimed at facilitating national and regional intercommunication.

Of course, all of the above comments are based upon the assumption that the average amount of terminal dues revenues accruing to LDC's is sufficiently large to have some impact on the quality of their postal systems, if applied for upgrading purposes. I do not know if this is so, since the authors do not offer any relevant facts and figures. On the other hand, they do make it clear that their analysis relies on two other assumptions—first, that terminal dues revenues are received by the postal administration itself in the LDC and, secondly, that they are used to improve service. Altogether, this is quite a bunch of assumptions for which facts are lacking and, as the authors note, research is needed. It would have helped, also, to have had one or more knowledgeable representatives of the LDC's present at this conference in order to provide us with some relevant infor mation. Perhaps next time.

References

Huq, M. M. 1989. The Economy of Ghana. London: Macmillan.
UNESCO. 1989.World Communications Report. Paris.
United Nations' Conference on Trade and Development. 1989.The LDC's: 1988 Report. New York: UN.

13
COMPETITIVE STRATEGY FOR NEW ZEALAND POST
Elmar Toime

1. Introduction

New Zealand Post is in world terms a relatively small company in a small country. However, it has a long tradition in providing postal services in New Zealand, as old as the Penny Black and Sir Rowland Hill's postal reforms in England. Both New Zealand and New Zealand Post also celebrate their 150th anniversary in 1990.

This paper aims to describe the performance and structure of New Zealand Post as a recently established corporation. With an environment heading for rapid deregulation and characterized by a high level of competition, service and innovation have become mandatory to meeting the company's goals of profitability and growth.

2. A State-Owned Enterprise

There is also much that is very new about New Zealand Post. It was established as a state-owned enterprise on April 1, 1987. In New Zealand, this major economic reform, which transformed a number of former government departments into commercial trading companies, was called "corporatisation". In Europe and North America, this process would be called "privatization".

As a state-owned enterprise, New Zealand Post is established as a limited liability company, headed by a board of directors. It operates in all respects as a private company, paying all taxes, including the Goods and Services Tax on postage, and returns a dividend to its owners.

Its shareholders are two Ministers of State, who hold shares on behalf of the people of New Zealand.

New Zealand Post is required by statute to operate as a successful business enterprise, that is to be as profitable as private companies. In this regard, the measures of performance used include: (1) profit after tax to shareholders funds;

(2) trading profit to turnover; and (3) profit before interest and tax to total tangible assets. This focus on profitability becomes the driving force for the board of directors and for the executive. It explains the progress of New Zealand Post to date; it explains its commitment to customers and service; and it explains its drive for marketing innovation.

In three years of trading, New Zealand Post has returned a very creditable profit performance, averaging 18% trading profit to turnover.

3. Regulatory Protection

Having briefly described the company structure of New Zealand Post and its financial performance goals, it is necessary to understand the structure of the regulatory protection provided in legislation, both as it exists now and as it will be in the future. Obviously the form of this protection will determine New Zealand Post's competitive strategy.

New Zealand Post was established with a degree of regulatory protection. Like all other postal administrations, the basic first-class letter service (which has been kept at 40c, or approximately (US) 22 cents, since February 1987) is protected from direct competition. This protection level was set by legislation at $1.75 and 500g.

This level of protection carried with it an obligation (but not a mandatory condition) to provide a universal letter service throughout New Zealand at a single price. This obligation is judged to be the price for statutory protection.

A number of exceptions to protection are provided for. Chief among these is express permission for the transfer of mail between "document exchanges".

The New Zealand Government did not have a long-term view on protection. It provided for a review of these statutory provisions within two years of the establishment of New Zealand Post in 1987. This review was indeed carried out and concluded in 1989. It provided for the phased reduction of protection in three steps: (1) to $1.25 and 200g immediately; (2) to $1.00 in December 1990; and (3) to $0.80 in December 1991.

Legislation to enact this change was passed by Parliament in August 1990. Competitors to New Zealand Post opposed the legislation, arguing that either New Zealand Post should be fully deregulated or that it should be excluded from providing competitive services.

Close attention was given to immediate deregulation. In the final analysis, Government decided that a phasing-in period was necessary to ensure the orderly transition to full competition, including time for New Zealand Post to restructure its asset base. Although not explicitly provided for, the expectation is that full deregulation would occur when the 80c level was reached.

The Government and New Zealand Post have also agreed on a Deed of Understanding to formalize service obligations in exchange for a continued level of protection. The main features of the Deed are: (1) to continue a universal letter service in New Zealand; (2) to maintain existing delivery service standards; (3) to place an initial price ceiling of "CPI-2%" on the basic (40c) first-class letter rate and an ongoing price ceiling of "CPI-1%" each year thereafter; and (4) to maintain a basic network of New Zealand Post and agency outlets.

4. The Competitive Environment in New Zealand

Competitors and potential competitors have begun to enter the market in anticipation of the new legislation which will reduce protection levels. Well-established competitors providing courier and parcels services, remail, unaddressed advertising mail, and document exchange services also operate with considerable vigor in a small market.

Even in segments where New Zealand Post is currently the dominant service provider, attention to the quality of service, to customer care, and to product innovation is the key growth and survival strategy in the face of deregulation.

Competitors dominant in the courier market, facing competition from fax services and electronic mail, are turning to traditional mail business opportunities for new growth. Costs of entry are low. Cream skimming of the more profitable sectors (main trunk routes, business-to-business mail) is widely practiced via the document exchange exemption in the legislation. As we say in New Zealand Post, it is competition aimed at our core.

Document exchange services operate on the basis of company subscription to a "mailbox." The subscription is proportional to estimated volume usage at prices which undercut the universal letter rates. Overnight service is provided to main centers with linehaul services provided by a group-operated common carrier (courier, parcels, and document service share). Document exchange services evolved from a narrowly-based legal document exchange operated between courts and members of the legal profession. In New Zealand, a much wider business market is being targeted.

Significant competition also exists in the circular/unaddressed mail market. Although prevented by the regulatory legislation from delivering addressed mail, circular distributors have an established low cost delivery network.

A final important area of allowed competition is an exemption provision which permits firms to deliver their own mail using employees. In New Zealand, a number of local government authorities and utilities deliver their own mail in this fashion.

5. New Zealand Post Performance

New Zealand Post had inherited a number of operating conditions, both positive and negative, which needed to be harnessed or changed. On the plus side, every New Zealander and every New Zealand company was a customer. New Zealand Post operating managers knew how to process and transport large volumes of mail, and the company had a solid delivery network. On the negative side, a lack of management systems, wrongly allocated assets (Post Office buildings instead of mail processing plant), and civil service attitudes meant fundamental change was needed. More importantly for the longer term, business and the public had a generally poor image of the postal service, while employees and management had still to savor and appreciate the rewards of success.

At its inception, New Zealand Post faced a number of challenges. The postal business of the former New Zealand Post Office suffered a $40 million loss in its last year of operation, and the early New Zealand Post budgets indicated that this trend was likely to continue.

The condition of the company in its first months determined priorities. The first year aimed to get costs under control and lay the foundations for the internal change program needed. On February 5, 1988, 432 company-owned Post Offices were closed and replaced with a network of private sector retail outlets.

This major shift away from company retail outlets to private sector agencies has continued until today. More than 80% of our 1400 outlets are privately-owned.

Further, staff numbers and recurring expenditure have been reduced by 30%. The company now has major costs under control and is able to turn its operational attention to ongoing productivity improvements.

The need for change has been widely communicated to staff and management, and this has been accepted as necessary for the ultimate good of the organization. Natural attrition and voluntary redundancy allowed an orderly downsizing of the workforce, and labor relations have been maintained at a very good level overall, through consultative mechanisms. There have been no mandays lost through industrial action since corporatisation.

With its short-term viability assured, New Zealand Post can now focus properly on marketing, customer service, and growth.

6. The Marketing Challenge

New Zealand Post's national sales manager illustrates the position very well when he says at sales conferences: New Zealand Post is the latest entrant in a market it has dominated for 150 years.

This statement expresses an unfortunate fact. Years of monopoly and dominance had evolved deep layers of bureaucratic process which had little to do with customer care and marketing innovation. Decisions to leave or contest particular markets were based on political influence or operational factors, not on competitive strategy.

On corporatisation, New Zealand Post assumed autonomous responsibility to set prices and to establish its own products and services. This independence in pricing is no more evident than in New Zealand Post's decision to cease registered publications discounts in October 1988. Under the old Post Office department, many attempts to remove these price discounts were vetoed by the Government of the day, no doubt a world-wide situation. The cross-subsidy remained as a carry over from situations no longer relevant today, and no commercial justification existed to continue it.

The challenge which faced New Zealand Post was that it needed to adopt a marketing and customer-driven outlook without having a marketing discipline and without having adequate customer knowledge.

These skills are being developed through the judicious recruitment from outside the company of sales and marketing professionals.

The company shaped a strategic marketing plan based on three key thrusts: (1) to protect its core business by developing competitive products and services; (2) to enhance service through customer care programs and by meeting high delivery performance standards; and (3) to provide for future growth, profitability, and competitiveness.

These points recognize that core letter business represents the largest profit source and thus needs to be secured in the expectation of deregulation and the immediate erosion of business mail to competitors targeting more profitable segments. At the same time, good operational performance needed to be guaranteed. This was to be the basis on which New Zealand Post could launch its marketing programs.

Some of New Zealand Post's marketing successes and initiatives derived from this strategy, we believe, represent service advances which are worth describing.

Delivery Performance

In common with many other postal administrations, New Zealand Post inherited a limited inland airmail service, a first-class letter service, and second-class services for bulk mail and small packets. Delivery standards were consistently in the 80-85% delivery-on-time range.

The first major product rationalization led to the removal of the second-class mail stream. All mail was to be first-class. Furthermore, mail processing centers were required to operate a clear floor policy. All mail lodged during the day is required to be dispatched that same day.

This led to a major resource realignment, but it removed the mountains of bags of mail which commonly used to be found in mail centers. Mail is not aged in New Zealand Post.

This operational initiative led to major service improvements. Coupled with better attention to networking, delivery standards now consistently reach 96-97% for all mail, and further improvement is targeted.

Size-Based Prices

Letter Post prices were originally based on weight. Although the bulk of mail still comprised ordinary letters, non-standard items needed to be weighed and airmail items were covered by a complex rating structure based on 10g steps.

Weight criteria for prices were removed for all enveloped mail and replaced by a 3 step price structure based on envelope size (medium, large, and extra large) corresponding to paper size standards.

This approach was adopted initially for inland mail, but has now been extended to international letters.

The change has been very successful, with a very high level of customer acceptance. Pricing is simple.

New Zealand Post's first major marketing promotional campaign centered on Fast Post, a next day delivery service for most towns and cities in New Zealand. This service replaced the little used airmail service, but was backed up by extensive advertising. Again, customer acceptance has been very high, with significant trade-up by customers to the new service.

For the first time businesses and the New Zealand public had service choices which performed.

BoxLink and Contract Services

BoxLink is a service unique to New Zealand Post. It is similar in some respects to a document exchange service, but has wider features. It is targeted at business customers for their commercial mail to other businesses.

BoxLink makes use of the fact that many businesses in New Zealand have Post Office box addresses. In quoting for a BoxLink contract, an estimate is made by survey of mail sent by the firm to Post Office box addresses anywhere in New Zealand. A single per annum price is quoted for this mail, based on estimated annual volume, size of articles, and distribution pattern.

Key to BoxLink's success is that it offers an overnight mail service across New Zealand. By carefully streaming BoxLink mail both in mail centers and in network used, it is assured a very high service performance. Furthermore, the customer need only separate BoxLink mail from other mail. Stamping or franking is not required. Because delivery is not by letter carrier (it is delivered to a Post Office box), pricing is able to be sharper and still retain margins.

The service has grown at a very rapid rate and is regarded by customers as a premium New Zealand Post service.

The success of BoxLink has manifested itself in demands from customers for a similar service for all mail, business and household.

As a consequence, New Zealand Post is currently offering a total mail service whereby commercial customers are charged an annual total fee for all postal services. Customers do not need to itemize any individual articles, nor are they required to stream mail into different channels. Mail is picked up by courier at pre-set times and processed by dedicated, skilled staff in the mail center.

It is worth dwelling on this service offering. Since the first message delivery services became systematized well over 150 years ago, pricing concerned itself with the efficiency trade off between pricing for individual items and pricing uniformity. Contract pricing, as it is offered by New Zealand Post, offers the ability to price differentially for service, distance, and any other factors, but removes the need to do this for each item sent.

The saving to customers in terms of their own mailroom processing is significant.

Facilities Management

An obvious area of expertise for a postal organization is in mailroom management.

New Zealand Post has gone even further in its total mail service. For a fee, New Zealand Post employees will be placed in a firm's mailroom, providing both internal mail processing facilities as well as controlling the receipt and dispatch of mail and courier items. In the jargon of hi-tech communications, we talk about network management, configuration planning, performance management, and so on.

The advantage to the firm is that it frees up overheads and receives professional attention in an important communications area. New Zealand Post's employees are expected to advise the firm on the best mailing options.

Since launching this service this year, a number of important facilities contracts have been signed. Interestingly enough, it is a highly contested area and New Zealand Post is facing considerable and effective competition for this business.

Integrated Services

The potential for success is considerable for a company which is able to offer a bundle of services which meet all of a customer's needs in any particular area.

New Zealand Post has certainly aimed at being a provider of integrated services. For example, a business customer will have access through New Zealand Post to bulk-mailing facilities, expedited mail, high quality courier and parcel services, as well as to value-added services such as direct mail consultancy, direct mail lists, and so on. Although New Zealand Post operates separate parcel and letter processing facilities, its linehaul network is integrated.

In a country with the demographic and economic characteristics of New Zealand, this integration is seen as a considerable strength.

In the retail area, although a major rationalization of Post Offices has been achieved, growth opportunities are still being sought. Merchandising in the so-called Post Shops is becoming a significant source of revenue.

New Zealand Post is currently marketing a financial transaction processing service whereby it can service the entire billing needs of a company. This is an example of an integrated service which makes use of the retail network, of the delivery network, and of the mail network.

Under this scheme, New Zealand Post is able, through a joint venture company, to prepare financial statements directly downloaded from a data link to a laser printer, to envelope the mail, and to transport and deliver it. Further, it will receive and process payments, either across the counter in post shops or by business reply post at a central processing center.

While none of these elements is new, the ability to put an integrated proposal together, based on interdependent pricing, is a considerable strength.

Unaddressed Mail Delivery

A final example of service innovation by New Zealand Post is in the unaddressed advertising mail area, branded AdPost.

This represents a large and profitable market segment, serviced by a number of local and national distributors. New Zealand Post has a small market share, limited by the capacity of its letter carrier workforce. Recognizing the business as a natural adjunct to its core letter delivery services, New Zealand Post acquired a small circular delivery company. Although it is a fully owned subsidiary, it is managed as an independent operation, with no shared resources.

This company has now grown into a major operation with very good delivery standards.

7. Conclusion

Visitors to New Zealand and to New Zealand Post talk about the "social laboratory" which has seen major economic reforms take place in a very short time.

The state-owned enterprise program set in place in 1987 has produced a dramatic turnaround in the profitability and efficiency of government-owned trading organizations.

New Zealand Post is one such enterprise which has enjoyed a high level of success-measured in terms of profitability, growth in the value of shareholder funds, returns to the people of New Zealand via taxes and dividends, and, last but not least, improved postal services.

Whilst a level of regulatory protection remains, New Zealand Post does not believe it has any natural monopoly features. Accordingly, it is preparing for full deregulation.

It has transformed its inland services, adopting price strategies and operational strategies which aim to simplify customer access to services and to ensure a high level of reliability in performance.

Competition in the profitable business-to-business letter segment is contested vigorously by both New Zealand Post and by document exchange services. Success in this market required the development of a new service stream, BoxLink, which was required to out-perform existing services.

This approach to meeting customer demands for service has led to the development of integrated services, based on contracts and volume estimates, rather than on mail itemization. Differential pricing has proved to be necessary in a market vulnerable to cream skimming.

Mail is being delivered in greater and greater quantities, for purposes and communications not possibly dreamt of by Sir Rowland Hill.

His reforms have served the world well for 150 years. New Zealand Post believes that a major new era of reform has begun.

COMMENTS
Ian Steele

1. Topsy Turvy

New Zealand is often said in this country to be upside down. There are socialists in the government, but they seem more Thatcherite than Thatcher and more into Reaganomics than Reagan. In the same way it was said that Nixon was the only United States President who could be trusted to open the doors to China and Russia, it could be argued that only socialist governments will be able to privatize postal services. Maybe we should be looking to Eastern Europe or the Soviet Union for the next initiative in this area.

Certainly it is odd to see that even in the United States—the home of free enterprise—they have not managed to privatize the posts. In fact, the United States has one of the most effective monopolies in the world.

It is probably too early to conclude whether or not the New Zealand changes have been successful, but the developments are certainly being watched closely, as they will have a major impact throughout the postal administrations if they are.

2. Measures of Success

It may not be easy to decide whether deregulation in New Zealand is successful. The measures listed in the paper—profit levels, the return to shareholders, and improved service—may not be enough to provide conclusive evidence.

2.1. Quality of Service

On the issue of improving services, it is going to be difficult to prove that they have improved, when the service specification has changed so radically. Most postal administrations have neglected the marketing of their services for so long that, when they are repositioned in the market, the perception of quality can be changed radically without altering the service very much. It would be interesting to know whether, in New Zealand, customers think they have been conned in the change from first and second class to first and fast classes. There was much laughter in Britain when the railways changed their service name from second to standard class.

In Britain, after 16 years of first and second class, most people think that first class is a guaranteed next day service. In fact, it was never intended to be more than 90 percent assured—but this was never made clear when it was introduced. In any country, a bit of "glasnost," advising customers what they can reasonably expect, could have more impact on the perception of quality than millions spent on improving systems.

2.2. Stakeholders

Profits and returns to shareholders are a very narrow definition of success. Shareholders, staff, and customers are all stakeholders in a commercial organization. A profitable change for one group may be seen in a different light by another.

2.2.1. On staff, it would be interesting to see how their morale, motivation, and effectiveness has changed over the past three years in New Zealand. Have, for instance, staff made redundant in retail closures taken on the franchises and become happy entrepreneurs? Those staff wanting higher risk, higher reward remuneration are likely to have done well from the changes. Not many staff, however, are likely to have joined the Post Office for its entrepreneurial possibilities.

2.2.2 For customers, their attitude to the changes are likely to depend on whether it has more closely met their needs. Different groups have different and often conflicting requirements—and different levels of influence over governments and postal administrations. Large mailers, for instance, may not care much about the few people who live in remote rural areas, as long as they are getting discounted deals well below universal pricing levels on their mailings to the bulk of their market. On the other hand, in most countries, farmers (in remote rural areas) have a disproportionate level of influence with governments and are likely to insist on continued cross-subsidization.

2.3. Market Share

The other measure of success normally used for "corporatized" organizations is the change in their market share. Market definitions are difficult in this arena, but it is difficult for anyone to argue these days that postal administrations have any real monopoly in the provision of services for the transmission of messages, documents, and packages.

However we define our market, the least ambitious commercial organization wants at least to maintain its share or to move into other markets. During deregulation, "corporatized" or "privatized" organizations are expected to accept the orderly handover of large parts of their markets to competitors. These are not the most motivating conditions in which to work.

New Zealand Post are obviously planning or expecting to lose market share. To maintain profitability, they will therefore have to improve profitability (either by motivating staff, improving their work methods, or reducing their rewards) or by increasing margins in the market as a whole. It is also almost certain that New Zealand Post will have to accept an increased complexity for its relationships with other business — by subcontracting and franchising out more of its work. Will this element still be included in their market share?

3. Innovation

The final element of Toime's paper that I wish to raise is that of innovation—the engine for increased market share in most commercial organizations.

I am sure that most postal administrations worldwide are jealous of New Zealand. They have been given the freedom, the environment, and the resources to introduce new products and organizational changes which we can only dream of. Because we are not given the freedom to raise capital, to change product specifications, or to allow existing products to die a natural death, it can take as long for us to change as it can for an oil tanker. When we are competing directly against fast-moving telecom companies and fleet-footed courier firms, we need to get a few speed-boats in the water as well.

4. Conclusion

New Zealand have got a flotilla of speed-boats in several stretches of unchartered water. They are doing for postal administrations what Captain Cook did for the domination of the world by Western Europe. We need to help them to pilot their course—to validate and quantify their progress.